# Legal Lexicography
## A Comparative Perspective



*Edited by*
MÁIRTÍN MAC AODHA
*Council of the European Union, Belgium*

Routledge
Taylor & Francis Group
LONDON AND NEW YORK

First published 2014 by Ashgate Publishing

Published 2016 by Routledge
2 Park Square, Milton Park, Abingdon, Oxfordshire OX14 4RN
711 Third Avenue, New York, NY 10017, USA

First issued in paperback 2016

*Routledge is an imprint of the Taylor & Francis Group, an informa business*



**British Library Cataloguing in Publication Data**
A catalogue record for this book is available from the British Library

**The Library of Congress has cataloged the printed edition as follows:**
Mac Aodha, Máirtín, author.
Legal lexicography : a comparative perspective / by Máirtín Mac Aodha.
pages cm. -- (Law, language, and communication)
In English; with some chapters in French.
Includes bibliographical references and index.
ISBN 978-1-4094-5441-0 (hardback)
1. Law--Language. 2. Law--Terminology. 3. Law--Dictionaries. I. Title.
K213.M275 2014
340'.14--dc23

2014015817

ISBN 13: 978-1-138-70077-2 (pbk)
ISBN 13: 978-1-4094-5441-0 (hbk)

# LEGAL LEXICOGRAPHY

*A reference book about legal lexicography was long overdue. With contributions by a number of highly respected experts in the field, this ground-breaking volume places equal emphasis on theory and practice and covers every aspect of the subject (lexicography and translation, monolingual and bilingual dictionaries, etc.), without neglecting the historical perspective. It will prove invaluable to legal translators, lexicographers and lawyers alike.*

Frédéric Houbert, freelance legal translator

*Since Antiquity, legal glossaries and dictionaries have been compiled but seldom analysed. This versatile book fills the gap. It is most useful not only for the professionals of lexicography and terminology work, but also for all lawyers who want to know better the relevant sources of lexical information in their field.*

Heikki E.S. Mattila, University of Lapland, Finland

*This important work on the connections between legal vocabulary and legal culture is a welcome addition to the literature in the growing field of "jurilingistics", a practical and theoretical discipline located at the confluence of law and language. An expert in legal translation and legal terminology who has worked in North America and Europe, editor Máirtín Mac Aodha presents a stimulating collection of essays from a wide range of common law and civil law jurisdictions that show how comparative law, legal history, legal traditions and multilingualism all inform the study of legal lexicography. As multilingual legal dictionaries are increasingly relied upon as points of entry for an understanding of the world's different legal systems, this book will be a source of insight and delight for lawyers, judges, translators, linguists and comparative law scholars working anywhere that law and languages interact.*

Nicholas Kasirer, Justice of the Quebec Court of Appeal, Canada

*The study of law often starts with a dictionary. Better law dictionaries provide substantial insight into the relationship between law and language. Wardens of legal language, they contribute to improving the quality of the language of law; transcripts of legal history, they help lawyers to develop clearer ideas, refreshing and sharpening their legal knowledge; and last but not least, they assist laypersons in their efforts to better understanding law. Máirtín Mac Aodha and his brilliant team of collaborators have to be thanked for putting to lawyers and laypersons alike the challenge of treating legal lexicography as a true social discipline.*

Jean-Claude Gémar, Université de Montréal, Canada

# Law, Language and Communication

Series Editors
Anne Wagner, Lille University – Nord de France, Centre for Legal Research and Perspectives of Law, René Demogue Group, France and Vijay Kumar Bhatia, City University of Hong Kong

This series encourages innovative and integrated perspectives within and across the boundaries of law, language and communication, with particular emphasis on issues of communication in specialized socio-legal and professional contexts. It seeks to bring together a range of diverse yet cumulative research traditions related to these fields in order to identify and encourage interdisciplinary research.

The series welcomes proposals – both edited collections as well as single-authored monographs – emphasizing critical approaches to law, language and communication, identifying and discussing issues, proposing solutions to problems, offering analyses in areas such as legal construction, interpretation, translation and de-codification.

*I ndilchuimhne ar mo mháthair agus ar m'athair*

# Contents


*List of Figures* *ix*
*List of Tables* *xi*
*Acknowledgements* *xiii*
*Notes on Contributors* *xv*
*Foreword* *xix*

Introduction 1

1 A View of French Legal Lexicography – Tradition and Change from a Doctrinal Genre to the Modern Era 11
*Pierre-Nicolas Barenot*

2 The Early Modern English Law Lexicon 31
*Ian Lancashire and Janet Damianopoulos*

3 Legal Lexicography: A View from the Front Lines 45
*Bryan A. Garner*

4 The Challenges of Compiling a Legal Dictionary 59
*Daniel Greenberg*

5 Bilingual Legal Dictionaries: Comparison Without Precision? 75
*Coen J.P. van Laer*

6 Pour des dictionnaires juridiques multilingues du citoyen de l'Union européenne 89
*Pierre Lerat*

7 Principes terminologiques pour la constitution d'une base de données pour la traduction juridique 103
*Thierry Grass*

8 Translation and the Law Dictionary 115
*Marta Chroma*

9 Multinational Legal Terminology in a Paper Dictionary? 141
*Peter Sandrini*

10 Database of Legal Terms for Communicative and Knowledge Information Tools 153
*Sandro Nielsen*

11 Defining Ordinary Words for Mundane Objects: Legal Lexicography, Ordinary Language and the Word Vehicle 177
*Christopher Hutton*

12 Establishing Meaning in a Bilingual and Bijural Context: Dictionary Use at the Supreme Court of Canada 201
*Mathieu Devinat*

13 La phraséologie chez des jurilexicographes: les exemples linguistiques dans la deuxième édition du Dictionnaire de droit privé et lexiques bilingues 223
*Patrick Forget*

14 Inconsistencies in the Sources and Use of Irish Legal Terminology 265
*Malachy O'Rourke*

15 The Struggle for Civic Space Between a Minority Legal Language and a Dominant Legal Language: The Case of Māori and English 289
*Māmari Stephens and Mary Boyce*

*Index for English Language Chapters* *321*
*Index for French Language Chapters* *335*

# List of Figures


8.1 The process of legal translation 122

10.1 Definitions help law students understand legal terms 164
10.2 Presentation of homonyms and polysemes 166
10.3 Data helping lawyers to write legal texts when the expression is known 167
10.4 Data giving help to acquire knowledge 168
10.5 Data providing help to find a term where the meaning is known 169
10.6 Data providing help to translate a legal term 170
10.7 Data providing help to translate collocations and phrases 171
10.8 Specific results of searches for collocations and phrases 172
10.9 Suggested translation supplemented by contrastive note 173
10.10 Data providing help to acquire knowledge 174

# List of Tables


3.1 A sample entry from *Black's Law Dictionary* 57

8.1 Example 3 134

11.1 The automobile exception and the status of the motor home 190

15.1 The complete Legal Māori Corpus by text category (numbers rounded) 292
15.2 Comparison of top 20 content words in selected texts of the Legal Māori Corpus and the MBC 298
15.3 The top ten 'borrowed' legal terms from each time period, with indicative glosses. Time period indicated by H – historical, M – mid-period, C – contemporary 306
15.4 The top ten 'borrowed' legal terms across time in rank frequency per sub-corpus 307
15.5 A comparison of the distribution of *moni* across the Legal Māori Corpus and Māori Broadcast Corpus 308
15.6 Spellings of *pūtea* 309
15.7 A comparison of the distribution of *pūtea* and *putea* across the Legal Māori Corpus and Māori Broadcast Corpus 309
15.8 Relative presence per million words of *pūtea* in the Legal Māori Corpus and the Māori Broadcast Corpus 310
15.9 Patterns of occurrence around *pūtea* in the Legal Māori Corpus mid-period 311

# Acknowledgments

Many people have contributed to this book and I should like to take this opportunity to thank them. I am indebted, first of all, to Professor Mathieu Devinat for his help with the original proposal. Thanks must also go to the contributors for sharing their passion and insights on matters jurilinguistic.

I would like to extend a word of sincere gratitude to my jurilinguistic family at the Paul-André Crépeau Centre for Private and Comparative Law, Faculty of Law, McGill University, and in particular, to its Director, Professor Lionel Smith for agreeing to pen the preface to this book.

Thanks are also due to Róisín Nic Cóil, and to Alison Kirk and Philip Stirups of Ashgate Publishing, for their excellent work on the manuscript.

The last acknowledgment is to Aifric, Tomás, Dónall, Fionnuala, Éamonn and Sinéad for their constant support and love.

# Notes on Contributors

**Pierre-Nicolas Barenot** is a PhD student in History of Law at University Montesquieu Bordeaux IV (France).

**Mary Boyce** is currently Māori Program Coordinator at the University of Hawai'i at Mānoa. She designs and compiles corpora of te reo Māori and uses these corpora to inform the creation of dictionaries and resources for the teaching and learning of Māori. She has also worked for Huia NZ Ltd, the leading Māori publisher, for Victoria University of Wellington in the School of Applied Linguistics and Language Studies and the Department of Māori Studies and as a primary school teacher.

**Marta Chroma** has been teaching legal English, legal linguistics and legal translation to both students of law and students of linguistics at Charles University in Prague for almost 25 years. Her research is based upon a comparative study of the Czech law and language, the Anglo-American system of law, European law and legal English used in those contexts. She focuses on the issues of linguistic and legal interpretation of legal concepts and texts for the purposes of translation, as well as the issues of equivalence and conceptual analysis for the purposes of lexicography. She has authored Czech-English and English-Czech legal dictionaries, textbooks of legal English and dozens of papers published in academic journals and books.

**Janet Damianopoulos** holds a Master's degree in psychology from the Vriej Universiteit in Amsterdam and a Bachelor's degree with double major in psychology and English literature from the University of Toronto, where she worked as a Research Assistant (2012–13) on the Lexicons of Early Modern English project.

**Mathieu Devinat** has been a full-time Professor at the Faculté de droit of Université de Sherbrooke since 2005. His teaching and research interests are in private law (property), legal methodology and comparative law. He has worked on the Private Law Dictionary/Dictionnaire de droit privé project, as a member of the Editorial Committee (Obligations, 2002 and Property, 2012). He is currently a visiting Fellow at the Faculté de droit of the Université de Larochelle (France).

**Patrick Forget** has been Professor in the Département des sciences juridiques de l'Université du Québec à Montréal since 2011. In 2009, he was appointed

Professor/Researcher in Jurilinguistics at the Université de Moncton's Faculté de droit and Centre de traduction et de terminologie juridiques. There, he took an active role in the terminology project aimed at the standardization of the French terminology of the common law vocabulary. Between 2001 and 2007, Patrick worked at the Quebec Research Centre of Private and Comparative Law (McGill University). He is notably the co-author of the *Dictionnaire de droit privé et lexiques bilingues – Les obligations/Private Law Dictionary and Bilingual Lexicons – Obligations*, published in 2003.

**Bryan A. Garner** (@BryanAGarner) is the President of LawProse, Inc. (www.lawprose.org). He is the author of many widely used books, including *Garner's Dictionary of Legal Usage*, *Garner's Modern American Usage* and *Legal Writing in Plain English*. He is the editor in chief of *Black's Law Dictionary*. He is the co-author, with Justice Antonin Scalia, of *Reading Law: The Interpretation of Legal Texts* and *Making Your Case: The Art of Persuading Judges*.

**Thierry Grass** is Full Professor at the Applied Languages and Humanities Faculty of the University of Strasbourg, where he is the director of various masters programmes in translation. He is currently Dean of the Applied Languages Department. He studied French, German, English, computer linguistics and law at the Universities of Erlangen-Nürnberg, Besançon, Strasbourg and Grenoble. He wrote his PhD on legal translation and the legal terminology of the language pair German-French. His research focuses on terminology, legal translation and translation tools.

**Daniel Greenberg** was Parliamentary Counsel (UK) from 1991 to 2010 and is now in the parliamentary team at Berwin Leighton Paisner LLP. He has edited *Stroud's Judicial Dictionary* since 1995, and was the general editor of the third edition of *Jowitt's Dictionary of English Law* in 2010; he is a consultant to the *Oxford English Dictionary*. He is also the editor of *Craies on Legislation*, the *Statute Law Review*, and an associate research fellow at the Institute of Advanced Legal Studies, University of London.

**Chris Hutton**'s research focuses on political issues in language and linguistics. At present he is investigating the links between linguistic theory and race theory, and the history of race theory, following on from his 1999 study of linguistics and ideology in Nazi Germany, *Linguistics and the Third Reich*. In addition to this interest in the history and politics of Western linguistics, he is pursuing various projects at the intersection of linguistics, law and intellectual history. Recent publications include *Race and the Third Reich* (2005), *Definition in Theory and Practice* (with Roy Harris, 2007), *Language, Meaning and the Law* (2009).

**Coen J.P. van Laer,** PhD (1952), studied law and philosophy at the University of Nijmegen, the Netherlands. In Nijmegen he obtained the degrees Magister iuris and Doctorandus philosophiae. He also wrote a doctoral dissertation about the suitability of comparative concepts for legal studies for which the degree of Doctor iuris was bestowed by Maastricht University. Today, he is an information expert and copyright adviser at Maastricht University, the Netherlands. He publishes regularly in the fields of comparative law, jurisprudence and librarianship. Email: c.vanlaer@maastrichtuniversity.nl.

**Pierre Lerat** is a specialist in legal language is Professor is professor emeritus at the university of Paris-North (Paris XIII). His main publications include: *Les langues spécialisées* (1995), *Las lenguas especializadas* (1997), *Livres juridiques: Le langage du droit* (1975, avec J.L. Sourioux), *Terminologie du contrat* (1994, with J.L. Sourioux) and *Vocabulaire du juriste débutant* (2007).

**Ian Lancashire** is Emeritus Professor of English at the University of Toronto. Ian is the editor of *Representative Poetry On-Line*, *Renaissance Electronic Texts* and *Lexicons of Early Modern English*. In addition to his editorial work, his publications include numerous book chapters and journal articles. He serves on the editorial boards of *Early Modern Literary Studies*, the *Records of Early English Drama* and the *Internet Shakespeare Editions*, as well as the advisory boards of Computing in the Humanities Working Papers, Digital Studies/Le Champ Numèrique, and the Society for Early English and Norse Electronic Texts.

**Sandro Nielsen** is affiliated with the Centre for Lexicography – Research into Needs-Adapted Information and Data Access, Aarhus School of Business and Social Sciences, Aarhus University, Denmark, where he is Associate Professor. He graduated with an MA in English (LSP for translators and interpreters) in 1987 and was awarded his PhD degree in specialized lexicography in 1992. He is the author and co-author of numerous publications on theoretical and practical lexicography, including *The Bilingual LSP Dictionary. Principles and Practice for Legal Language* (1994), a printed and an online bilingual law dictionary, three printed and five online accounting dictionaries and a major contributor to the *Manual of Specialised Lexicography* (1995). His main research areas are principles for online LSP dictionaries, user guides in dictionaries, lexicographic information costs and academic dictionary reviewing. His teaching interests focus on lexicography and legal translation for translators and interpreters. Sandro Nielsen is an officially sworn translator and interpreter.

**Malachy O'Rourke** is a former member of the translation service of the Council of Ministers of the European Union. Has written extensively on various aspects of Irish grammar. Iarbhall de Rannóg an Aistriúcháin i gComhairle na nAirí. Go leor scríofa aige faoi mhionghnéithe de ghramadach na Gaeilge.

**Peter Sandrini** has earned a degree in translation studies; his doctoral dissertation focused on legal terminology and terminography. He has published extensively on legal terminology, translation, website localisation and translation technology. He is currently attached to the Department of Translation Studies at the University of Innsbruck as an Assistant Professor where he lectures on Translation Technology, Terminology as well as LSP Translation. He is also the initiator of USBTrans and tuxtrans, a project which aims at bringing Open Source Software to translators' training and the translator.

**Māmari Stephens** is a Senior Lecturer with the Faculty of Law and, with Assistant Professor Mary Boyce of the University of Hawai'i, runs the Legal Māori Project. Her primary research interests are law and language, Māori and the New Zealand legal system and social security law. Māmari taught welfare law, criminal law and first year statutory interpretation in 2011.

# Foreword

The study of law often starts with a dictionary. The beginning law student, asked to read cases and textbooks, is thrown into a sea of strange vocabulary. Unfamiliar words are everywhere, and so too are familiar words used in unfamiliar ways. It is no surprise, then, that most students are advised to invest in a dictionary, and to use it. As Karl Llewellyn put it in the classic *The Bramble Bush*: 'You are outlanders in this country of the law. You do not know the speech. It must be learned. Like any other foreign tongue, it must be learned: by seeing words, by using them until they are familiar; meantime, by constant reference to the dictionary'.[1]

But it is not only the law student who needs a law dictionary. Law is a discipline, not of formulae or images, but of words. The practising lawyer, the academic jurist, the translator, and the judge all need dictionaries, and it is no surprise to find that dictionaries of legal terms are one of the oldest genres of legal literature. Nor is it surprising to find, as the chapter by Mathieu Devinat illustrates, that appellate judges at the highest level have resort to law dictionaries when faced with difficult questions of interpretation. It was Oliver Wendell Holmes, Jr., speaking for the Supreme Court of the United States, who expressed a view that perhaps every lexicographer would share: 'A word is not a crystal, transparent and unchanging, it is the skin of a living thought and may vary greatly in color and content according to the circumstances and time in which it is used'.[2]

The longstanding importance of legal dictionaries makes it all the more surprising that there is to date no book devoted to the scholarly analysis of different aspects of legal lexicography. How wonderful, then, to see this volume that Máirtín Mac Aodha has so carefully assembled. Anyone interested in the field will find this substantial collection to be filled with original and interesting perspectives on a whole range of issues arising at the intersection of lexicography and the law.

The Paul-André Crépeau Centre for Private and Comparative Law has always shared the view that legal dictionaries are a central genre of legal doctrine. The Centre has been publishing bilingual dictionaries of Quebec civil law since 1985, in this way seeking to contribute to a deeper understanding of the interaction of bilingualism and bijuralism, an interaction that makes Canada such a reference point for those with an interest in jurilinguistics.

It is a pleasure to see how many of the contributors to this volume have an affiliation with the Centre. Máirtín Mac Aodha was the researcher who was

1 K.N. Llewellyn, *The Bramble Bush: On Our Law and its Study*, rev. ed. (Dobbs Ferry, N.Y.: Oceana Publications, 1950), 41.

2 *Towne v Eisner, 245 U.S. 418* (1918), at 425.

primarily responsible for the Centre's publication, in 2007, of a new edition of Albert Mayrand's *Dictionnaire de maximes et locutions latines utilisées en droit*.[3] Patrick Forget and Mathieu Devinat were also both Assistant Directors and researchers at the Centre, who contributed substantially to its lexicographical undertakings.

Everyone who loves law and language will thank Máirtín Mac Aodha, and all of the contributors, for this innovative contribution to legal literature.

Lionel Smith
Director, Paul-André Crépeau Centre for Private and Comparative Law
Faculty of Law, McGill University

3 A. Mayrand, *Dictionnaire de maximes et locutions latines utilisées en droit*, 4e édition mise à jour par Máirtín Mac Aodha (Cowansville: Éditions Yvon Blais, 2007).

# Introduction

To access the law one must first pierce the linguistic cocoon that envelops it. Words are the lawyer's main tool, and Law is used, interpreted and manipulated through language. The nexus between language and Law sets it apart from other disciplines such as physics, mathematics or theology. Those disciplines have a common vocabulary that is shared throughout the scientific world. With Law, however, we are constantly reminded that language is firmly wedded to culture, and sublanguage to subculture. Legal terminology varies to a greater or lesser extent from country to country, leading some comparative lawyers to see in language one of the limitations of comparativism (Örücü 2004: 163–4).

Terms of art, ordinary words with uncommon meanings, obsolete words, formal words, Latin words and legal doublets congregate in legal texts, obscuring (sometimes deliberately) the meaning for practitioners, scholars and translators. It is not surprising, therefore, that legal lexicons have such ancient pedigree as a valuable aid. Indeed, the first such work, Gaius Aelius Gallus' *De verborum quae ad jus pertinent significatione* dates back to the first century B.C.[1] This tradition of legal lexicography was maintained in Byzance and in Eastern Europe. The first Western medieval law dictionaries were in Latin, and then dictionaries in the new national languages began to appear, contributing greatly to the development of those vernaculars.[2]

Given the richness and longevity of the dictionary-making tradition, it is surprising that legal lexicography has received relatively little academic attention. Legal lexicography has been largely ignored in other works on legal language and legal linguistics. Very few monographs are devoted to this subject. Notable exceptions include Sandro Nielsen's *The Bilingual LSP Dictionary: Principles and Practice for Legal Language* (1994), Reed and Groffier's *La lexicographie juridique* (1990), and Marta *Chroma's Legal Translation and the Dictionary* (2004). These lexicographical works, despite their utility, limit themselves to particular projects and specific languages.

This neglect may in part be due to the somewhat opaque and contradictory nature of lexicographical works themselves. Lexicographers, although engaged in scientific work, publish dictionaries for users whose pursuits are practical. This results in a paradox which Zgusta describes in these terms:

1 See Fiorelli 1947: 293 quoted in Mattila 2012: 9.

2 See Lancashire in this volume who shows how the gradual increase of headwords in legal lexicons contributed to the well-known sizable expansion of English vocabulary in that period.

> The basis of a sound and efficient lexicographic work is a good theory, but on the other hand, the dictionary is written for a user who will not primarily be seeking too much of lexicographic theory nor a wide array of lexicographic problems presented in it; the user will be interested in finding quite different information, viz. Indications concerning the facts of the respective language itself. In other words, the user of a dictionary does not wish, at least usually, to have the purely lexicographic problems presented but to have them solved (1971: 17).

For this reason the prefaces of legal dictionaries often ignore or are silent on their underlying principles. Even dictionary reviews are of limited value in this respect for as Hartmann (1996: 241) notes, dictionary criticism is an activity 'which has been beset by personal prejudice rather than noted for the application of objective criteria'.

One is also reminded that 'a living body of law is not a collection of doctrine, rules, terms and phrases. It is not a dictionary, but a culture and it has to be apprehended as such' (Friedmann 1990: 47). It is however this very living organism that law dictionaries must seek to capture between their covers (real or virtual). This task, already daunting for the editor of a monolingual dictionary, becomes all the more elusive in the case of bilingual dictionaries due to the system-bound nature of legal terminology as René David and John Brierley expertly outline in their comparative exegesis on French and English Law:

> Since there is no identity between such different legal ideas and concepts (although there may be some overlapping in functions they perform in each system), English legal terms cannot be translated effectively into French or some other Latin language. If a translation must be made, whatever the price, the meaning is most often completely distorted; the difficulty is usually no less even when it appears to be possible: the contract of English law is no more the equivalent of the *contrat* of French law than English equity is that of équité; administrative law does not mean *droit administratif*, nor can civil law be properly rendered as droit civil and common law does not mean *droit commun* (David 1985: 334–5).

This inherent difficulty is further amplified in the case of multilingual dictionaries.

The failure of legal dictionaries to overcome the problems posed by culture-bound legal terminology is, however, not just an obstacle to communication between lawyers but also poses a threat to legal certainty and legal clarity. In this context it is particularly interesting to note recent efforts to promote plain language at European level where the Union has embraced better and clearer legislation as one of its priorities.[3]

3 See for example the European Commission's Clearwriting campaign where clear official language is seen as a citizen's right and as a human right ('Trying to change the

Justice Holmes, referring to the Common Law, once wrote: 'In order to know what it is, we must know what it has been, and what it tends to become. We must alternately consult history and existing theories of legislation. But the most difficult labor will be to understand the combination of the two into new products at every stage'. A similarly inspired approach is adopted here – history is consulted, existing theories of legal lexicography are examined and their products (dictionaries) dissected. Drawing on the sound universal logic, our starting point are matters historical and theoretical from which we progress to more practical concerns. Jurilexicography, the interdiciplinary field par excellence, is found at the confluence of law and language.[4] Comparative Law, legal history, terminology, translation and linguistics all inform this discipline and are present in this volume.

It brings together 15 contributions from 10 jurisdictions. Topics covered include the history of French legal lexicography, ordinary language as defined by the courts, the use of law dictionaries by the judiciary, legal lexicography and translation, legal combinatrics and a proposed multilingual dictionary for the EU citizen. Most of the contributions can be considered as tributaries or affluents flowing into the parent river formed where law and language converge. One or two, however, might better be termed distributaries flowing away from the main stream but nonetheless a part of it for all that. The purpose of this book is not to pinpoint the exact orientation of each of these currents, but rather to suggest the depth and variety of the sources. A variety of perspectives, anachronic, diachronic, monolingual and bilingual, from both the Common Law and Civilian traditions are brought together here in an attempt to reflect current academic thinking. The defining common thread is the law dictionary in its manifold manifestations in numerous linguistic and legal situations.

The value of this volume lies in the richness and diversity of the lexical deposits that result from this confluence of language and law. The scope of this emerging discipline is suggested, its relationship with cognate social sciences reflected and potential areas for future research highlighted. There is a need for further examination of the relationship between general and legal lexicography. To what extent can the latter benefit from the contribution linguistics and particularly corpus linguistics have made to the former? The nexus between legal lexicography and Comparative Law also needs to be further explored. It is hoped that a jurilinguistic approach, comparing and contrasting the legal and linguistic content of legal concepts, will continue to inform today's lexicographers. Such an approach is essential given the centrality of legal terminology for lawyers, translators and civilians. *Da mihi verbum dabo tibi ius*: as the only slightly modified maxim would have it. This collection hopefully goes some way to meeting that imperative.

---

institutional culture: The European Commission's clear writing campaign', Clarity, Number 69, January 2013, 4–5).

4 Jurilexicograpy is a branch of jurilinguistics, which term originated in Canada and denotes the study of the relationship between language and law. See Gémar (1982), Gémar and Kasirer (2005), Mac Aodha (2008: 679) and Preite (2013).

Pierre-Nicolas Barenot opens this volume by leading us through the legal lexicographical landscape of France from its origins in the twelfth century to modern times. Our guide introduces us to the main landmarks along the way including Ferrière's *Repertoire universel et raisonne de jurisprudence* and Guyot's work of the same title under the Ancien Régime. These ambitious works blurred the distinction between dictionary and encyclopaedia and paved the way for the works that followed. In the period between the revolution and the promulgation of the Code we learn that works such as Tennesson's *Dictionnaire sur le nouveau droit civil* helped the transition between the *ancient droit* and *le droit intermédiaire*. The nineteenth century was the golden age for French legal lexicography and works such as Langlande's *Repertoire de la nouvelle legislation* and Meynial's *Jurisprudence generale du Royaume* (1825) provided the first real syntheses of the Law in its entirety. Our lexicographical journey brings with it some surprising lexicographical travel companions including the *arrêtistes* (case-reporters) of the eighteenth century and the compilers of some of the annotated codes in the nineteenth century. Our final post is the twentieth century where the earlier encyclopaedic tendencies are shed in favor of more utilitarian specialist works such as the *Repertoire pratique de legislation, de doctrine et de jurisprudence* (1910), a trend that mirrors the development in law itself.

The contribution of early modern law lexicons to the English language is the subject of Ian Lancashire's chapter. He explores the influence on the English vernacular of the works of lawyer-lexicographers such as John Ratsell, the author of the first monolingual dictionary (1523) whose lexicon was the subject of re-editions right up until the end of the seventeenth century, and those of John Cowell who integrated Civil and Common Law in his 1607 work, *The Interpreter*. The linguistic backdrop for this is one where English was only gradually displacing Law French and Latin. Indeed, the final death knell for Law French was only sounded in 1650 by a statute forbidding its use by the legal profession. The author shows the importance of patronage in the emergence of these new lexicographical works and how they were aimed at the education of a new legal profession 'conversant in the languages of European business and diplomacy'. These works extended beyond their own register, expanding the vocabulary of the general language and, in the case of *The Interpreter* with its use of quotations and references to other books, ultimately inspired the innovative structure of the major works of English lexicography that followed.

As editor of *Black's Law Dictionary*, Bryan Garner's perspective is that of a lexicographer on the front lines. He addresses the following core questions that all lexicographers from Ratsell to Black have had to grapple with:

a. To what extent should a law dictionary be a dictionary – as opposed to a legal encyclopaedia? That is, to what extent should it merely define terms, rather than expansively discuss the law relating to those terms?

b. To what extent is a law dictionary a work of original scholarship – as opposed to a compilation of definitions taken from judicial opinions and other legal sources?
c. To what extent should we worry about the formalities of defining words – that is, about getting the lexicography right as well as getting the law right?
d. To what extent can the modern lexicographer rely on the accuracy of predecessors?
e. How do you find the material to include in a dictionary?

Among the numerous gems unearthed in the response to those questions we discover the five tenets of defining words outlined by Landau (1971) and applied to legal terms:

- Make the definition substitutable for the word in context, so that the entry begins with the definition itself – never with a phrase such as 'a term meaning' or 'a term referring to'.
- Indicate every meaning of the headword in the field covered by the dictionary.
- Don't define self-explanatory phrases that aren't legitimate lexical units (including such phrases as living with husband).
- Define singular terms, not plurals, unless there's a good reason to do otherwise.
- Distinguish between definitions and encyclopaedic information (that is, textbook descriptions).

The singularity of the approach in the modern editions of Henry Campbell Black's dictionary is highlighted, including the citation of sentences, not just to illustrate the use of terms but the quotation of substantive experts precisely for their expertise, to lend greater historical and intellectual depth to the entries.

Daniel Greenberg's analysis is also that of a practitioner: he is editor of *Stroud's Judicial Dictionary* and general editor of *Jowitt's Dictionary of English Law*. He makes a distinction between law dictionaries (such as, for example, *Jowitt's* or *Black's Law Dictionary*) and judicial dictionaries as exemplified by *Stroud's*. The former defines terms that are relevant to the law, the latter terms that are used in the law. Like Garner he suggests that the boundary between dictionary and encyclopaedia is blurred: 'there is no real distinction between the parameters of a concept as part of the fabric of the law and the substance of the concept'. He also discusses what material should be included, and demonstrates, for example, the value of including seemingly obsolete terms. Such terms, for example, prove their use when lawyers are called upon to apply commercial or legislative documents of great age. As regards the inclusion of terms in foreign languages, the author shows how the concerns of legal lexicographers are largely those of all lexicographers but with a legal twist or two: namely the demands imposed by the existence of separate legal jurisdictions within the UK and by membership of the EU.

How can bilingual legal dictionaries be improved? This is the question addressed by Conrad Van Laer. The author argues that the provision of encyclopaedic material is essential. He specifically makes the case for the inclusion of juxtaposed legislative definitions from both the source and the target legal systems to enable the dictionary user to bridge the conceptual gap between diverging legal systems. A note of caution is struck, however, as an overabundance of such information can in fact obscure rather than highlight conceptual differences. Only when the correct balance is struck between concision and completeness, the author suggests, can the question of equivalence truly be resolved.

Pierre Lerat proposes a methodology for the creation of a database multilingual legal dictionary aimed at EU citizens who by virtue of their general and linguistic knowledge are 'semi-experts'. The author argues that such a project is all the more feasible given the degree of commonality between the basic legal concepts of French Law, German Law, Italian Law and even UK Law. He rejects thc traditional distinction between lexicography and terminography, insisting that all lexicography is to a greater or lesser extent specialist. The starting point for every entry should be the concept, and should progress from this global level to the local level (level of language), with a 'minimal definition' inserted between the onomasiological and semasiological levels. The author also sets out a list of desiderata for a legal terminological database including the indication of hyponymic relations, the limitation of grammatical information, the provision of typical collocates and so on.

The increasing internationalization of law makes the terminological needs of translators even greater. Thierry Grass advocates the use of ISO standards and the TBX framework (for the exchange of terminological data) in the creation of a FR-DE termbase of the core legal vocabulary of French and German Civil Law. ISO 1087 defines terminology as a 'set of designations belonging to one special language' and designations as 'representations of a concept by the sign which denotes it'. The author shows how this can be applied to legal language. He also shows how ISO 12620 (the international standard for the data categories used in termbases), ISO 12616 (terminology aimed at translation) and ISO 704 (which sets out the principles governing the formulation of designations and the formulation of definitions) can provide a structure for entries: the lexical level followed by the translation level and concluding with the level of language. The merits of the ISO approach, he argues, is that it provides uniformity of form while preserving complete freedom as to the contents of the terminological record.

Marta Chroma's contribution is also directed at the needs of translators and the implications thereof for lexicographers. Drawing on Jakobson's semiotic theory of translation (1959), the author characterizes law as 'a dual semiotic system composed of the language in which it is expressed, and the discursive system expressed by that language'. She points out the difficulties that arise from the artificial separation of words from their context. The lexicon is presented only at the level of language as a system. This inevitably results in what V.A. Gak calls 'the lamentable gap between what is proposed in dictionaries and the linguistic truth' (ce décalage tragique entre les recommendations lexicographiques et les réalités linguistiques) (1970: 105). This is a direct result of the 'frequent discrepancy between lexemes viewed in isolation and their usage as words in context' (Hornby 1990: 209). The problem of equivalence is also addressed with the author promoting the use of conceptual analysis to determine degrees of equivalence. The inclusion in law dictionaries of labels, usage notes, examples, selectional restrictions, information on jurisdiction and on geographical scope is encouraged.

Peter Sandrini demonstrates the inadequacy of paper law dictionaries to give an adequate portrait of legal terminology. These shortcomings result both from the very nature of terminology in general with its emphasis on the centrality of the concept, on the interrelatedness of concepts and on the principle of univocity, and also from the specific culture/system-bound character of legal terminology. Paper dictionaries propose equivalence where terminology rejects such a relationship, seeking instead to compare and contrast concepts in different legal systems. Traditional paper electronic dictionaries provide multiple equivalents whereas terminology theory holds that each concept should be designated by a single term. The author sets out the information requirements (including the hierarchy of concepts, the relationship between concepts, legal classification and so on), a multitude of data and cross-references that can only truly be represented electronically.

The death-knell for paper law dictionaries is also sounded by Sandro Nielsen. He examines how online legal dictionaries can be improved drawing on experience gained in an on-going lexicographical project at the Department of Business Communication, Aarhus University, Denmark, which combines two monolingual and two bilingual dictionaries for the language pair Danish and English in a tool containing a database, search engine and online dictionary. This dictionary takes account of the specific functions of dictionaries (communicative and cognitive) and matches them with the needs of users. This approach caters for both the encoding and decoding needs of users. A variety of search options including 'help to understand a term', 'help to find a term where the meaning is known', 'help to translate a term', 'help to translate a collocation or phrase' allow for a final multi-functional product that escapes the constraints of traditional paper dictionaries.

Ordinary language as understood within the culture of law is the subject of Christopher Hutton's chapter. The author examines the treatment of the word 'vehicle', as a representative of this class of language, in the major legal dictionaries and in case-law. The blurring of the boundaries between ordinary language and legal language is illustrated. It is argued that there is nothing ordinary about 'ordinary language': it is a fiction that is promoted by the courts to meet the interpretive needs of law. Ordinary language is shown to be no more than judge-made language.

Two ordinary languages or ordinary meanings exist in the specific bijural and bilingual context that Mathieu Devinat addresses. In Canadian Law, the official bilingualism and the principle of equal authority elaborated in case-law and underpinned by Section 18 of the Canadian Charter of Rights and Freedoms have important implications for the lexicographical approach adopted by the Courts in determining ordinary meaning. Failure by the courts to examine ordinary meaning in both linguistic versions of statutes (relying on lexicographic works from both linguistic and legal traditions) gives the erroneous impression that each linguistic version of a statute exists independently of the other. The author also exposes a judicial tendency not to differentiate between legal and general dictionaries. This flawed approach, the author argues, has the sole advantage of dethroning law dictionaries and relegating them to the status of mere sources of information on meaning.

Patrick Forget analyses phraseological units sourced in the linguistic examples found in the second edition of the *Dictionnaire de droit privé et lexiques bilingues* (Paul-André Crépeau Centre for Private and Comparative Law: 1991). The author shows how his review of this sample supports the view that phraseological units can be divided into two categories: lexical and conceptual. His definition of phraseological units is founded on idiomaticity, with what constitutes a phraseological unit in a given context being left ultimately to the determination of specialists in the given field. This study demonstrates the need for a re-appraisal of the relationship between legal and ordinary language.

The provision, dissemination and use of Irish legal terminology from the foundation of the State to the present day forms the subject of Malachy O'Rourke's contribution. The publication in 1957 of *Tearmaí Dlí*, the first official corpus of Irish legal terms, should have placed the Irish language on a more secure footing. The author explains why this did not transpire, a failure which has implications not only for translators in the Irish Parliament and at the European institutions but more importantly for the vitality of the language itself. Not only was this to prove to be the first and final edition of this work, but the neglect of this authenticated terminology in De Bhaldraithe's *English-Irish dictionary* and later in the *Foclóir Gaeilge-Béarla* deprived users of legal and linguistic certainty. The author acknowledges that the work itself had its failings, notably a dearth of information on the correct usage of the terms and on selectional restrictions, but points out that such shortcomings could have been remedied, with the aid of advances in linguistics, in future editions. The author also highlights grammatical inconsistences in the Irish language which mitigate against clarity. This analysis is particularly valuable in the context of Irish becoming an official EU language in 2007 with the concomitant need for terminological consistency in the authentic texts of EU laws in Irish.

Legal terminology of another lesser-used language, Māori, is analysed by Māmari Stephens and Mary Boyce. The authors look at the bilingual legal history of New Zealand and in particular at the relationship between English, the dominant legal language for special purposes (LSP) and Māori as revealed in the compilation of the Māori-English legal dictionary (*He Papakupu Reo Ture: A Dictionary of Māori Legal Terms*, LexisNexis 2013). The analysis reveals how customary legal concepts interact with and absorb Western legal concepts. The corpus created as part of the Legal Māori Project/He Kaupapa Reo ā-Ture suggests for example that the neologism *pūtea* (originally a bag or basket of fine woven flax, for clothes and so on) is gradually displacing *moni* (a transliteration from the English 'money'). Another illustration of the collision of two worldviews is the rendering of the Western concept of 'consideration' by the indigenous *utu* (reciprocity in exchange). It is hoped that the lexicographical insights gained in the course of this project can also be applied to similar undertakings in other jurisdictions.

## References

Chroma, Marta (2004) *Legal Translation and the Dictionary*. Tübingen: Max Niemeyer Verlag.

David, René (1985) *Major Legal Systems in the World Today: An Introduction to the Comparative Study of Law* (translated and adapted by John E.C. Brierley), 3rd ed., London: Stevens.

Friedman, Lawrence (1990) in Clark, David S (ed), *Comparative and Private International Law: Essays in Honor of John Henry Merryman on his Seventieth Birthday*. Berlin: Duncker & Humblot.

Gak, Vladimir 'La langue et le discours dans un dictionnaire bilingue', *Langages*, 19, 1970, pp. 103–15.

Gémar, J.-C. (dir.). (1982) *Langage du droit et traduction – Essais de jurilinguistique*. Montréal: Linguatech.

Gémar, Jean-Claude and Nicholas Kasirer (eds) (2005). *Jurilinguistique: entre langues et droits*. Montréal, Thémis, and Brusseld, Bruylant.

Groffier, Ethel and David Reed (1990), *La lexicographie juridique: principes et méthodes*. Cowansville, Les Éditions Yvon Blais inc.

Hartmann, R.K.K. (1996) 'Lexicography', in R.R.K. Hartmann (ed.) *Solving Language Problems*. Exeter: University of Exeter Press.

Hornby, S. (1990) 'Dynamics in meaning as a problem for bilingual lexicography', in Tomaszczzyk. J. and Lewandowska-Tomaszczzyk (eds) *Meaning and Lexicography*. Amsterdam: John Benjamins, pp. 209–26.

Mac Aodha, Mairtin, Review of J.-C. Gémar and N. Kasirer (dir.) (2005) 'Jurilinguistique: entre langues et droits. Jurilinguistics: Between Law and Language', Montréal, Thémis/Bruylant, *Meta*, vol. 53, no. 3, 2008, pp. 679–84.

Mattila, Heikki (2012) *Jurilinguistique comparée: Langage du droit, latin et langues modernes*. Éditions Yvon Blais, Montréal.

Nielsen, Sandro (1994) *The Bilingual LSP Dictionary. Principles and Practice for Legal Language*. Tübingen: Gunter Narr Verlag.

Örücü, Esin (2004) *The Enigma of Comparative Law. Variations on a Theme for the Twenty-first Century*. Leiden; Boston Martinus Nijhoff Publishers.

Preite, C. 'Des années 1970 au nouveau millénaire: essor de la jurilinguistique ou linguistique juridique', *Parallèles*, numéro 25, 2013, pp. 43–50.

Zgusta, Ladislav (1971) *Manual of Lexicography*. Praha: Academia, The Hague: Mouton.

# Chapter 1

# A View of French Legal Lexicography – Tradition and Change from a Doctrinal Genre to the Modern Era

Pierre-Nicolas Barenot[1]

According to an expression attributed to the Jurisconsult Javolenus, 'every definition in civil law is dangerous'.[2] However without the definition of legal concepts, an activity as basic as it is daunting, there could be no legal science.

From Roman to modern times, works of a lexicographical nature, in all their forms – glossaries, dictionaries, répertoires (repertories), encyclopaedias and so on – have gone hand in hand with, provided a structure for, refashioned and even sometimes directly led to the development of legal science and the refinement of practice in the most diverse of contexts (Carbasse 2004; Hayaert 2011; Delia 2011). The historical approach to the lexicography of law leads us accordingly to take a broad view of this doctrinal genre (Hakim 2010) which had such an influence on legal literature.

Before the systematization of Roman Law carried out by Gaius and prior to the first attempts at codification under the Late Roman Empire, the *Veteres* of the Republic, influenced by dialectics and Greek thinking (Gaudemet 1996; Villey 2006), had made significant efforts to define, classify and order the law. While Quintus Mucius Scaevola (140–82 B.C.) would appear to have been the first to have written a treatise on Civil law aimed at classifying legal transactions into kinds and types, it was C. Aelius Gallus, a contemporary of Cicero who compiled the first truly lexicographical work devoted to law, the *Verborum quae ad jus pertinent significatione*. But the flagship work of Roman legal lexicography, although not strictly a lexicon or a dictionary (Carbasse 2004: 6; Hayaert 2011: 316, 317), is still the title *De verborum significatione* of Justinian's *Digest* (D 50.16). The inspiration through the ages for numerous glosses, commentaries and alphabetical recasts, this disparate text's original purpose was to elucidate the meaning of legal terms occurring in 246 fragments taken from the leading Roman jurisconsults. The primary definitional purpose of the *De verborum*, and in particular the

1 The translation from the author's French original is by the editor. Thanks are also due to Professor Geoffrey Williams for proofing the final draft of this translation.

2 D 50.17.202, 'Omnis definitio in jure civili periculosa est'.

alphabetical and analytical works that followed it, make it the key and founding text of legal lexicography.

With the renaissance of Roman Law in the Middle Ages[3] and throughout the Ancien Régime, law dictionaries flourished and started to take on the traits they now possess. In the twelfth century the first medieval legal lexicons were produced by French lawyers and civilists, who remained true to their grammarian origins (Carbasse 2004: 10). The most famous of these were Aubert de Béziers, Jacques de Révigny and in particular Albéric de Rosate, author of the *Grand dictionnaire de droit civil et canonique* compiled circa 1350, and re-edited and recast in the sixteenth century by Decianus. This masterpiece is structured in alphabetical order and designed as a tool for practitioners. The myriad dictionaries that followed this work were conceived as practical works and borrowed heavily from their predecessors (2004: 12).

The Humanist approach to legal lexicography applied by Lorenzo Valla to the *De verborum*, or that of Maffeus Vergus or Cujas, was not, moreover, to change the aspect or the object of law dictionaries.

At the end of the sixteenth century, François Rageau's l'*Indice des droits royaux et seigneuriaux* became the first dictionary of 'French Law', jettisoning the Latin tongue for the vernacular. Re-edited by Eusèbe de Laurière in 1703, Rageau's *Indice* and Louis Charondas' *Mémorables* which appeared shortly afterwards marked the beginning of the new era of law dictionaries published in the seventeenth and eighteenth centuries. In was in this same period that lexicography became a true science with the foundation of the Académie française. It is interesting to note in this connection that the jurisconsults of the Ancien Régime often made reference in their works to 'general dictionaries' of the French language. Le *Dictionnaire de Trévoux* in particular was considered an authority because of the high quality of its articles on the words of the law.[4]

Dictionaries, legal encyclopaedias, thematic or alphabetical répertoires were from that time on an integral part of legal literature; many of those works, moreover, met with enduring success right up until the nineteenth century and

3 Professor Jean-Marie Carbasse points out that before the twelfth century two major works of legal lexicography were produced in the seventh and ninth centuries: Isidore de Séville's *Etymologies*, book V of which is devoted to law, and a major general dictionary entitled *Elementarium doctrinae rudimentum* produced in Italy by Papias, a proper lexicon focusing on the definition of words (2004: 8).

4 *Dictionnaire universel François et Latin, vulgairement appelé Dictionnaire de Trévoux* (Compagnie des libraires associés, Paris 1771). As the Preface to this work states, it is a 'dictionnaire de notions' which is neither purely grammatical, nor confined to 'la seule intelligence des termes de la Langue'. The *Dictionnaire de Trévoux* in fact provides 'detailed' and 'contextual' descriptions of words, hence its appeal to lawyers who found in it convenient syntheses or synopses of the major legal institutions.

were the subject of numerous re-editions (Bonin 2004; 2011).[5] In addition to those works should be mentioned the myriad of alphabetical reports[6] dedicated to case-law produced by *arrestographes*[7] (case reporters); these were even sometimes entitled 'dictionaries' of legal decisions – the most famous of which is that of de Brillon (1727). These laboriously compiled compilations of legal judgments, meticulously dissected, systematised and compared with other sources of law, follow in effect the model of general lexicographical works (Dauchy and Demars-Sion 2005).

Nevertheless, it is Joseph Ferrière's *Répertoire universel et raisonné de jurisprudence* which became *le Dictionnaire de droit et de pratique* under the editorship of first his son and then de Boucher d'Argis, along with Joseph-Nicolas Guyot's *Répertoire universel et raisonné de jurisprudence* which were to become the flagship works of legal lexicography under the Ancien Régime. These works of encyclopaedic scope established the general characteristics of this literary genre and served as models for the lexicographical works of the nineteenth century.

What then are the general and abiding traits which sustain this multiform doctrinal genre and which unite these lexicographical works beyond their sole definitional purpose?

To be useful from a practical as much as a scientific point of view is undoubtedly the primary aim of works of legal lexicography. Their main objective is to render legal norms, principles or institutions easy to understand, accessible and available for use – in other words they are primarily tools. This utilitarian purpose is evident firstly in the form of these works, organised alphabetically or according to subject and making use sometimes of tables or indices. In this respect, legal dictionaries,

---

5 The most famous of these works which were to be the subject of numerous re-editions in the last two centuries of the Ancien Régime include l'*Enchiridion* by Jean Imbert (1627); *Recueil de jurisprudence civile du pays de droit* écrit *et coutumier, par ordre alphabétique* by Rousseau de Lacombe (1736); *Dictionnaire de jurisprudence et des arrêts* by Prost de Royer (1781–87) and *Collection des décisions nouvelles et de notions relatives à la jurisprudence actuelle* by Jean-Baptiste Denisart (1754–71).

6 'Reports' is used here to refer to reports in the strict and traditional sense but also as what Wijffels and Ibetson describe as 'a convenient shorthand for what is usually referred to (in continental Europe) as recueils de jurisprudence (or, ... raccolte di giurisprudenza, Rechtsprechungssammlungen, rechtspraakverzamelingen), in early modern literature generally published under titles as Decisiones ..., Arrêts ..., or more original titles during the later centuries of the Ancien Régime, but forming, on the whole, a fairly established and more or less well-defined category for the purposes of legal-historical research' (1997: 15).

7 The term arrestographe is given by Antoine Furetière (1690) as a synonym of arrêtiste 'auteur qui a fait 'un recueil de plusieurs arrêts' (the author of a collection of several decisions) (Dauchy 2010: 1). Both terms are translated as case reporter here. The science of arrestographie, a term which is not listed in any dictionary and only appeared in the nineteenth century, denoted a 'selection of isolated case studies (decisions from one particular or several parliaments) that emphazised the legal arguments of the parties in order to discover the decision's ratio decidendi' (Dauchy 2011: 50, 56).

lexicons or répertoires can be likened to the codification process (Bureau 2003): for codes, like lexicographical works, aim at making the law more accessible, by bringing together and organizing separate legal texts in a single corpus. The sole purpose, moreover, of Gregorian and Hermogenian Codes was to be of use to practitioners by making available inaccessible imperial texts and constitutions (Gaudemet 1996: 24).

Unlike those codes, however, lexicographical works also seek to define the words of the law. It is not a question of simply uniting and making known the rules and the principles, their meaning and terms also have to be explained. It is worth re-emphasizing here that that 'definition' is never confined to a mere terminological account of the terms, which account would be of no use to lawyers. In this sense, legal lexicons have followed on from the Roman *definitiones*, which were not purely lexical definitions. It is more a question of 'principles, of legal rules, in other words of propositions regarding the institutions designated by the headwords rather than the words themselves' (Hayaert 2011: 316). A descriptive and synthetic approach to legal entities is still very much the preferred approach in legal lexicography. As a result as Valérie Hayaert points out, 'there is no watertight division in this type of work between dictionary of language and encyclopaedia' (ibid.). The exigencies of the legal subject-matter and the practical function of these works, depositaries of definitions, case-law, formulae and extracts from the case-law, cause a blurring of the traditional landmarks of metalexicography.

De Ferrière's *Dictionnaire* is a typical example. A collection of customary law, royal law, learned law and case-law, it places the emphasis more on description and analysis than on terminology and the definition of words, and is closer to a répertoire than a pure lexicon (Delia 2011: 337). The same applies to most of the major lexicographical works whose articles often range from learned syntheses, to technical articles and *forme brève* ('abbreviated form').

These works are usually directed at different types of users. However, the learned nature of some types of developments, sometimes recorded by the jurisprudence itself, shows that these works also had a scientific function and could go hand in hand with and serve the development of legal science. They were accordingly also written for the narrower public of university jurisconsults and legal writers.

The dictionaries, index and reports are also aimed at young lawyers embarking on a career or even those students already enrolled at l'École. By making access to the law easier and providing generally understood definitions of the concepts that make up the law, these legal lexicons by their very nature have a capacity to be *didactic* and *paedagogical* tools. In his *Instructions sur les études propres à former un magistrat*, d'Aguesseau gave the following advice to his son: 'The other thing which would be of great use to you is to read the last two titles of the *Digest*, which are akin to a supplement to the *Institutes*; one of these titles deals with legal rules, the other with the meaning of words'. Legal lexicons therefore became part of the training, be it theoretical or practical, of lawyers. This pedagogic function is explicitly stated in the preface to Claude de Ferrière's *Introduction* à *la pratique*, where its author writes '[this work] has no great scholarly pretensions and was only produced for 'those who are embarking on the study of case law' (Delia 2011: 330, 331).

The same is true of the alphabetical reports written in French which are primarily aimed at recently qualified practitioners as yet uninitiated in the subtleties of case-law and procedure, but also at trainee lawyers. In effect, after the decree of the Édit de Saint-Germain-en-Laye (1679) establishing the teaching of French Law in the universities, reports were to become powerful pedagogic tools, making known customs, laws and case-law through the prism of the judgments which were officially embedded in the curricula (Dauchyand Demars-Sion 2005: 13).

Finally, certain lexicographical works were intended for a wider public not just containing lawyers, to wit, readers who were just keen to know the *law*. It is in the eighteenth century under the influence of the Enlightenment and of Encyclopaedism, that those who are ignorant of the law, are invited to inform themselves about a law that is in the process of rationalization and that is accordingly becoming more accessible. For example, the *Dictionnaire de droit et de pratique* is also aimed at those 'who although their station does not require of them to be versed in law, [they do so] so that they can become familiar with certain rules that are in daily currency, and ignorance of which is shameful and of which every man should have a knowledge for the conduct of his affairs'. Law, although in competition with and supplanted by 'philosophy' and 'politics', was to remain an essential science at the heart of the training and culture of the learned. As for Godot's imposing Répertoire, its targeting of a wider public had a cautionary purpose in dissuading private citizens from embarking on expensive litigation where the outcome was in doubt or likely to be unfavourable (Guyot: XIII, XIV).[8]

Legal lexicographical works therefore contributed to the strides made to unify and rationalise French Law by providing ambitious syntheses of doctrine, practice and case-law and by making access to law, in all its forms, easier. The more comprehensive works could be viewed moreover as a first attempt at synthesis, accompanying and working towards the unification of national law, even though the plurality of sources and the regional particularities of the Ancien Régime made such an attempt daunting. Expressions of a form of legal rationality, at the same time practical, scientific and didactic, these works had as their primary goal to provide answers for the most immediate queries and problems faced by all types of jurisconsults, ranging from the novice to the most inveterate of scholars. Finally, lexicographical works with encyclopaedic pretensions, veritable 'swiss army knives' of the law, differ from other works of legal literature by their holistic approach.

Following on directly from their predecessors under the Ancien Régime, the lexicographic works of the nineteenth century were to add to the number of

---

8 Guyot, op. cit., XIII, XIV: 'Les particuliers eux-mêmes éclairés sur leurs vrais intérêts pourront apprécier la justice de leurs prétentions avant de les soumettre à la décision des tribunaux'.

different types of this doctrinal genre and bring them to their highest degree of perfection.

Although the initial aim of those dictionaries was to facilitate the transition and adjustment to the new law (I), legal lexicography was not to really achieve its highest degree of accomplishment until the final two-thirds of the century with the production of ambitious works of unprecedented scope (II).

## I) From the Revolution to the Civil Code, Lexicographical Works of Transition

With the advent of the Revolution and in the years that followed the promulgation of the Civil Code, the main purpose of lexicographical works was to facilitate the passage from the *ancien droit* to legal ecosystems constructed on new paradigms. Works of transition but also synthetic works revealing continuity and intangible principles, the dictionaries and repértoires of this period are amongst the rare works that can be directly exploited to provide a real overview of the law, rationalised and brought up to date. A valuable resource for practitioners, these works were part of the thankless but vital groundwork that first had to be carried out to pave the way for subsequent works on doctrine.

By its legicentric nature (Rials 1988) the unsettled period of the Intermediary Law resulted in total legislative chaos, a situation that was aggravated by the abrupt ideological turnabouts of the *Convention Nationale* and of the *Directoire*. While the Revolution made 'outlaws' of lawyers, placing them 'hors la loi' (Halpérin 1993: 55, 65), and strove to do away with the confusion of sources in favour of a single norm, a number of lexicons and dictionaries were produced to help citizens new to legal commerce, but also lawyers converted into *défenseurs officieux*, administrators and often appointed judges by reason of their expertise. The desire here once again was to make accessible and comprehensible, to organise or even rationalise a law that was more disparate and uncertain than ever. In 1791 Louis-François Jauffret in the *Gazette des Nouveaux Tribunaux* painted a grim picture of the administration of justice too often placed in the hands of untalented amateurs in a time of the utmost legal uncertainty. To remedy this situation, the jurisconsult set out to produce a dictionary aimed at clarifying and making accessible a law in the process of being substantially renewed: 'it is perhaps more important than we realise to illuminate the path of those charged with the precarious duty of applying the laws or we will soon witness a partial law where the arbitrary will cause irreparable damage. Books are needed! […] in response to the numerous requests I have received in the last six months, I have mapped out the basis for a crucial work but whose imminent publication my numerous other commitments may prevent. It is a *Dictionnaire raisonné du nouvel ordre judiciaire*, containing a clear and precise definition of the terms of the law and of practice and bringing the old law closer to the new law, retaining as always the alphabetical order'.[9] Although Jauffret's project was to remain unrealised, Tennesson for his part published the similarly conceived *Dictionnaire sur le nouveau droit civil*: 'In producing this little dictionary, we hoped to be of use to judges, to *défenseurs officieux* and to all citizens, sparing them the labour of researching the new laws on Civil Law. The subject-matter is organised in such a way to make it possible to instantly find a point of law requiring elucidation. Those most proficient in the law will find a handy répertoire to refresh their memory of what they have learnt and what they may have forgotten'. Although there are few definitions in this text, it does provide an alphabetical classification of the main concepts and ideas of the law in addition to the old and new laws that govern them, accompanied in some places by details on the difficulties they present.

With the promulgation of the Napoleonic Codes, it is interesting to reflect on the development of the lexicographical project. The question of how to make law accessible, of rationalizing and sytemizing law is not as determinate as it once was, or is not posed in the same way: the law is from that point on unified, organised in clear and concise articles, the glory of the Empire. The Civil Code, in particular, an essential part of every good citizen and paterfamilias' book collection was thought to contain the entirety of French Civil Law and to obviate the need for laborious research in previous lexicographical or doctrinal works. The supreme quality of the prose (Teissier-Esminger 2004),[10] its rationality and its systematic spirit made the law more accessible than ever.

However, as Portalis pointed out in the *discours préliminaire* to the first Civil Law project, the law cannot predict every situation. The first commentaries on the code, reviled by the Emperor, inevitably showed up the problems with the new law: its imprecisions and deficiencies.[11] The case-law, particularly the judgments of the *Cour de cassation* retranscribed and analysed in new reports that started to appear at the start of the century (Meynial 2004: 177; Serverin 1985: 97), provide a complement to, supplement and interpret the Code and adapt its rules on a daily basis. In less than a decade a rich and complex body of doctrine grew up around and complemented the codified law.

It was primarily the case-law, a reflection of the exigencies of legal trade, that provided the impetus for the production of the first lexicographical works of the nineteenth century. The immediate problems arising from the application and

9 Louis-François Jauffret [1791] *Gazette des Nouveaux Tribunaux* n°27, 11, 12.

10 On this topic, see, in particular, Anne Teissier-Esminger, *La fortune esthétique du Code civil des français* (La Mémoire du Droit, Paris 2004).

11 It is worth noting that all the seventeenth-century manuals, treatises and commentaries, with the exception of some later works including those of François Gény for example, commence with some introductory definitions of law, statute, case-law or natural law. Formal and nugatory or extensive and circumstantial, this attempt to define, often relying on directories and dictionaries, demonstrates that the jurists of the time were unwilling to treat legal objects without preliminary qualification, a process that is at the heart of legal science.

interpretation of the Code were added to by a significant amount of transitory litigation settled according to the customs and norms of the Ancien Régime and the *droit intermédiaire* during the first third of the century. These essentially practical problems were addressed by a category of lexicographical works which made possible the transition between the previous law and the Napoleonic Law, inscribing the works under the Empire into French legal history and tradition. The best known of these is the *Répertoire* of Merlin de Douai, a renowned jurisconsult and *procureur général près la Cour de cassation* (chief prosecutor) under the Empire, who penned a quarter of the articles in the second edition of the *Répertoire universel* Guyot (Clère 2007; Leuwers 1996). Entirely recast and augmented between the years 1807 and 1809, this voluminous work is complemented by the *Questions de droit* (1st ed. 1803), a work which is part alphabetical répertoire and part report and in which the judicial element is dominant. Merlin's lexicographical works represent transition between the Ancien Régime and the new law and met with unfailing success right up until the 1830s. To the articles on the history of institutions, or norms and the associated doctrine, on the principles and intangible rules of Roman Law, of Canon Law and of the Ancien Droit, Merlin adds the new developments of the Intermediary Law and of the Code. While the Répertoire seeks to situate law in its historical context, rules that have fallen into obsolescence are discarded. A cultural mediator, the jurisconsult provides with this work a fulcrum, a monument and a synthesis for all the people of the land in a time of fervent legal reform and uncertainty.

In 1804, Charles Dagar published a considerably more modest tome with a strictly utilitarian purpose, le *Nouveau Ferrière ou Dictionnaire de droit et de pratique*, emphasizing in its preface the still fragmentary state of the law in the wake of the promulgation of the Code: 'the Civil Code guarantees a legislation that is less uncertain than the one that preceded it. Thanks to this immortal work, the study of law is no longer a ghastly maize where all forms of human intelligence lose their way. But this will not be the case in the first few years following the publication of the Code, its provisions only govern the future; the past is subject to the laws that preceded the Code. We are unwillingly still obliged to rummage in that amorphous mass to arrive at decisions on cases that involve acts or events that occurred under the Empire; this unfortunate reality will be with us for some years still, and will only gradually cease to be'. Dagar, by describing the state of the law in different periods (*Droit ancien, Droit intermédiaire Droit nouveau*), traces the lineage of the norms and principles, making the transition to the codified law easier. As with Ferrière's *Dictionnaire* from which it borrows the content relating to the Ancien droit, this eponymous work was aimed at assisting all types of jurisconsult but also those citizens uninitiated in the mysteries of the law.[12]

12 Ibid., IV, V: 'Tous ceux qui veulent connaître le Droit de leur pays pour se conduire avec sûreté dans l'administration de leurs affaires, y trouveront facilement, et sans grande étude, ce qu'ils pourront désirer'.

These two works which differ greatly from each other in terms of their form, dimensions and contents, follow nevertheless in the line of great lexicographical authorities embodied by the *Guyot* and the *Ferrière* of which, moreover, they are no more than updated and augmented re-editions.

As works of transition, certain lexicons published under the Empire served to give legitimacy from an historical perspective to provisions of the Napoleonic Code drawing their sources from a glorious past. Fieffé-Lacroix's La *Clef des lois romaines*, published in 1809, is more than a basic vocabulary of Roman Law, as it also refers in each article to positive provisions of different codes of the Empire. These references have firstly a paedagogic function: for, under the Empire, Roman Law in conjunction with Civil Law is reinstated as part of the university curriculum. This being the case, Fieffé-Lacroix's work obviously serves to make the study of this formative technical law easier but it also served the interests of the hierarchy which viewed Roman Law as a powerful didactic tool, adding through its majesty to the aura surrounding the imperial Regime and its new judicial architecture.

The same period also saw the emergence of lexicographical works based on case-law. In 1805, Jean de Montainville published a *Dictionnaire de jurisprudence de la Cour de cassation* (preceded by a *traité sur la compétence des autorités judiciaires et des magistrats de l'Empire français*) which was intended to 'follow on from and supplement the dictionaries of the old case law handed down to us by MM. Brillon, Louet and Brodeau, Denisard and other similar reports', the aim being to furnish a diverse readership[13] with the main points (in alphabetical form) of the case-law of the *Cour de Cassation* from the year VIII to XIII. Making tedious research in the periodic reports unnecessary, this lexicographical work is the first overview of the case-law of that Court up until the Code. The *Dictionnaire des arrêts modernes* by Jean-Simon Loiseau (1809) is a more doctrinal work that attempts to expound the emerging case-law drawing on the unified law, referring in some places to the jurisprudential and critical analyses. Some of the entries are presented exactly as they would be in a general dictionary: the entry for 'absent', for example, starts with a definition of the term, then goes on to set out in detail the rules and the case-law on the 'statement and division of the property of the deceased' in the law that preceded and came after the Civil Code.

In 1817, the *arrêtiste* (case reporter) Jean-Baptiste Sirey published a work which was to form a separate genre within legal lexicography: the annotated Code or *Code annoté*. Unlike dictionaries or other classical répertoires this work follows the order of the Civil Code, enhancing its articles with succinct commentary and references to the case-law and doctrine. As yet rudimentary, this first *Code civil annoté* assuredly did not claim to be a dictionary but it does challenge our understanding of what legal lexicography is. Many similar works followed closely

13 Id., IV: 'Cet ouvrage étant destiné à ceux qui se livrent à l'étude du droit, à ceux qui, étant investis de l'autorité publique, soit comme juges, soit comme administrateurs, ont à prononcer journellement sur les contestations de tout genre que peuvent faire naître les différentes matières soumises à leur décision'.

on that of Sirey, works aimed at explaining the words of the law following the order and legal logic of the codes instead of the alphabetical or thematic order favoured by grammarians. A striking example is the *Code civil expliqué* produced by Rogron in collaboration with Ortolan in 1825, in which the preface clearly sets out the lexicographical aspect of the project '[while] the publication of our, [...] has enabled every citizen to have on his bookshelves a book containing all the laws of the land, these texts are often impenetrable for those who are not familiar with the principles and language of the law'. To remedy these problems and to make the law more accessible 'to those who want to understand the code without having to gain an in-depth knowledge of it', Rogon set out to clarify the provisions of the law following the stated plan of the legislator analysing the predominant general principles in each title and of course 'providing definitions which the legislator had eschewed as being of no use in the mandatory provisions of the law'. Aimed primarily at the uninitiated and law students but also at practitioners, this work is truly a law dictionary and is thus to be distinguished from the more technical *Codes annotés* published by Sirey and Dalloz throughout the century.

Usually these codes enhanced with definitions and references to case-law and jurisprudence were in a portable format[14] which makes them user-friendly and sets them apart from the more voluminous legal *Dictionnaires*, *Répertoires* or *Encyclopédies* (format *in-4°* or *in-2°*).

The result of editorial ingenuity, the *Codes annotés* or *expliqués* were an instant success that has endured ever since. Today Dalloz's *Méga-Code* represents the ultimate evolution of this type of legal lexicography which is at the border between dictionary, learned répertoire and strictly utilitarian work.

As regards administration law, the situation at the start of the nineteenth century was a singular one. In anticipation of the official *Code administratif* which was never to materialise, writers initially set about lexicographical work to lay the foundations for and rationalise a fragmented and highly complex subject-matter, by editing private dictionaries and private codes (*codes privés*) (Touzeil-Divina 2009: 38, 44). In effect, to facilitate the work of administrators, lawyers and the subjects themselves, it was above all else necessary to make known and to publicise a law that was at that time still not equipped with general theories and major principles.

Fleurigeon's *Code administratif* (2 vols., 1806), a pioneering work that met with the unequivocal approval of doctrinists, is neither a systematic code nor a real dictionary. Devised as a tool to aid the administration, it contains a summary of the major laws, sometimes accompanied by remarks 'all gleaned from the correspondence of various ministries' along with practical forms. To make the transition with the *droit ancien* possible, Fleurigeon also reproduces texts that had lapsed into oblivion, a feature that detracts from the purely utilitarian scope of the work. With its paucity of definitions Fleurigeon's Code is somewhere between an alphabetical compilation and a dictionary in the true sense of the word. Many

14 The Codes annotés are for the most part in eight-inch format.

subsequent authors produced codifications aimed at the public, usually employing alphabetical order, but which were not nevertheless real dictionaries (Blanchet 1839; Lalouette 1817; Solon 1848; Bonnin 1809) (See Touzeil-Divina: 42, 44).

These consolidating texts were soon followed by genuinely specialist répertoires on administration law. The *Questions de droit administratif* by Cormenin (1822) or even the *Traité général du droit administratif appliqué* by Gabriel Dufour (1843) adhered for example to the canons of legal lexicography: these works which are both theoretical and practical, and organised according to theme and subject, provide a particularly rich synthesis of the statute law, the doctrine and the case-law and are addressed at all categories of jurisconsults. The *Répertoire du droit administratif*, established in 1883 by the *conseiller d'État* Léon Becquet and carried on ten years later first by Édouard Laferrière and then by Paul Dislère (28 vol., 1883–1912), is one of the most accomplished works of legal lexicography of administrative law of the nineteenth century. An alphabetical work which systematically defines the terms it contains, along with the history of concepts and their principles, it is followed by a general and positive synthesis drawing on all the sources and aiming to serve practice and science. Public and administrative subjects are a favourite preoccupation of the general lexicographical works that begin to appear in the 1920s, the more renowned of which were completed at the dawn of the twentieth century. Both theoretical and practical at the same time, these encyclopaedic works had no less an ambition than to bring together the entirety of legal science (II).

## II) The Great Répertoires, or the Golden Age of Modern Legal Lexicography

The first substantial lexicographical work of the nineteenth century was the *Répertoire de la Nouvelle Législation civile, commerciale et administrative*, published in 1823 by Baron Favard de Langlade. This work, which enjoyed a considerable and enduring success, deals uniquely with the post-codification law. Such a work could only have been conceivable once a sufficient body of case-law and doctrine in the area had been created and once litigation regarding the old law had become less frequent: 'for some twelve years now I have had the idea for a *Répertoire de la nouvelle Législation civile, commerciale et administrative*, whose aim was to present the general principles of the laws that govern us along with their manner of application by the various judicial and administrative authorities; I had even drafted articles on the main subjects of the Civil Code and in particular on the law of successions and the law on hypothecs but the further my research advanced, the more necessary it became, in order to carry out my design, to wait for increased, more developed and more certain case-law on the Code. It is clear that until the law has been put to the test, it remains no more than pure theory; it is in a certain sense incomplete until its meaning and spirit have been teased out by jurisconsults and wisely settled by magistrates (Ibid.).

Whilst Merlin's *Répertoire* and the *Questions de droit*, cluttered with references that were becoming outdated, were found more and more wanting with regard to new problems arising in law, Favard de Langlade's *Répertoire* provided a *first* general synthesis of the positive law, that took into account the doctrinal and case-law architecture.[15]

The author's methodology is typical of exegesis: the essential is to explain the 'principles' of the Civil, procedural and commercial codes along with the connected 'lois', making reference to the old laws where these could add to our understanding of the new ones, but taking pains to avoid any discussion of repealed customs or objects no longer of real interest. In this task, the author was guided by the debates on each code by the *Conseil d'État* and the *Tribunat* but he also reproduces and classifies the judgments of the Cour de cassation under their corresponding articles. Administration law is also addressed from a legislative and jurisdictional perspective. The laws on the organization and jurisdiction of the administrative authorities are analysed along with the laws on litigation involving the administration. Favard de Langlade also reproduces the case-law of the Conseil d'État 'on the main questions that matters within its jurisdiction gave rise to'.

The place and the importance attached to case-law is a hallmark of great lexicographical works, which seek to provide as complete and up-to-date a synthesis as possible of all the sources of law. Practitioners, moreover, often need a preview of the current situation regarding questions falling for decision by the courts and general principles that can easily be applied rather than learned or theoretical developments in legal science. However, at the same time jurisprudence which hitherto had concerned itself primarily with the development of systems and theories on the substance of the Codes and of the Law began to take an interest in the contribution of the case-law of the courts. Amongst authors or in scientific journals such as *Thémis*, case-law was from that point on the subject of specific studies and the output of judges was increasingly taken into account by the *commentateurs*.

However the study of case-law was the guarded preserve of practitioners and in particular case reporters. To counteract the ambitions of doctrine, case reporters increased their production of lexicographical-type works and updated them at regular intervals. Theirs was a particularly ambitious project: to supply in a relatively small number of volumes the most complete synthesis possible of legal science aimed at practitioners as much as jurisconsults. These 'répertoires' are the scientific reflection of the great reports and display the know-how of the 'école practicienne'.

---

15 Ibid., VI: 'Dix années de méditations dans mes fonctions à la cour de cassation et au Conseil d'État, m'ont convaincu que leur jurisprudence s'était graduellement formée de manière à être invariable, sur les points les plus essentiels, et que les ordonnances du roi dans les matières contentieuses, comme les arrêts de la cour de cassation, devenaient un supplément naturel et nécessaire de notre législation'.

The most emblematic work of legal lexicography in the nineteenth century is that of the renowned case reporter, Désiré Dalloz, who started in 1825 to publish his alphabetical répertoire, *Jurisprudence Générale du Royaume* (Meynial: 188; de la Morandière 1950: 105, 108). It gathers together in 12 volumes all of the judgments prior to 1825 and forming part of the old periodic collection of the *Journal des Audiences*, arranging them in order of subject, those subjects being themselves organised in alphabetical order. In 1829 the Globe outlined the exacting method employed by Dalloz:

> The author begins each subject with an historical sketch, reviewing the monuments of old and modern legislation and faithfully reproducing in the notes the text of laws, decrees and by-laws still in force, without forgetting ministerial circulars or decisions reserving the right to oppose these same sources when they seem to be in conflict with the principles. After the historical exegesis, the author moves on to the doctrine showing the divisions and subdivisions within each subject, revealing in the order he has mapped out the principles of his subject and retraces, drawing on his own knowledge and that of the authors both ancient and modern that he has consulted, the often diverse Roman laws of the old and the new French law. Finally Mr Dalloz broaches judicial interpretation by means of a methodical classification under each of the jurisprudential divisions and subdivisions of all of the judicial monuments without exception, that are to be found in existing reports, but affording a truer and more concise account. Mr Dalloz does not confine himself to the methodical and analytical classification of the case law: he consults all the leading sources, seeking either to counter those judgments which appear to him to be at odds with sound doctrine, or to bolster those judgments which in his opinion have been subject to unfair criticism and unwarranted reticence.[16]

This work, the first tome of which appeared in 1831, was the subject of a major re-edition in 44 volumes begun in 1845 and completed in 1870. This re-edition considerably increased the size of Le *Répertoire* de *Dalloz* and was prefaced with an important *Essai sur l'histoire générale du droit Français*. As the author points out, the work has a triple nature – it is simultaneously a repertory of statute law, of doctrine and of case-law. For Dalloz, the combination of these three elements made the new edition akin to an encyclopaedia, and almost a collection of law books, which accounts for and justifies at the same time the significant number of volumes that it consists of.

A work which is both practical and useful, it makes access to information easier and is to be used in tandem with the periodical collection *Jurisprudence Générale du Royaume*. It stands apart, however, because of its global view of legal science, encompassing history, the philosophy of law, public law, case-law and all the branches of statute law. As Edmond Meynial pointed out, it 'will stand apart for many years because of its size and the quality of its contents' (2004: 90).

---

16 [19 juillet 1829], Journal Le Globe n° 57, vol VII, 453 et seq.

The legal répertoires that followed Dalloz were bestsellers. The tandem periodical-répertoire appealed to practitioners who could find in one half of the equation the most up-to-date information, and in the other a synthesis of the most prominent subjects at the Palais.

In 1845, Ledru-Rollin, then chief editor of the *Journal du Palais*, also published a *Répertoire* with identical ambitions to those of his rival Dalloz. History is also prominent in his work: 'Nothing less than a Répertoire was needed, containing history, statute law, doctrine and case law for all the general divisions of the law. It is just such a répertoire that we have provided for the public [...] as a comprehensive self-contained work, encompassing all the writings on law for the last half century on subjects whether they have been codified or not and which has required the collaboration of many in a toil of over three years' (I, II).

To borrow Edmond Meynial's felicitous turn of phrase, 'at that time it was felt amongst the enlightened bourgeoisie, that we had reached one of those beatific periods in the history of Man where after enduring a painful and protracted period of crisis, society can step back and from the edifice it laboriously constucted view the terrain thus far covered and contemplate the paths that lie ahead' (Meynial 2004: 190). These voluminous collections which are the very essence of legal lexicography are accompanied by a 'veritable forest' of ancillary specialist répertoires, which increased rapidly in number between 1830 and 1850. Meynal mentions in particular *Répertoire de la jurisprudence du notariat* by Rolland de Villargues (7 vols, 1827–31), the *Dictionnaire de procédure by* Bioche (5 vols. 1834–35) or even the *Dictionnaire du contentieux commercial by* Devilleneuve et Massé (1839).

Two dictionaries stand out from this mass of specialist dictionaries. The first of these is Armand Dalloz's *Dictionnaire Général* published in 1835. A distillation of legal science in five *in-quarto volumes*, this stand alone works also serves as a summary and complement to Désiré Dalloz's imposing *Répertoire* and his periodical collection. Sebire and Carteret's l'*Encyclopédie du droit* (7 vols., 1836–46), started at the same time but never completed, follows in the tradition of the great répertoires; 'we have tried to do for the contemporary law what Guyot achieved for the old statute-law and Merlin for the intermediary period which preceded and followed the publication of the Codes. Our *Encyclopédie*, accordingly, aims at occupying the place so deftly and useful held up until now by Merlin's *Répertoire*'.

An alphabetical work, l'*Encyclopédie* contains definitions and explanations of 'all the terms of law and of practice along with the historical and philosophical perspective of statute law on each subject. These elements are supplemented with a review of the doctrine, a summary of the private and public case law, a bibliographic note, and here and there, a real innovation for that time, elements of comparative law'.[17] The articles are also penned by a number of eminent jurists

17 Ibid., VIII, IX: 'On avait négligé jusqu'à ce jour de s'occuper, dans les ouvrages de droit, des législations étrangères; et cependant, par suite du principe qu'un acte est régi

including professors Antoine-Marie Demante and Foucart, the *bâtonnier* (chairman of the bar) Philippe Dupin, the lawyers Marie, Paillet, Simon and Odilon Barrot, or even the former ministers Mérilhou and Vatimesnil.

In 1886, the publishing house Sirey added a *Répertoire* to their collection, a 37-volume work published under the editorship of Fuzier-Hermann. In the preface, Adrien Carpentier and G. Frèrejouan-du-Saint recall the role and the functions occupied by this type of work enshrined in the history of legal literature:

> Repertories of case law have always held pride of place in the libraries of scholars and practitioners; in the recent past one could mention the renowned works of that genre handed down to us from Guyot, Merlin, Favard de Langlade, etc., and even today there is not a single jurisconsult who does not consult with success the répertoires that came to us from the editors of the *Journal du Palais* and the authors of the *Jurisprudence Générale*. [...] To bring together in a single work that indicates the texts and the principles, a comprehensive and reasoned review of the way those same texts and principles have been applied, to illuminate them through doctrinal criticism so that everyone can access, instantly as such, on any question whatsoever the most general and specific concepts in theory and in practice – that has been the abiding goal of those who embarked before us on the path we now enter.

Both a jurisprudential and practical work, the Répertoire is organised along the lines of its predecessors, following a schema that is aimed at facilitating research and access to the law.[18]

Although voluminous, Fuzier-Herman's *Répertoire* is of slightly smaller dimensions that its competitor Dalloz. Its spirit is more utilitarian as set out from the start in the preface: 'As regards the statute law we confined ourselves to texts that are currently in force and in the account of the subject we only borrowed from the history of law that which is strictly necessary for the understanding of the historical evolution of institutions or to help settle a disputed point'. Perpetuating the great tradition of legal répertoires, the *Fuzier-Hermann* favours a purely practical content. In so doing it sets itself apart from the other great répertoires

---

par la loi du pays où il a été passé, un grand nombre de contrats consentis hors de France doivent être appréciés par nos tribunaux suivant les lois étrangères. Il fallait combler cette lacune, au moins pour les contrats qui résultent le plus habituellement des rapports entre nationaux et étrangers, et surtout des relations commerciales'.

18 Id., II: 'A peine est-il besoin d'expliquer pourquoi nous nous sommes arrêtés à l'ordre alphabétique préférablement à l'ordre raisonné des matières. Le premier est le seul qui convienne à des travaux principalement destinés à faciliter les recherches: c'est aussi le seul qui ne prête à aucune équivoque. Il est pour ainsi dire le propre des répertoires, l'autre convient plutôt aux encyclopédies'. 'A l'intérieur de chaque article, la division adoptée est la division en titres, chapitres, sections, paragraphes. Quant aux numéros qui se suivent d'un bout à l'autre du mot, chacun d'eux correspond à une proposition complète, que cette proposition soit l'expression d'un principe ou seulement d'une application'.

of the Ancien Régime and even from those of the *Journal du Palais* which were intended as instruments of synthesis of legal culture in its entirety.

From 1886 to 1909 new reports, the *Pandectes françaises*, also published a répertoire in 59 volumes (to which were added three volumes) edited under the direction, firstly, of Hyppolyte-Férréol Rivière and then of André Weiss. The '*avertissement*' to the first volume is typical of the new utilitarian course followed by the great lexciographic works of the end of century: 'a répertoire is an astute and methodological compilation aimed at the easy discovery of information useful to traders and jurisconsults on all the questions that are settled in the doctrine and in the case law'.

Henceforth répertoires became tools aimed at the most immediate needs of professionals, in other words tools of the greatest utility, thereby shedding bit by bit their paralegal content such as legal history or the philosophy of law. In 1910 the *Répertoire pratique de législation, de doctrine et de jurisprudence* published by Dalloz under the direction firstly of Gaston Griolet and then of Charles Vergé completed this transformation. This new répertoire which only contains a 'small number of volumes' is according to its authors 'of a practical nature'. To achieve this new conception, it was necessary to purge the work of 'previous flaws': 'What people are looking for today in legal publications above everything else is specific solutions and information: theoretical developments and learned debate are of less and less interest. An account of the statute law in force, an analysis of cases in which it is interpreted should be given priority and cannot be too comprehensive'.

This transformation of legal lexicography is partly the result of a law that has become increasingly complex, rapidly evolving and specialist. Major collections of 'general legal culture' have become less and less useful to lawyers converted into technicians of the law, and who are more and more removed from the universal figure of the jurisconsult. At the turn of the twentieth century, legal lexicography favours the easily accessible specialist tool over cross-cutting works, legal vocabularies with standardised terminological definitions (Guillien and Vincent 1970; Cornu 1987) over verbose and context-bound developments.

The history of legal lexicography however shows us the other side of this doctrinal genre. Far from being rudimentary tools, the major lexicographical works provide us with a comprehensive overview of the law and can be regarded as doctrinal works in their own right in which reasoned syntheses are complemented with the personal views or theories of the authors. Too seldom studied as objects for analysis themselves, these works do not enjoy a reputation that befits their worth. Part of the reason for this may lie in the often unwarranted and excessive academic criticism directed at these easily accessible works. The meeting point of theory and practice, these lexicographic works and, in particular, those devoted to case-law have always been considered by the École as anti-scientific populist compilations, crude or strictly practical works (Dauchy: 14; Chene 1985: 179, 187). Edmond Meynial, although less severe in his judgment, still believes that the great dictionaries of the nineteenth century were instruments that were 'too convenient not to provoke idleness and apathy in those who were glad for professional reasons not to have to rely on pure speculation'. The author is of the opinion that these works even stifled intellectual thought amongst the jurisconsults of the Palais who were at that time at the cutting edge of legal science. Whilst recognizing the qualities of these works, he sees in them the principal instigator for the decline of practitioners and makes the case for their exclusion from legal science.

Moreover, once the École took over dictionaries and répertoires at the end of the century, it transformed them into mere tools, dispensing with the scientific and scholarly ambitions that were such a key part of this literary genre for centuries: in so doing it deprived hard-pressed practitioners of the cultural resources they were wont to mine in the great dictionaries and repertories of law.

The beginning of the twentieth century marked a turning point in the way legal lexicography is conceived. Extremely diverse, utilitarian, sometimes didactic and often specialist, this literary genre has left behind it once and for all the ideal of the entirety of the law being contained in the thick volumes of the great repertories. In this respect legal lexicography is a mirror of the current state of the law and legal thinking.

## References

S.-A. Blanchet, Code administratif (Dupont, Paris 1839).

P. Bonin, *Bourgeoisie et habitanage dans les villes du Languedoc sous l'Ancien régime* (Presses Universitaires d'Aix-Marseille, Aix-en-Provence 2005).

P. Bonin, 'La coutume entre pluralisme juridique, souveraineté étatique et projection historiographiques: les dictionnaires de l'Époque Moderne' in Corinne Leveleux-Teixeira, Anne Rousselet-Pimont, Pierre Bonin, Florent Garnier (eds), *Normes et normativité, études d'histoire du droit rassemblées en l'honneur d'Albert Rigaudière* (Economica, Paris 2009).

C.-J.B. Bonnin, Principes d'administration publique (Renaudière, Paris, 1809).

A.-G. Boucher d'Argis, *Dictionnaire de droit et de pratique, contenant l'explication des termes de droit, d'ordonnances, de coutumes & de pratique, par M. Claude-Joseph de Ferrière, nouvelle édition, revue, corrigée et augmentée* (Bauche, Paris 1771).

D. Bureau, 'Codification' in Stéphane Rials & Denis Alland (eds), *Dictionnaire de la culture juridique* (PUF, Paris 2003).

J.-M. Carbasse, 'De verborum significatione, quelques jalons pour une histoire des vocabulaires juridiques' [2004] Droits 3, 16.

C. Chene, 'L'arrestographie, science fort douteuse' in *Recueil des mémoires et travaux publiés par la Société d'Histoire du droit et des institutions des anciens pays de droit écrit* (Faculté de droit et des sciences économiques, Montpellier 1985) 179, 187.

J.-J. Clère, 'Philippe-Antoine Merlin' in Patrick Arabeyre, Jean-Louis Halpérin, Jacques Krynen (eds), *Dictionnaire historique des juristes français (XIIe-XXe siècle)* (PUF, Paris 2007).

C. Dagar, *Nouveau Ferrière ou Dictionnaire de droit et de pratique, civil, commercial, criminel et judiciaire; contenant l'explication de tous les termes du droit, anciens et modernes etc.* (1st, Dagar, Garnery, Levrault, Schoell et Cie, Paris 1804).

*Dictionnaire universel François et Latin, vulgairement appelé Dictionnaire de Trévoux* (2nd, Compagnie des libraires associés, Paris 1771).

A. Dalloz, *Dictionnaire général et raisonné de Législation, de Doctrine et de Jurisprudence en matière civile, commerciale, criminelle, administrative et de droit public, etc.* (Bureau de la Jurisprudence Générale, Paris 1835–41).

S. Dauchy, *L'arrestograhie, science fort douteuse*? (consulted at http://www.sartonchair.ugent.be/file/270), 2010.

S. Dauchy, « Legal interpretation in 18th century law reports », dans Y. Morigiwa, M. Stolleis et J.-L. Halpérin (éd.), Interpretation of Law in the Age of Enlightenment. From the Rule of the King to the Rule of Law, Springer, 2011 (Law and Philosophy Library 95), p. 45-60.

S. Dauchy and V. Demars-Sion (eds), *Les recueils d'arrêts et dictionnaires de Jurisprudence, XVIe-XVIIIe siècles* (La Mémoire du Droit, Paris 2005).

L. Julliot de la Morandière, 'Le centenaire du Dalloz' [1950] D.P. chronique XXIV 105.

L. Delia, 'L'encyclopédisme du Dictionnaire de droit et de pratique de Ferrière' in Martine Groult (ed.), *Les Encyclopédies: construction et circulation du savoir de l'Antiquité à Wikipédia* (L'Harmattan, Paris 2011).

C.-J. de Ferrière, *Dictionnaire de droit et de pratique, contenant l'explication des termes de droit, d'ordonnances, de coutumes & de pratique, nouvelle édition, revue, corrigée et augmentée* (Chez la veuve Brunet, Paris 1769).

G.-J. Favard de Langlade, *Répertoire de la Nouvelle Législation civile, commerciale et administrative, etc.* (Firmin Didot, Paris 1823).

Fleurigeon, *Code administratif, ou Recueil par ordre alphabétique de matières, de toutes les Lois nouvelles et anciennes etc.* (Garnery, Paris 1806).

Fuzier-Herman (eds), *Répertoire général alphabétique du droit français : contenant sur toutes les matières de la science et de la pratique juridiques l'exposé de la législation, l'analyse critique de la doctrine et les solutions de la jurisprudence, etc.* (L. Larose – Forcel, Paris 1886–1924), 37 vols.

J. Gaudemet, 'Tentatives de systématisation du droit à Rome' [1996] APD 11, 28.

G. Griolet and C. Vergé, *Répertoire pratique de législation, de doctrine et de jurisprudence* (Dalloz, Paris 1910).

J.-N. Guyot, *Répertoire universel et raisonné de jurisprudence civile, criminelle, canonique et bénéficiale, ouvrage de plusieurs jurisconsultes* (Panckoucke, Visse, Paris 1775–83).

J.-L. Halpérin, 'Haro sur les hommes de loi' [1993] *Droits* 55, 65

N. Hakim, 'Les genres doctrinaux' in La doctrine en droit administratif, Actes du colloque de l'AFDA des 11 et 12 juin 2009 à la Faculté de droit de Montpellier (Litec, Paris 2010).

V. Hayaert, 'Les lexiques juridiques: une ambition encyclopédique?' in Martine Groult (ed.), *Les Encyclopédies: construction et circulation du savoir de l'Antiquité à Wikipédia* (L'Harmattan, Paris 2011).

L.-F. Jauffret, [1791] Gazette des Nouveaux Tribunaux n°27, 11, 12.

C.-J. Lalouette, Classification des Lois administratives depuis 1789 jusqu'au 1er avril 1814 (A. Bavoux, Paris, 1817).

A. Ledru-Rollin, *Répertoire Général contenant la jurisprudence de 1791 à 1845, l'Histoire du droit, la Législation et la Doctrine des auteurs* (F.-F Patris, au Bureau du Journal du Palais, Paris 1845–47), 13 vol. et 2 suppl.

H. Leuwers, *Un juriste en politique: Merlin de Douai (1754–1838)* (Artois presses université, Arras 1996).

J.-S. Loiseau, *Dictionnaire des arrêts modernes, ou Répertoire analytique, sommaire et critique de la nouvelle jurisprudence française, civile et commerciale; contenant la Notice des Arrêts les plus importants de la Cour de cassation depuis 1790 jusqu'en 1809, et ceux des Cours d'Appel depuis la promulgation du Code Napoléon, etc.* (Archives du Droit Français, Clament frères - Libraires éditeurs, Paris 1809).

P.-A. Merlin, *Recueil alphabétique des Questions de Droit, qui se présentent le plus fréquemment dans les tribunaux; ouvrage dans lequel l'auteur a fondu et classé un grand nombre de ses plaidoyers et réquisitoires, avec le texte des arrêts de la Cour de cassation qui s'en sont ensuivis* (5th, Garnery, Paris 1827–30).

E. Meynial, 'Les recueils d'arrêts et les arrêtistes' in Dalloz (ed.), *Le Code civil 1804–1904, livre du centenaire* (1st, Paris 1904).

F. Jean de Montainville, *Dictionnaire de la jurisprudence de la Cour de cassation, précédé d'un traité sur la compétence des autorités judiciaires et des magistrats de l'Empire français, contenant littéralement les maximes, règles, principes de cette Cour...en matière civile et criminelle, etc.. Dictionnaire de la jurisprudence de la Cour de cassation ou les maximes, règles, principes de cette Cour depuis l'an VIII jusqu'en 1806 etc.* (Chez l'auteur, Trèves 1805–07), 5 vols.

J.-M. Pardessus, *Œuvres complètes du chancelier d'Aguesseau, nouvelle édition augmentée de pièces échappées aux premiers éditeurs, et d'un discours préliminaire, etc.* (Nicolle, Paris 1819).

*Pandectes françaises – Nouveau répertoire de doctrine, de législation et de jurisprudence* (Chevalier-Marescq, Paris 1886–1909), 62 vols.

S. Rials, *La déclaration des droits de l'Homme et du citoyen* (Hachette, Paris 1988).

Sebire et Carteret, *Encyclopédie du droit, ou répertoire raisonné de législation et de jurisprudence en matières civile, administrative, criminelle et commerciale, etc.* (Coulon, Videcoq Père & fils, Paris 1836–46).

E. Serverin, *De la jurisprudence en droit privé. Théorie d'une pratique* (Presses Universitaires de Lyon, Lyon, 1985).

J.-B. Sirey, *Code civil annoté des dispositions et décisions de la législation et de la jurisprudence, etc.* (1st, Bureau d'Administration du Recueil Général des Lois et des Arrêts, Paris 1817).

V.-H. Solon, Code administratif annoté (A. Durand, Paris, 1848).
A. Teissier-Esminger, *La fortune esthétique du Code civil des français* (La Mémoire du Droit, Paris 2004).
G.V. Tennesson, *Dictionnaire sur le nouveau droit civil* (Rousseau, Rondonneau, Garnery, Paris 1799).
M. Touzeil-Divina, *La doctrine publiciste, 1800-1880: éléments de patristique administrative* (La Mémoire du Droit, Paris 2009).
M. Villey, *La formation de la pensée juridique moderne* (PUF – Quadrige manuels, Paris 2006).
A. Wijiffels and D.Ibetson, Introduction to *Case Law in the Making: The Techniques and Methods of Judicial Records and Law Reports* (ed. A. Wijiffels), pp. 13–39.

# Chapter 2
# The Early Modern English Law Lexicon

Ian Lancashire and Janet Damianopoulos

## Introduction

No profession contributed more to an understanding of the English language in the Early Modern English period than law. The notion and publication of a monolingual English dictionary began with a lawyer, John Rastell, in the early 1520s, long before it occurred to Robert Cawdrey to bring out his celebrated hard-word dictionary in 1604. Of the 43 known members of the Elizabethan Society of Antiquaries (circa 1572–1604; Schoeck 1954), 38 were lawyers. Of these, 15 contributed to lexicography in the period.[1] Another five non-antiquarians – John and William Rastell, John Cowell, Sir Thomas Blount and Thomas Manley – produced long-lasting, very sizable dictionaries of law terms that built on, before 1520, only a single, short and somewhat enigmatic glossary (Skemer 1998 and 1999). This chapter is an introduction to their work.

## John Rastell

John Rastell (Geritz and Laine 1983), an English lawyer and playwright who married the sister of Sir Thomas More, published the first monolingual English dictionary about 1523. This is a notable first (Lancashire 2006; McConchie 2012). It glossed terms of Common Law in the original law-French and separately translated the whole glossary – headwords and explanations – into English. Rastell

1 The bibliographical indexes of *Lexicons of Early Modern English* (2006–) at leme.library.utoronto.ca name these individuals and their achievements. William Camden, in his *Remaines*, analyses old proper and place names in England, a subject also explored by Sir John Doddridge, William Lambarde and William Patten. Richard Carew is remembered for his eloquent defence of the English language, published in Camden's *Remaines*. Sir William Cecil, Lord Burghley, left a partial index of law terms in manuscript and patronized many lexicographical works. Sir John Davies was a Welsh lexicographer. Thomas Doyley advised Richard Perceval on Latin terms used in his Spanish-English dictionary (1591). William Fleetwood's research on forestry terminology exists in manuscript. Abraham Hartwell published on Persian and Turkish. John Holland and Francis Thynne annotated medieval terms in Chaucer's works, Sir Walter Raleigh studied alchemical symbols and John Selden published on the language of heraldry. Francis Tate compiled a dictionary of legal terms, surviving in manuscript.

had published some important legal works for working lawyers before, notably Anthony Fitzherbert's abridgements, but his little dictionary served novice English students of the Inns of Court who did not yet know law-French well. In explaining a lawyer's terms of art – his professional vocabulary – to non-lawyers, Rastell anticipated the popular purpose of law dictionaries to this day. Unsurprisingly, the chief legal historian of Early Modern English law, J.H. Baker devised a manual of law-French (1990), but he did not discuss law dictionaries in his study of early law publishing. Few barristers, solicitors and judges would use them.

Rastell's dictionary survived in several dozen editions until the mid-eighteenth century but the Inns of Court did not delight in using English. Late in the reign of Henry VIII, the king's ministers and courtiers actually tried to replace law-French with Latin and contemporary French. By the reign of James I, a professor of Civil Law, John Cowell, published *The Interpreter* (1607), which departed from the modestly explanatory word-entry to provide small scholarly essays with argumentation that tried to bring together the Civil and the Common Law: a merger that would have inevitably weakened law-French and injected mainstream Latin into the Inns of Court. Cowell's text survived into the late seventeenth century, when editors like Sir Thomas Blount and Thomas Manley, both of them lawyers, managed the merger in a way that protected the culture of the Common Law.

English monolingual dictionaries themselves came into being because Rastell supplied Inns of Court students with the tools to understand legal language. Those tools did not leverage change in the profession itself, which resisted encouragement to use English, regular French and correct Latin.

Why did the coroner in Coventry in 1506 move to London about three years later to set up a printing press for legal and humanist books, become an early Tudor playwright, open the first public theatre in London and introduce vernacular lexicography to England? His achievements mark a patriotic man of many parts who did not deserve to die in prison, impoverished, in 1536, a year after the king had executed his brother-in-law, Sir Thomas More, the former Chancellor, for treason.

Rastell appears to have had two motives. As an outer barrister of the Middle Temple in London by 1502, he wanted to make reference works for his fellow lawyers. His first great service to the profession was his printing of *La grande abbregement de la ley* by Anthony Fitzherbert (1514–16; STC 10954; cf. Graham and Heckel 1958). This went through successively larger editions until the *Magnum abbreuiamentum statutorum anglie* came out in 1528 with over 600 alphabetical headings. These served to organize information in its original language.

However, like More, Rastell also believed strongly in educating the English people, and his major achievement in doing so was to translate the law of the land into English. Rastell was in the vanguard of the Tudor humanists in this, following Henry VII himself, who ordered that any new statutes of the realm should be published in English (Graham 1966). In 1519, accordingly, Rastell published, in English, an abbreviation of the statutes as a whole, organized under 145 alphabetical headings from 'Accions popular' to 'vsery'. Henry VIII had perceived, Rastell said in his introduction, that 'our vulgare englysh to*n*g was maruelously ame*n*dyd & augmentyd by reaso*n* that dyuers clerkis & lerned men had translate & made many noble workis in to our englysh to*n*g wherby there was mych more plenty & habou*n*dau*n*ce off englysh vsyd tha*n* ther was in tymes past'. Rastell followed the king in good faith, an example that made William Tyndale's translation of the New Testament into English in the mid-1520s seem natural, even if Henry VIII afterwards pursued Tyndale to his execution.

John Rastell's dictionary also translated law-French, which was not taught in universities but only to those who became members of the Inns of Court. His first edition, in 1523, explained 165 'obscure and derke termys con*s*ernyng the lawis of thys realme'. Most were either law-French or Latin in etymology, although many were plain English, like 'Arest', 'Disceyt', 'Homage', 'Proteccion' and 'Treason'. Rastell's word-entries focused on things denoted by words rather than the words themselves: explanations were practical, often anecdotal rather than lexical discussions. For instance, Rastell describes a ceremony of giving 'Homage' rather than defining the term:

> Homage shalbe made in such maner / yt is to sey ye tenaunt in fee symple or fee tayle that holdyth by homage shall knele vppo*n* both hys knees & the lorde shall syt & shall hold the hand*es* of hys tenau*n*t betwene hys hand*es* and the tenant shall sey I becum your ma*n* from this day forward of lyfe & me*m*ber and of yerly honour and to you shalbe faythful and trew and shall berre to you fayth for the land*es* yt I clai*m*e to hold of you sauyng the fayth yt I owe to our lord the kyng / and than the lord so syttyng shall kysse hym but how fealte shalbe done loke before in fealte / and the stewerd of the lorde may take fealte bute not homage (e3v–e4r).

The *Oxford English Dictionary Online* today gives a succinct definition, 'Formal and public acknowledgement of allegiance, by which a male tenant declares himself the vassal of the king or lord from whom he holds land'. Nowhere in its full entry is there a description of the ceremony. *Ballantine's Law Dictionary* today, however, gives both a definition and an account of the ceremony, combining the encyclopaedic and the lexical as Rastell did.

## Thomas Cromwell

About 1536, Richard Morison (circa 1510–56), a propagandist working for the chief minister who ultimately succeeded Cardinal Wolsey, Thomas Cromwell, proposed a radical change in the Inns of Court, that barristers use Latin instead of law-French. In a manuscript treatise titled 'A Perswasion to the King that the Laws of the Realme Shulde be in Latin', Morison 'complained of lawyers who could not even draw deeds in Latin, but were forced to draw them in French and cause their clerks to turn them into Latin' (Baker 1998: 14; Woolfson 2004). No doubt, Morison did Cromwell's bidding in this, but why was the chief minister so concerned about the language of practice used in the Inns of Court? His former master, Wolsey, had no such scruple. If we accept Morison's arguments at face value, his motive must have simply been to bring law into the humanist fold.

Some two years later, however, Cromwell approached another three men, Thomas Denton, Nicholas Bacon and Robert Carey, to assess the curriculum of the Inns of Court, revise it and propose a new corporation be set up to implement the revision (Fisher Nov. 1977; Bland 1969). They recommended that a new fifth inn require the use of '*pure* French *and* Latine *tongues*' and that 'the inner Barristers shall plead in *Latine*, and the other Barristers reason in *French*; and that either of them shall do what they can to banish the corruption of both tongues' (Waterhouse 1663: 540). These recommendations presumably went to Henry VIII under Cromwell's name, although they died still-born when Cromwell fell from power and was executed.

It is a reasonable surmise that Cromwell's lobbying was part of a larger crown plan that had John Palsgrave bring out the first bilingual, English-French dictionary in 1530, and Sir Thomas Elyot, in 1538, issue the first Latin-English lexicon not indebted to the old medieval clerical compilations issued by Wynkyn de Worde in *Promptorium Parvulorum* and *Ortus Vocabulorum* (1499–1500). Henry VIII patronized the makers of both new dictionaries, Palsgrave being the French instructor of his sister, and Elyot having been urged personally by the king (who threw open his library to the lexicographer's use) to finish the job. Both works in effect purify these languages in England itself, Palsgrave's from the corrupt influence of law-French, and Elyot's from the influence of Catholic Rome. No longer could the Inns of Court have any excuse not to know better. Yet why, in the mind of the king, and of Wolsey's successor, did they need to?

After Henry VIII acquired a new fertile wife, Anne Boleyn, and recognition as head of the Church of England who could grant his own divorce from Catherine of Aragon, the king turned to the question of financing his new ecclesiastical responsibilities. He dissolved the monasteries and seized their assets, those very institutions whose Latin Elyot would replace. Next, Cromwell plotted to seize the Inns of Court, both for their wealth, although they held valuable London properties, and for their importance as a potential source for well-educated courtiers, administrators and diplomats. If they were to serve the king in Europe, however, they could not speak law-French but would have to use uncorrupted French and perfect Latin. Consequently, the Inns of Court would have to be reformed. Elyot had already intimated as much in his *The Governor* (1531).

The Tudors were always keenly appreciative of how much they depended on their ministers to prosper and survive. Typically, Henry VII used the Church and the Inns of Court, drawing John Morton (–1500) from Oxford and the clergy, and lawyer Richard Empson (circa 1450–1510) from the Middle Temple. Henry VIII promoted another churchman, Thomas Wolsey, who thrived under his master until he failed to deliver the divorce. Sir Thomas More, a Morton protégé from Oxford and then New Inn, came with a lawyer's education at the Inns of Court, and as part of his administration he implemented legal reforms on lawyers and judges. More's inability to approve of the king's spiritual and marital actions led to his execution in 1535, but that outcome evidently did not alter long-term crown policy: to abandon the clergy as a resource for ministers and servants, focusing instead on reformed educational institutions that taught the law.

Modern dictionaries, both monolingual and bilingual, started up abruptly in London from circa 1525 to 1538, if we are correct, primarily to solve problems at the Inns of Court. These were not professional issues of critical importance to lawyers. At stake was education of a new legal profession, not bound to an obscure register of old French but fully conversant in the languages of European business and diplomacy. The new lexicography did not owe its emergence to public demand but to royal patrons and their servants.

## Richard Tottel and the Company of Stationers

John Rastell's son, William Rastell, a judge, may have assisted in making the original *Exposition*, but after 1530 – when Palsgrave's French dictionary came out – this ultimately very popular law dictionary returned to print only after both the deaths of both Rastells in the reign of Elizabeth. The crown maintained control of the printing of law books by issuing a patent to a publisher who paid for the privilege. In 1553 Richard Tottel paid for this monopoly and held it for 40 years. After his death, the patent passed to several other printers for a short time before it was centralized in the Company of Stationers itself, in which Tottel had, over time, filled major positions, including master.[2]

Royal influence under Elizabeth was mediated through Lord Burghley, her first minister until the early 1590s, when his son Robert took over. Elizabeth kept securely at arm's length from patent decisions, but the two Cecils used the tool to raise funds for the crown. The father's entourage of civil servants had almost entirely Cambridge connections and he permitted dedications to him from but a few lexicographers, such as the Latinist Thomas Thomas in 1589 (who was Cambridge University printer). Burghley preferred herbals and other scientific books, and no new law dictionary was printed when he held sway. Tottel simply hired others to expand the Rastell glossary, a practice that continued for more than 100 years. Law-French maintained its ascendence in the Inns of Court, despite complaints about its corruption and continued lobbying by men such as Nicholas Bacon.

## Dr John Cowell

Cowell, a professor of Civil Law at Oxford, introduced the Civil Law to print in his *The Interpreter* (1607) and integrated it with discussion of the Common

2 See Bacon and Gwillim, V: 595 for bills by plaintiffs against the Company of Stationers for wrongfully printing law books in 15 James I and 13–14 Charles 2.

Law. Civil Law dealt with the admiralty and the Church and was taught in the universities only, and then in Latin, not French. Cowell's patron was impeccable, none other than the archbishop of Canterbury, but several slips impugning the authority of Parliament created a scandal, and none other than the king, James I, was forced to denounce Cowell's book and have all locatable copies burned. Cowell had made serious errors in thinking that he could support the divine right of kings in the face of a Parliament well populated by Inns of Court-educated lawyers of the Common Law. Sustained patronage was essential to the life of law dictionaries. Cowell's book failed drastically because of an unforgivably obtuse affront to king and Parliament and was not reissued until by Archbishop Laud in 1637 on the eve of the civil war. Disgraced Cowell died of a botched operation for kidney stones in 1610, his yeoman service to legal lexicography in ashes.

## Sir Thomas Blount and Thomas Manley

By 1660, with the return of Charles II, Sir Thomas Blount (1618–79; Mortimer 2004) attempted a second integration of the two laws, civil and common, first by revising the Rastell, and second by integrating Common Law terms in a revised Cowell. Blount was a member of the Inner Temple and was called to the bar in 1648, but he could not practise law because he was a Roman Catholic. In 1656 he published *Glossographia*, the largest hard-word English dictionary to date, and by the time Charles II was restored in 1660, there was a resurgence of Catholicism that benefited Blount. He issued various editions of *Glossographia* and redid both Rastell (1667) and Cowell (in *Nomo-Lexikon* 1670). Blount was unquestionably the most prolific and important lexicographer in England during those 15 years.

As the major law lexicon by the end of the Early Modern period, *Nomo-Lexikon* illustrates contemporary trends in lexicography. Blount dedicated it to Sir Orlando Bridgeman, Knight and Baronet, Lord Keeper of the Great Seal of England, Sir John Kelynge Knight, Lord Chief Justice of His Majesties Court of Kings Bench, and Sir John Vaughan Knight, Lord Chief Justice of His Majesties Court of Common Pleas. All three men were prominent judges who had long, distinguished careers behind them by the time. Their responsibility was not to grant funds to enable Blount to do the revision but rather to give authority to its statements.

Like *The Interpreter*, *Nomo-Lexikon* generously cites printed sources for its information. In this respect it became more an index of other books than Rastell's reflection on how law terms actually worked in the world. He wrote word-entries with an antiquarian's eye interested in local and ancient history, and in etymology. *Nomo-Lexikon* also successfully brought together the civil and Common Law into one volume. Unlike Cowell's original, however, Blount's revision avoided controversy. He wisely omitted Cowell's headword for the king.

Blount's scholarly objectives left him vulnerable to being exploited by other, much less accomplished men. Edward Phillips, John Milton's nephew and a protestant, plagiarized *Glossographia* in a rival dictionary issued only two years after it, in 1658. Thomas Manley likewise copied Blount's *Nomo-Lexikon* (1670) in *Nomothetes, the interpreter* (1672, 1684). Before being called to the bar in 1673, Manley had previously served in lesser capacities, to judge from his publications, The Sollicitor (1663) and The Clerk's Guide (1672; Cheesman 2004). Manley did not greatly expand Blount's word-entries, although he reintroduced ones by Cowell that Blount had omitted, including that for the king. Manley was no scholar (Bonagaerts 1978: 47), and so he sought out a powerful patron, Anthony Lord Ashley, Baron of Wimbourne St Giles, Chancellor of the Exchequer and a Lord of the king's Privy Council. Judges gave a satisfying authority to Blount's additions, but Manley may have wanted political protection from Blount, whom he had clearly plagiarized.

Cowell did more than his predecessors or his successors to develop legal word-entries. He expanded the simple word-entry in Rastell's law dictionaries by including discussion and bibliographical references. Compare what Rastell in 1525 says about *ad quod damnum*:

> … a wrytt of ad quod dampnum lyeth wher one wyll giue landys to an house of relygyon than this wryt shall go forth to the eschetor to enquere off what valew the land ys & preiudyce yt shall be to the kyng.

… with Cowell's much richer word-entry, which draws information from Sir Anthony Fitzherbert's lengthy French explanation in his *La Novelle Natura Brevium* (London: Thomas Berthelet, 1534), fols. 250–256:

> Ad quod damnum, is a writ that lyeth to the escheater to inquire what hurt it will be to the King, or other person, to graunt a Faire or market, or a mortmaine for any lands intended to be giuen in fee simple to any house of religion, or other body politicke. For in that case, the land so giuen is said to fal into a dead hand, that is, such an estate and condition, that the chiefe Lords do leese all hope of heriots, seruice of court, and escheates vpon any traiterous or felonious offence committed by the tenant. For a bodie politicke dieth not, neither can performe personall seruice, or commit treason or felonie, as a singular person may. And therefore it is reasonable, that before any such grant be made, it should be knowne, what preiudice it is like to worke to the graunter. Of this reade more in Fitzh. nat. breu. fol. 221. and look Mortmaine.

Both Blount and Manley copied Cowell almost verbatim, although Manley added a reference to *Les termes de la ley* (1671).

## The Growth and Spread of Legal Vocabulary

The Rastell editions, 27 in number from circa 1523 to 1685, reveal how gradually the legal lexicon expanded. If we look at the letter *R*, John Rastell's glossary of 1525 has just six entries, which increased to ten by the close of his printing career. Tottel did not expand *R* in his first four re-editions from 1563 to 1575, but by 1579 *R* grew to 16, and to 21 in 1592 and 1595. When Thomas Wright took over in 1598 and 1602, he obtained Me. Paget to revise the entries: *R* had 24 entries, which the six re-editions of the Company of Stationers from 1607 to 1629 only increased by one. The 1636 edition under John More boasted 150 new entries in all, 38 in *R*, a plateau lasting until 1659. When Thomas Blount re-edited Rastell in 1667 and 1671, *R* had 43–4 entries. The last seventeenth-century edition, in 1685, offered 51 entries. Over 160 years, Rastell's *R* grew from 6 to 51, a nine-fold increase.

One tool to measure the growth of Early Modern English vocabulary is *Lexicons of Early Modern English* (*LEME*), which Lancashire has edited since 2006. At present it lists 66 legal lexical texts in a total of 1,225 glossaries and dictionaries from 1475 to 1701. Of the 180 texts whose word-entries are in *LEME*, eight are principally legal in nature. They are John Rastell's first expositions (circa 1525), the glossary in his statutes (1527), the anonymous *Verba Obsoleta et Alia* in British Library Lansdowne MS 171 (later sixteenth century), Rastell's *Exposition* of 1579, John Cowell's *Interpreter* (1607), W. Folkingham's *Feudigraphia* (1610) and Henry Spelman's *Of the Original of Terms or Law-days* (1614). Currently we are adding Thomas Blount's *Nomo-Lexikon* (1670), possibly the last major law dictionary not yet in *LEME*.[3]

*LEME* gives explanations of words as living speakers of the period understood them. A word-search reveals the main senses that a word has by juxtaposing word-entries in which it is found. In this way researchers can trace to what extent terms of art in law-French belong, or came to belong, to the English language in general. Here are three examples.

The word 'remitter', the second term under Rastell's *R* of 1525, occurs six times, first in Rastell, then thrice in Cowell (1607), once in Edward Phillips (1658) and once in Elisha Coles (1676). Phillips and probably Coles abbreviated one of Cowell's entries. 'Remitter' did not enter any of the half-dozen hard-word dictionaries before Phillips and cannot be found in Kersey's general monolingual lexicon of 1701. None of the *LEME* entries appears in the *OED* entry, which records two senses (not one) and gives sample quotations from circa 1443 to 1992.

The word 'replication' turns up in all Rastell editions, 1525–1685, and 44 times in 19 *LEME* works from 1525 to 1701. Almost all hard-word lexicons give it as a headword, and sometimes bilingual dictionaries: Elyot (1538) and Florio (1598, 1611) use it as a synonym for 'repetition', in a rhetorical rather than a legal

3 Early English Books Online/Text Creation Partnership (EEBO/TCP) has digitized – in text form – more than 40,000 works in STC and Wing. Some of these are law dictionaries not yet in *LEME*. They include William Fulbecke's *A direction or preparatiue to the study of the lawe* (1600), *Edward Leigh's Philological Commentary* (1652), and Thomas Blount's *Nomo-Lexikon* (1670). Other dictionaries not yet digitized are by Manley and George Meriton (1685), and manuscript lexicons by John Joscelyn (Bately 1992; Tornaghi 2008), David Chalmers (1566), and Francis Tate (1600–11; see Lancashire 2005 and Considine 2012).

context. Again, no overlap exists between the *OED* and *LEME* citations, but *OED* gives more extensive ranges for these and other later senses.

The word 'replevin' appears in most Rastell editions, and in seven *LEME* works, beginning with Rastell (1525) and Cowell, and thereafter in hard-word dictionaries by Cockeram (1623), Blount (1656), Phillips (1658), Coles (1676) and Kersey (1702). Again, none of the *LEME* entries appears in the fuller *OED* entry, which detects similar legal senses except for 'The action or an act of bailing a prisoner' (1588–1784). Kersey mentions that a replevin responds to a writ of *replegiari facias*, a detail not in *OED*.

*OED* unquestionably gives the most complete picture of these three words, but it avoids quoting from dictionaries. While it is true that lexicographers copy from one another, they also make a decision whether or not to carry terms in early works forward or not. They are primary contemporary witnesses of meaning and explicitly explain words. It is valuable, as well, to know whether a legal term of art turns up in hard-word dictionaries. If not, the word has been isolated in its register.

## Conclusion

Early Modern English legal dictionaries made two significant contributions to the development of the language. Bilingual dictionaries had always been around, but not English-only ones. The Rastell lexicons of legal 'terms of art', from 1525 to the mid-seventeenth century, laid the groundwork for the emergence of monolingual English hard-word dictionaries by glossographers from Edmund Coote (1596) to Elisha Coles (1676). Secondly, John Cowell's *Interpreter* (1607) introduced word-entries that quoted from or referred extensively to books and manuscripts, a feature that Thomas Blount used in *Glossographia*, his hard-word dictionary, and in *Nomo-Lexicon*, his re-edition of Cowell. This technique anticipated the great innovation of Samuel Johnson's own dictionary (1747), which gave quotations from major Early Modern English authors to illustrate every sense and of course influenced the structure of the *Oxford English Dictionary* a century later.

Not to be forgotten are two further effects of Early Modern English law dictionaries. The gradual increase of headwords in legal lexicons, especially in the Rastell series, contributed to the well-known sizable expansion of English vocabulary in this period. This growth, also, owed much to the promotion of English by patrons. The monarchy and its chief advisers used their influence to have bilingual and terms-of-art lexicons written and published. Less well known as a tool of patronage are the monopolies on publishing certain types of books. Lord Burghley, Elizabeth's chief minister, extended these, and the Company of Stationers took over Rastell's law dictionary for much of its career.

Law has always been a prime mover in history owing to its role in allocating property and power. Language is one of the most crucial mechanisms of law, but that the legal profession gave so much to documenting and growing, not only its own register, but also languages in the Early Modern period, is not as well known as it deserves to be.

## References


Arber, E., *A Transcript of the Registers of the Company of Stationers of London, 1557–1640*, 5 vols. London: n.p., 1875–94.

Baker, John Hamilton. *Manual of Law French*. 2nd ed. London: Scolar Press, 1990.

——. 'English Law Books and Legal Publishing'. *The Book in Britain: Volume IV, 1557–1695*. Eds John Barnard and D.F. Mackenzie, assisted by Maureen Bell. Cambridge: Cambridge University Press, 2002, 474–503.

——. An Introduction to English Legal History. 2nd edn. London: Butterworths, 1979.

Ballentine, James A. *Ballentine's Law Dictionary*. 3rd edn. Ed. William S. Anderson. Rochester, NY: Lawyers Co-operative, 1969.

Bately, Janet. 'John Joscelyn and the Laws of the Anglo-Saxon Kings'. Words, texts, and manuscripts: studies in Anglo-Saxon culture presented to Helmut Gneuss on the occasion of his sixty-fifth birthday. Eds M. Korhammer, Karl Reichl and Hans Sauer. n.p., 1992, 435–66.

Bland, D.S. 'Henry VIII's Royal Commission on the Inns of Court'. *Journal of the Society of Public Teachers of Law* 10 (1969): 183–94.

——. 'Some Notes on the Evolution of the Legal Dictionary'. *The Journal of Legal History* 1.1 (1980): 75–84.

Blount, Thomas. *Glossographia*. London: Thomas Newcomb for Humphrey Moseley and George Sawbridge, 1656. Wing B 3334.

—. *NOMO-ΛΕΘΙΚΟΝ [Nomo-lexikon]: A Law-Dictionary. Interpreting such difficult and obscure Words and Terms As are found either in Our Common or Statute, Ancient or Modern Lawes: With References to the several Statutes, Records, Registers, Law-books, Charters, Ancient Deeds, and Manuscripts, wherein the Words are used: And Etymologies, where they properly occur.* London: Thomas Newcomb for John Martin and Henry Herringman, 1670. Wing B 3340.

Bush, Jonathan A. and Alain Wijffels. *Learning the Law: Teaching and the Transmission of the Law in England 1150–1900*. London and Rio Grande: Hambledon Press, 1999.

Chalmers, David. *Dictionary of Scots Law*. British Library Additional MS 27, 472. 22 July 1566.

Cheesman, C.E.A. 'Manley, Thomas (c.1628–1676)'. *Oxford Dictionary of National Biography*. Eds H.C.G. Matthew and Brian Harrison. Oxford: OUP, 2004. Online ed. Ed. Lawrence Goldman. Jan. 2008.

Chrimes, S.B. 'The Constitutional Ideas of Dr. John Cowell'. *The English Historical Review* 64.253 (1949): 461–87.

Cockeram, Henry. *English Dictionarie: or, an Interpreter of Hard English words*. London: Eliot's Court Press for N. Butter, 1623. *STC* 5461.

Coles, Elisha. *An English Dictionary, 1676*. Menston: Scolar Press, 1971.

Considine, John. *Ashgate Critical Essays on Early English Lexicographers. Volume 4: The Seventeenth Century*. Farnham: Ashgate, 2012.

Coquillette, Daniel R. 'Legal Ideology and Incorporation I: the English Civilian Writers, 1523–1607'. *Boston University Law Review* 61 (1981 January): 1–89.

Cowell, John. *The Interpreter: or Booke Containing the Signification of Words: Wherein is set foorth the true meaning of all, or the most part of such Words and Termes, as are mentioned in the Lawe Writers, or Statutes of this victorious and renowned Kingdome, requiring any Exposition or Interpretation*. Cambridge: John Legate, 1607. STC 5900.

Elyot, Sir Thomas. *The Dictionary of syr Thomas Eliot*. London: T. Bertheleti, 1538.

Fisher, R.M. 'Thomas Cromwell, Dissolution of the Monsteries, and the Inns of Court, 1534–1540'. *Journal of the Society of Public Teachers of Law* 14.2 (March 1977): 103–17.

——. 'Thomas Cromwell, Humanism and Educational Reform, 1530–40'. *Historical Research* 50.122 (November 1977): 151–63.

Florio, John. *Queen Anna's New World of Words*. London: Edward Blount and William Barret, 1611.

Fraunce, Abraham. *The Lawyer's Logic, 1588. English linguistics, 1500–1800, no. 174*. Menston: Scolar Press, 1969. STC 11344.

Fulbecke, William. 'A Table of certain words in the Interpretation whereof the Common Law of this Realme and the Ciuill Law doe seeme to agree'. *A Direction or Preparatiue to the Study of the Lawe. London: Adam Islip for Thomas Wight, 1600*. STC 11410.

Geritz, Albert J. and Amos Lee Laine. *John Rastell*. Boston: Twayne, 1983.

Graham, Howard Jay and John W. Heckel. 'The Book that "Made" the Common Law: The First Printing of Fitzherbert's La Graunde Abridgement, 1514–1516'. *Law Library Journal* 51 (1958): 100–16.

Graham, Howard Jay. 'The Englishing of English Law'. *Moreana* 11 (1966 September): 27–32.

Graham, Howard Jay. 'The Rastells and the Printed English Law Book of the Renaissance'. *Law Library Journal* 47 (1954): 6–25.

——. '"Our Tong Maternall Maruellously Amendyd and Augmentyd": The First Englishing and Printing of the Medieval Statutes at Large, 1530–1533'. *UCLA Law Review* 13 (1965–66): 58–98.

Hortus Vocabulorum. *English Linguistics, 1500–1800; no. 123*. Menston: Scolar Press, 1968.

Kersey, John. *English Dictionary: Or, a Compleat: COLLECTION Of the Most Proper and Significant Words, Commonly used in the LANGUAGE*. London: Henry Bonwicke and Robert Knaplock, 1702.

Lancashire, Ian. 'Dictionaries and Power from Palsgrave to Johnson'. *Anniversary Essays for Johnson's Dictionary*. Eds Jack Lynch and Anne McDermott. Cambridge: Cambridge University Press, 2005, 24–41.

——. '"Dumb Significants" and Early Modern English Definition'. In Jens Brockmeier, Min Wang, and David R. Olson, eds, *Literacy, Narrative and Culture*. Richmond, Surrey: Curzon, 2002: 131–54.

——. 'Law and Early Modern English Lexicons'. *HEL-LEX: New Approaches in English Historical Lexis*. Eds Roderick McConchie, Heli Tissari and Olga Timofeeva. Somerville, MA: Cascadilla Press, 2006.

——. 'William Cecil and the Rectification of English'. *The Languages of Nation: Attitudes and Norms. Ed. Carol Percy and Mary Catherine Davidson*. Bristol: Multilingual Matters, 2012, 39–62.

——, ed. *Lexicons of Early Modern English*. Toronto: University of Toronto Press and the University of Toronto Library, 2006–.

——. 'Lexicography in the Early Modern English Period: the Manuscript Record'. *Historical Lexicography*. Eds J. Coleman and A. MacDermott. Tübingen: Max Niermeyer, 2005. 19–30.

Leigh, Edward, *A Philologicall Commentary, Or, An Illustration of the most Obvious and Usefull Words in the Law. With their Distinctions and diverse Acceptations, as they are found as well in Reports Ancient and Modern, as in Records, and Memorials never Printed: Usefull for all young Students of the Law*. London: T. Mabb for Charles Adams, 1652. Wing L 997.

McConchie, Roderick. *Ashgate Critical Essays on Early English Lexicographers. Volume 3: The Sixteenth Century*. Farnham: Ashgate, 2012.

Meriton, George. *Nomenclatura Clericalis: Or, The Young Clerk's Vocabulary, in English and Latine*. London: Richard Lambert, 1685. Wing M1807.

Mortimer, Ian. 'Blount, Thomas (1618–1679)'. *Oxford Dictionary of National Biography*. Eds H.C.G. Matthew and Brian Harrison. Oxford: OUP, 2004. Online ed. Ed. Lawrence Goldman. Oct. 2008.

Palsgrave, John. *Lesclarcissement de la langue francoyse*. London: R. Pynson and J. Haukyns, 1530.

Phillips, Edward. *The New World of English Words, 1658*. Menston: Scolar Press, 1969.

*Promptorium Parvulorum 1499*. Introduction by R.C. Alston. Menston: Scolar Press, 1968.

Rastell, John. *Exposiciones terminorum legum Anglorum. Et natura breuium cum diuersis casibus regulis & fundamentis legum tam de libris Magistri Litteltoni quam de aliis legum libris collectis & breuiter compilatis pro Iuuinibus valde necessariis. THe exposicions of the termys of the law of englond & the nature of the wryttys wyth dyuers rulys and pryncyples of the law aswell out of the bokys of master lyttelton as of other bokys of the law gaderyd & breuely compilyd for yong men very necessary*. London: John Rastell, 1523. 1525–30: STC 2071, 2073, 2073.3.

——. *An exposition of certaine difficult and obscure wordes and termes of the lawes of this realme/John Rastell. The English experience, no. 210.* Amsterdam and New York: Theatrum Orbis Terrarum and Da Capo Press, 1969.

——. and William Rastell. *The Exposicions of the termes of the lawes of England, with diuers propre rules and principles of the lawe, as well out of the bookes of maister Littleton, as of other. Gathered both in French and English, for yong men very necessary. whereunto are added the olde tenures.* London: Rychard Tottel, 1563. STC 20703.5. Also 1567: STC 2074; 1572: STC 2075; 1575: STC 2076.

Rissanen, Matti. 'Standardisation and the Language of Early Statutes'. *The Development of Standard English, 1300–1800: Theories, Descriptions, Conflicts*. Ed. Laura Wright. Cambridge: Cambridge University Press, 2000, 117–30.

Schoeck, R.J. 'The Elizabethan Society of Antiquaries and Men of Law'. *Notes & Queries* 199 (1954): 417–21.

Skemer, Don C. 'Expositio Vocabulorum: a Medieval English Glossary as Archival Aid'. *Journal of the Society of Archivists* 19.1 (1998): 63–75.

——. 'Reading the Law: Statute Books and the Private Transmission of Legal Knowledge in Late Medieval England'. *Learning the Law: Teaching and the Transmission of Law in England 1150–1900*. Eds Jonathan A. Bush and Alain Wijffels. London: Hambledon, 1999.

Skene, John. 'De verborum significatione. The Exposition of the Termes and Difficill Wordes, contained in the foure buikes of Regiam Majestatem, and vthers, etc.'. *The Lawes and Actes of Parliament, maid be King Iames the First, and his successours Kinges of Scotland: visied, collected and extracted furth of the Register, etc.* Edinburgh: Robert Walde-Graue, 1597.

Tate, Francis. 'Lexicon Juris'. Cambridge University Library Ff.I.15. circa 1600–11.

Terrill, Richard J. 'Humanism and Rhetoric in Legal Education: The Contribution of Sir John Dodderidge (1555–1628)'. *The Journal of Legal History* 2.1 (1981): 30–44.

Tornaghi, Paola. 'On legal sources in the dictionaries of John Joscelyn and Sir Simonds D'Ewes'. *Thou sittest at another boke ...: English Studies in Honour of Domenico Pezzini*. Eds Giovanni Iamartino, Maria Luisa Maggioni and Roberta Facchinetti. Milan: Polimetrica, 2008, 331–54.

Woolfson, Jonathan. 'Morison, Sir Richard (c.1510–1556)'. *Oxford Dictionary of National Biography*. Eds H.C.G. Matthew and Brian Harrison. Oxford: OUP, 2004. Online ed. Ed. Lawrence Goldman. Jan. 2008.

## Chapter 3

# Legal Lexicography: A View from the Front Lines

Bryan A. Garner*

There are five big questions for the writer of a modern law dictionary – and they are pretty much the same questions faced by lexicographers of old, from Rastell to Jacob to Bouvier to Black. They are:

1. To what extent should a law dictionary be a dictionary – as opposed to a legal encyclopaedia? That is, to what extent should it merely define terms, rather than expansively discuss the law relating to those terms?
2. To what extent is a law dictionary a work of original scholarship – as opposed to a compilation of definitions taken from judicial opinions and other legal sources?
3. To what extent should we worry about the formalities of defining words – that is, about getting the lexicography right as well as getting the law right?
4. To what extent can the modern lexicographer rely on the accuracy of predecessors?
5. How do you find the material to include in a dictionary?

As a practicing lexicographer, I have had to answer those questions – and some of them I continue to answer ad hoc, from day to day and week to week. My answers largely explain why the seventh through ninth editions of *Black's Law Dictionary* (1999–2009) look so different from earlier editions. Let's take these questions one at a time.

### 1. To What Extent Should a Law Dictionary Contain Encyclopaedic Information?

Early law dictionaries were essentially glossaries, with short explanations of legal terms. In the eighteenth century, the English Lawyer Giles Jacob was the first

* Bryan Garner is the editor-in-chief of *Black's Law Dictionary*, president of LawProse, Inc. and author of many books on language, advocacy and interpretation. He is Distinguished Research Professor of Law at Southern Methodist University.

to combine a dictionary and an abridgment.[1] He was trying to expound the law according to an alphabetical arrangement. After all, the title of his dictionary is A Law-Dictionary: Containing the ... Whole Law... His entry for *jointenants* (which he spelled as one word, dropping one *t*) was an essay running to four long columns of small type, in which he set forth all the court holdings he could find on joint tenancy. This discursive essay is over 3,400 words long.

When Thomas Edlyne Tomlins, also English, took over Jacob's *Law Dictionary*, his first edition of 1797 more than doubled the entry on *jointenants* to some 7,500 words. He was writing more of an encyclopaedia – the kind of entry that *Corpus Juris Secundum* contains today. So it was also with most contemporaries of Jacob and Tomlins.

John Bouvier, the American, reacted against the encyclopaedic nature of his predecessors' dictionaries. In 1839, in the first edition of his *Law Dictionary*, he criticized other dictionaries: 'It is true such works contain a great mass of information, but from the manner in which they have been compiled, they sometimes embarrassed [the reader] more than if he had not consulted them' (p. v). His own entry for *joint tenants* (spelled as two words) runs only 46 words:

> JOINT TENANTS, estates, are two or more persons to whom are granted lands or tenements to hold in fee simple, fee tail, for life, for years, or at will. 2 Black. Com. 179. The estate which they thus hold is called an estate in joint tenancy.

The later editions of Bouvier's work, as expanded by others, rejected his concise approach and moved once again toward an overdeveloped encyclopaedic treatment. In the 1914 edition by Francis Rawle, one of the last editions, the entry for *joint tenants* ran to 512 words – more than ten times as long as the 1839 entry – and cited 11 case holdings, all of which look (to the modern eye) very antiquarian.

This kind of excessive growth occurred throughout Bouvier's dictionary after the first edition. I am convinced that hypertrophy is what led Bouvier's law dictionary to become obsolete. It could not accurately restate the whole law in two or three volumes. The essays had already been superseded by specialist treatises and by much bigger encyclopaedias. It became impossible to keep the essays up to date. So by the late 1930s, the publishers had abandoned Bouvier's dictionary as an unworkable venture.

There were other nineteenth-century dictionaries that appeared before and after *Black's Law Dictionary* was published in 1891, but none as important. Henry Campbell Black was a learned lawyer with varied interests. The list of his full-length treatises is impressive. He wrote full-length treatises on constitutional law,[2] on the removal of cases from state to federal court,[3] on the law of

1 Giles Jacob, *A New Law-Dictionary* (1729).

2 Henry Campbell Black, *Handbook of American Constitutional Law* (1897).

3 Henry Campbell Black, *Removal of Causes from State Courts to Federal Courts* (1889).

judgments,[4] on the rescission of contracts,[5] on bankruptcy,[6] on the income tax,[7] on tax titles,[8] on mortgages and deeds of trust[9] and on statutory interpretation.[10] He even wrote a book called *Black on Intoxicating Liquors*.[11] There can be little doubt that, perhaps apart from John Cowell, Black was the most erudite lawyer ever to write a dictionary. It's interesting to speculate whether he thought his law dictionary might become something of a household name.

Black's entry for *joint tenancy* ran to 153 words (citing two statutes and no cases). The entry characteristically begins with a definition and then expands modestly on it. While there's no attempt to restate the entire law, he does include some encyclopaedic information:

> JOINT TENANCY. An estate in joint tenancy is an estate in fee-simple, fee-tail, for life, for years, or at will, arising by purchase or grant to two or more persons. Joint tenants have one and the same interest, accruing by one and the same conveyance, commencing at one and the same time, and held by one and the same undivided possession. The grand incident of joint tenancy is survivorship, by which the entire tenancy on the decease of any joint tenant remains to the survivor. Pub. St Mass. 1882, p. 1292.
>
> A joint interest is one owned by several persons in equal shares, by a title created by a single will or transfer, when expressly declared in the will or transfer to be a joint tenancy, or when granted or devised to executors or trustees as joint tenants. Civil Code Cal. § 683.

In his second edition of 1910, Black wisely relegated the phrase *joint tenancy* to a subentry under *tenancy*. This was a smart move because it allowed the dictionary user to compare all the types of tenancy at a glance. Black carefully gave a cross-reference under J. and he added four case citations, to courts in Kansas, Indiana, Michigan and Pennsylvania.

When the sixth edition of *Black's Law Dictionary* appeared in 1990 – before I became involved in the project – the entry for *joint tenancy* remained pretty much as it had been in 1891, except that all the case-law was removed. Two new judicial definitions were added, one with a citation to a federal district court and one with a

---

4 Henry Campbell Black, *A Treatise on the Law of Judgments* (1891).

5 Henry Campbell Black, *A Treatise on the Rescission of Contracts* (2d ed. 1929).

6 Henry Campbell Black, *A Handbook of Bankruptcy Law* (1898).

7 Henry Campbell Black, *A Treatise on the Law of Income Taxation* (1913).

8 Henry Campbell Black, *A Treatise on the Law of Tax Titles* (1893).

9 Henry Campbell Black, *A Treatise on the Law of Mortgages and Deeds of Trust* (1903).

10 Henry Campbell Black, *Handbook on the Construction and Interpretation of the Laws* (1896).

11 Henry Campbell Black, *Black on Intoxicating Liquors* (1892).

citation to the Arizona Supreme Court. These judicial definitions mostly repeat the older definitions (in an earlier paragraph), using different words.

When I became editor-in-chief of *Black's Law Dictionary* in 1994, the prevailing view among lexicographers was that dictionaries should define – that they should not attempt to be encyclopaedias.[12] But there was a growing view that some encyclopaedic information is indispensable and that there's no easy dividing line between what is definitional and what is encyclopaedic. This was very much in line with Henry Campbell Black's approach. I developed a system for dividing definitions from discursive information: my colleagues and I used bullet dots to separate the two. And we came to refer, in our own in-house jargon, to 'BBS' (before-the-bullet stuff) and 'ABS' (after-the-bullet stuff). So the entry for joint tenancy reads:

> **joint tenancy**. A tenancy with two or more coowners who take identical interests simultaneously by the same instrument and with the same right of possession. • A joint tenancy differs from a tenancy in common because each joint tenant has a right of survivorship to the other's share (in some states, this right must be clearly expressed in the conveyance – otherwise the tenancy will be presumed to be a tenancy in common). See RIGHT OF SURVIVORSHIP. Cf. *tenancy in common.*
>
> 'The rules for creation of a joint tenancy are these: The joint tenants must get their interests at the same time. They must become entitled to possession at the same time. The interests must be physically undivided interests, and each undivided interest must be an equal fraction of the whole – e.g., a one-third undivided interest to each of three joint tenants. The joint tenants must get their interests by the same instrument – e.g., the same deed or will. The joint tenants must get the same kinds of estates – e.g., in fee simple, for life, and so on'. Thomas F. Bergin and Paul G. Haskell, *Preface to Estates in Land and Future Interests* 55 (2nd ed. 1984).[13]

The bullets allowed us to provide concise, substitutable definitions while including some encyclopaedic information – or ABS – whenever our research turned up something interesting or useful. This use of bullets was something of an innovation in lexicography.

There is something else new about that entry. West asked me to add citations to the entries where I could. I decided to integrate another level of encyclopaedic information by briefly quoting major authorities on various words and phrases.

---

12 See, for example, Sidney Landau, *Dictionaries: The Art and Craft of Lexicography* 5–6 (Cambridge University Press, 1984); Tom McArthur, *Worlds of Reference* 104 (Oxford University Press, 1986); R.R.K. Hartmann and Gregory James, *Dictionary of Lexicography* 48–50 (London and New York: Routledge/Taylor Francis, 1998).

13 Thomas F. Bergin and Paul G. Haskell, *Preface to Estates in Land and Future Interests* 55 (2nd ed. Brooklyn, NY: The Foundation Press 1984).

In the entry above, it is Bergin and Haskell on future interests. In other entries we quoted Blackstone on the law of England, Buckland on Roman Law, Chitty on criminal law, Dworkin on legal philosophy, Gilmore and Black on the law of admiralty, Wright on federal courts and so on. My colleagues and I looked for the most enlightening discussions of legal terminology, preferably from an acknowledged expert in the field. If the quotation happened to be from a leading judicial opinion, so much the better, but I gave no preference to judicial opinions.

One commentator has questioned why my editions of *Black's Law Dictionary* have more quotations from treatises than from cases. My answer is three-fold. First, a scholar who has studied and written extensively in a given field of law is more likely to have a solid, informed discussion of a legal term. I'd rather quote Douglas Laycock on the irreparable-injury rule (as the seventh and later editions do) than an intermediate court in Louisiana (as the sixth edition did). Doug Laycock knows more about this rule, and has written about it in far greater depth, than some appellate judge in Louisiana. Second, case-law is readily available and searchable electronically, whereas the treatises so frequently quoted in the current edition are not so accessible. Anyone wanting to research the case-law in a given jurisdiction can do so online. Third, the chances that a reader of *Black's Law Dictionary* is actually looking for a Louisiana precedent seems remote. Treatise-writers tend to be more expansive in their view and to discuss variations among jurisdictions: all this can be enormously helpful to a dictionary-user.

The quotations also lend a greater degree of scholarly reliability to the dictionary. Of course, the *Oxford English Dictionary* is famous for its illustrative quotations – sentences illustrating the actual use of a term through the centuries. Our quotations in *Black's* are rather different: my colleagues and I did not just quote a sentence to show how a term is used. Instead, we quoted substantive experts precisely for their expertise, and we typically quoted two to five sentences. This is something that a specialist dictionary can do to give the entries greater historical and intellectual depth. Once again, though, to my knowledge no previous dictionary had ever systematically used quotations in quite this way.

## 2. To What Extent Is a Law Dictionary a Work of Original Scholarship – as Opposed to a Compilation of Judicial Definitions?

There are two traditions in legal lexicography. There's the law dictionary, and there's the judicial dictionary – such as *Stroud's Judicial Dictionary* (a leading English authority since 1890) or *Words and Phrases* (a 90-volume collection of judicial pronouncements).

A judicial dictionary is both broader and narrower than a law dictionary because it collects whatever words and phrases judges have had occasion to define. It is broader in the sense that judges often, in deciding a case, are called on to define ordinary words. For example, one page of *Words and Phrases* (volume 5A) collects definitions for the terms *Boston cream pie*, *Boston Firemen's Relief Fund*, *bosun's chair* and *botanical garden* – none of which can properly be called a legal term. At the same time, judges are seldom called on to interpret certain legal terms. For example, one page of the current *Black's* has definitions for *legal realism*, *legal research*, *legal secretary*, *Legal Services Corporation* and *legal theory*. None of these appear in *Words and Phrases*; only two of them appeared in *Black's Sixth* (*legal secretary* and *Legal Services Corporation*).

At times, *Black's Law Dictionary* has erred on the side of being a judicial dictionary. For example, the fourth edition – the only one in print from 1951 to 1979 – had an entry for *Boston cream pie*, which it defined as follows: 'two layers of sponge cake with a layer of a sort of cream custard'. For that definition, the book cited an opinion from the District of Columbia Court of Municipal Appeals.

To round out *Black's Seventh* in 1999, I wanted to do three things. First, I wanted to be sure that *Black's* would not be a mere judicial dictionary. I wanted to define everything that might legitimately be called a legal term – whether it was about a judicially created doctrine or a type of legal philosophy that courts would never have occasion to address directly. Second, I wanted to be sure that my colleagues and I, as lexicographers and lawyers, did our best to define terms as fully and accurately as possible – without uncritically accepting some judicial pronouncement about what a word means. Third, I did not want to duplicate what *Words and Phrases* already does so comprehensively.

I, for one, consider lexicography to be serious scholarship. Samuel Johnson and Noah Webster amply demonstrated this; so did the editors of the *Oxford English Dictionary* and of the *Century Dictionary*, as well as the twentieth-century editors of the various editions of *Webster's International Dictionary* and of the *OED Supplement*. So I rejected the idea of being a mere compiler of judicial scraps, and I dismissed the idea of including non-legal terms: *Boston cream pie* is only one egregious example among many.

### 3. To What Extent Should We Worry about the Formalities of Defining Words – That Is, about Getting the Lexicography Right as Well as Getting the Law Right?

This is an interesting and a challenging question. Naturally, I wanted to get the lexicography right as well as the law.

But in legal lexicography, this is difficult. As a result of the two phenomena already discussed – the tradition of having legal encyclopaedias masquerade as law dictionaries, and the tradition of simply copying judicial definitions – most law dictionaries have been very loose in their defining. *Black's Law Dictionary*, as I inherited it, was no exception. Although Henry Campbell Black had been pretty systematic in his entries, the various contributors to the book in the third through sixth editions – most of whom were anonymous – had allowed the book to sprout all sorts of stylistic inconsistencies. Meanwhile, as far as I have been able to tell, they had not really been trained in lexicography.

In fact, five basic tenets of defining words seemed rarely to be followed. The tenets are:

- Make the definition substitutable for the word in context,[14] so that the entry begins with the definition itself – never with a phrase such as 'a term meaning' or 'a term referring to'.[15]
- Indicate every meaning of the headword in the field covered by the dictionary.[16]
- Don't define self-explanatory phrases that aren't legitimate lexical units (including such phrases as *living with husband*).[17]
- Define singular terms, not plurals, unless there's a good reason to do otherwise.
- Distinguish between definitions and encyclopaedicdic information (that is, textbook descriptions).[18]

These are challenging commands for the lexicographer – especially the first: substitutability. *Black's Sixth* had hundreds of entries that were not substitutable. They read, for example, after the headword: 'Exists where …',[19] 'Term refers to …',[20] 'Term used to describe …',[21] 'A Saxon term for …'[22] It had hundreds of other entries in which adjectives were defined as if they were nouns, and nouns as if they were adjectives. For example, *litigious*, an adjective, was defined as a noun: 'That which is the subject of a lawsuit or action'.[23] Henry Campbell Black wrote that definition in 1891, and it was carried through every edition up through the sixth in 1990. But examples like that one proliferated in the intervening years, and you'd find this sort of thing on almost every page of the sixth edition.

In fairness to those who worked on the third through the sixth editions of *Black's*, I can point to three mitigating facts. First, defining terms rigorously is not an easy matter. Even after months of training, most of my own assistants (past and present) have tended to stumble on the principle of substitutability, and I'm sure I've stumbled occasionally as well. Second, to the extent that the compilers used judicial pronouncements, and parroted ill-phrased definitions, they were just following the precedent of judges who were less than adept at defining. A good example of this is the Utah Supreme Court's definition of *hotel*, a non-legal

14 Sidney Landau, *Dictionaries: The Art and Craft of Lexicography* 164 (2nd ed., Cambridge University Press, 2001).

15 *Id.* at 163.

16 *Id.* at 187.

17 *Id.* at 187.

18 *Id.* at 187.

19 See, for example, *Black's Law Dictionary* 229, 935 (6th ed. 1990) (s.v. chain conspiracy, living separate and apart).

20 See, for example, *Black's Law Dictionary* 743, 796, 1425 (6th ed. 1990) (s.v. hybrid class action, insider trading, subject-matter jurisdiction).

21 See, for example, *Black's Law Dictionary* 1479 (6th ed. 1990) (s.v. third degree).

22 See, for example, *Black's Law Dictionary* 888 (6th ed. 1990) (s.v. lazzi).

23 *Law Dictionary* 934 (6th ed. 1990).

term included in *Black's Sixth*: 'a building held out to the public as a place where all transient persons who come will be received and entertained as guests for compensation and it opens its facilities to the public as a whole rather than limited accessibility to a well-defined private group'. In that example, a noun phrase turns into a clause in the latter part – and the definition itself is inaccurate, even if a state supreme court said it. As a third mitigating fact, the users of *Black's Law Dictionary* through the years seem never to have complained about one part of speech being defined as if it were another part of speech. It could be that only professional lexicographers complain about this sort of thing. Then again, it could be that users trust dictionary writers to get the definitions and parts of speech right.

Like the first tenet, substitutability, the other tenets are fairly routinely flouted in pre-seventh editions of *Black's*: meanings are not clearly enumerated,[24] many entries are not legitimate lexical units,[25] there are plural headwords and even plural definitions of singular terms,[26] there are entries in which verb definitions and noun definitions are run together without differentiation,[27] and many entries contain exclusively encyclopaedic information without any definitions at all.[28]

It was a major challenge putting the seventh edition of *Black's* into a consistent format and implementing the modern rules of lexicography. But I never doubted that this was the right course.

## 4. To What Extent Can the Modern Lexicographer Rely on the Accuracy of Predecessors?

As you might have guessed, I believe it's unwise to repeat predecessors' work. My policy has been, as much as possible, to research anew every entry in *Black's*. My colleagues and I did not merely rely on earlier editions. Within the time constraints we had, we researched every definition in every entry and generally wrote them from scratch. We rethought, second-guessed and re-researched everything in the dictionary, and we second-guessed everything.

I'll give you an interesting example of this. When I was working on the V's – a letter that grew enormously from the sixth edition to the seventh – I came upon the word *vitiligate*. There it was in *Black's Sixth*:

24 Compare *Black's Law Dictionary* 1026 (6th ed. 1990) (defining *natural* in two long unnumbered sentences from which two senses emerge) with *Black's Law Dictionary* 1048 (7th ed. 1999) (defining *natural* in seven numbered senses in about the same amount of space).

25 See, for example, *Black's Law Dictionary* 935 (6th ed. 1990) (s.v. living with husband).

26 See, for example, *Black's Law Dictionary* 897 (6th ed. 1990) (defining *legal usufruct* as 'usufructs established ...').

27 See, for example, *Black's Law Dictionary* 562 (6th ed. 1990) (s.v. exchange).

28 See, for example, *Black's Law Dictionary* 1479 (6th ed. 1990) (s.v. thin capitalization).

**vitiligate**. To litigate cavilously, vexatiously, or from merely quarrelsome motives.

Never having heard of this word, I thought it was an extraordinary discovery. Of course, I needed to verify its existence. So, as with almost every other entry, I checked the *OED*, and it was not there. Instead, the *OED* recorded *vitilitigate*, citing Blount's *Nomo-Lexicon* of 1670. Likewise, *Webster's Second New International Dictionary* (1933) recorded *vitilitigate*, and so did the *Century Dictionary* (1914). The meaning was the same.

Looking at many other sources confirmed that *vitiligate* was simply a typographical error in a headword. I looked in the first edition of *Black's* and found that it was correctly recorded there: *vitilitigate*, not *vitiligate*. So I wondered when the mistake had crept into the book. It appeared in the fifth edition (1979), in the fourth (1951), in the third (1933) and even in the second (1910). And the second edition, remember, was published in Henry Campbell Black's lifetime. The typesetter had apparently dropped a syllable in 1910, and this typographical error got perpetuated in every edition of *Black's* for the next 89 years. Fortunately, I could not find any case-law using the bastardized form in reliance on *Black's*. We put things right in *Black's Seventh*.

My decision to second-guess old research also took another form. *Black's Law Dictionary*, like most law dictionaries, is chock full of Roman Law terms and maxims. Being an American lawyer with a typical American legal education, I did not feel competent reviewing the Roman Law material. I had read a great deal about Roman Law, and I had built a small library of English-language materials on Roman Law, but still I knew that specialist reviewers would have to become involved.

So I went straight to the top of the field. I hired Professor Tony Honoré of Oxford University and Professor David Walker of the University of Glasgow to review every entry in the book. Not only did they correct a lot of the Roman Law material – from misrecorded Latin headwords to incomplete and inaccurate definitions – they also improved the treatment of English Law and Scots Law. There is not a single page of *Black's Seventh*, and therefore of all future editions, that was not improved by their erudition and industry.

Lawyers sometimes ask me why I added so much Roman Law material. The answer is simple: because Roman Law principles underlie many modern Civil Law and Common Law concepts, students of legal history often come across references to Roman legal terms. I had the opportunity, with the help of Honoré and Walker, to get things right. It would have been serious malfeasance not to take advantage of their suggested additions.

## 5. How Do You Find the Material to Include in a Dictionary?

One thing we tried to do in *Black's Seventh* and later editions was to improve the coverage of legal terms. You'll see this in various ways that are fairly easy to quantify. For example, the sixth edition had only five subentries under *interest rate* –

in other words, just five types of interest rates; *Black's Ninth* defines 15. Likewise, from the sixth edition to the ninth, *Black's* went from 75 subentries under *bond* to 122, from nine subentries under *marriage* to 33, from none under *reinsurance* to four, and from three under *veto* to eight.

So where did we find all this additional material? We did it partly, as lexicographers must, by examining other reference books. But the more important method was examining hornbooks and treatises that deal systematically with a given legal field. For more than 12 years, I've read and marked about one law book a month. I highlight potential headwords to be typed into a list followed by the illustrative quotations I've marked. Then either my assistants or I will use that information as the basis for further research and will draft an entry for each headword. Any good dictionary-maker must have some type of reading system for gathering new material in this way.

On the seventh edition, I had the help of three full-time lawyers that I had trained as lexicographers, including my senior assistant editor David W. Schultz. And for the more recent editions, I have had the help of four fine lawyer-lexicographers, Tiger Jackson, Jeffrey Newman, Karolyne H. Cheng and Becky R. McDaniel. Having a team, even a small one, is enormously useful.

With each new edition of *Black's*, I seek not only to add relevant new entries, but also to strengthen certain features of the book. Some of these innovations have attracted scholarly comment.[29]

In *Black's Seventh*, the primary focus was on (1) untangling the messy definitions of earlier editions and ensuring accuracy, (2) weeding out our non-logical headwords, (3) retranslating Latin maxims and collecting them in an appendix as opposed to spreading them throughout the main lexicon, (4) adding several thousand scholarly quotations and (5) improving the pronunciation system.

In *Black's Eighth*, the focus was on (1) enhancing the coverage of specialty areas, such as intellectual property, family law and criminal law; (2) double-checking the accuracy of Latin maxims, yet again; (3) adding several thousand headwords; (4) systematically supplying key-number citations that would be perpetually updated; and (5) redesigning the pages to make the book easier to use.

In *Black's Ninth* (2009), the focus was on (1) supplying the earliest known uses for the major terms; (2) revising all definitions for consistency of approach; and (3) continuing apace with each of the other innovations of the two prior editions, including the addition of thousands of key-number citations and thousands of new entries and subentries. Fred Shapiro of Yale Law Library has researched the earliest-recorded uses for thousands of terms – thereby conferring on the book a whole new level of scholarly reliability.

As for what's in store for *Black's Tenth*, that's a closely guarded trade secret. Sorry.

---

29 See, for example, Sarah Yates, *Black's Law Dictionary: The Making of an American Standard*, 103 Law Lib. J. 175(2011); Roy M. Mersky and Jeanne Price, *The Dictionary and the Man: The Eighth Edition of Black's Law Dictionary*, Edited by Bryan Garner, 63 Wash. & Lee L. Rev. 719 (2006); Peter Tiersma, *The New Black's*, 55 J. Legal Educ. 386 (2005).

With each successive edition I have enlisted the editorial assistance of more and more law professors and practicing lawyers. A proper dictionary must be based on the expertise of many people. For the seventh edition, I recruited 30 judges, lawyers, and academics to scrutinize our entries. For the eighth, I assembled a panel of 62 academic contributors and 13 practitioner contributors. By the ninth edition, the total number of law-trained editorial advisers had grown to 303. Specifically, the professors and practitioners were each sent 50–100-page batches of manuscript and asked to make editorial improvements, including the amplification and elaboration of entries, the tightening or sharpening of definitions and the addition of ABS (after-the-bullet) encyclopaedic information. My team in Dallas incorporated the best of these suggested edits.

In a few cases, I enlisted specialist reviewers – a task that requires much preparatory work for each batch. As an example, for the eighth edition E. Allen Farnsworth (1928-2005) of Columbia University agreed to review the contract law terminology. He painstakingly edited about 100 single-spaced pages of material, making invaluable improvements throughout the complex entries on permutations of acceptance and consideration and hundreds of specific doctrines (some of which were new even to him). In the final year of his life, he and I spent many hours on the phone as we hammered out improved definitions for dozens of terms.

Finally, I rely on the users of *Black's*, who are always welcome to suggest new entries and to comment on and critique existing ones. Anyone may contact me at bgarner@lawprose.org with submissions or requests – with the understanding that my colleagues and I seriously vet all suggestions against actual legal usage.

## Dashing One's Frame

Despite all the computers that make the job so much easier, the issues with which a modern legal lexicographer must deal are much like those that Rastell and Jacob and Bouvier and Black dealt with. My editorial decisions often depart from those of my precursors, but this is largely because of strides made in the field of lexicography.

Shortly before *Black's Seventh* was completed, my publishers at West, over dinner in St Paul, asked me how I would describe the book. I still have the dinner napkin on which I wrote: 'The seventh edition of *Black's Law Dictionary* is at once the most comprehensive, authoritative, scholarly, and accessible American law dictionary ever published'. Whether my colleagues and I met that goal with that edition, and later ones, only time will tell. I have tried here to give some explanation of why that claim might actually hold.

When you write a dictionary, especially in a field as wide-ranging as law, you are battling your own fallibility. I am constantly second-guessing my own work as well as that of my colleagues, and I have gone to great lengths to find other knowledgeable second-guessers. Only with that kind of vigilance can you feel confident about the scholarship.

Toward the end of his distinguished career as editor in chief of the *OED Supplement*, my friend Robert W. Burchfield wrote that it was 'discouraging to see the waves of new words lapping in behind as one dashed one's frame against the main flood'.[30] Perhaps it's a function of my age – and of the hope that I'll be able to supplement and perfect *Black's Law Dictionary* over the course of several more editions – but I welcome the flood of new legal terms and new legal meanings for old terms. And I imagine Henry Campbell Black felt the same way back in the 1890s.

## An Excerpt from the Preface of Black's Ninth

Since becoming editor in chief of *Black's Law Dictionary* in the mid-1990s, I've tried with each successive edition – the seventh, the eighth, and now the ninth – to make the book at once both more scholarly and more practical.

Anyone who cares to put this book alongside the sixth or earlier editions will discover that the book has been almost entirely rewritten, with an increase in precision and clarity. It's true that I've cut some definitions that appeared in the sixth and earlier editions. On a representative sample of two consecutive pages of the sixth can be found *botulism*, *bouche* (mouth), *bough of a tree, bought* (meaning 'purchased'), *bouncer* (referring to a nightclub employee), *bourg* (a village), *boulevard, bourgeois, brabant* (an obscure kind of ancient coin also called a *crocard*), *brabanter* (a mercenary soldier in the Middle Ages), and *brachium maris* (an arm of the sea). These can hardly be counted as legal terms worthy of inclusion in a true law dictionary, and *Black's* had been properly criticized for including headwords such as these.[31]

Meanwhile, though, within the same span of terms, I've added entries for three types of boundaries (*agreed boundary, land boundary, lost boundary*), as well as for *bounty hunter, bounty land, bounty-land warrant, boutique* (a specialized law firm), *box day* (a day historically set aside for filing papers in Scotland's Court of Session), *box-top license* (also known as a *shrink-wrap license*), *Boykin Act* (an intellectual-property statute enacted after World War II), *Boyle defense* (also known as the *government-contractor defense*), *bracket system* (the tax term), *Bracton* (the title of one of the earliest, most important English law books), and *Brady Act* (the federal law for background checks on handgun-purchasers). And all the other entries have been wholly revised – shortened here and amplified there to bring the book into better proportion.

Hence, in one brief span of entries, the sixth and ninth editions appear to be entirely different books. That's true throughout the work.

---

30 Robert W. Burchfield, *Unlocking the English Language* 176 (London: Faber and Faber, 1989).

31 Mellinkoff, *The Myth of Precision and the Law Dictionary*, 31 U.C.L.A. L. Rev. 423, 440 (1983).

**Table 3.1 A sample entry from *Black's Law Dictionary***

| ***Black's Law Dictionary* 1st ed. (1891)** | ***Black's Law Dictionary* 6th ed. (1990)** | ***Black's Law Dictionary* 9th ed. (2009)** |
|---|---|---|
| JOINT TENANCY. An estate in joint tenancy is an estate in fee-simple, fee-tail, for life, for years, or at will, arising by purchase or grant to two or more persons. Joint tenants have one and the same interest, accruing by one and the same conveyance, commencing at one and the same time, and held by one and the same undivided possession. The grand incident of joint tenancy is survivorship, by which the entire tenancy on the decease of any joint tenant remains to the survivor. Pub. St. Mass. 1882, p. 1292. A joint interest is one owned by several persons in equal shares, by a title created by a single will or transfer, when expressly declared in the will or transfer to be a joint tenancy, or when granted or devised to executors or trustees as joint tenants. Civil Code Cal. § 683. | Joint tenancy. An estate in fee-simple, fee-tail, for life, for years, or at will, arising by purchase or grant to two or more persons. Joint tenants have one and the same interest, accruing by one and the same conveyance, commencing at one and the same time, and held by one and the same undivided possession. The primary incident of joint tenancy is survivorship, by which the entire tenancy on the decease of any joint tenant remains to the survivors, and at length to the last survivor. Type of ownership of real or personal property by two or more persons in which each owns an undivided interest in the whole and attached to which is the right of survivorship. Single estate in property owned by two or more persons under one instrument or act. D'Ercole v. D'Ercole, D.C.Mass., 407 F.Supp. 1377, 1380. An estate held by two or more persons jointly, each having an individual interest in the whole and an equal right to its enjoyment during his or her life. In re Estelle's Estate, 593 P.2d 663, 665, 122 Ariz. 109. | joint tenancy. A tenancy* with two or more coowners who take identical interests simultaneously by the same instrument and with the same right of possession. · A joint tenancy differs from a tenancy in common because each joint tenant has a right of survivorship to the other's share (in some states, this right must be clearly expressed in the conveyance – otherwise, the tenancy will be presumed to be a tenancy in common). See right of survivorship. Cf. tenancy in common. 'The rules for creation of a joint tenancy are these: The joint tenants must get their interests at the same time. They must become entitled to possession at the same time. The interests must be physically undivided interests, and each undivided interest must be an equal fraction of the whole – e.g., a one-third undivided interest to each of three joint tenants. The joint tenants must get their interests by the same instrument– e.g., the same deed or will. The joint tenants must get the same kinds of estates – e.g., in fee simple, for life, and so on'. Thomas F. Bergin & Paul G. Haskell, Preface to Estates in Land and Future Interests 55 (2d ed. 1984). |

*Note:* * The genus *tenancy* having already been defined just above, in the main headword, the word may be used in defining the *species joint tenancy*.

# Chapter 4
# The Challenges of Compiling a Legal Dictionary

Daniel Greenberg*

## Introduction

This chapter is written from a purely practical perspective, by someone who became involved in the compilation of legal dictionaries without any theoretical training or background in lexicography. Much of what is said here will therefore appear naive to those with professional lexicographical knowledge and experience; but it is to be hoped that it will be naivety of the useful kind, where the neophyte's comments are at least refreshing and thought-provoking for those more steeped in the subject.

## What is a Legal Dictionary?

Assuming to begin with that one knows what a dictionary is – although that is of course something that becomes less clear the more one thinks about it, and I will return to it below – the question arises, how does a dictionary develop so as to deserve the description 'legal'?

Broadly speaking, there are two different ways in which a dictionary can be 'legal': it can elect to define terms that are relevant to the law, or it can elect to define terms as they are used in the law. The difference is much more than a semantic one: it is fundamental both to the choice of the terms to be defined in the dictionary and to the way in which the definitions are cast.

In the United Kingdom the distinction is illustrated by the difference between two dictionaries: *Jowitt's Dictionary of English Law* and *Stroud's Judicial Dictionary*. The former is a dictionary of law in the sense of defining expressions that form part of the law; the latter is a judicial dictionary in the sense that it defines expressions that may have nothing to do with the law in themselves, but which by being defined in the course of decided cases or statutes have acquired a meaning that has become part of the law.

---

* Parliamentary Counsel, Berwin Leighton Paisner LLP; Counsel, Legal Services Office, House of Commons; General Editor, Annotated Statutes, Westlaw UK; Editor-in-Chief, *Statute Law Review*; Editor, Craies on Legislation; Editor, *Stroud's Judicial Dictionary*; General Editor, *Jowitt's Dictionary of English Law*.

A legal dictionary requires to be clearly aware of which of these two kinds of dictionary it aims to be, or it risks falling between two stools and fulfilling neither function consistently and effectively. The distinction should therefore form a key plank of the editorial policy of any legal dictionary, and the suitability of each entry should be tested against it.

The practical result of the distinction is illustrated by the following extract from the preface to the third edition of *Jowitt's Dictionary of English Law*:

> The intention is for *Jowitt* to serve as a companion work to *Stroud's Judicial Dictionary*. As a legal dictionary, *Jowitt* lists expressions forming part of the mechanism of the law of England and Wales. As a judicial dictionary, *Stroud* lists words and phrases that have been defined by judicial dictum or legislative provision. There is some overlap, but less than might have been expected. So, for example, 'garden' appears in *Stroud* but not *Jowitt*; 'bounty' appears in *Jowitt* but not *Stroud*; and 'lease' appears in both. Where an expression listed in *Jowitt* receives particular added value from the judicial or legislative definitions in *Stroud*, the entry includes a cross-reference to that effect.

Although that serves as a reasonably effective editorial policy, and has been facilitated in practice by having a common component in the editorial teams of the two works, the reality is that the distinction is easier to state in theory than to operate in practice. At the two extremes, there are no difficulties: the word 'garden' has no technical legal resonance at all, and if it comes to be defined by the courts or by statute for a particular purpose of law, the definition can simply be included in a judicial dictionary and ignored in the legal dictionaries. Similarly, there are many expressions that form part of the fabric of English Law and therefore require definition in a legal dictionary but have never attracted the focus of the courts or statute in the sense of falling to be defined as such, although much may have been said about them: for example, legal professional privilege. But a vast number of expressions fall between these two extremes, being both demotic expressions whose parameters are bound to attract the attention of the courts and statute but which also have a precise technical resonance in law: for example, rape.

Although the editorial policy cited above is able to state simply that expressions in this area of overlap will be defined in both kinds of legal dictionary, the reality is more complex than that: the definition in the legal dictionary needs to take account of the nature of the definition in the judicial dictionary, and vice versa. Since each definition influences the other, it can be difficult to know when to stop on each side: in particular, at what point is the technical definition of rape in the legal dictionary accurate and comprehensive, without requiring further adjustment to reflect current judicial and legislative usage? And how does one choose in the judicial dictionary to quote or digest a judicial decision on rape so that it supplements the technical definition in the legal dictionary without appearing to purport to replace it? Judicial and legislative definitions are necessarily contextual, but they do not always appear to recognise their contextual limitations, and can be couched more in terms of a comprehensive technical definition for all legal purposes. The editor of the judicial dictionary therefore has to determine which to select as sufficiently formative and representative to serve the purpose of that dictionary; but the editor of the legal dictionary has the even more difficult task of determining to what extent they have modified or developed the key legal concept and therefore require to be reflected in the legal dictionary's definition as well.

## What is a Dictionary?

While grappling with the difficulty of determining what a legal dictionary is and, in particular, how to maintain the character of each dictionary in terms of the legal-judicial distinction, the compiler of the legal dictionary has constantly to grapple also with the difficulties familiar to all lexicographers of knowing exactly what a dictionary is. This issue has a number of separate aspects, which although common to all lexicography will have particular implications in the legal context.

## Dictionary v. Encyclopaedia

First in the 'What is a dictionary?' line of thought, is the difficulty of determining where a dictionary ends and an encyclopaedia begins. Just as a legal dictionary needs to determine early on whether it is to be a legal or a judicial dictionary lest by aiming at both it becomes neither, so too a legal dictionary needs constantly to struggle with the temptation to move from providing a thorough and authoritative dictionary to aiming at, and certainly failing, the provision of a legal encyclopaedia.

Again, this problem is touched on in the preface to the third edition of *Jowitt*:

> The editorial team decided at an early stage that *Jowitt* is a dictionary and not an encyclopaedia: it should explain the meaning of those terms that together form the structure of the law, rather than attempting to summarise the substantive law on every topic. A number of articles in the first two editions arguably crossed the line, being unnecessarily long for a mere explanation of the meaning and function of a term but unacceptably short for an authoritative exposition of all relevant law. There were also a considerable number of entries that arguably did not belong at all in a dictionary of legal words and phrases.

The real problem is that, again, while the distinction is easy to state in theory it is very difficult to apply rigorously in practice. In law, as doubtless in many other disciplines, there is no neat distinction between the parameters of a concept as part of the fabric of the law and the substance of the concept.

Taking the concept of 'rape' as an example again, the two extremes are easy to explain, but neither is appropriate for an authoritative dictionary: in a concise dictionary that does not aim to be comprehensive or authoritative, it will be enough to define the term in a few words, perhaps along the lines of 'The criminal offence of having sex with a person against their will'. But although that would suffice for someone who needs only a very vague idea of the meaning of the term, perhaps for a non-English speaker who simply needs to establish with which foreign offence the word 'rape' roughly corresponds – it will be immediately apparent that almost every word of the definition will not stand up to any kind of critical analysis: in particular, one could write pages about the concepts of 'having sex', 'person' and 'against their will' in the context of the law of rape. Which is what an encyclopaedia would set out to do: and it would not be unreasonable to expect the entry for 'rape' in an encyclopaedia to occupy several pages. But a dictionary cannot afford several pages for each entry of this kind, nor is it fulfilling its function as a reliable dictionary if it attempts to summarise the substantive law of rape, since the enterprise is doomed to failure by omission or misdescription, which risk turning a useful and authoritative dictionary into an inadequate and misleading encyclopaedia. The editors, therefore, have to do their best to identify those components of the substantive law of rape which can reasonably be regarded as part of the essential definition of rape as a concept.

Without a doubt, therefore, the most exacting task in the compilation of a legal dictionary is that of shortening or constraining entries so that they remain strictly definitions rather than summaries of the law. Nor is it possible to give contributing editors any very serviceable rules of thumb for how to effect this balance, since it varies so enormously from concept to concept according to the state of the substantive law. It is ultimately a question of feel, and one which calls for a consistent judgment to be applied throughout the dictionary as a whole.

## Avoiding the Normative

The second theme that the editor of a legal dictionary encounters in considering the essential nature of dictionaries is that they generally set out to perform a function different from that which is expected or assumed by many of those who use them. Readers of dictionaries frequently consult them in the hope of discovering what is 'good' or 'bad' English: the first lesson learned by a novice lexicographer, however, on consulting any of the expert practitioners in the field is that it is not the job of the dictionary to tell people how they should or should not speak or write, but to reflect faithfully how language is actually used in each relevant area.

In the *OED*, in particular, the definition passage is really no more than a summary of, or generalization based on, the usage examples which follow. As the usage examples develop over the years, the definition adapts to reflect them.

A legal dictionary has a particular difficulty in applying this principle because legal usage includes so many statements of judges or others whose purpose in using a term is expressly or implicitly normative. A judicial usage of a term may to a greater or lesser extent be intended to determine what it does or does not mean as a technical component of English Law. Those usage instances deserve to be given particular weight, since as a matter of law they are more authoritative than merely demotic uses even by legal professionals; so the dictionary has to reflect those usages, without ignoring the weight of usage which while not technically normative is in practice sufficiently determinative of how the expression is used to deserve and demand recognition in an authoritative dictionary. Put differently, while the *OED* can simply reflect increasing usage of what would once have been considered 'wrong' and thereby determine what is currently 'right', the legal dictionary has to accept that unthinking reflection of a preponderance of 'wrong' usage may be unhelpfully misleading in a context where there is or can be, unlike in general demotic English, a concept of what is 'right' and 'wrong' by reference to normative pronouncements of the courts or the legislature.

Again, it is impossible to give contributing editors much in the way of a rule of thumb for negotiating this difficulty; what is possible, however, in the course of a moderately lengthy article in a dictionary, is to begin with a description of the apparently authoritative usage, followed by an account of less authoritative or actually 'wrong' usage with an appropriate commentary that sets it into context for the reader, reporting it as found in reality but warning against assuming that it will be regarded as correct usage, or as correctly reflecting the underlying substantive law, by the courts or others whose task it is to construe or apply legal documents.

In selecting normative pronouncements for inclusion or reflection in a legal dictionary there is an additional complexity, that even amongst expressly normative statements about the legal meaning of a particular expression there are degrees of authority, for two reasons. First, the doctrine of precedent, according to which the higher courts have authority over the lower, needs to be followed through into the editorial decisions reflecting word usage: if a decision of a lower court shows that the judiciary are expressly or implicitly giving a particular meaning to a term, the dictionary needs to recognise and reflect that. If a later decision of a higher court falsifies that, the preponderance of usage suddenly becomes 'incorrect' in a technical legal context, and the definition has to be adjusted, while recognizing and reflecting the possibility of actual usage of the term in legal contexts changing only very slowly, and perhaps never entirely coming to reflect the decision of the higher courts, despite that having become 'the law'.

An example of this kind of process would be the term 'common law wife', which is not only used plentifully by non-lawyers writing about legal and other matters, but is also found plentifully in the writings and speeches of lawyers, sometimes in apparently technical contexts. The higher courts have from time to time expressly warned against using the term as if it carried any technical resonance, and yet usage continues in legal contexts, including usage by legal professionals. The definition in the third edition of *Jowitt's Dictionary of English Law* attempts to combine a reflection of the demotic usage with a firm steer on the lack of legal substance to the term:

> **Common law marriage; common law wife; common law husband; common law spouse.** Colloquial expressions commonly used to refer to unmarried persons

> living together as man and wife. But they have neither technical meaning nor substantive status in law, despite the fact that 'there is evidence of a wide-spread myth of the "common law marriage" in which unmarried couples acquire the same rights as married after a period of cohabitation' (*Stack v Dowden* [2007] UKHL 17 per Baroness Hale at para.45). See COHABITANTS; COHABITATION.

The second reason why expressly normative statements about definition have to be treated with caution is that English law differentiates between propositions which are part of the reasoning of a case and those which are *obiter dicta*, mentioned in passing. An *obiter dictum* may be expressed in very trenchant terms, but when other courts come to reflect upon the impact of the statement on the substance of the law they can be expected to detect its *obiter* status and reduce its authority accordingly, perhaps to nothing.

This is one example of the reasons why compilation of a legal dictionary requires significant legal expertise: the task is not confined to identifying and compiling instances of usage in a legal context, but requires an element of expertise in analysing what degree of authority to accord to particular usages or tranches of usage.

For example, consider the definition of 'palm tree justice' in *Jowitt*'s third edition:

> **Palm tree justice.** An expression used to describe a form of justice dispensed by a cadi sitting under a palm tree without the advantage of books or precedents. See, for an example of the use of the term, *Gissing v Gissing* [1969] 2 Ch. 85, per Edmund Davies L.J. See also 'However, simply to invoke the doctrine that "fraud unravels everything" would seem to me to involve palm tree justice. In other words, one would be relying on a general sense of morality or indignation, without regard to principle or the rule of law. Such a course would be inconsistent with principle, especially in the context of a taxing statute, and would effectively represent carte blanche for any tribunal to do what it likes'. – *Total Network SL v Her Majesty's Revenue and Customs* [2008] UKHL 19, per Lord Neuberger at [202].

One only needs to compare the opening definition with the example of the term being used by Lord Neuberger to show that the latter clearly had limited understanding of the historical or colloquial meaning of the term. But although this is a usage instance from one of the most senior judges speaking *ex cathedra*, its *obiter* nature would not have justified replacing the opening words, or adjusting them, to reflect the quasi-definition offered by Lord Neuberger. It helps, of course, that the term is unlikely to be considered a technical legal term or to be used in a technical legal context; but even if it were, the principle holds good that the editor's own assessment of the majority usage is to be preferred to a single reference by however senior a judge or legislator, which again shows the degree of analytical expertise required of contributing editors to a legal dictionary.

## The Influence of the Judiciary

In the case of a legal dictionary, the influence of the judiciary is, as discussed above, confined to their providing usage examples which require to be reflected alongside other usage, although at least in some contexts their usage will be particularly significant.

In the case of a judicial dictionary, of course, the primary focus is on judicial pronouncements, which cease to be mere usage examples and become the primary material of the work. This shows that, despite its name, a judicial dictionary is either much more than, or much less than, a dictionary, depending on one's point of view. It would be more accurate, perhaps, to describe a judicial dictionary simply as a list of occasions on which the judiciary have offered definitions of a particular expression.

The justification for having a judicial dictionary at all is that, while it may not serve the classic purpose of a dictionary by providing a balanced view of the meaning of all terms falling within an area of English usage, it reflects the fact that a definition of a term offered by a judge *ex cathedra* becomes part of the law. So although much less than a dictionary in one sense, a judicial dictionary is much more than a dictionary in another sense, being an authoritative account of the state of the law in a number of miscellaneous respects. It therefore has a normative character not generally, as discussed above, associated with a dictionary; not because of the nature of the dictionary but because of the authoritative nature of the statements which it records.

The result of this is that a judicial dictionary is treated by the judiciary and the legal profession in general in a different fashion from other legal dictionaries. Lawyers will consult it routinely to see whether there is a binding or persuasive precedent for the interpretation of an expression which is important to a case or matter with which they are dealing. And the courts will hear citations, and sometimes repeat them in judgments, both of actual quotations recorded in a judicial dictionary, and also of prose passages in a judicial dictionary which analyse or summarise the effect of a number of decisions on the construction of a particular expression. In effect, a judicial dictionary is or can be treated at least in part as a legal treatise on the meaning of certain words and phrases.

These considerations are likely to influence another choice that the editor of a dictionary has to make, whether to distil the effect of judicial pronouncements or to incorporate them verbatim by way of quotation. In the case of a legal dictionary, lengthy passages of text taken direct from judgments are likely to confuse the reader and obscure the purpose of the work, which is to present the editor's view of the state of the meaning of a particular term having regard to all the available usage evidence. In the case of a judicial dictionary, however, although distillation will frequently be necessary or desirable, since the primary purpose is to present the evidence usage, the most helpful way of doing that will often be by presenting quotations, often lengthy ones, from judicial pronouncements or from defining statutes.

## The Influence of the Legislature

Acts of Parliament routinely contain both express and implicit definitions of expressions, as does subordinate legislation. The issues determining the extent to which these definitions require to be reflected in a legal or judicial dictionary are similar to, but not entirely the same as, those relating to judicial pronouncements discussed above.

In particular, it is important to note that as a matter of law legislative definitions are capable of carrying either more or less weight than judicial pronouncements.

More weight, in the sense that the pronouncement of the legislature is necessarily superior to the pronouncement of the courts in a legal system based, as the United Kingdom's is, on Parliamentary supremacy. To the extent, therefore, that a dictionary is expressing a normative or legally authoritative definition, a legislative interpretation has to be treated as supremely authoritative. Less weight, in the sense that express legislative definitions are habitually given for very narrow and specific purposes, while judicial definitions are frequently designed to be, or taken as being, wider and more cross-contextual.

In the case of a legal dictionary whose function is, as discussed above, closer to that of other dictionaries than is a judicial dictionary's, legislative usage is merely a particular form of language usage which reflects how a term is used but does not necessarily have more authority than any other usage. The use of a term in legislation may be indicative of the degree to which, or manner in which, it has become embedded as a technical concept of the law; in which case it will be more influential usage than a casual reference in a legal journal or other legal context. But the mere fact that a particular term has been defined in a particular way in legislation does not mean that the compiler of a legal dictionary will necessarily wish to include the definition or even reflect it: indeed, that a term needs to be defined expressly in a particular way in a particular legislative context may amount to evidence that it does not have that meaning automatically as a technical component of English Law, and its inclusion in a legal dictionary will therefore be warranted only if the legislative context is sufficiently significant.

In a judicial dictionary, however, despite the traditional name, legislative definitions are as important as or more important than judicial pronouncements. One purpose of a judicial dictionary is to express the state of the law in respect of the meaning of a particular term in accordance with decided cases: but if the latest judicial definition has been superseded by statute, to list the cases and not the statute will be positively misleading. The common law spent centuries defining the concept of 'family', for example, for a variety of purposes: once statute had intervened in a particular area and established an exhaustive definition of 'family' for that purpose, however, to continue to list the earlier decisions without a reference to the statute would have falsified the entry. From its earliest years, therefore, *Stroud's Judicial Dictionary* included a selection of statutory definitions, particularly where it was necessary to draw the reader's attention to a shift from Common Law to statute in the interpretation of a particular term.

Two other points should be made about the inclusion of statutory material in a judicial dictionary.

First, as the present editorial policy of *Stroud* puts it, one of the purposes of a judicial dictionary is to be: 'a source of ideas useful in framing definitions of particular concepts in the drafting of contracts and other legal documents, and generally, a useful tool for legal practitioners of all kinds and for members of related professions'. With that in mind, it is not only the most recent legislative definitions that fall to be included, nor should they necessarily be removed simply because the legislation of which they form part is repealed: as the policy says, 'References to statutory definitions are included to show what can be and has been done by way of definition: they do not imply that the provisions cited are in force'.

Secondly, there is an area of overlap between the legislature and the judiciary when it comes to the inclusion of legislative references in a judicial dictionary: although the legislature is able to extinguish centuries of judicial creativity and uncertainty in the matter of a particular definition of an expression in a particular context, only the judiciary can determine to what extent, if any, that legislative definition is to be given a cross-contextual application outside its own limits. The judicial dictionary, therefore, and to some extent the legal dictionary, has both to include the legislative definition and also to include any judicial indications as to the extent of its influence on the law.

## Historical Terms

One of the principal challenges in the preparation of any new edition of any dictionary, of course, is to determine how the use of language has altered since the previous edition. The inclusion of new words and phrases is straightforward, being merely a question of reflecting new usage evidence. The difficult part is the assignment of classifications to reflect diminishing usage.

For dictionaries of demotic usage the problem may be relatively limited because obsolescence occurs so gradually; and it is probably rare that an entry needs to be moved from current to obsolete directly, without passing through a period of several decades marked as rare, a classification which is relatively easy to justify.

For a legal dictionary, however, the problem is extreme, in two ways.

First, at least in one sense an expression can become obsolete overnight. For example, the prerogative writs of the High Court were until recently known by their Latin names and were in such frequent use that many non-lawyers had heard of writs of mandamus, even if they might not have known exactly what they were. The Civil Procedure (Modification of Supreme Court Act 1981) Order 2004 provided that 'The orders of mandamus, prohibition and certiorari shall be known instead as mandatory, prohibiting and quashing orders respectively', thereby instantly consigning the original Latin terms to official obsolescence. A legal dictionary compiled or revised after 1st May 2004 therefore needs to list and define the modern phrases. It will, however, inevitably need to do so by reference to the former expressions, since the jurisdiction to make the new orders is expressly determined by reference to the old. A dictionary of vernacular usage cannot generally become suddenly so out of date as to be positively misleading: but a legal dictionary which after 1st May 2004 continues to list mandamus as if it were an available remedy and fails to list the term 'mandatory order' is seriously misleading its readership. The very concept of a sudden 'repeal' of a defining term is unknown to general linguistics, but is a powerful force within legal language that makes it peculiarly possible for a legal dictionary to become dangerously out of date literally from one day to the next.

Secondly, whether legal language moves gradually or in sudden moves as described above, expressions that have in one sense become obsolete continue to exert significant influence for decades, or even centuries. The example of the continued influence of mandamus serves as one illustration; but any serviceable legal dictionary abounds with expressions which nobody has used in the law for tens or hundreds of years but which may become of importance simply because lawyers regularly and frequently have to construe and apply commercial or legislative documents of considerable age. A will habitually sits for decades before being required to be construed, and the probate lawyer will therefore eventually need to be able to establish how legal (and indeed non-technical) language was used when it was written. But that is a relatively tame example of the kind of historical influence that is common in law: the Charter or trust deed of an educational foundation may lie dormant for literally centuries before a dispute emerges in the context of which it suddenly becomes necessary to discover and construe the intended meaning of the original grant. Local legislation providing for the construction of a bridge or some other kind of undertaking may by local Act of Parliament provide a power or duty that is intended to have perpetual effect and which, again, lies dormant for decades or centuries until as the result of a dispute or a desire to make some change it becomes necessary to establish the precise original legislative intent. With other examples like these being common, it becomes a necessary function of a serviceable legal dictionary to preserve the definitions of terms which may not have been the subject of original usage evidence for a very long time, but which may yet surface and need to be understood in their original meaning.

Even more challenging is the case of the many expressions which are used in law today and have been used in law for centuries, but whose meaning has changed beyond recognition during that time, so that the dictionary has to enable the lawyer confronted with usage in a particular commercial or legislative document to be able to determine which layer of meaning to apply by reference to the date of the document. An example of this kind of ageing is the term 'enfranchisement', which has been used without interruption for centuries but with a technical meaning which has changed at precise periods and in precise ways; there are other terms where the changes have been more gradual, through development of the Common Law, and are therefore even more difficult to track, such as 'engrossment'.

A particularly stark example is the Supreme Court, which since 1873 had a technical meaning as a term of the law of England and Wales, referring to the High Court, the Court of Appeal and the Crown Court; but the Constitutional Reform Act 2005 renamed these as the Senior Courts and created a new entity called the Supreme Court, which replaced the appellate jurisdiction of the House of Lords. Again, a legal dictionary which fails to record a change of that significance, together with an accurate account of the times at which and from which it took effect, is set to seriously mislead its readers.

The result of all this is that in compiling a new or revised legal dictionary the editors are compelled to add much and to change much, but to remove very little. How then does one prevent a legal dictionary from simply getting longer and longer until it becomes completely unmanageable?

In compiling the new edition, after a 30-year gap, of *Jowitt's Judicial Dictionary*, the editors took the following decision as reflected in the preface:

> So we set about the third edition with a revolutionary zeal, determined to cull a lot of extraneous material: but we quickly found that much of the material was too good to lose altogether and was not likely to be found anywhere else. For example, what place does a definition of 'Castleward' have in a modern legal dictionary? Probably none: but if we remove it, it is gone forever and lost to the one-in-a-million historical researcher who might need it. So *Jowitt* still betrays its origins to some extent: the preface to the first edition acknowledged how much the work owed to *Viner's Abridgement*, and the selection of entries still occasionally betrays the work's original debt to what was more an encyclopaedia – and not an exclusively legal encyclopaedia, at that – than a dictionary.
>
> In accepting this result we have relied to some extent on the fact that since dictionaries are alphabetical, it does not matter much if the contemporary entry you are looking for is flanked by a dozen entries on each side of only historical relevance – they will not significantly interfere with your finding the information you seek. And it is surprising how often archaic legal terms do turn up in contemporary documents. The historical entries of the dictionary also serve to show how many purported innovations turn out to be merely reinventions of once-familiar concepts, and how ideas thought archaic and discontinued are in fact more contemporary than one might think or like to think: so, for example, the entry for the much-vaunted *Explanatory Notes* for Parliamentary Bills is cross-referenced to the *Breviates* of which they are merely a belated revival, while the barbaric medieval *Castigatory* is cross-referenced to the equally barbaric, but disconcertingly contemporary, *Waterboarding*.

In other words, it does not really matter how long a legal dictionary becomes, or how many entries of purely historical relevance it contains, if each entry can be found by a simple alphabetical search. Even the sheer size of volumes on shelves becomes of less importance as dictionaries are increasingly accessed through their electronic versions.

Here, however, surfaces another practical difference between the legal dictionary and the judicial dictionary. The reader of a legal dictionary knows the term that he or she wishes to consult and should not be seriously inconvenienced by its being surrounded by a variety of obsolete terms, except perhaps in the sense of being distracted and diverted by how interesting some of them are and surfacing hours later rather shamefacedly to resume the search for the desired expression. The reader of a judicial dictionary, however, has to assimilate a set of entries showing usage; and the longer they are, the less effective is the help to be derived from the dictionary in terms of shortening and facilitating research and providing a serviceably certain definition. It is here that the editor's job becomes particularly challenging, requiring the retention of sufficient old usage to service modern research in historical contexts, while adding enough modern material to illustrate current usage, clarifying the entries where necessary to show the age and context to which they belong, and, most perilous of all, thinning out the entire entry to make it reasonably possible to navigate and absorb at a reasonably efficient pace.

The demands of that last exercise make it necessary from time to time to carry out a 'cull' of a judicial dictionary if it is not to cease being serviceable to its users. As the preface to the seventh edition of *Stroud's Judicial Dictionary* records:

> The last edition was the occasion for removing a considerable amount of material that was no longer likely to be of significant assistance for modern research, while preserving a certain amount of historical material that would be of occasional use and would be found nowhere else if not in *Stroud*. This edition has afforded an opportunity to examine a number of old entries, particularly those which have grown to an unwieldy length and which lack a helpful structure, to confirm their accuracy and to re-organise them in such a way as to facilitate logical and efficient research.

And yet a mere four years later the preface to the eighth edition was already warning of a new cull on the horizon:

> The sixth edition was the occasion for removing a considerable amount of material that was no longer likely to be of significant assistance for modern research, while preserving a certain amount of historical material that would be of occasional use and would be found nowhere else if not in *Stroud*. The seventh and eighth editions have seen renewed growth of the overall size of the dictionary, and another cull is probably inevitable next time around. For the present, however, the policy remains as a general rule to add material without making compensating omissions, on the grounds that Stroud is generally used as an opportunity for comprehensive initial research, following which readers are able to select for themselves which sources to investigate further. For that reason too, the practice for the last two editions has been to include full quotations

> and not mere citations wherever possible; although this accelerates the increase in the length of the work, it also helps readers to identify which sources are particularly promising in the context of their research.

One way of guarding against the perils of these necessary occasional culls, both for judicial dictionaries and to a lesser extent for legal dictionaries, is to acknowledge that earlier editions will continue to serve a significant research purpose. It has always been a tacit assumption that legal libraries will preserve old editions of dictionaries for purposes of specialist research; but the most recent editions of both *Jowitt* and *Stroud* make that assumption explicit, and in a number of places provide a basic definition of a term with primarily historical relevance, while referring the reader expressly to the previous edition of the work for an expanded definition in its historical context. Although this occurs only in a relatively small number of entries, it is a useful way of keeping down the overall length of what is necessarily a growing work, without the editor having to feel too guilty about having deprived the serious historical researcher of material that he or she will not find elsewhere easily or at all.

## Foreign Languages and Jurisdiction

In relation to foreign languages, the challenges confronting the legal lexicographer are the same as those confronting all lexicographers, with perhaps just one or two peculiarly legal twists. The basic test is reasonably simple to describe and apply: once an expression of a foreign language has been adopted so that it is commonly incorporated into an English sentence as a term of English Law, without translation or explanation, it deserves inclusion in an English legal or judicial dictionary. While it remains a term that would generally be accompanied by translation or explanation, or refers to a process found in a legal system outside the United Kingdom, it has no place in an English legal or judicial dictionary.

The first minor complication in this context for a legal dictionary relates to the existence within the United Kingdom of a number of separate legal jurisdictions. Scots Law, in particular, has a very large number of its own terms and expressions, some of which have no direct equivalent in the law of England and Wales or Northern Ireland. In this respect a legal dictionary therefore has to decide, first, whether it wishes to serve the United Kingdom as a whole or only the jurisdiction of England and Wales. (Northern Ireland, although technically a separate jurisdiction, does not have a sufficiently distinct legal vocabulary either to justify a separate dictionary or to make one designed primarily for England and Wales unhelpful for Northern Ireland.)

Secondly, even if a legal or judicial dictionary determines that it is confined to the law of England and Wales, it is inevitable that some entries will require modification by reference to Scots Law if the dictionary is to avoid seriously misleading readers. It is important, for example, to identify expressions that a person might come across and naturally assume to be expressions of English Law and to explain that they have reference exclusively to Scotland – for example, the Fatal Accident Inquiry, which is the Scottish equivalent of a coroner's inquest but which is occasionally used by writers who are obviously unaware of its territorial restriction.

Finally, terms of European Union Law, some of which derive from the French, effectively became terms of English Law by incorporation by virtue of the European Communities Act 1972, and will have to be reflected as appropriate in an English legal dictionary. This applies not merely to terms of obviously foreign derivation, but also to ordinary English words – like 'worker' – which have acquired technical meanings within the body of European Union Law and which therefore require exposition in both their domestic and European Union contexts in a dictionary of English Law.

## Who Should Write a Legal Dictionary?

There are a number of difficulties about determining who is reasonably competent to compile or revise a legal dictionary. The principal problem is simply that the training for each is so specialised and demanding that the author knows of nobody who has significant qualifications, or even experience, both in law and in lexicography, at least in the United Kingdom. The result is that legal dictionaries have tended to be compiled over the years, again at least so far as the United Kingdom is concerned, by lawyers with an amateur or peripheral interest in lexicography. The economics of the production of dictionaries have also meant that as a rule there has been little or no professional lexicographical contribution to the production of legal dictionaries in the United Kingdom; and, I would imagine, a lexicographical audience reading the last statement would be inclined to add 'and it shows!'.

On balance, however, if one or other expertise has to be used to the exclusion of the other, less harm is likely to be done by a lawyer 'dabbling' in lexicography than by a lexicographer dabbling in the law; and publishers have been right to leave the assessment of usage evidence in legal contexts to legal practitioners. The compilers of the *Oxford English Dictionary* habitually refer technical legal terms to lawyers for consideration of revised entries, and experience has shown that they are right to do so, in the sense that it is often possible to suggest nuances or to identify developments that would not have been apparent even to the most skilled of lexicographers.

Ideally, there is no doubt that the principal English legal dictionaries would benefit from lexicographical expertise, particularly when it comes to addressing some of the problems of ageing and development discussed above; and should a way be found in the future to provide a contribution from that profession in the revision of those dictionaries it would be likely to be greatly to their advantage.

The next problem that arises, having determined that by default one is required to have legal dictionaries written by lawyers, is that of determining what kind of lawyer should write them: in particular, generalists or specialists. Here at least, despite the commercial constraints, it has sometimes been possible to have the best of both worlds: the production of the third edition of *Jowitt's Dictionary of English Law* was overseen by generalist editors, but benefited from the involvement of around a hundred specialist editors, including judges, academics and practitioners from all areas of the law. As the foreword by Rt. Hon. Baroness Scotland of Asthal QC, HM Attorney General, says:

> The contributors to this new edition consist of a galaxy of talent drawn from all parts of the legal profession, including academics, present and former members of the Government Legal Service and lawyers in private practice.

The result of having such a breadth of experience means, of course, that it is difficult to ensure an overall consistency of treatment and coherence of the work; but while the general editor will do what he or she can in this respect, the need for it is limited by the fact that a dictionary can serve as a set of individually separate entries each of which is likely to be consulted individually and separately, so that most readers will be little distracted or disturbed by differences of style. The most important aspect of this coordination role will therefore be to ensure that consistency is applied in matters such as the treatment of obsolescence discussed above.

## Who Is the Audience?

All the questions discussed above need to be considered by the editor before he or she sets about writing or revising a legal or judicial dictionary. But there is one more, that if neglected could undermine the entire project: for whom is the dictionary being written? Although this will again be a question familiar to all prospective lexicographers, there is again a subtle but important legal twist in the case of a legal dictionary: in construing commercial or legislative documents the courts have some, although limited, regard to what is said about particular expressions in dictionaries. In construing an expression that has a natural English meaning the courts will sometimes rely on the definition in a standard dictionary, although normally in doing so they will remind themselves of the need for due caution in transposing the lexicographer's opinion onto the mind of the parties or the legislature. Legal and judicial dictionaries are likely to be accorded just a shade more deference, and therefore require to be compiled with more than a shade more caution.

## Conclusion

If the questions and issues discussed above require to be considered thoroughly before a legal dictionary is written or revised, it is perhaps not difficult to see why relatively few are written and why they are sometimes allowed unhappily to lapse into moribundity for want of regular and frequent updating. With a law that permeates all areas of life, however, and that relies so heavily on the use of technical language, legal and judicial dictionaries are clearly a necessary tool for lawyers and non-lawyers alike; and it is to be hoped that the enormous difficulties that attend their creation will not be too effective a discouragement for those who set out to try their hand.

# Chapter 5
# Bilingual Legal Dictionaries: Comparison Without Precision?

Coen J.P. van Laer*

## 1. Introduction

### *1.1. Encyclopaedic Information in Comparative Bilingual Law Dictionaries*

Bilingual legal dictionaries (BLDs) are useful in so far as they add explanations to their word lists but they still disappoint in that they do not fully meet all the requirements of legal translators. There are only a small number of outstanding, comparative BLDs that provide the comparative and contrastive material necessary for the translator to make informed decisions about equivalence. Since addressing the question of equivalence of legal terms is a fundamental desideratum of BLDs, this paper will focus on a sample of five comparative BLDs for European languages to assess whether and to what extent information permitting the determination of equivalence is provided. In so doing, this chapter seeks to evaluate the content and structure of the encyclopaedic information found in our sample as such information should enable the user to identify and, more importantly, to assess degrees of equivalence of legal terms used in different jurisdictions.

Translators of legal terminology are obliged to practice comparative law in order to find an equivalent in the target language legal system for the term of the source language legal system (De Groot and van Laer 2006: 66). As one would expect, BLDs that provide encyclopaedic information along with their translation suggestions are more effective because they facilitate the comparative law research the translator needs to carry out. In the absence of such supplementary information, the translator is forced to consult other sources such as monolingual legal dictionaries, online resources and even legal experts. BLDs that furnish this encyclopaedic information make this time-consuming research superfluous and thus become indispensable tools for the legal translator, seeking to make conceptual distinctions and to choose the right equivalent.[1]

---

* C.J.P. van Laer PhD, Maastricht University, The Netherlands. Email: c.vanlaer@maastrichtuniversity.nl. Coen J.P. van Laer wrote this chapter and is responsible for its contents; he is greatly indebted to Prof. G.R. de Groot.

1 Especially in the case of dictionaries that deal with culture-bound material such as law, encyclopaedic information is indispensable so that the translator is placed in a situation

### *1.2. Legislative Definitions in Encyclopaedic Information*

This chapter deals with problems involved in formulating encyclopaedic information related to reliable equivalents. Encyclopaedic information in comparative BLDs is useful if it clarifies the usage of terms and the contents of concepts in a reliable way. Preferably, encyclopaedic information should include authoritative information about national legal concepts in the form of legislative definitions excerpted from the relevant legislation. Explanations, although less precise, can help to indicate degrees of equivalence as well. However, most dictionary makers do not follow these recommended practices; they assume equivalence for their word lists (De Groot and van Laer 2006: 75).

The possible usefulness of definitions introduced in encyclopaedic information will be explored in the next section before examining sample entries for 'nationality' that will illustrate various practices found in a sample of leading comparative BLDs. As one would expect, these tools provide definitions as part of their encyclopaedic information in order to enable translators to measure equivalence as precisely as possible.

## 2. Background

### *2.1. Measuring Equivalence by Means of Definitions*

One of the main desiderata for reliable BLDs is that they meet the following requirement as much as possible: 'The dictionary should indicate the degree of equivalence: whether the translation suggestion is a full equivalent, the closest approximate equivalent (acceptable equivalent) or a partial equivalent' (De Groot and van Laer 2006: 73). The precision of encyclopaedic information is crucial in indicating degrees of equivalence between the concepts expressed by the terms in the source language and the target language. As a consequence, definitions are to be preferred since they establish the meaning of concepts in precise formulations but explanations of the usage of terms may also be productive.

Two definitions are needed to allow for comparison and to determine degrees of equivalence. The juxtaposition of legislative definitions may make explicit relevant similarities and differences between concepts not belonging to the same jurisdiction. This will be illustrated with two short definitions of national concepts of apartment right: the Dutch 'appartementsrecht' and the German

---

to correctly choose between the proposed equivalents and become aware of relevant distinctions. This is a translation of the following statement by Janker: 'Insbesondere in Wörterbüchern, die kulturabhängige Fächer wie das Recht behandeln, sind enzyklopädische Informationen unentbehrlich, damit die ÜbersetzerInnen in der Lage sind, die richtige Wahl zwischen den gegebenen Äquivalenten zu treffen und begriffliche Unterschiede erkennen zu können' (2012: 15–16).

'Wohnungseigentum'. The Dutch 'appartementsrecht' is defined as follows: 'An apartment right means a share in the property which is involved in the division and includes the right to the exclusive use of certain portions of the building which, as indicated by their layout, are intended to be used as separate units'.[2] By contrast, the German Condominium Act defines 'Wohnungseigentum' as: 'Residential property is the separate ownership of an apartment in connection with the co-ownership share of the joint property, to which it belongs'.[3]

The important distinction between both terms is that 'the right to the exclusive use', mentioned only by the Dutch legislator, does not imply the ownership of a specified part of the whole building, as is the case in German Law (Van Laer 2002: 4). The juxtaposition of the two definitions reveals, in addition to this difference, the common characteristic of 'co-ownership' which is an important similarity between the two concepts. Since the difference co-exists with this similarity, it can be stated that there is an acceptable or partial equivalence between the Dutch 'appartementsrecht' and the German 'Wohnungseigentum'.

Legislative definitions and their juxtaposition provide the translator with authoritative information which is useful to identify and to assess degrees of equivalence. BLDs which provide these juxtapositions do not suggest full or perfect equivalence but make the legal translator aware of the fact that the terms involved are not simply synonymous. This will enable the translator to avoid the pitfall of blindly substituting one term for another. Because of the context, however, it is possible that there is no need for detailed information about minor differences between terms in the source and target languages. Take for example the case where the Dutch document to be translated into German emphasizes 'the right to the exclusive use'. In this case, the translator should avoid creating the false impression that the document is about ownership of a specified part of the whole building. If the document to be translated, however, predominantly or exclusively deals with the common characteristic of co-ownership of the whole building, the Dutch term may be translated by the German 'Wohnungseigentum' because, in this context, the difference between both terms is not central.

### *2.2. How Much Encyclopaedic Information is Efficient?*

Legislative definitions can be more or less specific so it has to be considered whether the juxtaposition of more detailed definitions is too complicated for translators. If so, it is not certain that more encyclopaedic information in BLDs will contribute to the efficiency of the measurement of degrees of equivalence. The following definition will be used as a starting point to illustrate the limits of encyclopaedic

2 Netherlands Civil Code, book 5, s 106(4) is available on <http://wetten.overheid.nl/zoeken_op./BWBR0005288/Boek5/Titel9/Afdeling1/Artikel106/geldigheidsdatum_20–11–2013> translated by P.P.C. Haanappel and E. Mackaay; accessed 25 November 2013.

3 Gesetz über das Wohnungseigentum und das Dauerwohnrecht, s 1(2) is available on <http://www.gesetze-im-internet.de/woeigg/_1.html> accessed 25 November 2013.

information: 'Exploitation shall include, as a minimum, the exploitation of the prostitution of others or other forms of sexual exploitation, forced labour or services, including begging, slavery or practices similar to slavery, servitude, or the exploitation of criminal activities, or the removal of organs'.[4] To some extent, this non-exhaustive EU definition has been incorporated into the French and Dutch criminal provisions regarding human trafficking.[5] In this context, comparability is already a given because of the presence of the international definition (Van Laer and Xanthaki 2013: 136). For this reason, the EU definition can be used as a yardstick to measure the degree of equivalence present in both national definitions of exploitation.

Exploitation is the central element in the crime of trafficking in human beings. Comparing the French and Dutch definitions for 'exploitation' in the context of the provisions penalizing human trafficking requires that the translator examine all of the elements contained in the above definition. This initial examination suggests that the element 'removal of organs' is present in the French definition but absent in the Dutch one. This analysis will not be very time-consuming as none of the legislative definitions involved are over-long.

As far as the element 'removal of organs' is concerned, the EU definition appears, at first glance, not to have been transposed by the Dutch legislator. However, the element 'removal of organs' is in fact present in the Dutch criminal provision. After some study the translator will discover that the element 'removal of organs' is mentioned repeatedly in a separate, extended paragraph of the Dutch section on human trafficking.[6] Although the element of 'removal of organs' has not been incorporated into the Dutch definition, its inclusion in several other places in the provision may very well have the same effect as the French definition which appears to be more complete at first sight. For these reasons, even full equivalence may be deemed to exist, but the comparison is complicated by the diverging approaches adopted.

---

4 Directive 2011/36/EU of the European Parliament and of the Council of 5 April 2011 on preventing and combating trafficking in human beings and protecting its victims [2011] OJ L101/6, art 2 (3) <http://eur-lex.europa.eu/LexUriServ/LexUriServ.do?uri=OJ:L:2011:101:0001:0011:EN:PDF>accessed 25 November 2013. This definition of 'exploitation' contains 43 words.

5 Code pénal (French penal code), s 225–4-1 <http://www.legifrance.gouv.fr/affichCode.do;jsessionid=58D469ED85F27F299FE62ECD64DE179A.tpdjo12v_3?idSectionTA=LEGISCTA000006165299&cidTexte=LEGITEXT000006070719&dateTexte=20131115> accessed 25 November 2013. The definition of 'exploitation' given by s 225–4-1(I) contains 94 words. Wetboek van Strafrecht (Dutch penal code), s 273f <http://wetten.overheid.nl/BWBR0001854/TweedeBoek/TitelXVIII/Artikel273f/geldigheidsdatum_15–11–2013> accessed 25 November 2013. The definition of 'exploitation' given by s 273f(2) contains 39 words.

6 Wetboek van Strafrecht (Dutch penal code), s 273f(1) contains 488 words; the defining element 'removal of organs' has been mentioned in s 273f(1)(4), s 273f(1)(5), s 273f(1)(7), s 273f(1)(8) and s 273f(1)(9). See <http://wetten.overheid.nl/BWBR0001854/TweedeBoek/TitelXVIII/Artikel273f/geldigheidsdatum_15–11–2013>accessed 25 November 2013.

Encyclopaedic information may influence the so-called 'search-related information costs' or the 'comprehension-related information costs'. Search-related information costs are the costs related to the look-up activities users have to perform when consulting a dictionary to get access to the data they are searching for; for instance a high degree of textual condensation in definitions may increase the information costs (Nielsen 2009: 34). Comprehension-related information costs are the costs related to the user's ability to understand and interpret the data presented in a dictionary (Nielsen 2009: 34). Probably, comprehension-related information costs are not likely to be high for the special group of translators who are experts in comparative law research.

The main task of a translation tool is to supply the translator with as much information as possible to support the intellectual decision-making process (Sandrini 1999: 103). However, the amount of encyclopaedic information in comparative BLDs is not always efficient since it may cause a higher level of search-related information costs or comprehension-related information costs. In particular, legislative definitions may increase the search-related information costs and their juxtaposition may involve higher comprehension-related information costs as well. In a definition that is more than 600 words long, clarity and comprehension may have been sacrificed in an effort to be precise (Price 2013: 1023). For these reasons, the compiler of a comparative BLD may exercise restraint in quoting too long or too complex definitions in order to enable translators to measure the equivalence of terms. References to legislative sources may be preferable to reduce information costs and to augment efficiency for the user of the BLD. The test case which follows explores these aspects.

## 3. Test Case

### *3.1. Entries for 'Nationality' in Comparative Bilingual Law Dictionaries*

To test comparative BLDs, the entry for 'nationality' has been chosen since it expresses a basic legal concept that needs to be defined since it is intertwined with the almost synonymous term 'citizenship'. Within several languages, a complicated relationship between terms for 'nationality' (in the sense of a bond with the State) and 'citizenship' can be observed (De Groot 2012: 149). Great confusion exists as to the exact meaning of the terms 'nationality' and 'citizenship' because the terms do not have the same meaning in the different legal traditions (Vonk 2012: 19). In the absence of full or perfect equivalence, it is reasonable to expect that the supposedly superior comparative BLDs will define the existing dissimilarities in order to clarify them. Although the entry for 'nationality' features in only five printed BLDs that have been categorized as comparative BLDs,[7] this small sample

7 The categories Word List, Explanatory Dictionary and Comparative Dictionary have been defined and applied in an annotated bibliography (De Groot and van Laer 2011: 152

will allow us to draw some tentative conclusions about the content and structure of encyclopaedic information translators would like to see in comparative BLDs.

Before embarking on an analysis of the various entries for 'nationality', let us first note the five sample BLDs in question:

de Franchis, F.
*Dizionario giuridico*
Vol. 1: Inglese–Italiano
Milano, Italy: Giuffrè, 1984
XI + 1545 pp.
ISBN 8814003165

de Franchis, F.
*Dizionario giuridico*
Vol. 2: Italiano–Inglese
Milano, Italy: Giuffrè, 1996
1467 pp.
ISBN 8814050015

Gallegos, C.
*Bilingual Law Dictionary*
Chicago, IL, USA: Merl, 2005
XVI + 414 pp.
ISBN 1886347034=9781886347038

Hesseling, G.
*Juridisch woordenboek (Nederlands–Frans, met woordenlijst Frans–Nederlands) privaatrecht*
Antwerpen, Belgium: M. Kluwer, 1978
XXII + 513 pp.
ISBN 9062150020

Internationales Institut für Rechts- und Verwaltungssprache
*Ausländer- und Niederlassungsrecht*
Deutsch–Französisch

---

and passim). Comparative BLDs explain different meanings, illustrate the relevant linguistic context, refer to legal systems and/or legal sources and they distinguish between legal systems using the same language.

The number of truly comparative BLDs for one or two EU languages is greater than five, but not all of them contain an entry for 'nationality'.

The exploration has been extended to six BLDs that have been categorized as not fully comparative but more than just explanatory. It is notable that definitions of 'nationality' are absent in these six BLDs. This suggests that the five really comparative BLDs are a good sample.

Köln, Germany: Heymanns, 1990
159 pp.
ISBN 3452215784

Oosterveld-Egas Repáraz, M. C., et al.
*Juridisch woordenboek Nederlands–Spaans, met register Spaans–Nederlands*
Apeldoorn, The Netherlands: Maklu, 1990
XXXI + 371 pp.
ISBN 9062152716

The sample consists of five BLDs and six volumes in total (De Franchis is a two-volume work).

*3.2. Entries for 'Nationality': Analysis and Comments*

Each entry for 'nationality' will be reproduced before commenting on the encyclopaedic information and the definitions in particular.

*De Franchis* (De Groot and van Laer 2011: 175–6)

> **Nationality.** Nazionalità in genere. L'espressione è impiegata sia nel senso di cittadinanza (detta anche *citizenship*), come nel British Nationality Act 1948, sia nel senso di nazionalità o appartenenza ad un certa gruppo etnico, come nel Race Relations Act 1968 (De Franchis 1984: 1038).

De Franchis does not give the generic meaning of 'Nationality'. The term 'Nationality' is said to correspond to two different Italian legal terms, 'cittadinanza' and 'nazionalità'. According to De Franchis, the term 'nazionalità' denotes membership of a certain ethnical community. However, he does not explain the relationship between 'cittadinanza' and 'nazionalità' in the Italian legal system. Apparently, De Franchis suggests that 'nazionalità' is not an acceptable equivalent for 'nationality' because 'nazionalità' refers to the ethnic dimension of persons contrary to the Italian term 'cittadinanza'. Furthermore, information is absent on the precise relationship between 'nationality' in the sense of the British Nationality Act and 'citizenship' in the sense of the very same act. Nevertheless, when it comes to translation suggestions, De Franchis draws a parallel between the Italian 'cittadinanza' and the context of the British Nationality Act while 'nazionalità' has its proper place in the context of the Race Relations Act 1968. By drawing both parallels, De Franchis does not explicitly set out the exact context in which the Italian translations should be used.

> **Nationalità.** Nationality, nationhood; ma il primo termine indica anche la cittadinanza (De Franchis 1996: 998).

This counterpart of the English entry states in Italian that the first term (that is, 'Nationality') also denotes 'citizenship', without mentioning possible differences between the English terms 'nationality' and 'nationhood'. More significantly, this volume which is meant to be a tool for those translating into English, does not supply any information to enable the translator to choose between the terms 'nationality' and 'citizenship'. The translator may have recourse to the first volume of the dictionary to get additional information, but the entry 'Nationality' will not clarify the relationship between 'cittadinanza' and 'nazionalità' in the Italian legal system or the relationship between 'nationality' and 'citizenship' in the sense of the British Nationality Act. Ultimately, the consequence of this absence of definitions in De Franchis is that the translator is not equipped with the necessary information to determine degrees of equivalence between 'cittadinanza' and 'citizenship',[8] or between 'nazionalità' and 'nationality'.

Gallegos[9]

> **nationality** n. *nacionalidad.* The relationship between a person, sometimes an entity, and a nation. The status of belonging to a particular nation. (…) See: citizenship.
>
> **citizenship** n. *ciudadania, nacionalidad.* (…) The status of being a member in a political society or nation, implying a duty of allegiance on the part of the member, and a duty of protection on the part of the society or nation.
>
> **ciudadania** n. citizenship.
>
> **nacionalidad** n. *nationality, citizenship.* (…) Nacionalidad es el vinculo jurídico que une a una persona con el Estado al que pertenece (Gallegos 2005: 133, 39, 242, 330).

Surprisingly, Gallegos contains only three definitions, not four, since 'ciudadania' has not been defined. Regrettably, verifiable references are missing and Gallegos

8 Comparing the following entries in both volumes is not helpful either: see volume 1: Citizenship. Nationalità in genere; detta anche nationality (De Franchis 1984: 458), suggesting that 'citizenship' and 'nationality' have the same meaning in English. And, by contrast, volume 2: Cittadinanza. Citizenship; ma, non senza una certa confusione, si parla anche di nationality (De Franchis 1996: 501), suggesting that 'citizenship' and 'nationality' could have a different meaning in English.

9 For a detailed review of this volume, see De Groot and van Laer: 'The structure of the dictionary, with indication of the degree and the kind of equivalence, looks very promising. Gives frequent references to relevant articles of statutes, to case law, and to legal literature. Terms are often explained in comparative perspective' (2011: 176).

does not specify where his definitions come from.[10] Apart from these flaws, it is interesting to analyse the relationships between the four entries quoted above.

Regarding the relationship between ‘nationality’ and ‘citizenship’, the dictionary explicitly states that these English terms are synonymous.[11] However, the existence of such a relationship is dubious since the legal status of the individual is usually denoted by ‘nationality’, the consequences by ‘citizenship’ (Dörr 2006: A sub 2). And it is ‘Nationality’ that expresses a person’s legal bond with a particular State but not everyone who possesses the nationality of a particular State also enjoys full citizenship rights in that State (De Groot 2012: 148).[12] Nationality is necessary, but not sufficient to exercise all citizenship rights. Since both legal terms are system-bound and since both concepts are parts of the legal system of the United Kingdom, their systematic and structural embedding may be too diverse to justify their unconditional identification as synonyms.

In the same vein, it is not obvious that the terms ‘nacionalidad’ and ‘ciudadania’ are interchangeable in every Spanish-speaking jurisdiction. Nevertheless, Gallegos claims that ‘nationality’ and ‘citizenship’ are different terms for the same concept and ‘nacionalidad’ and ‘ciudadania’ are synonymous as well. On the national level, Gallegos assumes that both terms confer the same status on individuals and that conceptual distinctions are absent.

When it comes to comparing jurisdictions, Gallegos suggests that the English ‘nationality’ may be translated by the Spanish ‘nacionalidad’, although the English definition of ‘nationality’ (‘The relationship …’) is slightly different from the Spanish one (‘vinculo jurídico’). The translator faced with the Spanish ‘nacionalidad’ may choose between ‘nationality’ or ‘citizenship’ because of the assumption made in this BLD that these English terms are synonymous. However, the assumed synonymy of legal terms within one and the same jurisdiction is not sufficient to substantiate the equivalence of two pairs of terms belonging to two different legal systems. Although it may happen that two different terms are synonyms and express the same concept, comparative law research will probably preclude full equivalence because of the specificity of national concepts.

---

10 ‘Entries and their definitions are based on terms and expressions found in various legal sources such as scholarly works, legal dictionaries, court proceedings, case law, and statutory law’ (Gallegos 2005: viii).

11 Citizenship and nationality are synonymous terms which are used ambiguously. And: ‘While both refer to that existing link between a person and a nation or a state, there is a tendency to use citizenship in contexts where the term is applicable mostly to individuals and nationality when referring primarily to entities’ (Gallegos 2005: 39).

12 ‘In the English language, the relationship between the two terms “nationality” and “citizenship” is even more complicated in the context of nationality law itself. In the United Kingdom, the term “nationality” is used to indicate the formal link between a person and the State. The statute that regulates this status is the British Nationality Act 1981. The most privileged status to be acquired under this Act, however, is the status of “British citizen” (De Groot 2012: 149).

Hesseling[13]

**Nationaliteit** ***Nationalité (f)*** (Hesseling 1978: 197).[14]

This entry could feature in a word list since it assumes equivalence and does not provide definitions or explanations.

Internationales Institut für Rechts- und Verwaltungssprache[15]

**Staatsangehörigkeit** f. (= Nationalität)

(die rechtlich geordnete Form der Zugehörigkeit einer natürlichen Person zu einem Staat ...)

=

**nationalité** f.

(lien juridique qui unit une personne physique a un Etat determiné ...) (Internationales Institut für Rechts- und Verwaltungssprache 1990: 55).

According to the sign '=' used in this BLD, the German and the French term are synonymous or 100 per cent equivalent terms. The definitions for 'Staatsangehörigkeit' and for 'nationalité' are adduced to corroborate this claim. However, since no references to sources are provided, it is not clear whether the French definition is just a translation of the German one, belongs to the French legal system, is derived from international instruments like treaties or is an autonomous explanation not derived from any particular jurisdiction. Finally, the sign '=' suggests that the German terms 'Staatsangehörigkeit' and 'Nationalität' are synonymous, but that is not correct as 'Nationalität' has an ethnic connotation while 'Staatsangehörigkeit' describes a legal link between an individual and a State (Vonk 2012: 20).

---

13 For a detailed review, see De Groot and van Laer: 'Entry terms and translation suggestions are illustrated with quotations, the sources of most of which are given' (2011: 180).

14 More specific terms underneath the main entry are Dutch compound terms which have been translated into French terms with examples and other explanations in French.

15 For a detailed review: 'The dictionary is divided systematically with the terms being given a central place. The book contains gradations of equivalence and references to statutory provisions' (De Groot and van Laer 2011: 182).

Oosterveld[16]

**nationaliteit** nacionalidad, *V. CCiv 9 ss, 17 ss;* (Oosterveld 1990: 134).[17]

This entry does not provide any definitions. Familiarity with Dutch sources is assumed on the part of the translator and he is supposed to use the references to find the Spanish provisions that contain the term to be translated. However, the provisions referred to do not contain legislative definitions of the concept of nationality.[18]

## 4. Conclusions

### *4.1. Encyclopaedic Information Without Juxtaposition*

Where it comes to the juxtaposition of domestic and foreign elements, it is interesting to note the difference between the two bi-directional BLDs (De Franchis, Gallegos) on the one hand, and the three one-directional BLDs on the other. The preceding analysis shows that some comparative and contrastive materials are present in De Franchis (UK→IT; IT→UK) and in Gallegos (UK↔ES). However, such materials are absent in Hesseling (NL→FR), Internationales Institut für Rechts- und Verwaltungssprache (DE→FR) and Oosterveld (NL→ES). Hesseling does not provide any additional information which makes any comparison impossible; the Internationales Institut für Rechts- und Verwaltungssprache volume does not clarify whether elements from different jurisdictions have been used; and, finally, Oosterveld only refers to foreign sources, without citing Dutch legislation. These observations support the conclusion that the compilers of bi-directional comparative BLDs are more inclined to insert information on both languages while compilers of uni-directional BLDs are more prone to assume that additional information on one legal language is sufficient.

Both bi-directional BLDs offer encyclopaedic information in the form of elements from different jurisdictions but the juxtaposition of domestic and foreign definitions is missing. Since both De Franchis and Gallegos do not define legal concepts as parts of the wider conceptual structure of the jurisdictions to which they belong, they suggest that the term 'nationality' and the term 'citizenship' and their respective counterparts in other languages are interchangeable. Conceptual

16 For a detailed review: 'Excellent and exemplary dictionary, which combines translation and explanation, context, and references to sources. The translation suggestions of Dutch–Spanish are certainly scientifically sound' (De Groot and van Laer 2011: 198).

17 More specific terms beneath the main entry are Dutch compound terms which have been translated into Spanish.

18 The Spanish Civil Code is available at this link: <http://www.mjusticia.gob.es/cs/Satellite/en/1288774502225/TextoPublicaciones.html> accessed 5 November 2013.

differences between legal systems may have been underestimated in the entries that have been analysed.

Legislative definitions permitting a comparative and contrastive approach are absent in the entries for 'nationality' which have been sampled. The reason for this lack may be that the compilers of the five titles assumed a high or sufficient degree of terminological equivalence which, in their view, makes an explicit statement of shared characteristics unnecessary. Nevertheless, the absence of legislative definitions results in a dearth of precise information thereby forcing the translator to consult international instruments, monolingual dictionaries, textbooks and online sources.

### *4.2 Implications*

Based upon the analysis of our limited sample of five BLDs, a conclusion may be drawn that they differ in terms of the content and structure of their encyclopaedic information. Although the information provided in this sample is inadequate and the elements therein could be completed, it is clear that a common practice regarding the provision of encyclopaedic information has not yet been developed. Comparative BLDs should contain more legislative definitions where the degree of equivalence between terms is low. In addition, they should include definitions for core concepts that cover a set of rules belonging to a legal field. In the absence of such definitions or where these are unreliable, this study suggests that explanations can constitute an acceptable alternative means for indicating degrees of equivalence in such a way that the legal translator who is not a comparative lawyer can make an informed decision. Where definitions are present, they should be placed side by side and be accompanied preferably by linguistic examples and references to sources.[19]

Since most compilers of BLDs have to serve both language professionals and comparative law experts, they should find the best compromise between concise, abridged definitions and long, legislative definitions. Longer definitions are more similar to encyclopaedic information but shorter ones are easier to comprehend. Comparative BLDs should maintain their foundation in comparative law research but extended or detailed encyclopaedic information could lead to an information surfeit. Further research is needed to determine what encyclopaedic information should be provided to measure equivalence as precisely as possible and to develop universally accepted standards for assessing the quality of the contents and

19 'In view of the nature of legal terminologies and the need to consider the general reader, a useful bilingual legal dictionary should at least include the following data: (a) definitions of a legal term; (b) a context showing how a legal term is interpreted; and (c) sources of the relevant ordinances and cases. It would not be sufficient to include only a Chinese translation of the legal term with a definition of that legal term because even if a term is defined, the legal connotation in a definition will still not be clear to a general user' (Poon 2010: 91).

structure of that information in comparative BLDs. The juxtaposition of long or complex definitions may be inefficient and, as a consequence, not be accepted as a standard for encyclopaedic information in comparative BLDs.

## References

Dörr O, 'Nationality' in *Max Planck Encyclopedia of Public International Law* (OUP host 2006).

de Groot GR and van Laer CJP, 'The Dubious Quality of Legal Dictionaries' (2006) 34 *International Journal of Legal Information* 65 <http://arno.unimaas.nl/show.cgi?fid=5021> accessed 5 November 2013.

de Groot GR and van Laer CJP, 'Bilingual and Multilingual Legal Dictionaries in the European Union: An Updated Bibliography' (2011) 30 *Legal Reference Services Quarterly* 149.

de Groot GR, 'The Influence of Problems of Legal Translation on Comparative Law Research' in CJW. Baaij (ed.), *The Role of Legal Translation in Legal Harmonization* (Alphen aan den Rijn 2012).

Janker K, Zweisprachige Rechtswörterbücher als Hilfsmittel für die Rechtsübersetzung. Eine metalexikographische Analyse unter besonderer Berücksichtigung des Sprachenpaars Deutsch-Englisch (Masterarbeit, Universität Wien. Zentrum für Translationswissenschaft 2012) <http://othes.univie.ac.at/23282/1/2012–10–11_0603155.pdf> accessed 5 November 2013

van Laer CJP, 'Comparative Concepts and Connective Integration' in *Fifth Benelux-Scandinavian Conference on Legal Theory: European Legal Integration and Analytical Legal Theory* (Maastricht 2002) <http://arno.unimaas.nl/show.cgi?fid=21327> accessed 5 November 2013.

van Laer CJP and Xanthaki H, 'Legal Transplants and Comparative Concepts: Eclecticism Defeated?' (2013) 34 *Statute Law Review* 128.

Nielsen S, 'Reviewing printed and electronic dictionaries: A theoretical and practical framework' in Sandro Nielsen and Sven Tarp (eds), *Lexicography in the 21st century: In honour of Henning Bergenholtz* (Benjamins 2009).

Poon, Wai Yee E, 'Strategies for Creating A Bilingual Legal Dictionary' (2010) 23 *Int J Lexicography* 83.

Price JP, 'Wagging, Not Barking: Statutory Definitions' (2013) 60 *Cleveland State Law Review* 999.

Sandrini P, 'Legal Terminology: Some Aspects for a New Methodology' (1999) 22 *Hermes: Journal of Linguistics* 101<http://download2.hermes.asb.dk/archive/download/H22_06.pdf> accessed 5 November 2013.

Vonk OW, *Dual Nationality in the European Union: A Study on Changing Norms in Public and Private International Law and in the Municipal Laws of Four EU Member States* (Martinus Nijhoff 2012).

# Chapter 6
# Pour des dictionnaires juridiques multilingues du citoyen de l'Union européenne

Pierre Lerat

A methodology for the creation of a database multilingual legal dictionary aimed at EU citizens who by virtue of their general and linguistic knowledge are 'semi-experts' is proposed. The author argues that such a project is all the more feasible given the degree of commonality between the basic legal concepts of French Law, German Law, Italian Law and even UK Law. The traditional distinction between lexicography and terminography is rejected on the basis that all lexicography is to a greater or lesser extent specialist. The starting point for every entry should be the concept, and should progress from this global level to the local level (level of language), with a 'minimal definition' inserted between the onomasiological and semasiological levels. The author also sets out a list of desiderata for a legal terminological database including the indication of hyponymic relations, the limitation of grammatical information, the provision of typical collocates and so on.

## Introduction

L'idée de dictionnaires juridiques multilingues pour les citoyens de l'Union européenne est à la fois raisonnable et utile. Raisonnable, car les concepts juridiques partagés sont nombreux; 506 couples de langues, c'est beaucoup, mais l'impératif de s'entendre sur les termes est de bon conseil, et l'obligation de résultat est productive. Utile, car les citoyens des pays de l'UE sont aussi, bon gré mal gré, des citoyens de l'Union, avec des droits et des devoirs communs.

L'idée générale est que le citoyen de l'UE n'est pas une abstraction: statistiquement, et grâce à l'allongement, ici et là, de la durée des études, c'est quelqu'un qui a un minimum de culture générale et de compétence dans une langue au moins. C'est assez pour qu'on puisse espérer en faire un « semi-expert » dans une matière qui régit sa vie sociale, de la naissance à la mort.

Comment faire? On sait au moins ce qui est peu efficace: la lexicographie bilingue ou plurilingue sur support papier, dont les écueils sont la polysémie et la synonymie. En théorie, ces écueils devraient pouvoir être évités si l'on traite les concepts juridiques partagés selon un principe de la terminologie classique: la distinction entre concepts opératoires (consensuels et/ou stipulés) et signifié lexical (propre à une langue et une culture nationales). C'est possible à condition de construire des bases de données où la consultation se fasse sur des chaînes de caractères et non pas au fil d'une nomenclature soumise à l'ordre alphabétique.

Le pluriel du titre (« Pour des dictionnaires ») résulte du souci de ne pas mêler réflexion méthodologique et implémentation. Les exemples sont tirés d'un fichier personnel plurilingue (de., en., es., fr., it.) résultant d'expériences cumulées. Il invite soit à un auto-apprentissage personnalisable autant que de besoin (une sorte de « carnet de vocabulaire » sur traitement de texte) soit à des exploitations plus ambitieuses (permettant l'échange et le travail coopératif), pour lesquelles je ne suis pas qualifié.

Une autre limite de ce travail est celle de mon expérience. C'est celle de la lexicographie générale (comme réviseur au *Trésor de la langue française*), puis de la lexicographie spécialisée (Lerat et Sourioux 1994, Lerat 2007). Ce n'est pas une expérience de juriste, ni même de jurilinguiste au sens canadien, mais de linguiste qui depuis longtemps s'intéresse au « langage du droit » (voir Sourioux 2011). Dans ces conditions, il ne s'agit pas de vouloir transformer en juristes les traducteurs, rédacteurs et simples citoyens, mais seulement de leur fournir une assistance.

## Le citoyen de l'UE

Il existe des outils lexicographiques et terminologiques destinés aux traducteurs, notamment communautaires, à commencer par *IATE*. Il serait bon aussi que l'on s'intéresse aux citoyens de l'UE en tant que tels, pour autant que l'on peut les cibler. Ce ne sont des experts ni du droit ni des langues. Ils ne sont pas pour autant incapables de devenir des « semi-experts » (Bergenholtz et Kaufmann 1997: 117). Ils n'ont pas besoin de notions de droit communautaire au sens restrictif (appellations des entités administratives, procédures de toutes sortes, principes divers). Ce qu'ils ont besoin de maîtriser, c'est d'abord un vocabulaire juridique fondamental, c'est-à-dire des concepts juridiques de base et des façons de les nommer; en somme, une terminologie au sens de la tradition onomasiologique: la « conceptualisation que partage une communauté de pratiques » (Depecker et Roche 2007: 112). De quoi permettre d'être un citoyen-contribuable-électeur-justiciable informé et responsable.

## L'alphabétisation juridique

Quand Sourioux et moi avons utilisé pour la première fois le slogan de l' « alphabétisation juridique » (1975: 11), c'était dans une approche unilingue, et il s'agissait uniquement de termes juridiques français. Il ne nous échappait pas que ce qui fait le terme n'est pas la forme plus ou moins savante (morphologiquement) d'un mot mais le contenu de connaissances qu'il sert à véhiculer; toutefois, l'importance des définitions restait encore aussi philologique que logique: la signature (du législateur ou d'un auteur reconnu) importait autant, ou presque, que la recherche de conditions nécessaires et suffisantes.

Une ouverture sur le plurilinguisme, dans une terminologie des contrats en français, anglais et allemand (Lerat et Sourioux 1994), aurait pu conduire à une méthodologie plus appropriée à la recherche de points communs et de spécificités. En fait, nous n'avons pas échappé à la malédiction du dictionnaire papier, qui est l'unidirectionnalité à partir de la langue de départ (voir Kromann 1990). Le résultat est un ensemble de dénominations en français et de définitions également en français (tantôt légales, tantôt doctrinales), avec des « équivalents » attestés dans des sources faisant autorité (ONU, UE, Canada, législations nationales).

Un éditeur m'a demandé depuis lors un « vocabulaire du juriste débutant » (Lerat 2007). J'ai cru devoir préciser qu'il ne s'agirait pas d'un vocabulaire juridique du français, mais seulement d'un dictionnaire pour étudiants commençant des études de droit en France. C'est loin d'être dépourvu d'utilité, les bacheliers de France n'étant pas tous fils de notaires ni latinistes, mais il n'est pas question de répondre aux besoins de tout francophone, par exemple belge ou suisse. Un acquis de cette expérience de rédaction ciblée est la mise en évidence du besoin d'avoir en vue un destinataire bien précis avant d'entreprendre un dictionnaire spécialisé.

La fréquentation assidue des sites de l'UE, notamment au début des années 2000, où j'ai mis sur le web une ressource intitulée Quadrirédacteur, qui posait de sérieux problèmes de mise à jour et que j'ai vite retirée du site d'un laboratoire de l'Université Paris 13, m'a appris quelque chose de rassurant: il existe une forte intersection entre le droit français, le droit allemand, le droit italien et même le droit du Royaume Uni. Rien d'étonnant: ce qui gage la validité des versions parallèles des règlements et des directives, ce sont à la fois des connaissances explicitées (par des définitions plus ou moins stipulatives) et des connaissances implicites qui sont partagées dans l'UE. Il est clair qu'il existe des concepts propres à une langue et à une culture: ceux d' « equity », de « charia », de « Land », de « conseil général » etc.; aussi bien, dans ces cas, un seul terme correspond à un seul concept dans une seule langue, et les différences d'une langue à l'autre portent tout au plus sur la graphie des langues non européennes (charia ou sharia). Il existe aussi des différences doctrinales, mais il ne faut pas en survaloriser la réalité: de part et d'autre de la Manche (et de l'Atlantique), un bien reste un bien, une acquisition une acquisition, un achat un achat etc.

Les connaissances explicitées dans ce qu'il est convenu d'appeler la « législation communautaire » sont plus ou moins fondamentales. On s'intéresse ici à celles qui sont les plus importantes juridiquement (plutôt que politiquement, administrativement etc.). Les critères à retenir sont au nombre de deux, à tout le moins. Le premier est le critère statistique de la répartition, c'est-à-dire de la présence dans beaucoup de textes spécialisés destinés à réglementer, toutes thématiques confondues (du commerce du bois à la génétique); par exemple, le concept de « traçabilité » est devenu incontournable. Le second est le critère logique de la subsomption, qui fournit les définisseurs juridiques nécessaires; ainsi, pour « rétractation », « résiliation », et pour « résiliation », « annulation ».

## Les écueils du dictionnaire bilingue ou multilingue sur support papier

### *Deux exemples*

Prenons l'exemple d'un bilingue plusieurs fois réédité et considéré à juste titre comme une assez bonne ressource pour un italophone comme pour un francophone: le Tortora (1994). De fait, il échappe à plusieurs écueils, mais pas à tous, comme on va le voir. Voici comment sont traités les couples *compera / achat* et *acquisizione / acquisition.*

a. *compera*: (Comm.) *achat, acquisition*
b. *acquisizione*: (Civ.) V. *acquisto 1*
c. *acquisto 1*: (Civ.) *acquisition, acquêt; acquisto 2:* (Comm.) *achat*
d. *achat:* (Comm.) *acquisto, compera*
e. *acquisition:* (Civ.) *acquisizione, acquisto*
f. *acquêts:* (Civ.) *beni acquisiti in comunione*

Une source de perplexité possible résulte des indications de domaines. Ainsi, *acquisition* relèverait du droit commercial en a) et du droit civil en c); à supposer que le cumul soit possible, il n'intéresse que les professeurs et leurs étudiants, non les clients et les héritiers.

Un autre écueil est l'indifférence aux hiérarchies de concepts: l'achat est une acquisition à titre onéreux, donc un cas particulier d'acquisition. Linguistiquement, on dira qu'en l'occurrence une hyperonymie est confondue avec une synonymie.

Les acquêts sont des biens acquis, mais dans des limites que précise bien f); dans ces conditions, le c) est dangereux.

Enfin, on ne retrouve pas ici la différence qui est à la base de la macrostructure des articles *achat* et *acquisition* dans un dictionnaire unilingue général: celle qu'il y a entre l'opération et le résultat. Or cette différence est logiquement importante, puisque c'est celle entre une opération (prédicat) et un objet (argument).

Techniquement, le traitement lexicographique d'*achat* et d'*acquisition* est meilleur dans le Larišova (2008), parce que l'auteure distingue clairement le générique *acquisition* (cs. *nabytí*), y compris l'acquisition d'un droit (*nabytí práva*), et le spécifique *achat* (cs. *koupě*), y compris dans le cas d'une vente à l'essai. Mais l'absence de définition, comme chez Tortora, fait que le dictionnaire laisse implicites les conceptualisations partagées qui justifient les équivalences. Là aussi, la fonction de décodage est limitée par la pluralité des équivalents proposés (lequel choisir?), et celle d'encodage est complètement sacrifiée.

### *Signifié et concept*

Le défaut commun de ces deux bons dictionnaires – paix aux autres ! – est de partir des mots, et non pas des concepts (et des relations entre concepts). Cette confusion, pour être très courante, n'en est pas moins redoutable. D'un côté, le signifié colle aux mots (pour Saussure, c'est le pendant de leur forme), il est conditionné par un système linguistique et une culture; de l'autre, le concept, à base de connaissance des choses, est une somme de propriétés définitoires.

La différence a été mise en évidence par un linguiste avec une grande clarté:

> « Parler du sens (ou *signifié*) de *cheval* revient à envisager le contenu de cet item comme une unité linguistique (…); parler du concept de « cheval », par contre, revient à l'envisager comme une unité extralinguistique » (Kleiber 1981: 24–25)

Dès lors que l'on a affaire à une unité extralinguistique, on comprend que les univers de discours ont une importance considérable. Ainsi, il existe une conceptualisation du cheval comme équidé, une autre comme monture. On est face à des techniques différentes: celle d'une science classificatoire et celle de l'équitation.

Les lexicographes font une différence entre les dictionnaires de mots (ou dictionnaires de langue) et les dictionnaires de choses (ou encyclopédies). En première approche, la distinction est utile. Elle devrait conduire à des définitions différentes, mais ce n'est pas toujours le cas, en sorte que les vraies différences sont surtout ailleurs: présence ou non de noms propres et d'iconographie.

Un dictionnaire spécialisé n'est pas un compromis entre ces deux types, mais un dictionnaire où les définitions sont l'essentiel parce qu'elles visent à rendre opératoire le concept dans un usage professionnalisé. Il s'agit avant tout d'une « mise à plat » des propriétés distinctives des objets pertinents (concrets et, surtout dans le cas du droit, abstraits). Alors que dans un dictionnaire de langue générale on pourra voir dans le mot *subsidiarité* la propriété de tout ce qui est subsidiaire, sur le modèle de *familiarité* par rapport à *familier*, et que dans une encyclopédie juridique on pourra faire un historique remontant au traité d'Amsterdam et citer la jurisprudence de la Curia, dans un dictionnaire juridique par sa matière mais pédagogique par sa visée, comme celui que l'on a en vue ici, l'important sera une définition limitée à un principe: celui selon lequel il n'y a pas à traiter au niveau communautaire ce qui peut l'être suffisamment au niveau national. Une telle définition est peu savante pour un professeur de droit, mais suffisante pour un citoyen européen qui n'est pas son étudiant.

### *Droit et technicité*

Au fait, le droit est-il technique? Il l'a toujours été, en tant qu'ensemble évolutif de réponses à des états de choses prévisibles susceptibles d'avoir des effets sociaux. Ainsi, de tout temps, l'achat a été une acquisition non gratuite. Le client le sait et en tient compte et, s'il préfère le vol, des sanctions sont prévues. Une opération réservée à des professionnels, comme la saisie, le partage après décès ou la sentence, relève d'une culture plus spécialisée, mais qui inclut les connaissances basiques sur l'achat et l'acquisition, entre autres. Il y a donc un continuum entre culture générale et culture spécialisée (sinon il n'y aurait de possibilité ni de formation professionnelle ni de vulgarisation).

La discipline qui traite techniquement de tout ce qui est technique dans le vocabulaire est la terminologie. Elle est faite elle-même d'un ensemble de concepts opératoires, à commencer par celui de « concept »: « unité de connaissance créée par une combinaison unique de caractères » (ISO). Pour son premier théoricien, l'ingénieur et chef d'entreprise autrichien Eugen Wüster, la terminologie est avant tout une « conceptologie ». C'est irréaliste, car les concepts ont besoin d'être nommés. Ce qui est réaliste dans sa démarche, en revanche, c'est l'idée que les connaissances sont exactement les mêmes pour les professionnels de tous les pays qui partagent des outils et des méthodes bien définis. S'il n'y avait de tels concepts opératoires partagés, comment les naturalistes, les cavaliers et les juristes du monde entier pourraient-ils communiquer de plain-pied dans des rencontres internationales?

Il est de bon ton de dénoncer la prolifération des définitions dans les textes normatifs. C'est qu'il faut prévoir tous les effets de droit que suscitent les découvertes, les innovations et, plus simplement, la libre circulation des personnes et des biens. C'est bien entendu aux scientifiques qu'il appartient de définir avec précision ce qu'est un OGM ou un clonage, mais la sanction du législateur européen en fait des objets de connaissance suffisamment spécifiques pour que les risques de conflits soient prévus et réglés, notamment dans le monde de l'agro-alimentaire et dans celui de la pharmacie. Suffisamment, mais pas plus: « aux fins du présent règlement », comme il est dit avant les définitions stipulatives acceptées par les parlementaires européens comme par les experts. En d'autres termes, à un niveau « semi-expert ».

## Le bon usage du multilinguisme

Ce qui est remarquable, du point de vue d'une terminologie à base de concepts, c'est l'intérêt d'une approche multilingue pour la connaissance des droits nationaux eux-mêmes, qui apparaissent ainsi, contrastivement, comme des objets particuliers, et non pas comme des évidences. On comprend les réticences des spécialistes; il ne s'agit pourtant pas de doctrine, mais de connaissance scientifique (ce qu' « on » entend par x chez les professionnels à un moment donné).

La recherche de généralités empiriques (et non pas d'universaux du droit) incite à travailler sur des langues pour lesquelles existent des versions parallèles des mêmes textes. L'anglais, l'espagnol et le français bénéficient de la meilleure couverture à la FAO et sont parlés sur plusieurs continents. Pour ces deux raisons, ici, on privilégiera les exemples dans ces trois langues, par commodité. Un traducteur ou un linguiste peut grâce aux sites de l'UE ajouter la langue de son choix; ainsi, dans mon cas, ce sont l'allemand et l'italien qui m'aident à relativiser un peu plus mes évidences juridiques et linguistiques.

## Distinguer un niveau global et un niveau local

La distinction entre un niveau global et un niveau local est faite par Guadalupe Aguado-de-Cea (2009) dans un cadre théorique visant à articuler terminologie et ontologie, au sens de l'intelligence artificielle. Le niveau global, pour elle, est celui de l'ontologie, le niveau local celui des langues. Cette ambition est séduisante, mais suppose que la question des postulats de base fondant l'ontologie soit résolue et que l'on opte pour tel ou tel logiciel, ce qui conduit d'un côté vers des problèmes philosophiques (réalisme ou nominalisme) et de l'autre vers des options technologiques (où le turn-over est impressionnant). La différence, en revanche, est bonne à prendre pour la terminologie, en tant qu'invitation à commencer par une approche onomasiologique (les conceptualisations techniques partagées) et à procéder ensuite à un travail sémasiologique (sur les termes, tant officiels que non officiels).

Chez Aguado-de-Cea, l'exemple choisi est celui d'une des rares ontologies qui ne soient pas médicales (la mécanique automobile): *Wärmekraftmotor / heat engine / motor térmico*. Ces dénominations de l'allemand, de l'anglais et de l'espagnol servent deux fois: d'abord comme « étiquettes » d'un même concept (au niveau ontologique), ensuite comme termes dans les trois langues (au niveau linguistique). On pourrait, au niveau conceptuel, utiliser un codage numérique et non pas linguistique, pour rendre plus nette la différence; c'est ce que fait Wüster (1968). Dans son dictionnaire, par exemple, *513* est le concept partagé par le français *taquet* et l'anglais *trip dog* (ainsi que son synonyme *trip-over stop*). Cette méthode, inspirée de la documentation, est utile dans le cas des nomenclatures; ainsi, sans changer d'exemple, le définisseur du concept de « taquet » est « butée », celui de « trip dog » est « stop », et l'étiquette commune à ces deux définisseurs est *1179*. En outre, un schéma visualise la place de la butée dans le taquet. Il est clair qu'on ne saurait dessiner la citoyenneté, donc il faut procéder mutatis mutandis.

Laissons à d'autres les ontologies juridiques, en leur souhaitant bon courage, et prenons en compte une particularité du droit, qui est d'être une discipline « flexible » (Carbonnier 1969), y compris au sein d'une même culture nationale. On ferait déjà œuvre utile et gérable en voyant dans la culture juridique de base, dans chaque pays, une « lexiculture » au sens de Galisson (1988), c'est-à-dire celui de « charge culturelle partagée » d'un vocabulaire. Jamais la lexiculture du français « créance » ne sera celle de l'italien « credito », qui inclut aussi l'idée de « crédit », mais en confrontant les emplois communautaires des deux mots et leurs équivalents dans d'autres langues on doit pouvoir distinguer d'une part un ensemble de propriétés définitoires constituant une « charge conceptuelle partagée », d'autre part des spécificités de l'ordre de la « langue-culture » (connotations comprises).

Pour que les concepts soient à coup sûr partagés, il faut et il suffit que les propriétés constitutives d'une définition commune fassent l'objet d'un consensus dans une communauté internationale d'experts. Il s'agit seulement d'un « noyau dur », qui n'exclut nullement des spécificités au niveau « local ». Voici un exemple, avec des étiquettes signalées comme telles par des majuscules, respectivement en français, anglais et espagnol:

–étiquettes: ACOMPTE_ADVANCE_ANTICIPO

–définition partagée (formulée ici en français, mais avec des définisseurs (en italique) qui sont eux-mêmes des étiquettes de concepts): *montant* partiel versé en attendant un *paiement* total–termes correspondants: en. *advance* et *deposit*, fr. *acompte*, *avance* et *arrhes*

–spécificité « locale »: les arrhes ne sont pas remboursables

Le « noyau dur » peut se limiter à une définition minimale.

–Ex.: INCAPACITÉ JURIDIQUE_LEGAL INCAPACITY_ INCAPACIDAD JURÍDICA

–définition partagée: privation de *droits*–spécificité locale: "personnes frappées d'*incapacité juridique* selon *leur législation nationale*" (Article 4 paragraphe 2 du directive 97/7/CE))

La distinction entre un niveau global (onomasiologique) et un niveau local (sémasiologique), séparés par une définition minimale qui est l'articulation des deux niveaux, est de bonne méthode pour plusieurs raisons:

–elle délivre de la polysémie en ne distinguant pas de simples acceptions de mots mais des concepts techniques (communs aux spécialistes et leur permettant de travailler efficacement)

–elle permet de prendre comme étiquette une périphrase descriptive, sans préjudice du vocabulaire effectivement en usage

–elle autorise des regroupements de termes plus ou moins synonymes au niveau « local »

Le premier avantage peut être illustré par les deux concepts d' « incapacité ».
Ex. 1: INCAPACITÉ JURIDIQUE_LEGAL INCAPACITY_ INCAPACIDAD JURÍDICA
Ex. 2: INCAPACITÉ DE TRAVAIL_INCAPACITY FOR WORK_ INCAPACIDAD LABORAL

Dans la pratique, on utilise souvent *incapacité* tout seul, le contexte étant généralement éclairant. Ainsi, on trouve dans une législation nationale « incapacité du mandant » (O: 108), et un peu partout « incapacité de longue durée »; on peut être à la fois, au moins théoriquement, un mandant frappé d'incapacité et un travailleur en incapacité de longue durée, mais il s'agit alors d'un cumul de deux sortes d'incapacités.

Le deuxième avantage, l'indistinction, au niveau global, entre termes au sens restrictif (unités lexicales simples ou polylexicales) et périphrase descriptive, peut être illustré par l'exemple suivant:

ANTIDATER_PRE-DATE_INDICAR UNA FECHA ANTERIOR

Le troisième avantage a déjà été mis en évidence par l'exemple d'ACOMPTE, qui permet de traiter dans un même article lexicographique sans renvois « analogiques » (au demeurant précieux dans un dictionnaire papier, et ils ont à juste titre contribué au succès du *Petit Robert*) les termes *acompte, avance*, et même, moyennant une note, *arrhes*.

Un quatrième avantage, dont l'intérêt sera démontré plus loin, est la possibilité de regroupements selon les concepts, et non pas selon la grammaire (*s'obliger* sous OBLIGATION, *valable* sous VALIDITÉ).

## Méthodologie lexicographique

Qu'attend-on d'un dictionnaire juridique pour le citoyen européen? Surtout des informations sur le sens des mots juridiques et sur le(s) sens juridique(s) des mots ordinaires. Le niveau global importe donc peu pour lui. En revanche, la distinction est importante pour l'organisation d'une base de données terminologiques juridiques, pour les raisons indiquées plus haut. Elle aide également le traducteur à prendre en compte ce qui est partagé et ce qui est complément de définition, exception ou régime juridique particulier.

Le fait que certains concepts juridiques soient propres à des « lexicultures » nationales les rend ici marginaux, ce qui ne veut pas dire à exclure. Ainsi, le pacte civil de solidarité, ou pacs, est une spécificité française, ayant vocation à être « en français dans le texte », quelle que soit la langue considérée, mais il peut intéresser hors de France, par exemple pour son statut fiscal, ou pour évaluer l'intérêt de régimes comparables, entre mariage et concubinage. En pareil cas, l'étiquette sera unique (sauf en italien, pour lequel existe un calque lexical bien attesté).

Les entrées conceptuelles prioritaires (étiquettes qui ne sont pas forcément les dénominations les plus importantes au titre de la fréquence ou de l'officialité) sont celles qui sont génériques, et qui fournissent donc le plus de définisseurs. Ainsi, STATUT ET RÉGIME sont prioritaires par rapport à PACS, CONCUBINAGE et MARIAGE, pour des raisons de statistique lexicale et non pas de sociologie. En revanche, les termes en tant que mots méritent un travail lexicographique au moins aussi attentif que dans un bon dictionnaire de langue. Voici quelques exigences susceptibles de faciliter la navigation dans une base de données terminologiques juridiques (et également non juridiques).

*Hiérarchiser les termes*

Si les entrées sont les étiquettes de concepts, les sous-entrées sont les dénominations usuelles de ces concepts. Autrement dit, la macrostructure a un fondement onomasiologique, la microstructure est sémasiologique. Par quel terme commencer la microstructure dans chacune des langues considérées? Priorité aux normes? Si oui, lesquelles? Priorité aux usages courants? Si oui, lesquels? Le traducteur et le rédacteur ont besoin que l'on distingue (typographiquement ou autrement) ce qui est recommandable par défaut et ce qui est dépendant des types de discours: en premier, *crédit-bail* ou *leasing?*

*Limiter la grammaire à l'essentiel*

Les mots juridiques sont surtout des noms (plutôt au masculin dans le cas des noms d'agents, mais le féminin progresse), des verbes (surtout à l'infinitif et à la 3ème personne de l'indicatif) et des adjectifs. Il importe que les difficultés morphologiques (ex.: *bail / baux*, *bailleur / bailleresse*) soient signalées, mais aussi les séries terminologiques. Il s'agit là d'un sous-ensemble de la famille morphologique d'un mot spécialisé; ce sous-ensemble correspond à un concept et à un seul.

Ex.: *saisir-saisie*, *saisir-saisine* – mais pas *saisissant* dans son emploi qualificatif

On peut à ce propos parler de « série terminologique » (Chabridon et Lerat 1993), y compris dans le cas des complémentarités grammaticales tels que *détention-détenu-carcéral*.

*Signaler les collocations typiques*

La phraséologie juridique est une difficulté durable, confondue souvent à tort avec la langue de bois. Le temps n'est plus où des copistes s'ingéniaient à figer ce qui n'a pas de raisons sérieuses de l'être, mais les professionnels du droit résistent aux rares tentatives d'humanisation de leurs discours. Il ne s'agit pas de savoir pourquoi l'on dit *apposer les scellés* et *to place official seals*, *apposer sa signature* et *to append signature*, mais de savoir ce qu'il faut écrire si l'on veut faire professionnel. Au reste, il n'est pas rare que les collocations aient une valeur distinctive; ainsi, nous l'avons vu, être *frappé d'incapacité* sous-entend « juridique », être *en incapacité* sous-entend « de travail ».

*Signaler les relations génériques*

C'est une relation privilégiée: le « genre prochain » (de préférence immédiat)

Ex.: une *allégation* est une *déclaration* (qui demande à être vérifiée)

*Signaler les relations partitives*

Reconnaissons-le, ce type de relation est plus important dans les terminologies des métiers manuels, comme ceux du bois, mais elle a son intérêt pour tout ce qui est organisation structurée (comme une *session*, de son *ouverture* à sa *clôture*).

*Signaler les relations séquentielles*

Tout ce qui est procédure est soumis à la considération d'un avant et d'un après. Ex.: l'achat d'un bien ou d'un service sur Internet.

*Signaler les relations fonctionnelles*

Il y a longtemps que je milite pour la prise en compte privilégiée des relations entre des actions spécialisées et leurs arguments typiques (acteurs requis, objets requis, circonstances requises). En utilisant la notation polonaise, qui réduit les propositions logiques à leur squelette en les rendant très lisibles, on peut visualiser commodément ce qui est expression prédicative (verbe, adjectif qualificatif, nominalisation ou autre mot ayant besoin d'être « saturé », comme *droit de* et *droit* à) et ce qui ne l'est pas (entre parenthèses).

Ex.: incapacité (être humain, droits) / incapacité (travailleur, travail)

*Sélectionner des citations pertinentes*

À quoi peuvent servir des citations bien choisies (et le choix des possibles est vaste dans les corpus des institutions européennes, de l'ONU, de la FAO, sur les sites des cabinets d'avocats, des agents immobiliers etc.)? La réponse est apportée par Bergenholtz et Kaufmann (1997: 117):

> « information on citation examples may be understood as implicit information on grammar and collocation, it may also contain further encyclopaedic information ».

Ex. 1 (grammaire): « en matière de droits réels immobiliers et de *baux* d'immeubles » (Article 22, point 1 du règlement (CE) 44/2001)
Ex. 2 (collocation): « frappé de droits de douane », « frappé de sanctions commerciales », « frapper de mesures discriminatoires » (FAO)
Ex. 3 (encyclopédie): "long-term land lease – for 50 or even 99 *years*" (FAO)

*Assurer la traçabilité des sources*

Ce principe ancien, qui remonte à la philologie classique, est plus que jamais nécessaire dans la civilisation du Net, où il n'est pas toujours possible de dater autrement que par une date de consultation, qui n'est pas forcément ce qu'il y a de plus pertinent, et où l'indication d'un site est surtout la preuve qu'il ne s'agit pas d'un exemple forgé, mais d'un usage réel.

*Compter sur la navigation interne*

Les lexicographes appellent « mots cachés » ceux qui ne font pas l'objet d'entrées d'articles et qui figurent seulement dans une rubrique de la microstructure. Il est clair que dans un dictionnaire à entrées conceptuelles les mots cachés sont particulièrement nombreux. D'abord, il y a ceux des différents synonymes et quasi-synonymes qui ne sont pas utilisés comme étiquettes. Ensuite, il y a ceux qui ne sont pas des termes, mais seulement du vocabulaire d'accompagnement, comme *frappé de*, qui apparaîtra au voisinage de termes autant de fois qu'il figurera dans la base.

*Témoigner de l'usage actuel*

C'est ici que le bât blesse: il faudrait idéalement des mises à jour permanentes, avec des entrées conceptuelles nouvelles, et aussi des sorties d'informations obsolètes ou redondantes qui créent du « bruit » dans la consultation.

## Conclusion

Les idées présentées ici n'ont pas la prétention de constituer un cahier des charges pour tout dictionnaire juridique communautaire à venir, mais sont conformes à une méthodologie et à une pratique mûries au cours d'une expérience professionnelle significative. Aussi bien, autant les recommandations ci-dessus semblent utiles si l'on a en vue un fichier individuel sur traitement de texte à des fins d'auto-formation, de traduction ou de rédaction, autant il faudrait poser en termes de technologie la question des moyens à mettre en œuvre pour en tirer un instrument de travail coopératif. Sous la pression des ingénieurs, l'accent a surtout été mis sur ces derniers jusqu'à ce jour; il est logiquement prioritaire de s'interroger sur les contenus, comme on a tenté de le faire ici. Résumons-nous:

–même pour une lexicographie spécialisée unilingue, il est bon de bénéficier d'une culture multilingue

–seule la comparaison est le gage d'un accès à des concepts opératoires, et non pas seulement aux signifiés lexicaux dans une langue

–il n'y a pas à opposer lexicographie et terminographie: il y a seulement une lexicographie plus ou moins spécialisée (totalement, si les définitions sont très techniques et les citations exclusivement professionnelles)

–une différence plus importante est celle entre une sémasiologie tributaire de l'ordre alphabétique dans une langue source et une langue cible et une onomasiologie étiquetant de façon multilingue des propriétés définitoires partagées

–la priorité donnée à l'approche onomasiologique ne vise absolument pas à négliger les termes en tant que mots, qui sont notre lot culturel situé, et qui méritent la plus grande attention

–le ciblage sur un lecteur « semi-expert » ou en mesure de le devenir autorise une part d'implicite dans les citations

–les citations sont précieuses au moins autant par ce dont elles témoignent, en matière d'information sur les choses et sur les langues, que par la représentativité de leurs sources

## Références


Guadalupe Aguado- de- Cea, « Terminología, ontologías y multilingualidad » (2009) *Puntoycoma* 115 S, 1–10 <http://ec.europa.eu/translation/bulletins/puntoycoma/115/pyc115su consulté le 5 mai 2012.

Henning Bergenholtz et Uhwe Kaufmann, "Terminography and Lexicography" (1997) *Hermes* n° 18, 91–125 <http://research.asb.dk consulté le 5 mai 2012.

Jean Carbonnier, *Flexible droit: pour une sociologie du droit sans rigueur*, Paris, LGDJ, 1969.

Jacky Chabridon et Pierre Lerat, « Terme et famille de termes » (1993) *La banque des mots* n° spécial 5, 55–63.

Loïc Depecker et Christophe Roche, « Entre idée et concept: l'ontologie » (2007) *Langages* (n° 168), 106–114.

Robert Galisson, « Culture et lexiculture partagées: les mots comme lieux d'observation des faits culturels », *Etudes de linguistique appliquée* (1988) 69, 74–90.

Georges Kleiber, *Problèmes de référence. Descriptions définies et noms propres, Recherches Linguistiques n° VI, Etudes publiées par le Centre d'Analyse Syntaxique de l'Université de Metz, Paris, Klincksieck*, 1981.

Hans-Peder Kromann, « Selection and presentation of translational equivalents in monofunctional and bifunctional dictionaries » (1990) *Cahiers de lexicologie* 56–57, 17–26.

Markéta Larišová, *Francouzsko-Český/*Česko-Francouzský *Právnický Slovník*, Aleš Čeněk 2008.

Pierre Lerat, *Vocabulaire du juriste débutant*, Paris, Ellipses, 2007.

Pierre Lerat et Jean-Louis Sourioux, *Dictionnaire juridique. Terminologie du contrat*, Conseil international de langue française, 1994.

Jean-Louis Sourioux, *Par le droit, au-delà du droit*, Paris, LexisNexis 2011.
Jean-Louis Sourioux et Pierre Lerat, *Le langage du droit*, Paris, Presses Universitaires de France 1975.
Giovanni Tortora, *Dizionario giuridico: italiano francese/francese-italiano*, 3 edizione, Milano, Giuffrè, 1994.
Eugen Wüster, *Dictionnaire multilingue de la machine-outil. Notions fondamentales définies et illustrées*, Oxford, Technical Press, 1968.

*Documents cités*

FAO: textes divers accessibles sur le site <http://www.fao.org/docrep
O: Obligationenrecht/Code des obligations/Codice delle obbligazzioni, Chancellerie Fédérale de Berne 1992–93
Principes terminologiques pour la constitution d'une base de données pour la traduction juridique

Chapter 7

# Principes terminologiques pour la constitution d'une base de données pour la traduction juridique

Thierry Grass

The increasing internationalization of law makes the terminological needs of translators even greater. The author advocates the use of ISO standards and the TBX framework (for the exchange of terminological data) in the creation of a FR-DE termbase of the core legal vocabulary of French and German civil law. ISO 1087 defines terminology as a 'set of designations belonging to one special language' and designations as 'representations of a concept by the sign which denotes it'. The author shows how this can be applied to legal language. It is also shown how ISO 12620 (the international standard for the data categories used in termbases), ISO 12616 (terminology aimed at translation) and ISO 704 (which sets out the principles governing the formulation of designations and the formulation of definitions) can provide a structure for entries: the lexical level followed by the translation level and concluding with the level of language. The merit of the ISO approach, it is argued here, is that it provides uniformity of form while preserving complete freedom as to the contents of the terminological record.

Toutes les écoles de traduction et les universités ne préparent pas les traducteurs à l'exercice périlleux de la traduction juridique, en partie parce que celle-ci ne constitue pas forcément, en volume, la principale activité du traducteur moyen et ensuite, parce qu'elle suppose, plus que toute autre traduction spécialisée, une compréhension d'ensemble des systèmes juridiques sous-jacents à la langue source et à la langue cible. Il ne s'agit pas ici de rentrer dans le débat de savoir s'il faut ou non être juriste pour être un bon traducteur juridique (nous sommes d'avis que non à condition d'avoir de bons outils), mais de se pencher sur un modèle de représentation terminologique sensé améliorer la compréhension d'ensemble d'un terme juridique. Les bases de données lexicales en ligne comme le *Grand dictionnaire terminologique* du Québec, *IATE* ou encore *Termium*, sans doute la mieux structurée et la plus détaillée, sont encore insuffisantes pour avoir une vision d'ensemble du vocabulaire juridique. Nous proposerons ici un modèle de structure de base de données lexicales pour la traduction des termes du droit civil français reposant en allemand sur le modèle défini par l'ISO (International Organization for Standardization) et la norme TBX (Term Base eXchange).

## 1. La norme ISO 1087 relative à la terminologie est-elle applicable à la langue juridique?

La norme ISO 1087 définit la terminologie comme la « désignation au moyen d'une unité linguistique d'une notion définie dans une langue de spécialité. » Cette norme part d'une conception purement lexicale du terme reposant sur une approche structuraliste, fidèle à la théorie d'Eugen Wüster, fondateur de la terminologie, pour laquelle chaque terme constitue une unité à deux faces correspondant non pas comme chez Saussure à un *concept* et une *image acoustique*, mais à une *notion* et une *dénomination*. Comme les seuls moyens d'expression de la terminologie sont la langue et les symboles, comme ses concepts sont linguistiques, la terminologie constitue ce que l'on peut appeler un métalangage dont la fonction est de traiter et d'interpréter le langage lui-même. La langue juridique est, elle aussi, un métalangage dont la fonction est de rassembler, de synthétiser et de codifier un ensemble de notions culturelles sur la vie en société, les droits et les obligations de l'individu vis-à-vis de la communauté, ces notions remontent pour l'Occident à la lointaine Antiquité. La langue juridique est bien antérieure à la terminologie, les concepts se sont formés parfois il y a fort longtemps et ont évolué dans le temps. Dans les pays de la famille romano-germanique qui s'inspirent du droit romain, du droit canonique et du droit coutumier germanique, il existe certaines similitudes, mais aussi certaines différences au niveau des notions d'un pays à l'autre.

A un tout autre niveau, le but poursuivi par l'ISO est celui de l'unification dans un cadre mondial. Les travaux du *Comité Technique 37*, initiés avant la Seconde Guerre mondiale visaient à l'uniformisation des normes industrielles et petit à petit, au fil des années, les normes se sont glissées dans la plupart des activités humaines, ce qui allait de paire avec le développement croissant des échanges internationaux. Certes, le droit et la langue juridique, d'essence nationale sont longtemps restés réticents à toute évolution, mais la vie moderne s'internationalise de plus en plus, le traité est supérieur à la loi et les nécessités d'interprétations communes de textes contraignants d'un état à l'autre s'accroissent. Le droit a aussi subi les conséquences de la mondialisation avec un accroissement de la circulation de marchandises et des personnes, hors de la sphère d'influence proprement nationale, d'où la nécessité à la fois de créer des concepts transnationaux comme c'est le cas en droit européen, un droit centrifuge d'expression plurilingue ainsi que de s'adapter aux influences venues de l'étranger. Ainsi, pour prendre un exemple trivial issu du droit privé, un juge allemand pourra par exemple être amené à statuer en appliquant le droit civil français pour prononcer le divorce d'un couple binational marié en France sous un régime matrimonial français, or, de par sa formation et sa culture, ce même juge allemand est formé à juger dans son système conceptuel. Les procédures ayant un caractère international impliquant à la fois le système judiciaire et les traducteurs augmentent donc avec les échanges internationaux et requièrent des ressources terminologiques fiables et accessibles. Le but n'est bien entendu pas de plier le droit à la norme ISO, ce qui serait une entreprise à la fois arrogante et ridicule pour un linguiste, mais de voir comment intégrer certains travaux menés en description terminologique dans l'aide à la traduction juridique.

Les dictionnaires juridiques sont souvent présentés comme des nomenclatures bilingues, des recueils de termes ayant des équivalences multiples en fonction des sous-domaines du droit considérées. Or, le terme juridique ne se rencontre pas isolément, mais en contexte, que ce soit dans une convention, un texte normatif ou une décision de justice. Le lexique juridique, dont l'évolution diachronique ne s'inscrit pas à proprement parler dans une démarche terminologique issue de l'industrialisation de la société, reflète l'hétérogénéité de concepts en pleine mouvance. Nous tenterons de voir comment ceux-ci peuvent être traités au niveau lexical dans la paire de langues allemand-français. Travaillant dans une optique de traduction, donc bilingue, nous verrons qu'il est indispensable d'insérer au niveau de la translation, niveau translingue entre le niveau lexical, le niveau de la langue et le niveau conceptuel traditionnellement monolingues pour aboutir à une fiche de données terminologiques conforme.

## 2. Le niveau lexical

Le niveau lexical est le niveau du terme que Wüster (1991: 165) décrivait par sa célèbre équation d'inspiration structuraliste où l'on retrouvait une entité à deux faces composée d'une notion et d'une dénomination. Pour Guy Rondeau, autre terminologue de renom, (1981: 25), « la terminologie a pour objet, en effet, la dénomination des notions » et selon l'ISO 1087, « un terme peut être constitué d'un ou de plusieurs mots [terme simple ou terme complexe] et même de symboles. » Dans une base de données, le niveau lexical est toujours monolingue.

Si l'on considère les différentes classes de mots, la langue spécialisée juridique n'échappe pas aux règles qui prévalent dans différents autres domaines et la terminologie s'exprime à trois niveaux:

Tout d'abord et à titre essentiel au niveau nominal: les noms, qu'ils soient des termes simples comme *dol*, *lésion*, *préciput* ou des termes complexes comme *avancement d'hoirie*, *quotité disponible*, *exploit d'huissier* constituent en volume la plus grande partie du domaine de spécialité avec des cas de polysémie à la fois interne comme *garde* (d'un enfant ou d'une chose) correspondant à deux concepts juridiques distincts et externe (la *garde* juridique et la *garde* d'un vin p.ex.).

Ensuite au niveau verbal: les verbes du droit sont nombreux et peuvent avoir un sens uniquement juridique comme *débouter*, *interjeter* ou encore un sens différent en langue spécialisée et en langue générale comme *expirer* qui a deux sens selon qu'il s'agit d'un *bail* ou d'une *personne*.

Enfin au niveau de la locution, catégorie fourre-tout qui inclut quelques conjonctions juridiques comme « attendu que » dans les arrêts de la Cour de cassation française, « considérant que » dans les arrêts du Conseil d'État, des collocations comme *ester en justice*, *interjeter appel*, des formules toutes faites comme « *par ces motifs, rejette/casse et annule* » et pourquoi pas des adages juridiques tels que « *en matière de meubles, possession vaut titre* » ou « *nul n'est censé ignorer la loi* ». Même des locutions prépositionnelles comme « *en vertu de* » sont assimilables à cette catégorie.

Les noms et les verbes du droit ont fait l'objet d'assez nombreuses études mono- ou multilingues et il existe différents modèles théoriques permettant d'appréhender la collocation au niveau juridique. Dans une thèse de 1996 parue en 1999, nous avions utilisé le modèle des fonctions lexicales utilisées par Igor Mel'čuk dans son Dictionnaire explicatif et combinatoire du français contemporain (1981–1999) et nous avions même essayé d'en faire un dictionnaire français-allemand à partir du Dictionnaire juridique et économique Doucet/Fleck pour finir par y renoncer vu la complication pratique de la tâche: lorsqu'il préexiste un dictionnaire comportant plus de 20 000 entrées, il est difficile voire impossible pour une personne de relier le tout en terme de fonctions lexicales, sauf à refaire complètement ce même dictionnaire, même si encore une fois le modèle du Dictionnaire explicatif et combinatoire du français contemporain est tout à fait convaincant, mais Mel'čuk et son équipe montréalaise n'est parvenu en une vingtaine d'années qu'à décrire un peu plus d'une centaine de mots vedettes impliquant certes plusieurs milliers d'autres mots, mais tout de même : la complexité du formalisme est telle que sa mise en application suppose des moyens humains dépassant la portée de l'entreprise. Cette expérience nous a aussi montré que la conception de la macrostructure et surtout de la microstructure d'un dictionnaire devait obéir à des règles prédéfinies pour permettre une évolution ultérieure. Il ne reste de ce travail qu'un prototype autour du champ lexical de quatre-vingts « termes premiers » du droit civil impliquant plus de 2000 termes sous la forme d'une base de données somme toute classique dans son développement (Grass, 1999 et 2010). La leçon retenue de ce travail est que la mise en application d'un modèle théorique de dictionnaire n'est pas possible sans que certains préalables méthodologiques soient réunis. Nous avons donc réduit la voilure et nous proposons pour la description d'un terme les mentions conformes à la norme ISO 12620 relative à la catégorisation des données qui sont a minima:

terme (terme vedette),

grammaire (informations grammaticales telles que la classe de mots et une description sommaire des catégories afférentes comme le genre et le nombre pour les noms, la transitivité pour les verbes, etc.),

contexte (correspondant à « au moins un contexte d'attestation suivi de sa source » en fonction de l'ISO 12620, il s'agit en fait d'une sorte d'exemple), source (la source du contexte) et note d'usage (un « champ d'énoncé libre » en fonction de l'ISO 12620 permettant notamment de faire des remarques contrastives dans notre cas précis).

Dans son Manuel pratique de terminologie, Dubuc (1985: 62) définit le contexte comme « l'énoncé qui entoure le terme repéré tout en exprimant une idée complète ». Par ailleurs, il identifie trois types spécifiques de contextes:

Le contexte définitoire se rapproche de la définition elle-même et énumère les caractéristiques sémantiques principales du terme spécifié.

Le contexte explicatif n'évoque quant à lui que certains aspects du terme de façon plus ou moins exhaustive.

Enfin, le contexte associatif comporte des descripteurs permettant d'identifier le champ d'application du terme sans comporter d'éléments définitoires.

Si les contextes propres à éclairer le traducteur sont soit de nature définitoire, soit explicative, les contextes associatifs permettent eux une catégorisation du domaine ou sous-domaine d'application, comme dans l'exemple suivant:

<terme_fr> jouissance (1) [le terme étant polysémique, il y aura aussi une entrée « jouissance (2) »)

<grammaire_terme_fr> nf [nom féminin]

<contexte_terme_fr> La jouissance du local étant indivise, la nullité de la procédure de révision doit être prononcée au profit des deux locataires. [Il s'agit ici d'un contexte associatif où d'autres termes comme *local* et *locataire* permettent d'identifier le domaine du droit civil et des biens]

<source_contexte_terme_fr> Civ. 3ème, 21/12/1993. Arrêt 2003)

<note_usage_terme> Jouissance est un terme largement polysémique en français, on oppose classiquement la jouissance d'un bien à celle d'un droit.

A ces cinq champs, nous adjoindrons des champs de description sémantiques issus des fonctions lexicales de Mel'čuk et issues elles-mêmes du modèle logique en lexicologie. Ces champs ont la particularité d'avoir une fonction de situation des termes les uns par rapport aux autres dans la langue juridique, les voici:

<synonyme_terme_fr> Ce champ comprend les synonymes au sens large du terme vedette: *offre* a pour synonyme en droit français le terme de *pollicitation*

<hypéronyme_terme_fr> Ce champ comprend le terme directement superordonné au terme vedette (genre proche), le *bail* a pour hypéronyme *contrat de louage*.

<co-hyponyme_terme_fr> Ce champ comporte les termes complémentaires venant caractériser la notion, ainsi, le terme d'*usus* (droit d'usage) est co-hyponyme des termes *fructus* (droit de recueillir les fruits) et *abusus* (droit d'aliéner) une chose.

Comme la plupart des termes juridiques sont des noms dits prédicatifs, ils engagent plusieurs participants dans le cadre d'une situation juridique, ces participants sont fréquemment au nombre de trois, le *bail* portant sur un *immeuble*, les participants au procès (prédicat) sont au nombre de trois:

<agent_terme_fr> *preneur* ou *locataire*

<objet_terme_fr> *immeuble*

<bénéficiaire_terme_fr> *bailleur* ou *propriétaire*

Tous ces champs sont accompagnés d'indications grammaticales de la même forme que le champs <grammaire_terme_fr>. Les champs comprenant des entrées multiples sont dupliqués, de manière à ne jamais avoir deux termes dans un même champ. Cette structuration suppose une certaine hiérarchisation où l'entrée en tant que terme n'est réservée qu'à la dénomination de certaines notions privilégiées. Pour notre travail sur les termes du droit civil français, nous avions choisi les principales notions développées dans le *Code civil.* Si l'on voulait travailler depuis l'allemand, il faudrait en faire de même avec les principales notions du *Bürgerliches Gesetzbuch*, le code civil allemand.

## Le niveau de la translation

La norme ISO 12616 (terminographie orientée vers la traduction) traite de la structuration des données terminologiques pour la traduction. La terminographie orientée vers la traduction se caractérise par l'utilisation de corpus parallèles bilingues où multilingues traduits par des humains à partir desquels sont construits des glossaires de segments équivalents. Dans le domaine juridique, l'Acquis communautaire constitue une source fiable pour le droit européen. Il en va différemment pour le droit privé où dans une large mesure ces corpus parallèles font défaut, sauf dans les États bilingues plurilingues comme le Canada ou la Suisse. Comme la traduction fonctionne par paires de langues, le niveau de la translation est en fait un niveau intermédiaire entre le niveau lexical et le niveau de la langue, puisqu'il a trait aux idiosyncrasies qui s'expriment dans toutes les langues et aux traductions de celles-ci. Or, les idiosyncrasies s'expriment généralement dans la collocation. Essentielle en traduction, la création d'équivalences pour les collocations reflète l'idiomaticité de la langue. La collocation est le lieu où le terme apparaît in vivo, où il est « actualisé ». La fonction d'un champ réservé à la collocation est essentielle pour un traducteur et permet d'éclairer le terme en fonction de la co-occurrence, c'est-à-dire de l'environnement privilégié du terme. Là encore, il n'est pas inutile de rappeler que la traduction humaine est une activité impliquant uniquement deux langues, une langue source et une langue cible et que les difficultés de traduction prennent exclusivement en compte la problématique de la translation de la langue de départ vers la langue d'arrivée. Ainsi, la perspective multilingue en terminologie qui vise à donner toutes les informations d'un terme dans sa langue et seulement au regard de cette langue fait fi de la contrastivité entre deux langues. Il s'ensuit qu'aux champs précédemment évoqués, nous proposons d'ajouter un champ réservé aux collocations et à leurs équivalences bilingues ainsi qu'un autre consacré à des remarques contrastives d'emploi, dans une optique d'aide à la traduction. Précisons qu'il est inutile que le champ réservé aux collocations soit réversible puisque la collocation n'intervient que dans la langue cible et son équivalence, même s'il peut aussi s'agir d'une collocation, n'en est pas nécessairement une. Mais dans tous les cas, « il faut traduire », même si la notion traitée en langue source n'existe pas en langue cible.

> <collocation_fr-de> abus de jouissance = übermäßige Fruchtziehung, übermäßiger Nießbrauch, avoir la jouissance = die Nutzungsbefugnis an einer Sache innehaben, apport en jouissance = Einlage in Form einer Nutzungsbefugnis, (… / …)

> <remarque_contrastive_fr-de> Le droit allemand ne comporte pas de notion comparable.

Il va de soi que ce niveau de description consistant à inventorier dans la plupart des cas les verbes les plus fréquents entrant dans l'environnement d'un terme donné dépasse le simple niveau lexical. Là encore, les dictionnaires existants donnent de telles indications, mais de manière insuffisante. C'est surtout au niveau des verbes supports que les dictionnaires juridiques présentent les insuffisances les plus marquantes. A leur décharge, il faut reconnaître que l'insertion des verbes supports dans l'article d'un dictionnaire papier n'est pas pratique puisqu'elle vient bouleverser la présentation alphabétique de l'entrée, cet inconvénient disparaît dans les dictionnaires électroniques.

Pour résumer, dans une base de données lexicale pour la traduction, la présence de deux champs par langue est nécessaire: le contexte définitoire ou explicatif d'une part, le contexte verbal d'autre part.

## Le niveau de la langue

La norme ISO 704 relative aux *principes et méthodes de la terminologie* définit la définition comme « la description complète d'une notion à l'aide de notions connues, exprimées le plus souvent par des moyens verbaux.» Le niveau de la langue est celui de la description du concept dans un espace culturel linguistique donné exprimé formellement par le code ISO 639 de la langue et le code de région (de-ch pour de l'allemand de Suisse p.ex.). En vertu de l'ISO 704, les définitions des concepts sont formulées dans les langues traitées en suivant les principes qui y sont développés. La définition juridique, d'origine légale, jurisprudentielle ou doctrinale, n'obéit pas toujours aux principes aristotéliciens énoncés dans l'ISO 704: « énumération des caractères de la notion à définir, (...) description de la compréhension de la notion. À cette fin, on mentionne la notion générique la plus proche (le genre), qui est, soit déjà définie, soit supposée généralement connue, et le(s) caractère(s) particulier(s) (déterminatif(s)) qui ramène(nt) ce genre à une espèce ». Les dictionnaires destinés à la traduction, même s'ils donnent des termes parfois assortis d'explications succinctes n'obéissent pas davantage à ces principes. Le *Dictionnaire juridique et économique français-allemand* dans son édition de 2009 formule même de courtes définitions lorsqu'il s'agit de termes jugés spécialement difficiles par l'auteur, voici, à titre d'exemple, l'entrée correspondant à *mesure conservatoire:*

> **mesure conservatoire** (1) (ZPR: *opération juridique tendant à la sauvegarde d'un droit*) Maßnahme zur Erhaltung (eines Rechts), Sicherungsmaßnahme, Schutzmaßnahme, sichernde Maßnahme, (2) (ZPR: *mesure urgente judiciaire pour sauvegarder des biens*) vorsorgliche dringende Maßnahme, gerichtliche Verwahrungsmaßnahme, (3) (SchuldR, VersR) Schadensminderungsmaßnahme; Abwendungspflicht.

L'article du dictionnaire fait apparaître la polysémie interne qui intervient à un double niveau. Le terme varie ainsi en fonction du sous-domaine juridique: *procédure civile* (ZPR) d'une part, *droit de la responsabilité* (SchuldR) et *droit des assurances* (VersR) d'autre part. Mais le terme varie aussi en fonction du domaine d'application de la notion: *sauvegarde d'un droit* d'une part et *sauvegarde d'un bien* d'autre part. Ces distinctions supposent un haut niveau de technicité et ne sauraient être désambiguïsées à l'aide du seul dictionnaire bilingue, aussi détaillé soit-il. Nous remarquerons aussi que dans chaque cas, plusieurs équivalences sont proposées, alors laquelle choisir? C'est dans cet ordre d'idées qu'apparaît le niveau de la langue sous la forme d'informations destinées à désambiguïser les termes particulièrement délicats à traduire hors contexte. Quoiqu'il en soit, un dictionnaire juridique pour la traduction digne de ce nom se doit d'intégrer des définitions ainsi que des explications dans ses entrées, peut-être pas systématiquement, mais au moins pour les termes soit polysémiques, soit difficile à manier parce que ne correspondant pas à une même réalité (c'est-à-dire à un même concept) dans le système juridique de la langue cible ou n'ayant pas à proprement parler d'équivalence.

Nous avons illustré dans l'exemple précédent le premier cas de figure, voyons le cas du terme polysémique dans la langue source et monosémique dans la langue cible. Pour la paire de langues français-allemand, il existe un exemple trivial, celui du terme *Gericht* qui en plus de constituer un cas de polysémie externe (*Gericht* a aussi le sens de *plat* dans un repas) se traduit en français tantôt par *tribunal*, tantôt par *cour* et désigne aussi le bâtiment que l'on appelle en français, non sans une certaine emphase, *palais de justice*. Dans l'édition du *Dictionnaire juridique et économique allemand-français* datant de 2002, Klaus Fleck propose l'entrée suivante:

> **Gericht** *n* (1) *(Organ der Rechtssprechung, allg.)* juridiction *f*, (2) *(Gericht erster Instanz)* tribunal *m*, (3) *(Berufungs- od. Revisionsgericht)* cour *f* (de justice), (4) *(Gerichtsgebäude)palais* m (de justice), tribunal (en tant que lieu où l'on rend la justice); [ … ]

Ces courtes explications formulées en langue source, même si elles ne répondent pas aux canons formulés dans les normes ISO 704, 1087 et 10241 présentent un intérêt indéniable pour aiguiller le traducteur vers le choix du terme correct en langue cible. Dans la norme ISO 12620, l'explication est un « énoncé qui décrit une notion et la rend compréhensible, mais qui [contrairement à la définition] ne permet pas nécessairement de la différencier des autres notions. »

Dans la fiche terminologique, les informations selon la langue pourront donc comprendre les champs suivants pour le terme *jouissance*:

> <code_langue_région>fr-fr (français de France)
>
> <définition_fr> Utilisation d'une chose dont on perçoit les fruits.
>
> <source_définition_fr> Lexique de termes juridiques Dalloz
>
> <explication_fr> La jouissance englobe les bénéfices et avantages divers attachés à la possession d'un bien ou d'un patrimoine. (a) Dans un sens strict, la jouissance désigne le droit de percevoir les fruits d'un bien comme le loyer d'un immeuble et d'en disposer sans en être comptable. (b) Dans un sens plus large, la jouissance englobe aussi l'usage. (c) Enfin, dans certaines expressions courantes, la jouissance correspond seulement à l'usage.

## Le niveau conceptuel

Dans la théorie terminologique, le niveau du concept est extérieur à la langue. Le concept a une dimension immatérielle et abstraite, Depecker (2010: 18) rapporte que « *concept* désigne toute unité de connaissance » et indique que dans les travaux de l'ISO 704–2001 « Nous avons finalement tranché en faveur de *concept* (…) alors que *notion* y était utilisé depuis des décennies ». *Concept* est un terme utilisé dans les milieux scientifiques et de l'industrie, moins dans le domaine juridique. Dans une base de données multilingue, le truchement d'une langue à l'autre a lieu par l'intermédiaire du concept représenté sous la forme d'un identifiant unique. Dans une base de données juridique, il est donc possible de partir du concept de « *mariage* » – et non du terme – en tant qu'unité culturelle dont les expressions juridiques et linguistiques varieront en fonction des langues et des régions, un identifiant numérique vient représenter ce concept pour bien montrer qu'il s'agit d'une abstraction qui aura pour dénominations différents termes dans les langues concernées. Certains concepts pourront exister dans un système juridique et pas dans un autre, comme la « *lésion* » propre au droit civil français, qui pourra avoir des équivalences au niveau lexical (parce qu'il faut bien traduire), mais pas au niveau de la langue. Du point de vue formel, le concept est exprimé dans une base de données par un identifiant unique numérique (ID). Pour ce qui est de la structure de la base de données, c'est aussi à ce niveau que sont présentes les métadonnées concernant l'auteur de la fiche terminologique et la date de rédaction/révision.

## Le format TBX pour la représentation des données terminologiques

Les langages déclaratifs sont apparus pour automatiser et structurer l'échange de données. Le format Term Base eXchange connu sous le sigle TBX est devenu le standard en matière de représentation des données, ce format repose sur ce que l'on appelle un « substrat », traduction de « framework », sur lequel, comme l'indiquent Vaucelle et Hudrisier (2010), « l'utilisateur va pouvoir ajouter ‹entre et dans les balises› ses propres couches d'information, de références, de structures et de sémantiques ». Ces langages fonctionnent comme des coquilles (*shells* en anglais) ou le terminologue va pouvoir ajouter ses propres informations qui pourront à la fois être lues par l'humain et par la machine et sont à la base de la documentation moderne. Le TBX est désormais une norme définie à l'origine par LISA (Localization Industry Standards Association) et décrite dans l'ISO 30042. Le format TBX distingue entre certaines catégories de données qui sont obligatoires pour garantir l'interopérabilité et d'autres qui sont définies en fonction du projet. Le TBX distingue entre niveau du terme, niveau de la langue et niveau du concept et définit les balises XML (eXtended Markup Language) devant être utilisées à tel ou tel niveau.

## Conclusion

La standardisation de la terminologie joue un rôle pivot dans communication interlangue et interculturelle, tant au niveau des spécialistes du droit que de celui des traducteurs et des interprètes. L'Union européenne a mis en place des ressources qui fonctionnent pour le droit européen, droit centrifuge qui s'applique également dans l'Union, quelle que soit le pays ou la langue. En revanche, cette standardisation ne s'est pas imposée pour le droit privé et le droit public dans les rapports entre États-membres ayant des langues ou des systèmes juridiques distincts. L'entreprise va bien sûr au-delà d'un simple projet sur une paire de langues, mais la méthode et la structure, même si elles sont encore imparfaites méritent d'être évoquées, d'autant que la démarche retenue pour l'ISO dans l'industrie se veut unificatrice dans la forme tout en gardant une totale liberté et indépendance dans les contenus.

## Structure de la fiche terminologique (XML)

*Niveau de la langue (monolingue)*

<terme>
<code_langue_région_terme>
<grammaire_terme>
<définition_terme>
<source_définition>
<contexte_terme>
<source_contexte_terme>
<note_usage_terme>
<explication_terme>
<synonyme_terme>
<hypéronyme_terme>
<co-hyponyme_terme>
<agent_terme>
<objet_terme>
<bénéficiaire_terme>

*Niveau de la translation (bilingue)*

<collocation_terme_langue_A_langue_B>
<remarque_contrastive_langue_A_langue_B>

## Références

Depecker, L. 2010. Comment aborder le concept d'un point de vue linguistique? in *Terminologie (I): analyser des termes et des concepts*, edited by J.-J. Briu. Bern: Peter Lang: 17–32.

Doucet, M., Fleck, K. E. W. 2002. *Dictionnaire juridique et économique allemand-français.* 6th Edition. München: Beck.

Doucet, M., Fleck, K. E. W. 2009. *Dictionnaire juridique et économique français-allemand.* 6th Edition. München: Beck.

Dubuc, R. 1985. *Manuel pratique de terminologie.* 2nd Edition. Québec: Linguatech.

Grass, T. 1999. *La traduction juridique bilingue français-allemand: problématique et résolution des ambiguïtés terminologiques*. Bonn: Romanistischer Verlag.

Grass, T. 2010. Fonctions lexicales et traduction juridique français-allemand, in *Terminologie (I): analyser des termes et des concepts*, edited by J.-J. Briu. Bern: Peter Lang: 57–82.

ISO 639:1998, 2002, 2007, 2008, 2009, 2010 – Codes pour la représentation des noms de langue.

ISO 704:2009 – Travail terminologique – Principes et méthodes

ISO 1087–1:2000 – Travaux terminologiques -- Vocabulaire -- Partie 1: Théorie et application.

ISO 10241:1992 – International terminology standards – Preparation and layout

ISO 12616:2002 – Terminographie orientée vers la traduction.

ISO 12620:1999 – Terminologie et autres ressources langagières et ressources de contenu – Spécification de catégories de données.

ISO 30042:2008 – Systèmes de gestion de la terminologie, de la connaissance et du contenu -- TermBase eXchange (TBX).

Mel'čuk, I. et al. 1984-I, 1988-II, 1992-III, 1999-IV. *Dictionnaire explicatif et combinatoire du français contemporain*. Montréal: Les presses de l'Université de Montréal.

Rondeau, G. 1981. *Introduction à la terminologie*, Bibliothèque nationale du Québec.

Vaucelle, A., Hudrisier, H. 2010. Langages structurés et lien social. *tic&société*, Vol. 4, n° 1, available at: http://ticetsociete.revues.org/790 [accessed 30 October 2012].

Wüster, E. 1991. *Einführung in die allgemeine Terminologielehre und terminologische Lexikographie*. 3rd Edition. Bonn: Romanistischer Verlag.

# Chapter 8
# Translation and the Law Dictionary

Marta Chroma[1]

## 1. Introduction

Twenty years ago, in the early days of a new democratic Czechoslovakia and with the revival of a free economy, a massive need for various (not only legal) texts to be translated into Czech and Slovak emerged; the influx of texts coming from the democratic West had to be translated for information, pedagogical reasons and sometimes to have a binding effect on their potential Czech or Slovak addressees. In general, translators were unprepared for this deluge, particularly when faced with English-language legal texts from the Anglo-Amercian system of law based on the Common Law. Many factors (educational, academic, political and so on) contributed to insufficient preparedness of both local lawyers and translators to produce quality legal translation in those early days. There were neither manuals for legal translation, nor helpful bilingual dictionaries available to ease translators' burden. However, some Czech lawyers who had studied in the US in the period 1967–69[2] recalled how useful *Black's Law Dictionary* had proven as an aid for understanding and interpreting American Law, and suggested that the American dictionary should be translated into Czech to serve two general purposes – to facilitate the understanding of Anglo-American Law and to assist legal translators in their selection of relevant equivalents.

The sixth edition of *Black's* was therefore translated into Czech and published in two volumes in 1993.[3] What was preserved in English was the headword in each entry and subentry; definitions and explanations were translated into Czech. Law professionals, students, academics and translators were finally provided with an eagerly awaited tool. Great credit is due to its authors for their courage, perseverance and assiduity. However voluminous and praiseworthy the Czech version of *Black's Dictionary* might have been, it became clear very shortly after its publication that

---

1 This chapter was drafted as part of PRVOUK 06 (Public Law in the Context of Europeanization and Globalization) within Charles University Research Development Schemes.

2 Dozens of Czech students in various branches of knowledge had a chance to spend some time at universities in the West as a result of the relaxation of political restrictions in Czechoslovakia in the second half of the 1960s, culminating in Prague Spring 1968.

3 Blackův Právnický Slovník. Volume I (A–I), Volume II (J–Z). Praha: Victoria Publishing, 1993.

not many initial expectations would be met. Basic conceptual problems surfaced in that definitions explaining institutions of US Law and Common Law in general were translated into legal Czech built upon the continental law tradition, that is, not yet conceptually and terminologically prepared for a philosophically different legal system and tradition. Lawyers ignorant of Common Law quite often came to the usually improper and misleading conclusion that differences between continental law and the law in English-speaking countries were marginal. Other terminological irregularities resulted from inconsistency in the translational equivalents provided over the two volumes, apparently due to insufficient final editing and terminological consolidation of all entries. Translators were quite often totally lost in their attempts to choose a proper translational solution for their source language term, since definitions in the dictionary, translated into Czech, regularly failed to provide *the* equivalent of a particular definiendum; translators (linguists by education and non-lawyers) quite legitimately claimed they were unable to identify in the definition a word or expression in Czech that might serve as an equivalent of the English headword. Since then, the experience, knowledge and education of both Czech lawyers and translators has improved, many more sources for legal translation and translational legal lexicography have became available and new approaches to both disciplines have been necessitated. Nevertheless, the general quality of legal translation and translational dictionaries, including those where Czech is either the source or the target language, is far from ideal. In this chapter some issues relating to the quality of law dictionaries will be dealt with in two parts; one devoted to the process of translation, the other to the way that process, or those processes, can be reflected in the compilation of a translational legal dictionary serving the needs of not only, but primarily, legal translators.

## 2. Legal Translation

*The Oxford English Dictionary* provides 13 definitions of the word *translation*. What is semantically common to all meanings is the process of transference, conveyance or change from one form, medium or position to another. One may assume that translation between languages is as old as languages themselves as, historically, there must have always been territories where two or more tribes, groups or families using different language codes met and had to effect a certain level of communication, translation being one of the non-violent means available. With time, verbal contacts among holders and users of different language codes developed and translation became a more conscious activity. However, it was the practice, not theory, of translation that was debated over the centuries.[4] As late as the twentieth century, coherent theories of translation were conceived, developed and taught. The internationalization of all fields of human life caused translation to play an increasingly significant role in professional settings, in which law is

4 For more details see, for example, Munday (2001); Nord (1997).

included, and shifted the focus of the theory of translation from belles-lettres to professional discourse.[5]

Various translational theories have attempted to critically analyse existing translational practices and to set principles, methods or even rules to help improve the practice of translation and the competence of translators. Discussions have revolved around the 'invisibility' or 'visibility' of the translator in a translated text, that is, to what extent translation should read fluently (like a piece of domestic culture), or should remind the reader of its foreign origin.[6] Although an unequivocal response to the general question of what a 'good' translation is has not been found (cf. Malmkjær 2005: 5–8), there are several determinants, such as (a) the function of the source text (ST) in the source culture, including the respective communicative functions of its source language (SL) in the Jakobsonian sense;[7] (b) reasons for translation of the ST into the target language (TL); (c) the function of the target text (TT) in the target culture; (d) typological remoteness of the SL and the TL; or (e) ideological and philosophical remoteness of the source and target cultures. The answer to whether a particular piece of translation is or is not 'good' often takes in the purpose of the translation, which may significantly determine the evaluation of its quality.

Although the practice of legal translation has existed for centuries, its theory has spanned just decades. The seminal book in this area, *New Approach to Legal Translation* by Susan Šarčević (1997), greatly increased the profile of interlingual translation in the domain of law, focusing primarily on the issue of equivalence and promoting a conceptual and functional approach to the search for adequate translational solutions particularly where legal terminology is at issue.

Legal translation implies both a comparative study of different legal systems and an awareness of the problems created by the absence of equivalent concepts, legal institutions, terms and other linguistic units. As pointed out by Kischel (2009: 7), 'the question in legal translation is not which translation is right, but, more modestly, which one is less wrong'. Naturally, legal translation is a very specific and complex type of activity which has been subject to various analyses from various perspectives (see, for example, Baaij 2012; Olsen, Lorz and Stein 2009; Cao 2007; de Groot 2006; Gémar 2001).

---

5 However, the practice of translation for professional purposes dates back to Roman times where every public official had members in his staff who acted as interpreters/translators (*interpretes* in Latin) in the communications of their superiors with the Greeks (Skřejpek 2007: 29).

6 Cf., for example, Venuti (1995), and a review of the first edition: Pym (1996: 165–77); or Lane-Mercier (1997: 43–68).

7 Jakobson defined six such communicative functions: 1. referential (the subject-matter of communication), 2. emotive (expressing the feelings of the addresser), 3. conative (aimed at influencing the addressee), 4. poetic (or aesthetic), 5. phatic (maintaining interaction between partners in communication) and 6. metalingual (reflecting the relationship between the language code and the natural language means) (Jakobson 1960).

Modern law in the developed world has interlinked with, and been based upon, social sciences (for example Knapp 1995: 4–5); therefore law always depends on the political environment of the society to which it belongs. The legal lexicon is based on abstract expressions which, however, bear quite a precise meaning in concrete situations. Each system of law, as well as the language through which the law is communicated to the persons on whom it is binding, is determined by, and often limited to, the history, traditions and culture of the society in question, and to the legal culture developed within that society (jurisdiction). Kischel (2009: 16) notes that '… each legal culture has a specific mode of talking', and two lawyers sharing the same general language (for example English) would very quickly identify (not because of different pronunciation or accent) whether they come from the same or different jurisdiction (for example the UK and the USA). Although the issue of globalization of legal language has been whispered,[8] the everyday practice of legal translators proves that they have to cope with many cross-cultural clashes even between legal systems from the same family (for example Austrian or German Law on the one hand and Czech Law on the other) – and all the more so, if philosophically different or remote legal systems are at issue (for example Common Law v. Civil Law v. sharia).

### *2.1 The Process*

Each legal text is produced for a certain purpose (such as to determine the rights and duties of parties to a contract) and to fulfil a certain function (for example to serve as proof that the contract has been made). Each legal culture (or legal system), however, establishes its own rules, for example, for how to make a contract or how to draft a law and what essential elements to include, so that the contract or the law can be considered valid, that is, binding and enforceable. Translating legal texts means transferring legal information from one language and culture into another language and culture, taking into account the differences in the legal systems, the purpose of translation and the related expectations regarding the role of the translated text in the target (legal) environment.

Since Jakobson's semiotic theory of translation (1959), the concept of intersemiotic translation has been imbued with greater implications for legal translation, particularly in relation to the development of legal semiotics as an extension to general legal theory: law may be regarded as a dual semiotic system composed of the language in which it is expressed, and the discursive system expressed by that language (Jackson 1997: 3). As a result, interlingual translation of a legal text is intersemiotic translation (Tomášek 1991: 147) as it represents a process where one dual semiotic system is to be replaced by the other; the issue, however, is to what extent all component parts of the ST (both legal and linguistic) can and should be transmitted into the TL in order to meet the expectations and

---

8 Cf. Tiersma (2012: 25).

requirements of the recipient of the translation (the extent may differ depending on the purpose of the translation).

This is the context which the Canadian Government calls 'bijuralism'.[9] Strictly speaking, any translation of a legal text may be called bijural since there is always a difference in the source legal and linguistic environment and background and the target legal and linguistic environment and background, caused by the system-specificity of the legal language (de Groot 2006: 423).

The language of law may be tackled from various perspectives. However, not all languages in their respective legal domains have been subject to such deep and extensive investigation as legal English has; one of the latest publications in this area – the *Oxford Handbook of Languages and Law* (2012) – provides a comprehensive analysis of English in Law, summarizing, to a certain extent, recent developments in this field. Placing legal language within a respective linguistic system, one may speak of a language for special or specific purposes, or of a sublanguage, scientific language or specialized language (Pearson 1998: 28). Widdowson (1979: 24) characterizes such subcategories of language 'not as formally defined varieties of English, but as realizations of universal sets of concepts and methods or procedures which define disciplines or areas of enquiry independently of any particular language'. This is what Sinclair (2007: 34) calls *local grammar* describing the specificity of the language in a particular subject area, and what Jackson (1997: 111) terms *legal grammar* when analysing the semiotics of legislative texts.

The general understanding of what is 'legal' about the language of law is usually confined to legal vocabulary, sometimes referred to as 'technical words', although terminology as part of vocabulary in legal texts creates no more than one-third of the narrative of any legal text and its quantity varies in different text-types as suggested in our earlier research (Chromá 2008: 311).[10] Although the attention of researchers (both in comparative law and translation studies) is usually drawn to legal vocabulary, it is not just terminology that may cause an obstacle to understanding a legal text. Translators quite often have to deal with texts where the structure and sense are far from clear. The following paragraph is from an authentic will drafted in the US (capitalized words were used in the English original).

**Example 1**

> I BEQUEATH all my personal chattels as defined by Section 55 (1) (x) of the Administration of Estates Act 1925 not hereby and by all codicils hereto otherwise

9 Canadian Legislative Bijuralism was officially launched more than ten years ago although the first attempts to raise awareness of the tight interconnection between 'drafting', 'interpreting' and 'translating' between the two Canadian legal systems occurred in the 1970s (White 1994: 243).

10 Newmark (1988: 160) estimates that terminology makes up 5–10 per cent of a text.

> disposed of free of all duties and taxes payable in respect thereof on my death to Ladislav absolutely but if he shall have died in my lifetime leaving a child or children living at my death then I BEQUEATH my personal chattels as aforesaid to such child or children and if more than one in shares of equal value as far as reasonably possible absolutely AND I DECLARE that if at the date of my death any such child shall be under the age of twenty one years the receipt of his or her parent or guardian shall be a good discharge to my Trustees SUBJECT AS aforesaid I BEQUEATH my personal chattels as aforesaid to my son Peter absolutely.

There are not many difficult terms in the paragraph to be looked up in translational dictionaries; translators can usually pick correct Czech equivalents of *bequeath*, *codicil*, *personal chattels* or *trustee*, although the underlying concepts do not exist in Czech Law (with the exception of *codicil*). What causes difficulty here is the elliptic structure of the phrases linking those terms and encompassed in one sentence without any separators (commas or semicolons); the translator should cut the one-sentence paragraph into logical segments in order to restore what belongs to what and, possibly, what has been hidden or unsaid.

The principle of interpretation by context (cf. Jackson 1997: 129) is used here in order to pick the relational meaning of individual parts of this long sentence; comments in italics and the symbol for missing commas are added to indicate the line of interpretation:

> I BEQUEATH all my personal chattels as defined by Section 55 (1) (x) of the Administration of Estates Act 1925
>
> *that are not* hereby and by all codicils hereto otherwise disposed of┐ free of all duties and taxes payable in respect thereof (*that is, in respect of the chattels bequeathed*)
>
> on my death to Ladislav absolutely
>
> but
>
> if he shall have died in my lifetime leaving a child or children living at my death
>
> then
>
> I BEQUEATH my personal chattels as aforesaid to such child or children┐
>
> and
>
> if more than one (*child exists then I bequeath my property*)
>
> in shares of equal value as far as reasonably possible absolutely

AND

I DECLARE that

if at the date of my death any such child shall be under the age of twenty one years

the receipt of his or her parent or guardian shall be a good discharge to my Trustees (*that is, the parent or guardian become Trustees with respect to the personal chattels in this particular situation, or, alternatively, the Trustees appointed in the will must give the respective personal chattels to the parent or guardian who is to hold the chattels in trust*)

SUBJECT AS aforesaid (*in the event that Ladislav has died and that Ladislav has no children*)

I BEQUEATH my personal chattels as aforesaid to my son Peter absolutely.

The interpretive analysis of a source text at all its applicable levels (for example lexical units, clauses, sentences, paragraphs, higher units) is one of the most important component parts of the process of interlingual translation. The analysis is to be pursued in the context of the source legal discourse (source legal system), the respective branch of law, the purpose of interaction (that is, why the ST was produced), the relating genre (that is, the text-type, such as a contract, testament, legislation) and the topic (subject-matter); a dispositional level of the text may also be relevant with respect to certain text-types (such as the last will) as it encompasses the author's intention and/or attitudes. The main aim of interpretation should be that the translator understands the text as a whole and that the text makes sense to him or her; only then is the translator ready to transmit the legal information into the target language and process the transmission accordingly.

Figure 8.1 attempts to schematize the entire process of translation in legal settings. The source legal text essentially becomes a concrete outcome of the semiotic intersection between the source language and source law. The middle circle describes the basic steps in a translator's treatment of the ST. As has already been emphasized, the translator's competent interpretation of the ST within the context of source law creates a *conditio sine qua non* for any competent legal and linguistic transmission of the interpreted information into the target text. The right circle is to indicate that the position of the target text, depending on its content and purpose, is balancing between two extremes: (a) its becoming a regular part of target law (typically, local versions of European legislation where all translated laws are considered authentic texts[11] or contracts where both language versions are stipulated by the parties as authentic and the contract is governed by target law) or (b) its becoming part of the general language informing of a certain

11 See, for example, Strandvik (2012: 25–50).

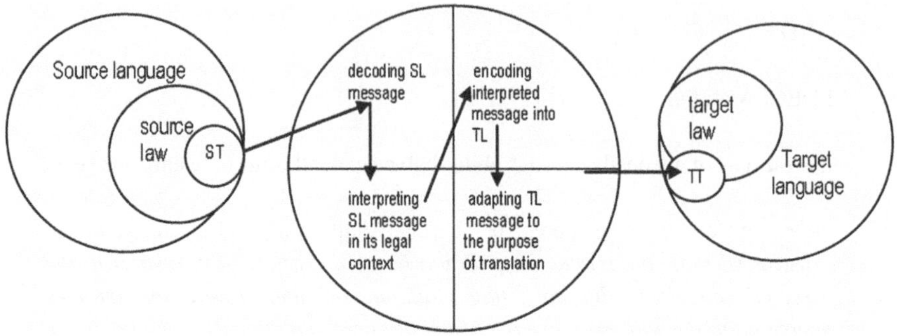


**Figure 8.1 The process of legal translation**

foreign reality (for example a testament written by a US citizen disposing of the property located in the US but establishing a Czech citizen to be the heir). Naturally, there is a wide range of translated texts within public and private law oscillating between these two margins. One of the special groups of texts not explicitly covered by Figure 8.1 includes legal documents drafted in a language not authentic for the law contained in the document and/or not the drafter's mother tongue. Recently, a German lawyer produced in English his legal opinion (two pages long) commenting on some specific issues of German law relevant for a contract to be concluded between the Czech Government and a German company; an English-to-Czech translator (with no German background) was commissioned to translate the opinion, and assigned just two hours for the task. However, the ultimate recipient (a Czech law firm) returned the translation to the translator, citing its poor quality as parts of it were unintelligible. Although some English terminological units in the opinion were complemented with their German originals (in brackets), the translator, in good faith, fully relied on the meaning of terms in English, supposing they had been meaningfully translated into English; moreover, she also complemented her translation of those terms into Czech with their German originals in brackets. Analysing the original and the translation, many translational 'mistakes' were caused by the erroneous use of terminology in English (for example confusing EU Directives with EU Regulations), incorrect use of prepositions (for example 'out of a legal perspective'), ambiguous use of English terms (for example '[the company] is the executor of such law') and by expressing typical German legal institutions in English in a way hindering their competent interpretation (for example 'a partial legal institution under direct government control' for 'teilrechtsfähige Anstalt des öffentlichen Rechts'[12]). In such cases, no extensive and well-compiled English-Czech legal dictionary would help the translator pick a proper Czech equivalent which would make sense to the ultimate recipient.

12 The German term 'teilrechtsfähige Anstalt des öffentlichen Rechts' would be better rendered in English as 'public/law/institution with partial legal personality'.

Another special group is composed of texts already translated, that is, the target legal text in one legal environment becomes a source legal text in another (a form of relay translation quite often spanning a long period of time);[13] needless to say, the effect of relay on the 'end product' may be calamitous; again, consulting bilingual legal dictionaries would not provide any guarantee that concepts in the first source legal text (the original) would be expressed in the last target text by terms representing the same concepts or legal institutions.

### *2.2 The Actors*

Bilingual translation as social interaction is fully dependent on a go-between or intermediary – the translator. Legal texts within a local legal system are primarily drafted by individual lawyers, team(s) of lawyers or teams made up of lawyers and subject-area experts to address persons (whether natural or juridical) in the local jurisdiction, all speaking one language.[14] Regarding the issue of translation, essentially two basic situations may occur:

a. the source legal text is drafted for the (intended) recipient not proficient in the SL (irrespective of whether legally proficient), that is, translation is presumed from the beginning and the purpose of both the ST and the TT would be essentially identical (for example contracts executed in two languages, EU legislation translated into the languages of EU Member States, an international treaty translated into the language of the Contracting State and so on); here the translator acts as a real intermediary; communication between the sender and the intended receiver is interrupted, but remains linear and the intended meaning of communication in a Gricean sense is recognized by the intended receiver (see Jackson 1995: 68).
b. the source legal text is drafted in the SL within the source legal environment for standard source law recipients, but, subsequently, the need for its translation into the TL emerges. The translator becomes a secondary, but unintended, receiver and one should speak of signification[15] rather than communication between the author of the ST and the recipient of the TT (Jackson 1995: 68); signification is the process of making sense of the target legal text entirely from the receiver's perspective because there was no intention on the part of the original sender to convey the sense of his/

13 For interpretation of a translated legal text see, for example, Chromá 2012: 113–4.

14 The situation in plurilingual and multilingual, yet unijural legal systems (for example Switzerland and Belgium or the EU respectively) is very different. See, for example, S. Šarčević 1997: 36–41 and 49–53, or Baaij 2012.

15 Cf. Grice (1991: 359–68).

her message through a different language to a receiver in a different legal environment.[16] Two situations may occur:

(i) the purpose of the TT differs from that of the ST; for example, the US Constitution translated into any other language would serve educational or documentary purposes, but not as a binding piece of legislation; and
(ii) the purpose of the TT is close to, or even identical with that of the ST; for example, a judgment issued in one EU Member State should be translated into the language of a Member State where it is to be enforceable under EU Law (for example in the case of a judgment determining maintenance obligations of a parent residing in a Member State different from the Member State where the judgment was issued and the other parent and the child reside[17]).

Moreover, the time of drafting a legal text and the time of its translation may span centuries or even millennia (take for example modern translations of the Codes of Justinian or Hammurabi). Nevertheless, most legal translations of texts built upon valid legislation are quite proximate in time (usually computed in weeks, months, or years at most).

The core factor of legal translation is the translator's ability to understand the source text and to reasonably interpret it, that is, to carry out an 'intra-language translation' in a Jakobsonian sense. As most translators are non-lawyers with a linguistic background, it may be assumed that they possess a certain degree of what James Boyd White calls 'legal literacy' (1985: 60). This term spans two extremes: (a) full competence in legal discourse both as a reader and a writer; in this sense it is a subject of professional education of lawyers; and (b) the capacity to 'recognize legal words and locutions as foreign to oneself, as part of the World of Law' including 'that degree of competence in legal discourse required for meaningful and active life in our increasingly legalistic and litigious culture' (1985: 61). It is not just the translator's ability to recognize words and style, but also to identify the genre of a legal discourse, the genre of a source text (text-

16 For the distinction from various perspectives about how the meaning of a message can be construed and the sense is made of it, see, for example, Eco (1994: 44–63); Phillips (2003: 83–99) regarding the distinction between (a) *intentio auctoris* (author's intention), (b) *intentio operis* (what the text actually says) and (c) *intentio lectoris* (what sense the text makes to the reader); a slightly modified approach to meaning construction is taken by Daniel Chandler (1995. 4–7) disregarding the author of a text in its interpretation: (a) objectivist theory claims that meaning is entirely in the text (that is, transmitted meaning); (b) constructivist theory sees the meaning in interplay between the text and its reader (that is, negotiated meaning), and (c) subjectivist theory relies entirely on interpretation by the reader (re-created meaning); Grice (1991: 86–137) focuses on a dichotomy of 'utterer's meaning' and 'sentence meaning', the latter in the sense of the propositional meaning of utterance.

17 See Council Regulation (EC) No 4/2009 on jurisdiction, applicable law, recognition and enforcement of decisions and cooperation in matters relating to maintenance obligations.

type), its narrative repertoire, legal concepts and their reflection in terminology and so on. Only then may the translator transmit the interpreted information into the target language, trying to re-create the text in the other legal and linguistic environment, keeping in mind the purpose of translation and the expectations and needs of the ultimate recipient. This is the stage of legal translation when the translator would consult his or her legal dictionary for the first time to look for the meaning of SL terms unknown to him or her. Although one would expect a monolingual (encyclopaedic) legal dictionary to be consulted first in order to get an explanation or even a definition of an unknown concept, translators even at this stage of interpretation resort to bilingual legal dictionaries, most frequently for the sake of saving time (as they themselves admit).

## 3. A Dictionary for Legal Translation

As has already been suggested, legal vocabulary as an archetypal component of legal language and legal discourse has been subject to both theoretical and empirical research by lawyers and linguists for decades. The most visible outcomes of such research are monolingual,[18] bilingual or multilingual legal dictionaries.

The theory of legal lexicography covers both monolingual dictionaries (for example Garner 2003), encompassing legal concepts and institutions of a particular legal system and their definitions, explanations and, if relevant, examples of their practical application, and bilingual legal dictionaries (for example De Groot 2006; Nielsen 2003) aimed primarily at helping translators in their jurilinguistic battle.

Although the purpose, content and potential users of monolingual and bilingual legal dictionaries differ, there are some common issues faced by authors of both types. Bryan Garner (2003: 151) posed five questions, and provided five analytical answers, in response to various reactions of audiences to the new appearance of the 7th edition of *Black's Law Dictionary* in 1999. Two of the questions, considered from a different perspective, are relevant in compiling a translational legal dictionary:[19]

- How do you find the material to include in a dictionary?

---

18 The most famous English monolingual dictionaries of law, which still retain their prestigious lexicographical position, were published at the end of the nineteenth century: Stroud (1890, 1903), and *Black's Law Dictionary* (1891).

Surprisingly, the first law dictionary in Czech in five volumes was compiled in the 1890s although no Czech State existed at that time, the Czech lands were under the jurisdiction of the Hapsburg Empire and despite officially declared language equality German was the language of all branches of law and administration (see *Příruční slovník práva soukromého a veřejného* I-V by František Xaver Veselý, 1894–99).

19 The original order of questions is changed to reflect their relevance to bilingual legal lexicography.

- To what extent can the modern lexicographer rely on the accuracy of predecessors?

Naturally, there are many more issues, both lexicographical and jurilinguistic, to be decided by the author of a bilingual legal dictionary (cf., for example, Poon 2010); their analysis would go beyond the scope of this paper. However, one more question should be dealt with:

- To what extent should a lexicographer concentrate on legal terminology, as opposed to other (larger) segments of the language of law (potentially causing problems in translation)?

Answering these questions will outline some aspects relevant within the basic lexicographical framework for compiling a bilingual legal dictionary.

### *3.1 To What Extent Should a Lexicographer Concentrate on Legal Terminology, as Opposed to Other (Larger) Segments of the Language of Law?*

*3.1.1 Structure of legal terminology* Traditionally, bilingual dictionaries for specialized (professional) subject-areas (sometimes called technical dictionaries irrespective of the domain they cover, whether medicine, law or mechanical engineering), have been tasks for, and products of terminography (cf. Felber 1982, 1984; Bergenholtz and Tarp 1995) rather than lexicography in its general sense. The reason for such an assertion is quite obvious: most compilers of bilingual dictionaries for translation of texts within professional domains focus on lexical units (items) considered or recognized to be terms in the respective subject-area. Moreover, not a negligible number of law practitioners, as well as many lay people, would still consider *legal terminology* as a synonym for *legal language* believing that it is only terminology that makes discourse 'legal'. On the other hand, to define which lexical units[20] are legal terms and which are not may be quite difficult since legal terminology is not confined to nomenclatures as is often the case with natural or exact sciences (cf. Pearson 1998). The traditional onomasiological postulate that a *term* is accurate, concise, linguistically correct, allowing for the formation of derivatives (Felber 1984: 181–2), and, preferably, should be monosemous and at the same time mononymous (Thomas 1993: 46) may apply to some terms only but does not essentially apply to the whole category of legal terminology. As suggested in our earlier research (Chromá 2011: 37), a rough estimate of entries under the letter P contained in the *Black's Law Dictionary*

20 Semanticists such as Saeed (2003: 56–7), Murphy (2008: 15), Halliday (2004: 2), or Hoey (2006: 156) distinguish between *word* (as an independent unit for paradigmatic and morphological purposes) and *lexical unit* (having not only a particular form but also a particular sense). Löbner (2002: 40) calls expressions with a lexical meaning *lexemes* or *lexical items* and for Murphy (2008: 144) a *lexical unit* is the instantiation of a *lexical item*.

(9th ed., pp. 1217–357) suggests that the proportion of one-word terms and multi-word terms is 20 per cent and 80 per cent respectively.[21] Moreover, some multi-word terminological phrases can have more than one legal meaning and their exact meaning in a particular context is sometimes quite hard to identify; for example, the translation of *legal remedy* in general legal contexts, that is, a remedy under any law not necessarily relating to Anglo-American (AA) law, differs from its translation in the context of the law of equity as a source of English Law, that is, a remedy under Common Law as opposed to that available in equity. In addition, mononymous terms can have a multi-word TL equivalent; for example, *infanticide* is the crime of *vražda novorozeného dítěte matkou* in the Czech Criminal Code, all the four words, expressly denoting essential elements of the concept ('murder of a newly born child by its mother'), constitute the Czech term. In compiling a bilingual legal dictionary, multi-word terms and terminological phrases always require that the lexicographer should make an initial 'macrostructural' decision whether (a) a multi-word term would constitute a separate entry, or (b) a multi-word term should appear in an entry with the lemma corresponding to the head (base) of the multi-word term. Either approach is practicable, with the former being more 'space-consuming' in the case of printed, non-electronic, versions of a dictionary.

Vocabulary used in law can be classified from different perspectives. Mellinkoff (2004: 11) groups the vocabulary into eight categories;[22] Riley (1995: 73–9) distributes the legal lexicon among three wider groups;[23] Hughes and Alcaraz (2002: 16–18) assign the same three groups of legal vocabulary slightly modified names, but essentially preserving the characteristics suggested by Riley.[24] Moreover, as Phillips points out (2003: 48), '[…] many words appear in ordinary speech before importation into the discourse of the law. Many also make the return journey or even a single journey starting from legal language to the ordinary vocabulary'. And he adds that 'in crossing over in either direction [legal language ↔ natural language] words

21 The total number of entries and subentries under letter 'P' is 4645. There are 784 one-word terms, 3210 multi-word terms. Latin terminological phrases (576) as well as abbreviations and acronyms (75) were excluded from calculation.

22 (a) common words with uncommon meanings/*prayer* as a form of pleading/, (b) Old English and Middle English words /*witnesseth*/, (c) Latin words and phrases/*lex fori*/, (d) words of Old French and Anglo-Norman origin/*plaintiff*/, (e) terms of arts /*fee simple*/, (f) argot/*taking the fifth*/, (g) formal phrases /*approach the bench*/ and (h) lexical units with flexible meanings/*reasonable*/.

23 (a) 'Pure' legal terminology as a scarce group of lexical units or phrases not used outside the branch of law unless stylistically marked (e.g. detinue), including Old and Middle English words and legal Latin; (b) Legal terminology found in everyday speech (e.g. negligence); (c) Everyday words which are assigned a special connotation in a given legal context.

24 (a) purely technical terms (meaning the lexical units and phrases found only in the legal setting, that is, having no application outside law); (b) semi-technical or mixed terms; and (c) everyday vocabulary frequently found in legal texts.

and phrases undergo semantic transformation'. Although all the above authors analysed English in law, similar conclusions with respect to essentially a three-tier classification of legal vocabulary were arrived at during the compilation of bilingual lexicons for Czech law students in the 1980s.[25] Whatever classification is retained, it is clear (and our own practical experience in legal translation bears this out) that the second category encompassing specialized vocabulary acquiring its precise legal meaning in a particular legal context is the most difficult for a translator to tackle and transmit into the target text properly. A lexicographer can ease this process through various contextualizing labels, determining geographical occurrence or jurisdictional uniqueness, branches of law, register and so on.

Unlike the first category encompassing lexical units 'looking legal' at first sight, the second group includes units very often concealing their actual legal sense under the veil of their common meaning applicable to the general language. For example, *joint tenancy* and *tenancy in common* are two different legal concepts within the Anglo-American system of law (the former non-existent in Czech Law since the Common Law institution of leasehold has no conceptual counterpart in Czech Law). A translator insufficiently aware of the legal difference between the two English terms might rely on the semantic similarity of the attributes in general English (*joint* and *common* are in fact synonyms), particularly if the target legal system is lacking the same conceptual dichotomy in property holding. The lexicographer, having completed conceptual analysis of these terms, should decide how to treat the situation where no equivalent legal concept exists in the target law, that is, no equivalent TL legal term can be provided. In addition, the lexicographer should shape the entries so that a translator would be able to distinguish between the two terms (See Example 2).

The issue of equivalence relevant for the legal language has been subject to many analyses (for example Šarčević 1997; De Groot 2006; Baaij 2012; cf. Adamska-Salaciak 2010 for general language). Following Löbner (2002: 20–21), the definiendum of the term *concept* is mental description or meaning, whilst *term* is its written (spelling) or oral (sound) form. This is why *conceptual* analysis should be pursued in order to select a suitable equivalent term in the target language, representing a concept in the target legal system which is closest to the concept in the source legal system denoted by the term in the source text subject to translation.

Attaining equivalence in the translation of legal terms, whether for the purposes of compiling a bilingual law dictionary or immediate translation of a legal text, should be accompanied not only with a comparative conceptual analysis of the source term and its potential equivalent in the target language and/or legal system, but also with a comparative research into a wider (extra-linguistic and possibly extra-legal) context. Although these requirements may represent a substantial workload if met through traditional methods of library research, both legal

25 Russian-Czech legal lexicon in 1984, German-Czech 1985, French-Czech 1986 and English-Czech in 1987.

translators and lexicographers may significantly accelerate the process of looking for, and analysing, suitable equivalents by using Internet sources (cf. Church 2008); needless to say, electronic sources found through various search engines should be treated *merely* as sources of information (not providers of ready-made equivalents and solutions) with which the lexicographer should analyse the concept under consideration and decide what degree of equivalence is relevant in the particular case and what TL equivalent can be provided in the dictionary.

The selection of 'proper' equivalents of the SL lexical units is one of the most important requirements for compiling a good (reliable) bilingual legal dictionary. There are no exact computational means of measuring the degree of equivalence. Susan Šarčević in her construction of three degrees of equivalence – near, partial and non-equivalence (1997: 238) – builds upon the variable proportion of 'essential elements' and 'accidental characteristics' in the SL concept and its potential TL representative; however, to identify which elements are essential and what are just complementary may be rather difficult. One example of a conceptual analysis of potential equivalents may illustrate the issue: a violation of traffic regulations subsisting in parking a car in places where parking is forbidden by local law is considered a crime in all English-speaking countries (*parking offence*). The same conduct – unauthorized parking – if committed in the Czech Republic, is not a crime but falls within the ambit of administrative law (*přestupek*). One essential element of the concept of a parking offence is the unlawful conduct – breaching parking regulations (that is, a point of fact) – the other is the legal qualification of that conduct (that is, a point of law – a criminal act within Anglo-American Law and a transgression of administrative law in the Czech Republic). An accidental feature would be the punishment for such conduct, which is a fine as a primary sanction in both systems, expanded to imprisonment under specific circumstances only within Anglo-American Law. Strictly speaking from a legal perspective, no unlawful conduct resulting in a breach of parking regulations – a *parking offence* in English – may be translated as *přestupek* in Czech, and no Czech *přestupek* should be translated as a *parking offence*, as there is no equivalence in the legal characteristics of such conduct between Anglo-American Law and Czech Law. As a result, no responsible compiler of an English-Czech legal dictionary would offer *přestupek* as an equivalent for *parking offence* as, technically, there is no legal equivalence between those terms. However, there are many semi-legal and non-legal contexts (for example mass media, movies) where just one essential element – breaching parking regulations – along with one accidental characteristic – imposing a fine for the breach – suffices for non-lawyers to translate *parking offence* as *přestupek* in Czech and it generally makes sense to the Czech (lay) audience.

The first two types of equivalence (near and partial) could be solved using a functional or substantive equivalent in the target law. For example, British *third-party debt order* has *exekuce přikázáním pohledávky* as its functional/substantive/equivalent in Czech Law, as it serves the same function in judgment enforcement; on the other hand, a Czech-English law dictionary would provide several equivalents in English for *exekuce přikázáním pohledávky*, depending on the jurisdiction in question: third-party debt order (UK), writ of garnishment (US), attachment/of debt/order (AU), garnishee order (I.E.), garnishment order (CA).

Non-equivalence could be compensated for by the addition of an explanatory (explicative) or descriptive phrase in lieu of a TL equivalent, as is usually the case with legal realia (for example terms denoting local institutions, such as TheOld Bailey rendered by the translation 'London Criminal Court' in the TL). The above-mentioned Czech term *přestupek* could be provided with an explicative 'equivalent' of *transgression under administrative law* or *administrative transgression*. On the other hand, the Czech term *jazykové právo*, strictly speaking, has no equivalent in English: the Czech term *právo* on its own can be either *right* or *law* depending on the context; quite uniquely in Czech law, the terminological phrase *jazykové právo* encompasses both meanings of *právo* and the only possibility of transmitting its essential elements and accidental features into English would be to use *language law and rights*, although in some contexts one or the other meaning is to be preferred. English *arraignment* has no procedural equivalent in Czech Law; in a dictionary, an explanatory phrase (for example *the defendant's answering the charge before court*) following the English term in lieu of its precise definition could, if translated into Czech, serve as its explicative 'equivalent'.

*3.1.1 Structure of a dictionary entry* The structure of a dictionary entry is the outcome of the microstructural design reflecting macrostructural lexicographic decisions; it is determined by both objective and subjective factors (the latter usually confined to individual preferences and the translation experience of the lexicographer). Objective factors include the intended users of a bilingual legal dictionary, whether the text is to be used by translators or by (comparative) lawyers as their needs and expectations may differ. The former group would look for ready-made TL equivalents to be inserted in their translations, whereas the latter would appreciate a dictionary actually comparing source law and target law concepts and institutions in their natural legal and linguistic environment (cf. de Groot 2006: 430, on the question of verifiability: 'the relation of the entries and their proposed translations to their respective legal system must be explicit by offering references to relevant legal sources, linguistic context and sometimes encyclopaedic and bibliographic references, thus ensuring verifiability'). Our focus here is on a dictionary primarily serving the needs of legal translators; but even this preference involves considerations, such as to what extent encyclopaedic information (definition, explanation) should be added? SL lexical units representing the concepts of source law, and their TL equivalents (whether conceptual, explicative or, possibly, transplanted[26] in TL), and what grammatical (linguistic) indicators should be used within an entry. As many terms acquire their precise meaning, that is, correct concepts are linked with the terms, in a particular legal and linguistic context the lexicographer should use an adequate

26 More on legal transplants can be found, for example, at Watson (2006); Langer (2004: 1–64); Legrand (1997: 111–24). Cf. Triebel (2009: 147–81).

lexicographical metalanguage in order to indicate the high degree of contextuality of legal terminology. The metalanguage encompasses indicators, tags and labels explaining the legal (including geographical or jurisdictional) and linguistic context of SL terminological units and their potential TL equivalents. It is usually the author of a bilingual legal dictionary who creates the metalanguage for his or her dictionary, preferably corresponding with potential users' reference skills. In doing so, the author can draw from, and be directed by, various authoritative manuals of lexicography; however, one issue, which, to our knowledge and as pointed out by Overgaard Ptaszynski (2010: 418), has been omitted is a natural language in which the metalanguage should be expressed in bilingual or multilingual dictionaries (whether the SL or the TL). Our own lexicographical experience culminated with the use a bilingual version of the metalanguage: lexicographical information relating to the jurilingual features of SL lexical units is in the SL, and lexicographic information regarding their TL equivalents (including a special set of contextualizing abbreviations and acronyms) is in the TL in order to make the SL part and the TL part of an entry linguistically compact. Example 2 illustrates some simple metalinguistic components in the excerpt of an entry in the planned 'English-Czech Law Dictionary with Explanations'.[27]

**Example 2:**

> **tenancy** (AA) occupation or possession of property conveyed by a lease (a leasehold interest) *vysv.* držba věci v dlouhodobém nájmu; **joint** ~ identical undivided interests in property of two or more co-owners based upon the right of survivorship *vysv.* spoluvlastnictví bez možnosti volně nakládat s vlastním dílem při úmrtí jednoho ze spoluvlastníků přechází jeho díl na přeživší spoluvlastníky; neexistuje v *CZ*; ~ **by the entirety/entireties** undivided interests in property of spouses based upon the right of survivorship *vysv.* bezpodílové spoluvlastnictví manželů; ~ **in common** *přibl.* spoluvlastnictví s možnosti volně nakládat s vlastním dílem

**Explanations**

(AA) stands for the Anglo-American system of law; this acronym suggests that the term is used in the same meaning virtually in all English-speaking legal systems based upon Common Law and that it is not typical just of the United States (US), Britain (UK), Australia (AU) and so on; *přibl.* is an abbreviation of Czech *přibližně* (approximately) and suggests that there is partial equivalence between SL and TL terms; *vysv.* is abbreviated Czech *vysvětlení* (explanation), suggesting

27 The term 'explanations' in the title of the dictionary covers both purely legal definitions of terms and their equivalents and simpler (generalizing) explanations, where these are required usually due to the conceptual differences between legal systems.

an explanatory gloss rather than an equivalent; an explanation or definition, following the lemma and multiverbal terms in the same entry having the lemma as head (base) of the terminological phrase, is in small print.

Strictly speaking from a legal perspective, the term *tenancy* should not be offered as an English equivalent of any Czech term in a Czech-English law dictionary as the concept of leasehold does not exist in Czech Law (assuming the Czech part of the dictionary covers only Czech Law). Since *tenancy* may, in legal English, be substituted for *occupation* or *possession* in various contexts, it may be generally understood as their legal synonym and emerge as a translational equivalent for the Czech *držba* although *possession* would be a true legal equivalent of that Czech term.

### *3.2 How to Find the Material to Include in a Dictionary?*

This question is closely related to the decision as to which language of the two in a bilingual legal dictionary should be the source language introducing source law and its conceptual and terminological entourage, and which should act as a conveyor of their sense to the users of the dictionary. Quite straightforward work would be required where concepts and terms of one unijural and unilingual (historically established and geographically limited) system are to be introduced into another unijural and unilingual (historically established and geographically limited) system, such as Polish Law and language and Czech Law and language, both built upon more or less identical continental legal maxims and governed by a very similar system of legislation in private and public law. As soon as there is an imbalance between the SL and TL in that one is reduced to just one legal system and territory (for example Czech), and the other is the language of more than one jurisdiction often tending to create local jurilingual varieties (for example English, German, Spanish), the decision-making by the lexicographer becomes rather complex.

In the case of an English-Czech law dictionary, the creation of an initial corpus should be preceded by careful consideration of the sources and branches of law to be covered. Common Law is relevant in six major English-speaking countries and dozens of smaller jurisdictions where English is the language of law (for example the British Commonwealth); all these countries have more or less autonomous legal systems, although case-law of any Common Law country seems to be relevant and applicable within the whole Common Law world. Legal English is usually modified locally to respond better to the particular jurilinguistic environment. Secondly, the law of the European Union is an autonomous legal system expressed in 23 official languages including English; the divergence between EU legal English and Common Law English is obvious and logical. Another field where English is used as a primary means of legal communication is public international law with most treaties drafted and adopted in English and only subsequently translated into the languages of contracting states for ratification.

Branches of law where texts are most frequently subject to translation include business law in its widest sense (including companies, business transactions and contracts, negotiable instruments and so on) and criminal law; however, property, succession or family law should not be omitted as they have been becoming more and more relevant in an increasingly globalized and borderless world. How can we find a reasonable cross-section between the wide range of jurisdictions and the range of branches of law so as to determine the relevant sources of excerpts for the initial corpus of English terms, terminological phrases and other collocations? To our knowledge, no theory of bilingual lexicography, or individual experience of a particular lexicographer, has provided a reasonable answer; each lexicographer, particularly when faced with a minor language as the TL, should decide for him or herself, calling on their own experience in translation and relying on their individual talent. A practical initial method is to resort to recognized monolingual dictionaries as sources of lemmata, definitions of concepts and their terminological representations (this is not a throw-back to the days of translating *Black's Dictionary* mentioned in the introduction). Law dictionaries, such as *Black's*, *Bouvier*, *Webster's* (all originally American), or *Stroud's*, *Oxford*, *Mozley and Whiteley's*, *Curzons* (originally British), provide a solid basis for the selection of terms, their definitions and other translationally relevant collocations to establish the initial SL corpus. Our own experience suggests that textbooks in major legal branches spanning private law and public law, both of American and British origin and possibly from other major jurisdictions, should be included as a source of excerpts in the initial corpus as they refer to relevant local legislation and case-law. Another quite useful source of English legal texts can be sets of standard legal forms usually available on the Internet on websites of law firms in English-speaking countries; the forms very often serve as a source of legalese (despite various campaigns for plain English in law), but translators must often deal with legalese in their source legal texts.

The corpus is to be a structured (electronic) database with precise indicators of the source of a particular term, terminological phrases and their definitions, and of other translationally relevant collocations (for example a particular law, textbook or dictionary, its page, date of excerpt and so on). The database is to be arranged alphabetically; multi-word terminological phrases would be ordered according to the first letter of their head (base). A generally available electronic database software (for example MS Access, Paradox) can be used for this purpose and the compiler of a dictionary may define and operate the database by him or herself. As soon as the initial SL corpus has been compiled by means of an electronic database, the long process of finding and testing the appropriateness of Czech equivalents begins.

Example 3 provides an outline of basic fields in the database; other fields may be added (for example who entered the excerpt in the database, should more than one person be engaged in the dictionary-making):

**Table 8.1 Example 3**

| Base | Term | Definition | Collocation | Source | Page | Date | CE | E type | C source |
|---|---|---|---|---|---|---|---|---|---|
| Tenancy | Tenancy | Holding of land in leasehold | Establish a tenancy | MWLD | 355 | | | | |
| Tenancy | Tenancy in common | Each co-owner holds his/her interest separately; can be disposed of by will | | MWLD | 62 | | | | |
| Tenancy | Joint tenancy | Property acquired by two or more persons in the same land, by the same title, at the same time; on death the share accrues to the other(s) by survivorship | | MWLD | 192 | | | | |

## Explanations

The field 'collocation' contains phrases excerpted from the same source where the defined term occurs. In sources other than law dictionaries (for example law textbooks) it may happen that no definition of the term would be provided but several collocations (relevant for proper translation) may be excerpted; MWLD – *Mozley and Whiteley Law Dictionary* (12th ed. 2001); date – the date when the excerpt was put in the database; CE – Czech equivalent; E type – the type of equivalent (full, partial, explicative); C source – the source of a Czech equivalent (legislation, law textbooks, case-law, proposed by the dictionary author and so on).

Excerpted definitions should be in a format allowing for the identification of essential elements of the concept and accidental characteristics, if applicable. The lexicographer compares the definitions of a particular English concept in all sources in the database and decides what legal features must (should or need not) be preserved in the TL equivalent.

In the case of a Czech-English law dictionary, a corpus of terms and their definitions, frequent collocations and phrases, which are difficult to translate but have their structural and substantive counterparts in English, would be compiled through excerpting basic pieces of legislation governing areas most frequently subject to translation. As the position of case-law within Czech Law, as is the case in the entire continental system of law, is much weaker than in countries whose legal systems are based on Common Law, there are not many Czech judgments of higher courts redefining statutory terms which would have to be included in the corpus. What should be included as a source of excerpts for the creation of an initial corpus are law textbooks and monolingual Czech law dictionaries drafted by recognized academic lawyers; as soon as the database has been completed, the search for English equivalents begins. It should be primarily directed at original English sources (not those translated from various languages into English), and only then to international documents written in English. Quite a useful source of potential equivalents of Czech legal terms in English is legislation (and also case-law) in jurisdictions within English-speaking countries whose legal system is based on continental law, that is, Louisiana and Quebec (particularly their civil codes constructed upon the French Code civil or Code Napoléon). But, as pointed out by Volker Triebel (2009: 149), 'legal English and common law grew up together', so Common Law sources cannot be omitted in the search for English equivalents of Czech terms. There are legal branches within Common Law with concepts which have analogous counterparts in Czech Law (for example Criminal Law or Constitutional Law). Contrast that however with the property law of Common Law jurisdictions which, due to its specific historical development, fails to yield many conceptual counterparts of Czech terms; this deficit can be compensated by, for example, looking to the Louisiana Civil Code. In fact, there is a bifurcated English terminology in property law depending on whether the source is Common Law or continental law: real property – immovable thing/property; personal property – movable thing/property; tangible property – corporeal things; intangible property – incorporeal things and so on.[28]

### *3.3 To What Extent Can the Modern Lexicographer Rely on the Accuracy of Predecessors?*

Garner's response to this question was logically negative (2003: 157) supported by one example of a mistyped headword, carried over from one edition of *Black's* to another until the error was eliminated by Bryan Garner in the 7th edition.

Unlike the case of monolingual legal dictionaries, there are not many bilingual legal dictionaries to rely on. The practice of bilingual legal lexicography is quite a recent (historical) phenomenon and not many countries can offer a diachronic series of bilingual legal dictionaries having, for example, English as the source language and their local language as the TL. Some lexicographers rely not on previous lexicographical solutions, but rather on certain widely used translational solutions, yet without any substantive second-guessing of their correctness or appropriateness, thus conserving in their dictionary potentially confusing or even incorrect equivalents.

Another (third-language) approach includes consulting a dictionary where either the source law or target law (depending on what is relevant in a particular situation) is close to the legal system dealt with by the lexicographer; for example, the compiler of an English-Czech legal dictionary seeking for the Czech equivalent of *interpleader* would look at its solution in an English-German legal dictionary

28 See, for example, bijural terminology records retrievable at http://www.justice.gc.ca/eng/pi/bj/harm/table.html

for guidance partly in this particular case and partly in the general approach to similar situations.

Finally, translational terminological databases deserve mention, but it should be noted that a bilingual or multilingual terminological database is not a translational dictionary. It is essentially a corpus from which a dictionary observing basic lexicographic requirements could be made. Of the numerous terminological projects launched in the 1980s,[29] few survive today. However, terminological databases such as the Canadian Termium[30] (in English and French, Portuguese and Spanish) or the United Nations Multilingual Terminology Database for their six official languages (English, French, Spanish, Russian, Chinese, Arabic) are widely consulted;[31] these databases can be helpful or provide inspiration but are (a) not created as databanks of legal terminology, and (b) limited to a few international languages. On the other hand, the IATE project (InterActive Terminology for Europe)[32] is a database encompassing all terminology used within the *acquis communautaire* (that is, not just legislation but all documents having some legal relevance). Although the database is constantly updated and the public has a limited access to it, it can be (critically) used as a source of inspiration for translational equivalents (in all 23 EU official languages even for the translation of texts on topics not relating to EU Law).

## 4. Conclusion

Both legal translation and the making of a bilingual legal dictionary are based upon a comparative study of the source and target legal systems; both translators and lexicographers should be well aware of the problems created by the absence of equivalent concepts, legal institutions or terms between the systems. The difference between the two tasks is the extent and scope of the jurilinguistic research required for their successful completion; a bilingual legal dictionary is expected to provide more comprehensive information so that a legally literate translator can reasonably decide what equivalents offered in the dictionary will best suit the legal context of his or her translation.

Each system of law, as well as the language through which the law is communicated, is determined by, and confined to, the history, traditions and culture of the society in question, and to the legal culture developed within that society (jurisdiction). In this sense, it creates a dual semiotic system. As a result, bijural translation is intersemiotic translation where one dual semiotic system (source law and language) should be 'replaced' by the other (target law and language). The translator should not only transfer legal information from one language and

29 For example, McNaught (1981: 297–308); Candeland (1987: 3–20).

30 http://www.termiumplus.gc.ca/site/termium.php?cont=001&lang=eng

31 http://unterm.un.org/

32 http://iate.europa.eu/iatediff/SearchByQueryLoad.do?method=load

culture into another language and culture, taking into account the jurilinguistic differences, the purpose of the translation, and so on, but his or her translation should make sense to the ultimate recipient.

As a result, there is a certain tension between the expectations and needs of legal translators, and the potential of translational legal dictionaries, whose quality is dependent upon the lexicographical expertise and translational experience of dictionary-makers. The contextuality of the process of legal translation, whose primary purpose appears to be the transmission of the sense of the source text as a whole and of its parts, thus slightly suppressing the relevance of the meaning of individual words or even phrases, should be reflected by the lexicographer in his or her initial decision-making with respect to the macrostructure and microstructure of a formally constrained dictionary. Subsequently, providing explanations or definitions of terms or terminological phrases both on the SL and the TL sides, providing examples of the use of a particular term in nominal and verbal collocations or clause patterns, which may be difficult to translate, and selecting a form of a lexicographical metalanguage enabling translators to identify the jurilinguistic context of a SL item and its potential TL equivalent would help translators make competent choices.

## References

Adamska-Salaciak, Arleta. 2010. Examining Equivalence. *International Journal of Lexicography*, Vol. 23, No. 4, 387–409.

Baaij, C.J.W. (ed.) 2012. *The Role of Legal Translation in Legal Harmonization.* Alphen aan den Rijn: Kluwer Law International.

Bergenholtz, H., Tarp, S. 1995. *Manual of Specialised Lexicography.* John Benjamins Publishing Company.

*Black's Law Dictionary*, 1891. 1st ed. St Paul, MI: West Publishing.

Candeland, Richard. 1987. The British Term Bank project: A prototype software. *Machine Translation*, Vol. 2, No. 1, 3–20.

Cao, Deborah. 2007. *Translating Law.* Clevedon, Buffalo, Toronto: Multilingual Matters Ltd.

Chandler, Daniel. 1995. *The Act of Writing: A Media Theory Approach.* Cardiff: The University of Wales Press.

Chromá, Marta. 2008. Translating terminology in arbitration discourse. In: *Legal Discourse Across Cultures and Systems*, edited by V. Bhatia, Ch. Candlin and J. Engberg, 309–27. Hong Kong: Hong Kong University Press.

Chromá, Marta. 2011. Synonymy and Polysemy in Legal Terminology and their Applications to Bilingual and Bijural Translation. *Research in Language*, Vol. 9, No. 1. 31–50.

Chromá, Marta. 2012. A Dictionary for Legal Translation. In: *The Role of Legal Translation in Legal Harmonization*, edited by C.J.W. Baaij, Alphen aan den Rijn: Kluwer Law International.

Church, Kenneth W. 2008. Approximate Lexicography and Web Search. *International Journal of Lexicography*, Vol. 21, No.3, 325–36.
Eco, Umberto, E. 1994. *The Limits of Interpretation*. Bloomington: Indiana University Press, 44–63.
Felber, Helmut. 1982. The General Theory of Terminology and Terminography. Anticipated Developments in the Eighties. In: Terminologies for the Eighties, Infoterm Series 7, edited by W. Nedobity, 119–36. Munich: K.G. Saur.
Felber, Helmut. 1984. *Terminology Manual*. Paris: UNESCO and INFOTERM.
Garner, Bryan. 2003. *Legal Lexicography: A View from the Front Lines*. 6 Green Bag 2d, Winter 2003, 151–61.
Gémar, Jean-Claude 2001. Seven Pillars for the Legal Translator: Knowledge, Know-how and Art. In: Legal Translation, Preparation for Accession to the European Union, edited by S. Šarčević. Rijeka: University of Rijeka, 111–38.
Grice, P. 1991. *Studies in the Way of Words*. Cambridge, MA: Harvard University Press, 359–68.
Groot, Gérard-René de 1987. Problems of Legal Translation from the Point of View of a Comparative Lawyer. *Cahiers de droit*, 28, 813–44.
Groot, Gérard-René de. 2006. Legal Translation. In: *Elgar Encyclopedia of Comparative Law*, edited by Jan M. Smits, Maastricht: Maastricht University.
Halliday, M.A.K., Teubert, Wolfgang, Yallop, Colin and Čermáková, Anna. 2004. *Lexicology and Corpus Linguistics*. London, New York: Continuum.
Hoey, Michael. 2006. *Lexical Priming*. London, New York: Routledge.
Hughes, Brian, Alcaraz, Enrique. 2002. *Legal Translation Explained*. Manchester: St. Jerome Publishing.
Jackson, Bernard, S. 1985, 1997. *Semiotics and Legal Theory*. Liverpool: Deborah Charles Publications.
Jackson, Bernard, S. 1995. *Making Sense in Law*. Liverpool: Deborah Charles Publications.
Jakobson, Roman. 1959. On Linguistic Aspects of Translation. In: *On Translation*, edited by R.A. Brower, 232–39. Cambridge, MA: Harvard University Press [Reprinted in Venuti 2003].
Jakobson, Roman. 1960. Closing Statement: Linguistics and Poetics. In: *Style in Language*, edited by T. Sebeok, 350–377. Cambridge, MA: MIT Press.
Kischel, Uwe. 2009. Legal Cultures – Legal Languages. In: *Translation Issues in Language and Law*, edited by F. Olsen, A. Lorz and D. Stein, Basinstoke: Palgrave Macmillan, 7–17.
Knapp, Viktor. 1995. *Teorie práva*. Praha: C.H. Beck.
Lane-Mercier, G. 1997. Translating the Untranslatable: The Translator's Aesthetic, Ideological and Political Responsibility, *Target* 9/1, 43–68.
Langer, Máximo. 2004. From Legal Transplants to Legal Translations: The Globalization of Plea Bargaining and the Americanization Thesis in Criminal Procedure. *Harvard International Law Journal*, Vol. 45, No. 1, 1–64.
Legrand, Pierre. 1997. The Impossibility of 'Legal Transplants'. *Maastricht Journal of European and Comparative Law*, 1997, 111–24.

Löbner, Sebastian. 2002. *Understanding Semantics*. London: Arnold, Hodder Headline Group.

Malmkjær, Kirsten. 2005. *Linguistics and the Language of Translation*. Edinburgh: Edinburgh University Press.

McNaught, John. 1981. Terminological Data Banks: a model for a British Linguistic Data Bank (LDB). *ASLIB Proceedings*, Vol. 33, No. 7/8, 297–308.

Mellinkoff, David. 1963, 2004. *The Language of the Law*. Eugene, OR: Resource Publications.

Munday, J. 2001. *Introducing Translation Studies. Theories and Applications*. London and New York: Routledge.

Murphy, M. Lynne. 2008. *Semantic Relations and the Lexicon*. Cambridge: Cambridge University Press.

Newmark, Peter. 1988. *A Textbook of Translation*. 1st ed. London: Prentice Hall Europe, 7th Impression Harlow: Pearson Education, 2003.

Nielsen, Sandro. 2003. Towards a General Theory of Bilingual Legal Lexicography. In: *LSP Translation in the New Millennium. A Cross-Baltic Symposium on Didactics and Research*, edited by P. Kastberg. Aarhus: Hermes Skriftserie, 165–88.

Nord, C. 1997 (2001, 2007). *Translating as Purposeful Activity. Functionalist Approach Explained*. Manchester: St Jerome Publishing.

Olsen, Frances, Lorz, Alexander and Stein, Dieter (eds). 2009. *Translation Issues in Language and Law*. Basingstoke: Palgrave Macmillan.

Overgaard Ptaszynski, Marcin. 2010. Theoretical Considerations for the Improvement of Usage Labelling in Dictionaries: A Combined Formal-Functional Approach. *International Journal of Lexicography*, Vol. 23, No. 4, 411–42.

Pearson, Jennifer. 1998. *Terms in Context*. Amsterdam: John Benjamins Publishing Company.

Phillips, Alfred. 2003. *Lawyer's Language. How and why legal language is different*. London: Routledge, 83–99.

Poon, Wai Yee Emily. 2010. Strategies for Creating a Bilingual Legal Dictionary. *International Journal of Lexicography*, Vol. 23, No. 1, 83–103.

Pym, A. 1996. Venuti's Visibility. *Target* 8/2, 165–77.

Riley, Alison. 1995. The Meaning of Words in English Legal Texts: Mastering the Vocabulary of the Law – A Legal Task. *Law Teacher*, 29–30, 68–83. London: Sweet & Maxwell.

Saeed, John I. 2003. *Semantics*. 2nd ed. Oxford: Blackwell Publishing.

Šarčević, Susan. 1997, 2000. *New Approach to Legal Translation*. The Hague: Kluwer Law International.

Sinclair, John. 2007. Language and computing, past and present. In: *Evidence-based LSP. Translation, Text and Terminology*, edited by K. Ahmad and M. Rogers, 21–52. Bern: Peter Lang.

Skřejpek, Michal. 2007. Státní úřady a úředníci v antickém Římě. In: *Právnický stav a právnické profese v minulosti*. Praha: Havlíček Brain Team, 15–34.

Strandvik, I. 2012. Legal Harmonization Through Legal Translation: Texts that Say the Same Thing? In: *The Role of Legal Translation in Legal Harmonization*, edited by C.J.W. Baaij, Alphen aan den Rijn: Kluwer Law International, 25–50.

Stroud, F. 1890. *The Judicial Dictionary of Words and Phrases Judicially Interpreted*. London: Sweet & Maxwell, Limited.

Stroud, F. 1903. *The Judicial Dictionary, or words and phrases judicially interpreted, to which has been added statutory definitions*. 2nd ed. London: Sweet & Maxwell, Limited.

Thomas, Patricia. 1993. Choosing Headwords from Language-for-Special-Purposes LSP. Collocations for Entry into a Terminology Data Bank. Term Bank. In: *Terminology: Applications in Interdisciplinary Communication*, edited by H.S. Sonneveld and K.L. Loening, 43–68. Amsterdam: John Benjamins Publishing Company.

Tomášek, Michal. 1991. *Právo – interpretace a překlad*. Translatologica Pragensia V, Acta Universitatis Carolinae Philologica 4–5/1991, Praha: Karolinum, 147–54.

Tiersma, Peter and Solan, Lawrence (eds) 2012. *The Oxford Handbook of Language and Law*. Oxford, New York: Oxford University Press.

Tiersma, P. 2012. A History of the Languages of Law. In: *The Oxford Handbook of Language and Law*, edited by Peter M. Tiersma and Lawrence M. Solan, Oxford: Oxford University Press, 2012, 25.

Triebel, Volker, 2009. Pitfalls of English as a Contract Language. In: *Translation Issues in Language and Law*, edited by F. Olsen, A. Lorz and D. Stein, Basinstoke: Palgrave Macmillan, 147–81.

Venuti, L. 1995 (2008). *The Translator's Invisibility. A History of Translation*. London, New York: Routledge.

Watson, Alan. 2006. *Legal Transplants and European Private Law*, Belgrade: University of Belgrade retrieved from <http://www.alanwatson.org>

White, James Boyd. 1985. *Heracles' Bow: Essays On The Rhetoric & Poetics of the Law*. Madison: The University of Wisconsin Press.

White, James Boyd. 1994. *Justice as Translation. An Essay in Cultural and Legal Criticism*. Chicago, London: The University of Chicago Press.

Widdowson, Henry G. 1979. *Explorations in Applied Linguistics*. Oxford: Oxford University Press.

Chapter 9

# Multinational Legal Terminology in a Paper Dictionary?

Peter Sandrini

The intentional scepticism of the title expressed by the question mark at the end raises the question whether terminology from different legal systems can be conveyed successfully in a paper dictionary. The following draws on terminology theory and the specific character of legal reasoning and legal language in an attempt to settle the debate over the feasibility of presenting legal concepts from diverging legal traditions and their linguistic representations in an alphabetical, paper-bound dictionary.

Our arguments in support of this derive from the following central tenets of terminology theory:

1. the centrality of the concept
2. the interrelatedness of concepts
3. the principle of univocity.

In the following, these three basic beliefs of terminology theory will be discussed with special regard to what is meant by legal terminology and different legal traditions. The consequences for the compilation of terminological products will be assessed in the context of the current lexicographical approach to the representation of equivalence.

## Terminology

Terminology theory was founded long before lexicography started to deal with language for special purposes (LSP) (Picht 1998, 117) and many of its early researchers were not linguists but practitioners (for example Eugen Wüster, see Lang 1998). They felt the necessity to document and harmonise the terminology they were using in their specific disciplines so that communication could be optimised and strengthened within their working environment as well as at international level. This is why they were so concerned about the concepts of their disciplines: identical things must be named with the same words and words in foreign languages must refer to these same things. Therefore, language, words and terms are mere instruments to help experts in their communication about the concepts of their disciplines. From this starting point, terminology has looked for ways to control, systematise and master concepts and their denominations in the various subject fields by developing an adequate methodology (See also Wright 1991):

> Terminology has developed theories and methods that are distinguishable from those of its most related discipline, lexicology. Terminology deals with concepts and their designations, whereas lexicology deals with words and their meanings. Terminology produces conceptually-based resources, usually in the form of a database, whereas lexicology produces dictionaries. These two diametrically-opposed perspectives require equally distinct methodologies (http://www.ailia.ca/Terminology, accessed 7/2012).

## 1. Centrality of the Concept

As a consequence of the centrality of the concept, the basic unit of description in terminology is the concept, never a term or a word. This results in some fundamental differences between terminology and lexicology in terms of their methodology, as well as between terminography and lexicography in the layout of dictionaries, glossaries and term banks.

Terminology tries to analyse, document and describe the concepts of a specific discipline, in the case of legal terminology, the concepts of a branch of law or legal discipline. Discussions about legal language and the importance of language in law should not distract from the fact that legal concepts pre-exist and predate language, for example as codes of action, signs and ethical concepts (Sacco 2000). Law is a subject field and discipline in its own right, as Sacco, a well-known scholar of comparative law, put it: ‘Il diritto non ha bisogno della parola. Il diritto preesiste alla parola articolata’ (‘Law has no need of language. Law precedes the spoken or written word’) (Sacco 2000, 122). Legal concepts exist independently of language and assigning a term is arbitrary. As such, a term is the designation of a concept belonging to a specific legal subject field; it is, therefore, part of a Language for Special Purposes (LSP) or legal language: each term is a lexical unit, but not all lexical units are terms. Legal concepts represent units of knowledge that are part of a system of law which has evolved over time in a specific society. Mattila (2006) defines legal concepts as ‘crystallisations of legal rules’ (Mattila 2006, 105). Today such legal systems are confined to political entities, but there were times when Roman Law was common to all European countries, for instance, or Islamic Law was applied in many African and Arab political units.

Legal concepts, their definition and scope are essentially characterised by their being part of a legal system and as such they are defined by their legal context, that is, their relation to neighbouring concepts as well as their embeddedness in a specific legal setting. Terminology holds that concepts should be viewed from the perspective of a subject field. The relations between concepts of a certain subject field may be illustrated in graphical concept maps or represented as specific links in terminological products. In Law the subject field may be a specific branch of law, such as the law of successions, business law, electoral law and so on. It is, however, most important to determine the general framework of the legal system in which such a division can be made. Apart from a handful of internationally established branches of law, there is no general electoral law and hence no common or universal terminology, but only the electoral law of the USA, of Italy or of any other country-specific legal system.

This system-specificity, as de Groot/van Laer (2008, FN1) call it, brings forth a fundamental disparity between concepts of different legal systems, because every concept will be embedded in a system of other concepts of the same legal system, which may greatly differ from the apparatus of concepts of another legal system. Affiliation to a legal system is therefore the key parameter for legal terminology, more crucial than the language or subject field. It governs the process of establishing equivalences between concepts, since we may compare concepts belonging to different legal systems independently from the language of their terms: for example German vs Austrian vs Swiss hereditary law concepts in German only, but with regard to three distinct legal systems, or we may compile a terminology of succession law in German, Italian and French related to Switzerland, that is, within one legal system.

## 2. Interrelatedness of Legal Concepts

A legal system may be viewed as a network of beliefs, ideas and moral notions that govern a society. All legal concepts form part of this system and it is therefore of utmost importance in terminology to interconnect concepts and to represent them as part of a network of concepts. Full understanding of a legal concept and interpretation of its meaning may only be achieved by differentiating it from the concepts surrounding it and framing it on the basis of its function and position within a legal setting. Concepts act as constitutive elements of a legal solution to a social problem. A good dictionary should provide information on this interdependence of concepts. Indeed, it is a special characteristic of terminological products to include concept relations, either in the form of concept maps used as a tool that may be adjusted in the course of the research or as data categories that reflect the specific relation to a super-/co- or subordinate concept in term bases.

## 3. The Principle of Univocity

The third pillar of terminology concerns the relation between concept and term. The necessity for unambiguity and precision in LSP communication in the subject fields makes synonyms and homonyms an obstacle and the unambiguous assignment of a term to a concept the proper remedy accomplished either by linguistic usage, experts or terminology commissions. Univocity refers to the notion that each concept should be designed by only one term and one term should only refer to one concept. This would eliminate all cases of synonymy and homonymy/polysemy.

Many linguists have opposed this terminology principle, arguing that language cannot be standardised and that synonyms may be functional in LSP discourse (Temmerman 2000, 12). Wüster himself saw the principle of univocity not so much as an ideal state of terminology but rather as a goal to strive for, keeping in mind that it will always remain an impossible task: 'Auch in der Terminologie muss das Verlangen nach vollständiger Eindeutigkeit ein frommer Wunsch bleiben' (Wüster 1991, 79). (Even in terminology the quest for complete univocity must remain wishful thinking.) One of the most important functions of a terminological product or a dictionary is to convey the meaning of a legal concept as well as to present the term or terms used for it. In legal language, synonymy plays a major role only when different layers of language are used, as is the case in English, whereas polysemy and homonymy are more widespread: 'The phenomenon of polysemy is rather the rule than the exception in legal language' (Mattila 2006, 109). Univocity is of special importance in legal language as the precise understanding of normative concepts is a prerequisite for legal certainty. In legal language we have thus an intrinsic conflict between the broad applicability of a norm or a concept, which would require it to be as general as possible, that is, between vagueness on the one hand and legal certainty on the other, which would require precisely defined concepts (for a more detailed discussion of the notion of vagueness in normative texts, see Bhatia et al. 2005; for some insights into the notion of indeterminacy in terminology, see Antia 2007).

Although univocity seems to constitute a worthwhile goal for terminology projects in the sciences, it should be emphasised that in law the concept of univocity is confined to each individual legal system. This is important for languages that are used in more than one legal system: each country using German as a legal language, for example, chooses its own terms and would not let itself be restricted in its choice by the fact that another German-speaking country uses the same term in another context, that is, for a concept with other features. If legal terms are system-bound it makes no sense to pursue univocity internationally within one language.

## Functional Requirements for Legal Dictionaries

Who are the users of dictionaries and what are their needs or what kind of information do they need? We may identify three major user groups for legal dictionaries: translators who need to translate a legal text into another language, legal experts who need to understand a legal text from another legal system, lay persons needing to use a legal text in their everyday life as persons affected by contracts, online terms and conditions or other legal acts written in a foreign language.

The differences between those user groups with respect to legal dictionaries are smaller than their common requirements: all of the groups of users need to fully understand the legal concepts present in the source text, their legal implications and the way the concepts influence the meaning of the text. These concepts and their terms may be unfamiliar to them where they belong to a foreign legal system or the foreign terms refer to familiar concepts, in the case of a multilingual legal system. Both translators and legal experts establish a cognitive relation between the concepts in the foreign language text and the knowledge elements they are familiar with. Translators, for example, must be familiar with the legal system to which the concepts in the source text belong as well as the legal system to which the concepts in the target text belong.

## One Concept – One Entry

To help users understand legal terms it must be clear what concept the term is referring to. This is the main task of a work of reference, keeping in mind that understanding is the main requirement for any reader.

Terminography is concept-oriented. Each concept will be described and documented in a single entry with a specific set of data categories. The dictionary user is interested in the meaning of the concept within a specific legal topic, that is, the subject of the text they are trying to interpret. So the dictionary user is not looking for the general linguistic meaning of a term, nor for potential homonyms in general language or other subject fields, but principally for the specific legal concept that constitutes part of the cognitive structure of the text. A useful work of reference explains the concept as a knowledge unit within the legal system, it allows the user to access the concept using the term or using a hierarchical concept system or a knowledge classification which illustrates the network of relations within a legal system.

Starting from the recognition of the concept, a user may need to know all the terms that are used for this concept in one language and in a specific legal system. Synonyms refer to the same concept and belong to the same entry whereas homonyms are to be treated in different entries. This principle is very unfamiliar to multilingual dictionaries in general. So, for example, in the *Conte/Boss Dizionario giuridico ed economico* we find the entry:

> licenziamento m Entlassung f Kündigung f

where the two German terms refer to two distinct concepts in German Labour Law and the dictionary user is given no information that might help him/her to discriminate between them and determine which might be the correct solution for his/her particular text.

## Thorough Documentation of the Concept

The understanding or interpretation of the source text, a common need for all user groups of legal dictionaries, may differ between the groups only in terms of their extent (Engberg 2002, 376). There is, however, no doubt that translators need to interpret the source text to be able to make decisions about the target text.

Legal dictionaries must therefore convey the concept behind a term, they must be able to situate the legal concept within the framework of the legal system it belongs to. With regard to the first terminological principle, the centrality of the concept, an entry in a legal dictionary has to delineate what the term in question is referring to and in what context. An intensional definition with the properties of the legal concept or citing a definition from a statute may characterise the concept. To specify clearly what the entry is referring to, however, it is also necessary to indicate the legal system the concept belongs to and give information about its usage within a specified branch of law (Simonnæs 2010, 40). Such an entry would more or less resemble the data found in a monolingual specialised dictionary, with the exception that extensive encyclopaedic information would be kept to a minimum.

All the collected information about a concept is structured according to specific data categories. This can be attributed to the fact that terminology adopted the use of electronic media at a very early stage, so much so that today almost every terminographical product is computer-based, with paper output as a secondary format (Lauren, Myking and Picht 1998, 306). The importance of a thorough concept documentation is underlined by the multiplicity of terminographical data categories available; these are compiled in a particular database called ISOCAT (see isocat.org).

The question is where does the meaning of a legal text come from? Is there objective meaning or does meaning come from language and its use, that is, context? Much has been written about meaning in law and we will not enter into this debate here as it would divert from our main topic: what and how can paper dictionaries contribute to our understanding of legal texts? Nonetheless, a critical analysis of the concept of context seems important for our line of argumentation. Overall we agree that meaning as well as understanding is context-dependent:

> This means that the translator must be aware of the fact that he cannot depend solely on context-free knowledge of what specific words mean in legal texts. He must at all times discover what specific words and terms mean in the concrete situation. (Engberg 2002: 385).

The different aspects of context have been clearly set out by Melby and Foster who propose a five-part definition of the concept: co-text – the surrounding text within a specific document; chron-text – diachronic versions of the document; rel-text – related documents and other resources; bi-text – aligned bilingual information; non-text – real-world setting of a document including technical knowledge (Melby and Foster 2010). The meaning of specific words and terms in the concrete situation of a text comes from the function of the text, from its embeddedness in a specific legal context which is why the fifth type of context is the most relevant one from a conceptual perspective.

It is this legal aspect that can be covered in a lexicographical/terminographical product by the documentation of the concept. All other aspects of context are contingent upon the text and have to do with the concrete communicative situation, unknown and unpredictable to the terminographer or lexicographer.

## The Misconception of Equivalence

Decisions about which words and terms to use in a particular communicative event are based on situational parameters; in a multilingual setting equivalence is one of these. Multilingual paper dictionaries are based on equivalences insofar as each term or word from the source language has a direct counterpart in the other language(s). This might work within general language, but in a specialised environment such as legal language this approach seems inappropriate: 'Where the source and target language relate to different legal systems, equivalence is rare' and 'virtual full equivalence proves to be a problem' (de Groot and van Laer 2008, fn. 5). Given what we said about legal concepts and especially the terminographical principle of one concept per entry, equivalence between concepts originating from different legal systems becomes impossible:

> Where the concepts of two legal systems differ, the semantic domains of legal terms do not correspond with one another (Mattila 2006, 105).

De Groot and van Laer list two exceptions to this general principle or cases in which near-full equivalence may still occur between different legal systems: when there is a partial unification of legal areas with regard to the legal systems in question, or when a concept has been adopted from another legal system and still functions in the same way (de Groot and van Laer 2008, footnote 8). In all other cases it would be impossible to speak of equivalence in the terminological sense.

Terminology defines equivalence as the coincidence of conceptual characteristics. When all concept features overlap, the concepts are considered equivalents or the same, resulting in one concept with its defined set of characteristics, with equivalent terms in two or more languages: 'The preeminent goal of descriptive terminology is to describe relations between the concepts of a defined subject field and to identify the terms in two or more languages which designate one concept' (Cole 1991, 400). When we contrast concepts and their terms in law, we cannot identify a common defined subject field, since every legal system is a distinct reality. Furthermore, there can be no common concepts to identify, only idiosyncratic concepts to compare. Compilers of multilingual legal dictionaries are hard pressed to find substitutable equivalents.

Many dictionaries offer a list of equivalents without any indication as to their use or the context in which these terms are used:

> Räumung n (f) removal; vacating; clearance; eviction; evacuation;
>
> Bürgschaft n (f) surety; guarantee; guaranty; security; sponsorship; suretyship; warranty obligation (Schulte 2007).

This not only violates the principle of one entry per concept but also gives the misleading impression that any of these equivalents could be used. Such dictionaries lack a clear basis for establishing equivalence relations and this is indeed the most criticised aspect of legal dictionaries (de Groot and van Laer 2008, 1999; Sandrini 1996; Šarčević 1988).

Equivalence, however defined, cannot therefore form the basis for the comparison of concepts from different legal systems. Every legal system has its own tradition and each has undergone a unique historic evolution leading to singular notions and a specific array of concepts, which are classified according to idiosyncratic criteria, very different systematic and structural embeddings. Instead of equivalence in law we prefer to speak of comparison. When we cannot establish strict equivalence relations, we need information about the concepts in their legal environment, about differences, common traits in relation to the concepts of another legal system. In electronic media that information can be dealt with in additional data categories (Lauren, Myking and Picht 1999, 309). Strictly speaking, there should not be one common concept entry for concepts from different legal systems because there can never be complete equivalence: a judge, for instance, will have completely different competencies and responsibilities – even the exact moment of the birth or death of a person will be defined according to different criteria in each legal system.

The misconception of equivalence originates from the erroneous belief that a dictionary can suggest immediately substitutable equivalents. For a term to be used in a translation, however, a series of parameters have to be taken into consideration, parameters which relate to the text as well as to the communicative embeddedness of the target text. As we may deduce from the definition of context by Melby and Foster (2010), only the non-text part which refers to the legal embeddedness of a term can be prepared by the terminographer, as the remaining four parts of context are all subject to situational factors.

A realistic alternative would be to see the function of dictionaries or terminographical products as the provision of as much information as possible. In Law they should provide accurate legal information useful for the understanding of the source text and helpful for the decisions to be taken with regard to situation-dependent communicative factors while composing the target text.

## Comparative Approach

A comparative approach to legal terminology may provide just such information. It involves documenting the concepts and terms of one legal system and their structural interrelations independently from the concepts and terms of another legal system, as well as comparing the concepts to identify similarities and differences; for a detailed account of such an approach see Sandrini (1996, 1999 and 2009) and the implementation described by Våge (2010). The results of such a procedure would differ from a traditional dictionary entry by the complexity of the information about equivalence relations. While concept documentation data categories are well established in terminography as well as in lexicography, there is no general practice for documenting the complex relations between similar concepts. Some legal dictionaries – all of them are ranked amongst the best comparative dictionaries by de Groot and van Laer (2008) – use some sort of signs to describe the nature of the equivalence relation: the European Glossaries of legal and administrative terminology published by Heymanns, for instance, apply the following signs: = concepts and expressions are synonymous in the two languages; +/- concepts and expressions are comparable or similar; ≠ no equivalents, explanations and translations underneath.

These signs are certainly useful and express the results of a comparative approach; a summary check of the occurrence of each sign in one of the glossaries of this series (Local Government Terminology, Vol. 14) reveals the importance of such a comparison in law: out of a total of 472 entries, 203 or 43 per cent have no equivalents (≠), 72 or 15 per cent are more or less similar concepts (+/-) and 197 or 42 per cent direct matches (=). Even if we take the cases of direct equivalence for granted (which is highly disputable in the case of two different legal systems), for more than half of the concept entries in this dictionary, the user would need additional information, either about the reason why there is no equivalent in the other legal system or on how the other legal system has solved the underlying social problem and with which concepts and terms, and what differentiates the legal concepts which are marked as more or less similar. Explanations and commentaries are essential in this regard, even more than the subdivision of equivalence relations into the three categories expressed by arbitrary signs. However, the representation in a dictionary of the results yielded from such a comparative approach is problematic.

Offering literal translations and other less common solutions when a direct translation is not possible, such as neologisms, and so on, as described in de Groot and van Laer (2008), is not the main focus of conceptual terminology for two main reasons: first, the use of foreign language terms by translators or text producers is heavily influenced by communicative parameters and the function of the text in which they are to be used and therefore outside the scope of systematic terminography; and secondly, if the user is provided with the appropriate legal knowledge of the target legal system and has a good command of the target language, it should be no problem for him/her to find adequate linguistic solutions.

Nevertheless, these may be indicated where appropriate but always with the necessary specification that it is a translation of the source language term or a neologism and not a naturally occurring term of the target legal system.

## Conclusions

In light of the above we may formulate the general requirements for the documentation of legal concepts and their respective terms. As a matter of course, every piece of research should adhere to the common principles of the verifiability of information, such as providing sources and references and the necessary diligence in documenting each concept (de Groot and van Laer 2008). The specific information units that the documentation of a legal concept requires are:

1. indication of the legal system
2. indication of the branch of law
3. indication of relevant legal sources
4. explanation of the concept
5. provision of the term and alternative terms used to denote this concept in the same legal system
6. indication of related concepts within the same legal system.

These requirements need to be applied to all concept entries for each legal system that is covered by the dictionary. A major advantage of such a conceptual approach and the application of the principle of 'one concept – one entry' is the attribution of each term to a specific concept as well as to a specific legal context within a specific legal system so that the user has a clear image of the structural embeddedness of the concept and the terms used to designate it. This may be implemented in a dictionary without problems as attested by the number of good monolingual works of reference on the market. For multinational legal terminology, however, the concept entries must be compared and contrasted, a process which requires the following relevant information: indication of the most closely related concept in the target legal system; explanation of differences and similarities where major differences exist; a knowledge link (concept hierarchy, legal classification) to the relevant concepts should be provided.

To represent these requirements in a traditional paper dictionary is a very challenging task, especially the flexible handling of equivalence relations. If the terms and concepts of both legal systems are recorded independently – a longstanding requirement in terminography (see Arntz, Picht and Mayer 2002, 225) – and equivalent relations are recorded afterwards, a lot of possible relationships may occur that have to be documented. Modern tools, such as data banks and digital media, offer better options to represent flexible entry structures and hyperlinks between legal systems avoiding direct equivalents; for a comprehensive model of a legal terminological data bank, see Sandrini (1996). In particular, the linking features of hypertext and structural flexibility of digital formats such as XML allow for the adequate representation of comparative legal terminology. In the presence of such technical aids and the vast publication possibilities of the World Wide Web, a legal dictionary in paper format no longer seems appropriate to fulfil the requirements of demanding users and the days of the paper law dictionary are definitely numbered.

**References**

Bassey Edem Antia, *Indeterminacy in Terminology and LSP: Studies in Honour of Heribert Picht* (John Benjamins 2007).

R Arntz, H Picht and F Mayer, *Einführung in die Terminologiearbeit* (Olms 2002).

V Bhatia and J Engberg and M Gotti and D Heller (eds), 'Vagueness in normative texts' (*Linguistic Insights* 23, Peter Lang 2005).

WD Cole, 'Descriptive Terminology: Some theoretical implications' (*Meta* 36, 1991) 16, 22.

G Conte and H Boss, *Dizionario giuridico ed economico – Wörterbuch der Rechtsund Wirtschaftssprache* (5th edition, C.H. Beck 2001).

Gerard René de Groot, 'Translating Legal Informations' in Giuseppe Zaccaria (ed.), Übersetzung *im Recht Translation in Law* (Jahrbuch für juristische Hermeneutik Yearbook of Legal Hermeneutics 2000) 131, 149.

Gerard-René de Groot, Conrad JP van Laer, 'The Quality of Legal Dictionaries: an assessment' (Maastricht Faculty of Law Working Paper 2008/6).

Jan Engberg, 'Legal Meaning Assumptions – What are the Consequences for Legal Interpretation and Legal Translation?' (*International Journal for the Semiotics of Law Revue Internationale de Sémiotique Juridique*, 15 2002) 375, 388.

Friedrich Lang, 'Eugen Wüster – His Life and Work until 1963' in E Oeser and C Galinski (eds), *Eugen Wüster: His Life and Work, an Austrian Pioneer of the Information Society* (TermNet 1998) 13, 26C.

Lauren and J Myking and H Picht (eds), *Terminologie unter der Lupe. Vom Grenzgebiet zum Wissenschaftszweig* (TermNet 1998).

Heikki E Mattila, *Comparative Legal Linguistics* (Ashgate 2006).

A Melby and C Foster, 'Context in translation: Definition, access and teamwork' (*Translation & Interpreting* 2, 2010) 1, 15.

Heribert Picht (ed.), *Modern Approaches to Terminological Theories and Applications* (Peter Lang 2006).

Heribert Picht, 'Terminology and Specialised Communication' in E Oeser, C Galinski (eds), *Eugen Wüster: His Life and Work, an Austrian Pioneer of the Information Society* (TermNet 1998) 117, 131.

Rodolfo Sacco, 'Language and Law' in Giuseppe Zaccaria (ed.), *Übersetzung im Recht Translation in Law* (Jahrbuch für juristische Hermeneutik Yearbook of Legal Hermeneutics 2000) 113, 129.

Peter Sandrini, *Terminologiearbeit im Recht. Deskriptiver, begriffsorientierter Ansatz vom Standpunkt des Übersetzers* (IITF Series 8, TermNet 1996).
Peter Sandrini, 'Legal Terminology. Some Aspects for a New Methodology' (*Hermes Journal of Linguistics* 22, Aarhus School of Business 1999) 101, 112
Peter Sandrini, 'Der transkulturelle Vergleich von Rechtsbegriffen' in S Šarčević (ed.), *Legal Language in Action: Translation, Terminology, Drafting and Procedural Issues* (Globus 2009) 151, 165.
Susan Šarčević, 'The Challenge of Legal Lexicography: Implications for Bilingual and Multilingual Dictionaries' in M Snell Hornby (ed.), *ZüriLEX '86 Proceedings. Papers at Euralex International Congress* (Narr 1988) 307, 314KW.
K-W Schulte, A Lee and E Paul, *Real Estate Dictionary – Wörterbuch Immobilienwirtschaft* (IZ Immobilien Zeitung Verlagsgesellschaft mbH. 2007).
Ingrid Simonnæs, 'Grundlegendes zur zweisprachigen Fachlexikographie aus der Sicht des Fachübersetzers' (*Synaps* 25 2010) 33, 44.
Rita Temmerman, *Towards New Ways of Terminology Description: The Sociocognitive Approach* (John Benjamins 2000).
Ole Våge, 'Legal Concepts in aquaculture in Norwegian and Chilean Spanish: a brief discussion on two approaches' (*Synaps* 25 2010) 45, 51.
Sue-Ellen Wright, 'Lexicography v Terminology', *ASTM Standardization News*, December 1991, 40, 45.
Eugen Wüster, *Einführung in die allgemeine Terminologielehre und terminologische Lexikographie* (Romainstischer Verlag 3rd edn 1991).

Chapter 10

# Database of Legal Terms for Communicative and Knowledge Information Tools

Sandro Nielsen

> If we were to combine the best features of the monolingual and the bilingual dictionaries, we should produce a much more flexible teaching aid. Such a work would be possible now in book form – and how much more possible when electronically accessed reference works are the norm.[1]

## 1. Introduction

Law dictionaries provide help to many people in many types of situation. Legal practitioners, scholars and law students often consult monolingual dictionaries because they need to understand words and phrases found in texts; professional and student translators often consult bilingual dictionaries in search of help to complete translation tasks; and anyone may look up legal words in dictionaries in order to acquire knowledge about legal topics they have come across, whether in their professional or private capacities. Until the 1990s, these dictionaries were exclusively printed books, but now many are available in various electronic forms and, therefore, a closer look at recent developments in theoretical and practical lexicography concerning Internet dictionaries may help lay the foundation for the future.

Advanced online dictionaries can give users access to data related directly to the specific needs users have in different situations. However, two recent studies examine a number of specialized online dictionaries and conclude that they do not provide optimal access to their data.[2] The dictionaries examined do not properly

1 Beryl Atkins, 'Monolingual and Bilingual Learners' Dictionaries: A Comparison', in C.J. Brumfit (ed.), *Dictionaries, Lexicography and Language Learning*, Oxford, Pergamon Press (in association with the British Council), 1985, 15–24, p. 22.

2 Verónica Pastor and Amparo Alcina, 'Search Techniques in Electronic Dictionaries: A Classification for Translators' (2010) 23(3) *International Journal of Lexicography* 307; Pedro A Fuertes-Olivera and Sandro Nielsen, 'Online Dictionaries for Assisting Translators of LSP Texts: The Accounting Dictionaries' (2012) 25(2) *International Journal of Lexicography* 196. See also Gerard-René De Groot and Conrad J.P. van Laer, 'The Dubious Quality of Legal Dictionaries' (2006) *International Journal of Legal Information*, 34(1); Dennis Kim-Prieto and Conrad J.P. van Laer, 'The Possible Dream: Perfecting Bilingual

distinguish between the different types of situation in which help is needed and, therefore, tend to provide masses of (frequently irrelevant) data. By focusing on the needs of users in specific types of situation, legal lexicographers can allow users to access and retrieve data that satisfy a specific type of need and ensure that the data are presented in such a way that users can easily convert them into useful information. This involves analysing, the functions of law dictionaries, the lexicographically relevant needs of users, the types of data needed by users in different situations, as well as the ways in which users have access to these data. Examples from an on-going project at the Department of Business Communication, Aarhus University, Denmark, to develop a database for a set of online law dictionaries are called upon to illustrate the general argument.

## 2. Introducing the Project

The digitalization of information activities and information tools is a factor that has greatly influenced lexicography. One consequence of this general trend is that printed dictionaries will gradually be replaced by online dictionaries. In today's knowledge and information society we are constantly exposed to huge amounts of data from many different sources, in particular the Internet, and this information blitz will likely continue in the future. Online dictionaries compete with Internet search engines as providers of data (and hence information), but Internet search engines tend to provide too many results from searches in an immense environment of unstructured data, and the results are often irrelevant to searches for specific information. One way in which lexicographers can overcome this problem is to develop theories and principles that allow them to design and produce online dictionaries that give users the opportunity to access structured data with targeted searches and enable compilers to present search results in structured ways that tell users exactly what they need to know.

When describing a project involving an online dictionary, lexicographers should start by determining the dictionary function(s). This is an appropriate place to begin for two reasons. First, the dictionary function(s) chosen by the lexicographers provides the basis for all other lexicographic decisions; including the initial selection of entry words, the selection of data types and the final presentation of the data. Second, lexicographers should determine the basic needs of the intended users and attempt to match those needs with the dictionary function(s). This is in line with modern lexicographic principles, which do not see dictionaries as linguistic constructs but regard print and online dictionaries as information tools that have been designed to fulfil one or more functions that are

Law Dictionaries by Distinguishing Better Examples from Bad' (2011) *Social Science Research Networking Papers* <http://ssrn.com/abstract=1859400> accessed 15 July 2012.

related to specific types of usage situations[3] (the nature of dictionary functions is examined in detail in Section 4).

The dictionary project discussed can be summarized as follows. It aims to develop a database that can serve as the core of a set of two monolingual and two bilingual dictionaries designed to help specific types of users to understand Danish and English legal texts, write legal texts in Danish and English, translate Danish legal texts into English and vice versa and acquire knowledge about Danish and English legal matters. The intended user groups consist of Danish lawyers (practitioners and scholars), professional translators and law students. These three groups all need help in general types of situation involving Danish and English Law and in which law dictionaries may provide help, for example representing clients in international contexts, reading legal textbooks and writing legal essays in English. At the time of writing (November 2012), the project has reached the end of phase one, which establishes the lexicographic foundation on which the database and dictionaries will be built.

By adopting a lexicographic approach to dictionary-making rather than a linguistic approach, it is possible to provide a useful definition of dictionaries within the field of law. Law dictionaries – whether print or electronic – are information tools which provide help to intended users in general types of communicative and cognitive situations relating to (in this particular case Danish and English) law. In order to create such information tools, it is relevant to study the lexicographic principles underlying the work.

## 3. The Data Repository for the Dictionaries

At the heart of any online dictionary lies the database. This is particularly evident when dictionaries are regarded as technology-based information tools, and in order to make good online dictionaries, lexicographers should build their work on a sound theoretical foundation. When talking about online dictionaries, we often have in mind a database consulted by users from an interface that gives direct access to the database and its articles. The database contains records' headed by entry words and with fixed data fields containing, for example, definitional, grammatical and syntactic data. Users who consult these 'database dictionaries' are presented with the record for the entry word searched for, usually in the form of a traditional dictionary article: database and dictionary are one and the same thing.

However, the technological options available enable lexicographers to design dictionaries with different overall structures. Nielsen and Almind discuss a set of fully operational accounting dictionaries and explain that online dictionaries

3 Sandro Nielsen, 'LSP lexicography and typology of specialized dictionaries' in Gerhardt Budin, Christer Laurén and John Humbly (eds), *Language for Special Purposes. An International Handbook* (de Gruyter forthcoming).

can be designed as complex lexicographic tools with three main components.[4] The first one is a database with specially selected data that have been structured in a way that ensures easy access to and retrieval of data. This type of database is divided into discrete data fields each containing a specific type of data, and examples include fields that contain entry words, fields that contain definitions, fields that contain grammatical data (for example inflectional paradigms) and fields that contain collocations and phrases. These fields are connected through links establishing a relationship between the field containing a specific entry word and the field with the appropriate definition, the field with the appropriate grammatical data and so on. The important point is that this type of relational database enables lexicographers to present users with different search options and results that match user needs.

Secondly, the database may serve more than one dictionary. For instance, a database may serve as the core of both a defining dictionary and a text production dictionary. The database and the dictionary will appear to users as one entity, but compilers should treat them as two separate and interacting components. The dictionary thus includes a user interface giving access to data and a database that functions as an electronic repository of structured data.

The third component is a search engine operating as an intermediary between the user interface and the database. This component allows users to search in the individual data fields in the database, retrieve the relevant data and present them according to a setup chosen by the compilers, that is, compilers can adopt different setups for different users and different dictionary functions. Defining dictionaries will show, for example, entry words and definitions, whereas text production dictionaries will show, for example, entry words, definitions, inflectional paradigms, collocations and phrases. In this type of structural setup, the database, the search engine and the dictionary together form a whole which is *the* dictionary.

A lexicographic basis with three main components has both practical and theoretical implications. One is that the database may serve several dictionaries, each with its own search engine that allows users to make targeted searches in specific data fields. Furthermore, online dictionaries may contain several independent lexicographic sections, as the search engine can give direct access to dictionary sections that support the function(s) and use of dictionaries, for instance user guides, subject-field sections that give a carefully arranged introduction to the field of law, sections providing help to translate linguistic structures and genre conventions, and sections with translated statutes.[5] Finally, online dictionaries based on complex

4 Sandro Nielsen and Richard Almind, 'From Data to Dictionary' in Pedro A Fuertes-Olivera and Henning Bergenholtz (eds), *e-Lexicography: The Internet, Digital Initiatives and Lexicography* (Continuum 2011). See also Dennis Spohr, 'A multi-layer architecture for "pluri-monofunctional" dictionaries' in Pedro A Fuertes-Olivera and Henning Bergenholtz (eds), e-Lexicography (Continuum 2011).

5 Sandro Nielsen, *The Bilingual LSP Dictionary. Principles and Practice for Legal Language* (Gunter Narr 1994) 85–104; Henning Bergenholtz and Sandro Nielsen, 'Subject-

relational databases have no alphabetically arranged wordlists in the traditional sense, because they let compilers fill in the data fields in random order, allow users to access data in the individual data fields and enable compilers to present the search results in various ways such as traditional dictionary articles or as mere lists of collocations and phrases (for further examples, see Section 6). This means that an advanced online dictionary is supported technically by an output device that arranges the data retrieved from the database according to type, and presents them in a predetermined order that matches user needs. These practical and theoretical challenges call for a set of principles that can guide compilers of law dictionaries.

## 4. The Theory Gives Special Attention to User Needs

A theoretical basis with focus on user needs and possible lexicographic responses is an appropriate means for developing modern information tools. Here, the function theory of lexicography provides a framework within which to place the dictionaries.[6] Bergenholtz and Tarp define a dictionary function as 'the satisfaction of the specific types of lexicographically relevant needs that may arise in a specific type of potential user in a specific type of extra-lexicographical situation'.[7] So before they put data into the database, lexicographers should identify the desired output of dictionaries and work their way backwards from user needs to database entries.

Dictionaries are designed for various functions that represent types of usage situation. In some situations users need information for acts of communication. One example is where lawyers are writing texts, either in their native language or in a foreign language, and they want to consult their dictionary in order to find help to complete the writing task. Language staff, such as translators, revisers and

---

field Components as Integrated Parts of LSP Dictionaries' (2006) 12(2) *Terminology* 281; Pedro A Fuertes-Olivera, 'Systematic introductions in specialised dictionaries' in Sandro Nielsen and Sven Tarp (eds), *Lexicography in the 21st Century. In honour of Henning Bergenholtz* (Benjamins 2009); Sandro Nielsen, 'Specialised Translation Dictionaries for Learners' in Pedro A Fuertes-Olivera (ed.), *Specialised Dictionaries for Learners* (de Gruyter 2010); Sandro Nielsen, 'Online Law Dictionaries: how to provide help for EFL text production by law students' (2012) 3–4 *Fachsprache/Journal of Specialized Communication*, 112–24.

6 Henning Bergenholtz and Sven Tarp, 'Die moderne lexikographische Funktionslehre. Diskussionsbeitrag zu neuen und alten Paradigmen, die Wörterbücher als Gebrauchsgegenstände verstehen' (2002) 18 *Lexicographica* 253; Sandro Nielsen and Lise Mourier, 'Design of a Function-based Internet Accounting Dictionary' in Henrik Gottlieb and Jens E Mogensen (eds), Dictionary Visions, Research and Practice (John Benjamins 2007); Sven Tarp, 'Functions of Specialised Learners' Dictionaries' in Pedro A Fuertes–Olivera (ed.), *Specialised Dictionaries for Learners* (de Gruyter 2010).

7 Henning Bergenholtz and Sven Tarp, 'LSP Lexicography or Terminography? The lexicographer's point of view' in Pedro A Fuertes-Olivera (ed.), *Specialised Dictionaries for Learners* (de Gruyter 2010) 30.

copy-editors, in legal offices may be revising or editing texts written by lawyers in their native language or a foreign language and consult dictionaries to find help. Similarly, law lecturers correcting essays or grading examination papers may need to check something in a dictionary, either related to linguistic or factual matters. Professional translators often use bilingual dictionaries when translating legal texts from or into their native language. Both bilingual and monolingual law dictionaries may be used by lawyers and students reading texts and who need to consult a dictionary in order to understand a word or a phrase. These types of usage situations are all catered for by dictionaries, and the relevant dictionary functions are called *communicative functions*.

Other dictionary functions are independent of on-going communicative acts. Lawyers and law students may want to acquire general knowledge about something related to law or legal language in order to broaden their knowledge bases. Legal practitioners and language staff may want to acquire specific knowledge about a particular topic, for instance the inflectional pattern of an irregular verb or the correct spelling of a legal phrase in Latin. Finally, lawyers and professional translators may want to learn something specific about language usage so that they will be prepared for discussions with colleagues, presentations of papers, interpreting in court and so on. These types of usage situations are also catered for by dictionaries and the relevant dictionary functions are called *cognitive functions*, because dictionaries offer assistance in situations where users are deriving and verifying propositional knowledge as well as acquiring factual and/or linguistic knowledge.

The identification of these two general types of function enables lexicographers to make multifunctional law dictionaries. As indicated above, the types of situation in which the planned dictionaries are intended to provide help are communicative and cognitive, which mirror the functions of the dictionaries,[8] which are to:

- provide help to understand Danish and English legal texts;
- provide help to write legal texts in Danish and English;
- provide help to translate legal texts into and from Danish and English;
- provide help to acquire general and specific knowledge about legal and linguistic matters in Danish and English.

It is important to note that usage situations occur in what is referred to as an extra-lexicographic environment. For example, lawyers who are writing texts are in an extra-lexicographic environment, that is, an environment that exists independently of dictionaries, as they are writers of texts and, at this point, merely potential dictionary users. They may encounter a problem related to legal text production and think they can find a solution in a dictionary at some point during the writing process. When consulting the dictionary, they have entered the lexicographic environment as actual dictionary users, and once they have found the help they

8 See also Lev V. Ščerba, 'Towards a general theory of lexicography' (1995) 8(4) *International Journal of Lexicography*, 314–50.

need, they leave the lexicographic environment and go back to writing their texts in the extra-lexicographic environment. This sequence of events is likely to be repeated several times until the writing task has been completed satisfactorily.

Communication activities within the field of law often involve several types of actors. Legal texts written by lawyers in their native or a foreign language are often subject to a quality assurance process undertaken by linguists who proof and revise texts. Similarly, legal texts translated into the native language of translators are often subject to a quality assurance process undertaken by lawyers, who see to it that the translations are factually and terminologically correct. This means that online dictionaries designed to provide help in legal communicative and cognitive situations need databases that contain the appropriate types of data, and the next step for lexicographers is to link usage situations and user needs to user types.

The various types of competence of intended dictionary users play a significant role, because competences may either help users or place them at a disadvantage in a specific situation. The levels of competence indicate which lexicographically relevant information needs the intended users have and provide valuable guidance for selecting the data necessary for responding to such needs.[9] The intended user groups of the planned legal dictionaries can be specified as:

- Legal experts and semi-experts
- Professional translators
- Law students.

These are diverse groups and their members have different cultural, factual, linguistic, translation and writing competences; the dictionaries therefore need to contain data that help users whose competences are inadequate. The function theory of lexicography can guide lexicographers in their attempt to identify user competences and one way to do so is through user profiling. Bergenholtz and Nielsen suggest that user competences can be characterized by answering a list of questions like the following:[10]

- Which language is their native language?
- At what level do they master their native language?
- At what level do they master a foreign language?
- How extensive is their experience in translating between the languages in question?
- What is the level of their general cultural and factual knowledge?

---

9 Sandro Nielsen, *The Bilingual LSP Dictionary. Principles and Practice for Legal language* (Gunter Narr 1994) 8–12; Henning Bergenholtz and Uwe Kaufmann, 'Terminography and lexicography. A critical survey of dictionaries from a single specialized field' (1997) 18 *Hermes – Journal of Linguistics* 91.

10 Henning Bergenholtz and Sandro Nielsen, 'Subject-field Components as Integrated Parts of LSP Dictionaries' (2006) 12(2) *Terminology* 281, 285.

- At what level do they master the subject field of law?
- At what level do they master legal language in their native language?
- At what level do they master legal language in the foreign language?
- At what level do they master writing legal texts in their native language?
- At what level do they master writing legal texts in the foreign language?

The answers to these questions will indicate which general types and levels of competence the intended users of a dictionary have and enable lexicographers to put data into the dictionary that will help users whose competences are insufficient. It is practically impossible to identify and group the individual competences of each potential dictionary user, so general characteristics of ideal types of users will suffice, at least at the preliminary stage of the dictionary project.[11] It is reasonable to assume that, as an ideal type, legal experts and semi-experts generally have a considerable factual knowledge of their own legal system but small to medium knowledge of facts in the foreign legal system concerned, that they have a small to medium linguistic competence in relation to a foreign language and little or no translation competence, that they have medium to high competence in writing native-language legal texts and little or no competence in writing general and legal texts in a foreign language. Professional translators have a considerable general linguistic competence and a medium to high competence in legal language, factual knowledge of law ranging from small to in-depth, considerable translation competence and considerable competence in writing general and legal texts in their native language as well as a foreign language. Law students can generally be assumed to have small to medium competence in all listed cases and will therefore share many levels of competence with the two other groups. Consequently, professional translators and law students will need more data on factual legal matters in the two systems than legal experts and semi-experts, whereas lawyers and law students will need more data that can help them with linguistic, writing and translation problems. All user groups will need data on conceptual differences between terms and their equivalents as well as legal specifics in the foreign culture, as they cannot be expected to possess such specific knowledge. As a result, several types of data warrant consideration in order to satisfy the needs of dictionary users with asymmetric competence and knowledge levels.

## 5. Selecting Function-specific Data

When choosing entry words for law dictionaries, lexicographers should base their selection criteria on dictionary functions. A study of Swedish specialized language shows that terms account for less than 20 per cent of the words in legal

11 Jonathan Grix, *The Foundations of Research* (Palgrave Macmillan 2004) 23.

texts,[12] which indicates that dictionaries should not only contain terms but several parts of speech relevant to the communicative and cognitive functions described in Section 4 above. Nouns are obvious candidates for selection including single-word units, multi-word units and proper names (for example acquittal, bankruptcy order, company limited by guarantee, Court of Justice of the European Union). The dictionaries should also include other parts of speech, as these are relevant for writing, editing and translating legal texts: adjectives, adverbs and verbs, including phrasal verbs (for example implied, impliedly, repudiate, set forth). Abbreviations should also be included (for example, FSA, that is, Financial Services Authority in the UK) as should spelling variants (for example authorise, authorize; encumbrance, incumbrance; movable property, moveable property) because they are likely to occur in legal texts read or written by the intended user groups.[13] In order to provide the required help, users will be able to search for inflected forms of all entry words. Furthermore, each dictionary contains collocations, phrases, examples and notes on usage restrictions, and the bilingual dictionaries contain their translations into Danish and English, respectively, in order to help users write, translate and understand legal texts as well as acquiring general or specific knowledge about legal matters.

When preparing the basis for law dictionaries, it is important to remember that law is fundamentally a jurisdiction-dependent domain. Each jurisdiction structures its legal system in a way that suits only that jurisdiction and the legal language used reflects the structure of the individual system. The term *English* used in legal contexts may, therefore, not only refer to the legal framework of a particular country, such as US English or UK English, but may refer to varieties of English used in communication involving different legal systems. In international contexts a variety of English, which can best be described as international English, is used in treaties and conventions, such as the United Nations Convention on Contracts for the International Sale of Goods (CISG). These texts aim to describe regulatory frameworks in a language that can be understood by and is acceptable to as many as possible no matter which legal system they belong to. Online law dictionaries should therefore specify their geographical and jurisdictional constraints and in this project English refers to the language used in the following jurisdictions and indicating their abbreviated codes: England and Wales (EN), Scotland (SCOT), the EU (EU), the USA (US) and international English (INT). The importance of this distinction may be illustrated by an example: in England and Wales a *public company* can also be referred to as a *public limited company* and a *cwmni cyfyngedig cyhoeddus*, whereas the equivalent term in EU legal acts is *public limited liability company*.[14]

---

12 Christer Laurén, *Fackspråk. Form, innhåll, funktion* [*Specialized Language. Form, content, function*] (Studenterlitteratur 1993) 99–101.

13 Rupert Haigh, *Legal English* (2nd edn, Routledge-Cavendish 2009) 6–20.

14 Under section 59 of the Companies Act 2006 (UK), a company registered in Wales can choose either the English term or its Welsh equivalent in its name. In the US there may be terminological differences between the federal and state systems, for example the US Supreme

The entire process of selecting data, not merely entry words, is governed by the *principle of relevance*. In connection with lexicographic selection, relevance means the quality of being directly connected with the subject field in question, the function(s) of the dictionary, the types of usage situation in which the dictionary is intended to be used and the various competences of intended users.[15] Relevance is a qualitative characteristic as it can be used to collect and collate *useful lexicographic data*, that is, data that directly support a dictionary function. For example, data showing the inflectional paradigms of entry words and equivalents are relevant because of the insufficient linguistic competences of intended users when editing, translating and writing legal texts. Similarly, collocations and phrases are selected because they are important when writing and translating legal texts (and often because they are difficult to translate from Danish into English or vice versa), and examples are selected because they specifically show how to write and translate legal texts as well as provide data for knowledge acquisition. The concept of relevance thus helps lexicographers decide which data types to include in dictionaries to support specific dictionary functions, and how to present the data in a way that satisfies user needs.

Based on the competences revealed by the profiling of intended users, the following data types have been selected for inclusion in the database:

a. Entry word (including homonym index where relevant)
b. Grammatical data relating to entry word (inflection, countability, active and passive forms)
c. Equivalent(s)
d. Grammatical data relating to equivalent(s) (inflection, countability, active and passive forms)
e. Definition (including language code and polysemy index where relevant)
f. Collocations (short and long combinations of words but not full sentences)
g. Examples (full sentences)
h. Antonyms and synonyms (addressed to entry word and/or equivalent)
i. Source (reference and/or link)
j. Grammar note (addressed to entry word or equivalent)
k. Usage note (addressed to entry word or equivalent)
l. Contrastive note (conceptual differences between entry word and equivalent)
m. Cross-reference (to relevant data)

Court is the highest court in the federal system, whereas the New York Supreme Court is a court of first instance. The document initiating ordinary civil proceedings is called a claim form in England and Wales, an initial writ (sheriff court) and summons (Court of Sessions) in Scotland, and usually a complaint in the US; in divorce proceedings the functionally equivalent document is called a petition in England and Wales as well as in many US states.

15 Pedro A Fuertes-Olivera and Sandro Nielsen, 'The Dynamics of Terms in Accounting: What the Construction of the Accounting Dictionaries Reveals about Metaphorical Terms in Culture-Bound Subject Fields' (2011) *Terminology* 17(1) 157, 162.

As illustrated below, the data set presented on a given dictionary consultation depends on the search option selected by users.

## 6. Search Options Reflect User Needs

Users can access the data in the planned law dictionaries according to their needs. By focusing on the needs of users in various types of usage situation, lexicographers can ensure that the data satisfy a specific type of user need and that the data are presented in such a way that they can easily be turned into useful information. This goal can be achieved by making dictionaries that offer users search options related to the situations users are in when consulting the dictionaries. In a particular type of usage situation, users will need help of a specific kind and consult the dictionary they believe is most likely to help them. The monolingual law dictionaries will offer users the following kinds of assistance:

- Help to understand a term
- Help to write a text where the expression is known
- Help to find a term where the meaning is known
- Help to acquire knowledge.

The bilingual law dictionaries will offer the following kinds of assistance:

- Help to translate a term
- Help to translate a collocation or phrase
- Help to acquire knowledge.

The law dictionaries will be designed so that they are easy to use, no matter what type of help is sought. When they consult a dictionary, users go to the dictionary website where the search engine will access the database and retrieve the relevant data. These data will be presented to users on the screen in a predetermined order and format. Even though the project has only reached the end of phase one, the following discussion illustrates how the dictionaries will work when fully developed and how the database will interact with the dictionaries. The examples below are prototypes and exemplify how the search engine can be manipulated by lexicographers to retrieve the types of data that users need in various usage situations.

Law students who want to know the meaning of the intellectual property law term *trademark* found in an English legal text may consult the *English Law Dictionary* and select the option ‘help to understand a term’. The search engine will make a targeted search, that is, in predetermined data fields only, for the term in the database in the fields containing inflectional data. This data type includes the canonical form of entry words as well as their inflected forms and this allows users to search for inflected word forms, so that they can merely copy the term they encounter in the texts. The search engine will retrieve the data addressed to the search word, which for this particular function includes the entry word, homonym index (if any), polysemy index (if any) and definition. Figure 10.1 shows the search result and the prototypical presentation in the dictionary.

**trademark**

Definition
A trademark is a sign that is used by a trader as a mark to distinguish the trader's goods or services from those of other traders. Signs can be words, letters, numerals, designs, the shape of goods, or their packaging. The owners of trademarks have the right to the exclusive use of the trademark in connection with their goods and services.

**Figure 10.1 Definitions help law students understand legal terms**

The search result in Figure 10.1 contains definitional data that are intended to help students understand terms found in legal texts: the meaning of the term searched for, as this was what the students wanted. However, definitions written exclusively for legal experts will often be too difficult to understand for all intended users, so the definitions have been written with the identified user competences in mind (see Section 4). The aim is to write definitions that accurately reflect the meanings of the terms as defined by legal experts and in order to focus on explaining the meanings of terms, definitions will generally answer two questions: What is it? What is its function? The overall principle is that of referential focus, which implies that definitions in the legal domain have narrow and specific referential focus, because they contain the conceptual features that are found in the legal domain in contextualized communication.[16] Finally, all definitions are written as full sentences using natural language so as to minimize users' information costs.[17]

Lexicographic databases can contain different types of definitions. It is theoretically as well as practically possible to have different versions of each definition in the sense that the definition of a term can be written in three versions: one for legal experts, one for semi-experts, and one for students. However, this procedure was not adopted for this project, because the levels of factual and English language competences of the intended user groups are deemed sufficient to understand the definitions.[18] Furthermore, it is possible

16 Roy Harris and Christopher Hutton, *Definition in Theory and Practice. Language, Lexicography and the Law* (Continuum 2007) 210–215.

17 Sandro Nielsen, 'The Effect of Lexicographical Information Costs on Dictionary Making and Use' (2008) 18 *Lexikos* 170.

18 Sandro Nielsen, 'Function- and user-related definitions in online dictionaries' in: F.I. Kartashkova (ed.), *Ivanovskaya leksikografischeskaya shkola: traditsii i innovatsii*

to have English definitions and their translations into the native language of intended users, in this case English definitions of English legal terms and the Danish translations of these definitions,[19] but the lexicographers opted out of this solution for the above reasons. Finally, the decisive factor is not whether definitions are long or short but whether they contain data that satisfy user needs. In order to achieve this goal, lexicographers may consider whether all data have to be placed in definitions or whether complementary and supplementary data should be placed in separate subject-field sections to which users are directed through cross-references with embedded links.[20] This will reduce the length and complexities of definitions.

Important aspects in connection with understanding the meaning of legal terms are homonymy and polysemy. In order to properly understand a legal term, users must be able to identify the correct meaning of words that are spelt identically (homographs)[21] but have different referential foci. The syntagmatic criterion 'part of speech' is used to distinguish between homographs belonging to different word classes, for example the noun *contract* and the verb *contract*, whereas morphological criteria are generally used in cases of polysemy, so that nouns that can be both countable and uncountable are treated as polysemes, for example, the noun *liability* ('being legally responsible for something' (uncountable) and 'amount of money owed by a company or person' (countable)). The implementation of these principles is illustrated in Figure 10.2.

In a few cases the criterion is referential focus, for example where the meaning is subject to jurisdictional constraints: the term *deed* can be a general term referring to legal documents meeting specific formal requirements (EN) and it can be a specific term referring to documents transferring ownership of land (US).[22] Since the intended users cannot be expected to know this, the dictionary should explicitly inform them of such instances. Definitions are often regarded as help to understand texts but they also support other dictionary functions.

Lawyers may require assistance to write texts in English and need to know how they can use the term *trademark*. In this case, they will select the option 'help

---

[*Ivanovo School of Lexicography: Traditions and Innovations*]: *A Festschrift in Honour of Professor Olga Karpova* (Ivanovo State University 2011).

19 Deny Kwary 'Adaptive hypermedia and user-oriented data for online dictionaries: a case study on an English dictionary of finance for Indonesian students' (2012) 25(1) *International Journal of Lexicography* 30. See also Sandro Nielsen, *The Bilingual LSP Dictionary. Principles and Practice for Legal Language* (Gunter Narr 1994) 254.

20 Sandro Nielsen, *The Bilingual LSP Dictionary. Principles and Practice for Legal language* (Gunter Narr 1994) 98–104; Henning Bergenholtz and Sandro Nielsen, 'Subject-field Components as Integrated Parts of LSP Dictionaries' (2006) 12(2) *Terminology* 281.

21 Homographs are words that have the same written form and constitute a subgroup of what is called homonyms, which are words with the same written or spoken form. Words with the same spoken form are called homographs.

22 Bryan A Garner, *A Dictionary of Modern Legal Usage* (2nd edn, Oxford University Press 1995).

**contract** 1 *noun*

1 Definition
A contract is a legally binding agreement made orally or in writing between two or more parties. The terms of the contract create legally enforceable obligations for the parties to do or not to do something.

2 Definition
A contract, or construction contract, is a legally binding agreement in which the parties have specified their particular obligations regarding the construction, repair, renovation or restoration of an asset or a combination of assets.

3 Definition
The term contract refers to the legal relationship between the parties to a contract, i.e. the terms of the contract itself as well as the case law and statute law governing the relationship.

**contract** 2 *verb*

Definition
To contract means to enter into a legally binding agreement that creates obligations for the parties to do or not to do something.

**Figure 10.2 Presentation of homonyms and polysemes**

to write a text where the expression is known' as they have identified the term they want to use. The database will be searched for three types of data: inflection, collocation and example. The following data types addressed to the search word will be retrieved (as applicable): the entry word, homonym index, polysemy index, definition, inflection, collocations, examples, synonyms, antonyms. Lawyers will be presented with the result shown in Figure 10.3.

The data types in Figure 10.3 support the function of providing help to write legal texts in English. The definition is necessary to determine that the word has the right meaning for the context and the inflectional data, the synonym, usage note, collocations and examples support the writing process. It can generally be said that the writing of texts involves a planning stage, an execution stage and a finalization stage, and for practical purposes Nielsen suggests that lexicographers should focus on providing help in the execution and finalization stages.[23] The execution stage involves the writing of drafts, the design of texts, as well as copyediting, which concerns checking texts to make sure that grammar and spelling rules are complied with, as well as revision, which ensures that terminology is consistent and that texts are free from errors.[24] These activities concern lexis and syntax (for example terminology and phraseology), grammar and syntax (for example coherence and cohesion) and pragmatics (for example communicational inferences and presuppositions). Dictionaries intended to provide help with writing legal

23 Sandro Nielsen, 'Monolingual accounting dictionaries for EFL text production' (2006) 12 *Ibérica* 49.

24 Carolyn D Rude (ed.), *Technical Editing* (Longman 2002) 15–16; Brian Mossop, *Revising and Editing for Translators* (St. Jerome 2007) 23–8.

**trademark** *noun* ‹a trademark; the trademark; trademarks; the trademarks›

Definition
A trademark is a sign that is used by a trader as a mark to distinguish the trader's goods or services from those of other traders. Signs can be words, letters, numerals, designs, the shape of goods, or their packaging. The owners of trademarks have the right to the exclusive use of the trademark in connection with their goods and services.

Synonyms
trade mark

Usage note
In US English the preferred spelling is in one word, i.e. trademark, while the preferred spelling in EN and EU English is in two words: trade mark.

Collocations
abandon a trademark
apply to register a trademark
exclusive right to use a trademark
non-use of a trademark
register a trademark
renew a trademark
surrender a trademark
the owner of the trademark
the rights conferred by the trademark

Examples
The proposal does not address substantive rules related to trademarks.
The trademark was struck off the register.

**Figure 10.3 Data helping lawyers to write legal texts when the expression is known**

texts should contain such types of data that help lawyers and language staff to successfully complete the individual steps of the writing process.

The *English Law Dictionary* can also assist users in cognitive situations. Lawyers, translators and students may want to acquire general or specific knowledge about the company law concept *uncalled share capital* and select the search option 'help to acquire knowledge'; this option will present all data addressed to the entry word. The search engine will make a targeted search in the database in two types of data, namely inflection and definition, and retrieve the relevant data types (as applicable): the entry word, homonym index, polysemy index, inflection, definition, synonyms, antonyms,, collocations, examples, cross-references (including homonymy and polysemy indices) sources (including links) and usage notes (Figure 10.4).

The definition in Figure 10.4 explains the meaning of the term accompanied by an example; and the provision of synonyms and antonyms help lawyers, translators and students place the term *uncalled share capital* in its terminological hierarchy in the legal universe. The grammatical data show linguistic properties that are relevant to lawyers, translators and students, because the data explain the inflectional restrictions of this term. The cross-references (*See also*) include two

**uncalled share** capital ‹no indefinite article, the uncalled share capital, no plural›

Definition EN

The uncalled share capital of a company is that part of the issued share capital that shareholders have not paid because it has not been required to be paid, i.e. called up.

Synonyms

uncalled capital

Antonyms

called-up share capital

Collocations

make a call on uncalled share capital

the uncalled share capital of the company

Examples

The amount of any uncalled share capital must be shown separately.

See also

issued share capital

share capital

Sources

Companies Act 2006, s. 547.

**Figure 10.4 Data giving help to acquire knowledge**

terms with embedded links and when they click these links, users are directed to the articles *issued share capital* and *share capital* where relevant additional data can be found; similarly, the item indicating the source of the definition is clickable as it contains an embedded link and will send users to a website where the Companies Act 2006 (UK) is found. There users can find more information about the entry word. Where relevant, lexicographers should consider including cross-references through links to specially prepared dictionary sections dealing with such matters as (comparative) introductions to the field of law, guidance on translating domain-specific linguistic structures and genre conventions and informative illustrations (for example pictures, podcasts and videos).

Lawyers, translators and students who are writing or translating legal texts may not know the exact word to use because they only know the meaning of what they want to write and therefore consult the *English Law Dictionary*. Those who want to use the correct word for the meaning 'to annul something' can type this phrase into the search box and select the search option 'help to find a term where the meaning is known'. The search engine will search the following data types in the database: definition, usage note, synonym and antonym. Users will be provided with the following data types (as applicable): the entry word, homonym index, polysemy index, definition, inflection, collocations, example, synonym and antonym, as shown in Figure 10.5.

Figure 10.5 contains two appropriate words and the data help lawyers, translators and students in the execution and finalization stages of writing texts by showing inflection (active and passive verb forms), collocations and example sentences. For instance, the dictionary makes it clear that the correct way of expressing the meaning 'to annul a will' is to write or say 'to revoke a will'. The search could also have been

**revoke** *verb* ‹revokes; revoked; has revoked; revoking› passive ‹is revoked; was revoked›
Definition
To revoke means to annul something that you have previously done.
Collocations
intention to revoke
revoke an offer
revoke a will
with the intention to revoke the will
Examples
An offer cannot be revoked if it indicates that it is irrevocable.
I hereby revoke all former testamentary dispositions made by me.

**withdraw** 1 *verb* ‹withdraws; withdrawn; has withdrawn; withdrawing› passive ‹is withdrawn; was withdrawn›
Definition
To withdraw means to annul something that you have previously done or to no longer be part of something.
Collocations
withdraw an acceptance
withdraw an offer
withdraw from the contract
Examples
An offer may be withdrawn if the withdrawal reaches the offeree before or at the same time as the offer.
You have the right to withdraw from the contract within a period of 14 calendar days.

**Figure 10.5 Data providing help to find a term where the meaning is known**

performed with Boolean operators, for example 'annul + will', and the dictionary would then have presented only the data relating to *revoke*.

The interaction between the database and the bilingual dictionaries is similar to that between the database and the monolingual dictionaries. It should be pointed out that searches are conducted in and the results retrieved from one and the same database, whether dictionaries are bilingual or monolingual. Danish users who translate legal texts may need to know how to translate the English term *trademark* and consult the *English-Danish Law Dictionary*. They will select the search option 'help to translate a term', and the database is searched for one type of data: inflection. The output unit will present data addressed to the entry word and the equivalent (as applicable): the entry word, homonym index, polysemy index, language code, definition, inflection, synonym, antonym, collocations and examples, all addressed to the entry word; and equivalent as well as inflection, contrastive note, usage note, translation of collocations, translation of examples, synonym and antonym, all addressed to the equivalent. Furthermore, there may be cross-references to relevant terms and an indication of a source with an embedded link. Figure 10.6 shows the search result for *trademark*.

**trademark** *noun* ‹a trademark; the trademark; trademarks; the trademarks›
Definition
A trademark is a sign that is used by a trader as a mark to distinguish the trader's goods or services from those of other traders. Signs can be words, letters, numerals, designs, the shape of goods, or their packaging. The owners of trademarks have the right to the exclusive use of the trademark in connection with their goods and services.
Synonyms
trade mark

**varemærke** *substantiv* ‹et varemærke; varemærket; varemærker; varemærkerne›
Collocations
abandon a trademark
opgive et varemærke
apply to register a trademark
indgive anmeldelse om registrering af varemærke
exclusive right to use a trademark
eneret til et varemærke
non-use of a trademark
manglende brug af et varemærke
register a trademark
registrere et varemærke
renew a trademark
forny et varemærke
surrender a trademark
give afkald på et varemærk
the owner of the trademark
mærkeindehaveren
the rights conferred by the trademark
de rettigheder, der er knyttet til varemærket
Examples
The proposal does not address substantive rules related to trademarks.
Forslaget berører ikke de materielle bestemmelser om varemærker.
The trademark was struck off the register.
Varemærket blev udslettet.

**Figure 10.6 Data providing help to translate a legal term**

Figure 10.6 shows how specific data types can benefit professional translators, and lawyers, who translate legal texts into Danish. In addition to an equivalent, English collocations and examples with their translations into Danish are types of data that assist users in translating legal texts. Moreover, the data presented in Figure 10.6 benefit translators and lawyers who write, proof and revise Danish legal texts based on information and knowledge acquired from reading English texts.

Translators often need help to combine terms with other words to form collocations and phrases in a foreign language. Danish translators who have to translate word combinations containing the company law term *præferenceaktie* may consult the *Danish-English Law Dictionary* and select the option 'help to translate a collocation or phrase', and the database is searched for two data types: collocation and example. The dictionary will show the following types of data addressed to the search word (as applicable): the entry word, homonym index, polysemy index, definition, collocations and phrases with translations, language code, examples with translations, equivalent(s) to entry word and inflection of equivalent(s). Queries for word combinations containing a specific term search in all collocations and examples in the database, and it is therefore likely that the searches will find the term in collocations and examples addressed to the term searched for as well as in collocations and examples addressed to other entry words. Figure 10.7 shows the relevant data types presented by the dictionary relating to collocations and phrases addressed to the search word.

**præferenceaktie** *substantiv*
Definition
Præferenceaktier er aktier, der giver aktionærerne en fortrinsret, hyppigst en fortrinsstilling ved udbetaling af udbytte, men ofte uden tilknyttet stemmeret.
**preference share** ‹a preference share; the preference share; preference shares; the preference shares›
**preferred stock** US ‹a preferred stock; the preferred stock; no plural›
Collocations
indløse præferenceaktier
redeem preference shares
redeem preferred stock (US)
præferenceaktier med en kort restløbetid på overtagelsestidspunktet
preference shares acquired within a short period of their maturity
preferred stock acquired within a short period of their maturity (US)
præferenceaktier med fast indløsningsdato
preference shares with a specified redemption date
preferred stock with a specified redemption date (US)
sælge præferenceaktierne til underkurs
sell the preference shares at a discount
sell the preferred stock at a discount (US)
tilbagekøbe præferenceaktier
buy back preference shares
buy back preferred stock (US)
udstede præferenceaktier
issue preference shares
issue preferred stock (US)
Examples
Investorerne blev kompenseret for deres køb af præferenceaktierne til overkurs.
The investors were compensated for purchasing preference shares at a premium.

**Figure 10.7 Data providing help to translate collocations and phrases**

One point to note in Figure 10.7 is that all Danish collocations and phrases are translated twice to match the two English equivalents offered. The unmarked equivalent and translations of collocations are generally unrestricted in use, whereas the equivalent and translations marked with the jurisdictional code US have restricted usage range. This helps translators to adapt their translations of collocations and phrases to the expected readers, and the data also help lawyers and translators draft, transfer meaning, copy edit and revise texts in the foreign language. As the search for help to translate collocations and phrases is likely to find the search word in word combinations addressed to terms other than the one in Figure 10.7, the dictionary will present such additional results along the lines illustrated in Figure 10.8.

**præferenceudbytte** *substantiv*
Definition
Udbytte, der udbetales til ejere af præferenceaktier, kaldes for præferenceudbytte.
**preference dividend** ‹a preference dividend; the preference dividend; preference dividends; the preference dividends›
**preferred dividend** US ‹a preferred dividend; the preferred dividend; preferred dividends; the preferred dividends›
Collocations
præferenceudbytte til kumulative præferenceaktier
the amount of preference dividends for cumulative preference shares
the amount of preferred dividends for cumulative preferred stock (US)

**nominel værdi**
Definition
Den nominelle værdi er det beløb, der står skrevet på et finansielt instrument, fx en obligation eller en aktie.
**nominal value** ‹a nominal value; the nominal value; nominal values; the nominal values›
Examples
De privatejede præferenceaktier havde en nominel værdi på 100 mio. EUR.
The privately-owned preference shares had a nominal value of EUR 100 million.

**Figure 10.8 Specific results of searches for collocations and phrases**

The first half of Figure 10.8 shows one instance of the search word found in a collocation addressed to the term *preference dividend*, and in order to keep the focus on the translation of collocations and phrases containing the search word, the dictionary will only show the relevant one and not any other collocations addressed to the entry word *preference dividend*. The second half of Figure 10.8 shows one instance with the search word found in an example sentence addressed to the term *nominal value*. The focus is still on translating examples containing the search word and, therefore, any other example sentences addressed to the entry word *nominal value*, and which do not contain the search word, are not presented by the dictionary.

As the legal domain is jurisdiction-dependent, Danish terms may not have any (direct) equivalents in English. Nevertheless, lawyers, translators and students may have to write about such legal concepts in or translate them into English and in order to help them, the *Danish-English Law Dictionary* offers suggested translations supplemented by contrastive notes explaining that the English equivalents offered are suggested translations, as illustrated in Figure 10.9.

**fordringshavermora** *substantiv* ‹ingen ubestemt artikel; fordringshavermoraen; ingen flertal›

Definition:
Fordringshavermora betegner et forhold hos fordringshaveren (kreditoren), der bevirker, at debitor forhindres i at præstere sin ydelse og dermed blive frigjort for sin forpligtelse over for fordringshaveren.

**failure in accepting performance** DK

Kontrastiv anmærkning:
I engelsk og amerikansk ret findes der ingen direkte ækvivalent til det danske begreb. Udtrykket 'failure in accepting performance' er et forslag til oversættelse, som dækker betydningen af den danske term. Efter dansk ret har en kontraktpart ikke en ubetinget pligt til at acceptere modpartens tilbudte, kontraktmæssige ydelse i modsætning til anglo-amerikansk ret, hvor et sådant forhold vil blive betragtet som misligholdelse.
EN and US law have no direct equivalent to the Danish concept. The expression 'failure in accepting performance' is a suggested translation covering the meaning of the Danish term. There is no obligation in Danish law for a party to a contract to accept the proper performance offered by the other party to the contract, whereas Anglo-American law will treat such a situation as breach of contract.

**Figure 10.9 Suggested translation supplemented by contrastive note**

In contrast to the rules of Anglo-American Law, there is no absolute obligation in Danish Law for a contractual party to accept the performance offered by the other party to the contract. When they occur, such events are treated as breach of contract in Anglo-American Law, and therefore an explanatory equivalent is offered so that lawyers, translators and students can write about and translate such concepts. The position is somewhat different in international sales law, as Articles 85–88 of the United Nations Convention on Contracts for the International Sale of Goods (CISG) contain provisions similar to the Danish rules. Furthermore, the suggested equivalent is marked DK, which does not mean that the equivalent is a Danish term but that the equivalent is a translation of a specific Danish concept. Finally, the contrastive note is not only written in Danish (for the benefit of Danish users) but also translated into English, thereby providing further help with writing about, translating and explaining a specific Danish legal concept in a foreign language.

Like the monolingual ones, the bilingual law dictionaries can assist users in cognitive situations. Lawyers, students and translators may want to acquire general or specific knowledge about the company law concept *turnover* and select the search option 'help to acquire knowledge'. The database will be searched for two types of data, namely inflection and definition, and all data addressed to the entry word will be retrieved (as applicable): the entry word, homonym index, polysemy index, definition, inflection, cross-references (including homonymy and polysemy indices), collocations, examples, synonyms, antonyms, sources, grammar notes, usage notes, contrastive notes, equivalent(s) and translations (Figure 10.10).

**turnover** *noun* ‹a turnover; the turnover; no plural›

Definition EN
The turnover of a company is the total sales revenue of goods and services falling within the company's ordinary activities over a specific period less any trade discounts, value added tax, and other taxes based on the sales revenue. The turnover is a basic element in calculating the profit or loss of a company for a specific period.

Synonyms
revenue INT, US
sales US

**nettoomsætning** *substantiv* ‹en nettoomsætning; nettoomsætningen; nettoomsætninger; nettoomsætningerne›
Definition
Et selskabs nettoomsætning er salgsværdien af produkter og tjenesteydelser fra selskabets ordinære aktiviteter i en bestemt periode med fradrag af prisnedslag, merværdiafgift og anden skat, der er direkte forbundet med salgsbeløbet. Nettoomsætningen udgør grundlaget for at beregne et selskabs over- eller underskud i en bestemt periode.

Synonyms
omsætning

Collocations
a decline in turnover
et fald i nettoomsætningen
an increase in turnover
en stigning i nettoomsætningen
operating profit as a percentage of turnover
driftsresultat i procent af omsætningen
turnover for the year
årets nettoomsætning
turnover in terms of volume
den mængdemæssige nettoomæstning
turnover per employee
nettoomsætning pr. medarbejder

Examples
The reporting system may be limited to enterprises with an annual turnover of more than EUR 100 million.
Rapporteringssystemet kan begrænses til at omfatte virksomheder med en årlig omsætning på over EUR 100 mio.

Sources
Companies Act 2006, s. 474(1)(i)
Årsregnskabsloven, bilag 1, C11

**Figure 10.10 Data providing help to acquire knowledge**

The prototype of data presentation intended for knowledge acquisition in Figure 10.10 is a rather simple example. However, it shows how it is possible to combine Danish and English data in a meaningful way. First of all, the two definitions explain the meaning of the entry word in English and its equivalent in Danish and reveal that the Danish and English terms are virtually identical in meaning and function. Secondly, the two English synonyms are accompanied by jurisdictional codes, thereby comparing the EN term with US and INT terminology. Finally, the sources tell users that Danish and English Law are structured differently in that the relevant statutory provisions are found in the Companies Act 2006 (UK), whereas the Danish rules are found in the Danish Financial Statements (Consolidated) Act 2011.

## 7. Concluding Remarks

On-line law dictionaries based on traditional linguistic and text linguistic approaches do not fully satisfy the needs for help lawyers, students and professional translators have in specific types of situation. This state of affairs can be remedied by re-assessing the practical and theoretical foundations of online dictionaries in light of the technical options available for on-line information tools combined with modern lexicographic principles. The above discussion indicates that the legal database is a repository of structured data serving online dictionaries that search for data in databases, retrieve the relevant data and present them to users in predetermined ways. Lawyers, students and translators can thus access the data through targeted searches relating directly to the problems they need to solve, because search engines are designed according to dictionary functions, that is, the type of help dictionaries can provide in certain types of situation. The dictionaries have both communicative and cognitive functions in that they help users to solve problems in communicative situations such as understanding, writing and translating legal texts and help users acquire knowledge about general or specific legal matters in cognitive situations. The theoretical foundation and practical implications of this type of online law dictionaries enable lexicographers to provide dictionaries that are practical information tools that satisfy the needs of lawyers, students and translators.

Chapter 11

# Defining Ordinary Words for Mundane Objects: Legal Lexicography, Ordinary Language and the Word *Vehicle*

Christopher Hutton[1]

## Introduction

This chapter concerns the category of 'ordinary language' as it is understood within the linguistic culture of law. Ordinary language, as contrasted with legal language (*facially overbroad*, *estoppel*, *ejusdem generis*), is represented in this discussion by the class of terms for mundane objects. That class in turn is represented here by the word *vehicle*: 'A means of conveyance provided with wheels or runners and used for the carriage of persons or goods; a carriage, cart, wagon, sledge, or similar contrivance' (*OED*).[2] Just as there exists (presumptively) a phenomenon known as 'ordinary language' and a more specialized linguistic variety known as 'legal language', so there are general as opposed to legal dictionaries. And just as there are (presumptively) words and things, so there are dictionaries (legal or general) as against encyclopaedias. The dictionary deals primarily with conceptual meaning ('lexical definition'), whereas the encyclopaedia describes or defines things, people and events ('real definition').

Such distinctions involve important methodological and theoretical considerations, but they are also drawn as a matter of practicality. A medium-sized or even large dictionary of English cannot do justice to every term of art in the common law tradition. Legal dictionaries may aim to define terms according to their general understanding within law, or may seek to cover much more fully the doctrinal framework, including a survey of relevant case-law. But even an encyclopaedic dictionary of legal terminology cannot define every word or phrase or phenomenon that was ever the subject of legal discussion. General dictionaries likewise vary in their understanding of, and attitude to, encyclopaedic knowledge. They differ, for example, in respect of the inclusion of proper names. *Webster's* 1923 edition included a page of pictures of 'typical forms' of automobiles ('roadster',

1 I hereby acknowledge the support of Hong Kong RGC GRF award HKU 745412H.

2 *Oxford English Dictionary*, available at http://www.oed.com. Almost every aspect of this definition is potentially problematic in a legal context, for example whether a vehicle is primarily for the carrying of people or people *and* goods.

'speedster', 'four-passenger roadster', 'runabout' and so on), as well as two highly detailed diagrams ('sectional elevation' and 'plan') of the workings of the gasoline automobile, with accompanying technical explanation.[3] Some definitional styles incorporate scientific classifications and other frameworks which are not strictly conceptual – if by 'conceptual' is meant the basic understanding of a word available to the ordinary speaker.

High lexicographical practice, such as that associated with the *Oxford English Dictionary* (*OED*), is analogous to legal drafting, in that the lexicographer seeks to define and map out a semantic space in a coherent and comprehensive fashion, even at the cost of the proliferation of complex subcategories and definitional detail. The *OED* entry for *vehicle* is organized into sections (I, II), sub-sections (1, 2, 3) and sub-sub-sections (a, b, c). This style of lexicography creates texts which are analogous in appearance and arrangement to statutes. Like comprehensive lexicography, legal drafting aims for 'all-embracing and mutually exclusive definitions' intended 'to cover the whole ground'.[4] The COBUILD dictionary marks a conscious break with this scholastic-legalistic tradition of lexicography: 'A *vehicle* is a machine such as a car, bus, or truck which has an engine and is used to carry people from place to place'.[5] The normativity of the dictionary and that of the law are in many respects analogous, and in adjudicative practice frequently intertwined. The act of definition, whatever the style of dictionary, inevitably acquires a flavour of legalism.

## The Scope of the Legal Dictionary

In its origins the law dictionary was a guide to the technical jargon of law, either as a subcategory in a lexicon of 'hard words' or 'difficult terms'[6] or in works of 'difficult and obscure' terms devoted to law exclusively.[7] The law dictionary might

---

3 W.T. Harris and F. Sturges Allen, eds, *Webster's New International Dictionary of the English Language* (Merriam 1923). The 1934 *Webster's* has two pages of pictures, distinguishing 'early automobiles' from current models, but no technical diagrams (William A. Neilson, ed., *Webster's New International Dictionary of the English Language* (2nd edn Merriam 1934, reprinted 1958).

4 *Canadian National Railway Co. v Board of Commissioners of Public Utilities* [1976] 2 SCR 112, 135.

5 http://dictionary.reverso.net/english-cobuild/vehicle, accessed 10 October 2012.

6 Thomas Blount, *Glossographia, or, A Dictionary Interpreting all such Hard Words of Whatsoever Language now Used in our Refined English tongue* [...] (1661); John Coles, *An English Dictionary: Explaining the Difficult Terms that are Used in Divinity, Husbandry, Physick, Phylosophy, Law, Navigation, Mathematicks, and Other Arts and Sciences* (Peter Parker 1676).

7 John Cowell, *The Interpreter or Booke containing the Signification of Words wherein is set foorth the True Meaning of all, or the most Part of such Words and Termes, as are mentioned in the Lawe Writers, or Statutes of this Victorious and Renowned Kingdome,*

be intended primarily for the practitioner, but many were also marketed at lay people who were encouraged to obtain a 'critical knowledge' of matters 'relating to their lives, properties, and other essential interests'.[8] The history of the legal dictionary is characterized by large-scale interbreeding among reference works which have undergone complex incorporations, acquisitions and mergers. The primary object of analysis has often been previous dictionaries: 'I am indebted to Burrill, as Burrill was to Spelman'.[9] But systemic inertia has been punctuated by genuine interventions involving methodological and conceptual re-engineering. This has taken the form of radical purging, as whole domains of terms or sub-domains are deemed irrelevant to the 'true' law dictionary or outmoded for the practitioner. Reference works such as *Black's Law Dictionary*, inaugurated in 1891,[10] survive, but they become brands behind which the content is periodically reinvented so as to create what is in effect a completely new work.[11]

Certain law dictionaries are in essence glossaries of word-for-word equivalences; others have encyclopaedic ambitions, to include 'not only a definition and explanation of the terms used in the science of the English law, but also a general summary of the theory and the practice of the law itself'.[12] The inclusion of 'older and obsolete words' has been defended as making a particular legal dictionary more useful to beginners, by giving the novice reader a sense of the history and evolution of legal language, even if this meant including apparently 'dead' material.[13] It is far from clear in any case which legal terms are current and which are conclusively out

---

*Requiring any Exposition or Interpretation* (John Legate 1607); Thomas Blount, *Nomo-Lexikon, a Law-Dictionary Interpreting such Difficult and Obscure Words and Terms as are Found either in our Common or Statute, Ancient or Modern Laws* (Thomas Newcomb 1670).

8 Richard Burn, *A New Law Dictionary: Intended for General Use, as well as for Gentlemen of the Profession* (2 vols, London 1792), v; Thomas Potts, *A Compendious Law Dictionary, Containing Both An Explanation Of The Terms And The Law Itself: Intended For The Use Of The Country Gentleman, The Merchant, And The Professional Man* (1815); Sir Thomas Edlyne Tomlins, *A Popular Law-Dictionary, Familiarly Explaining the Terms and Nature of English law: Adapted to the Comprehension of Persons not Educated for the Legal Profession, and Affording Information Peculiarly Useful to Magistrates, Merchants, Parochial Officers, and Others* (Longman, Orme, Brown, Green, & Longmans 1838).

9 J. Kendrick Kinney, *A Law Dictionary and Glossary for the Use of Students but Adapted also to the Use of Profession at Large* (Callaghan 1893), iv.

10 Henry Campbell Black ed., *Black's Law Dictionary* (West 1891).

11 See Bryan A. Garner ed., *Black's Law Dictionary* (9th edn, West 2009) and 'Legal Lexicography: A View from the Front Lines' (2003) 19 *English Today* 33.

12 William Sheppard, *An Epitome of All the Common & Statute Laws of This Nation Now in Force: Wherein More Than Fifteen Hundred of the Hardest Words or Terms of the Law are Explained* (Lee and Pakeman 1656); Timothy Cunningham, *A New and Complete Law-Dictionary, or, General Abridgement of the Law* (Crowder 1764–65); Sir Thomas Edlyne Tomlins, *The Law-Dictionary: Explaining* the Rise, Progress, and Present State of the English Law; defining and Interpreting the Terms or Words of Art (6 vols, Riley 1811), iii.

13 J. Kendrick Kinney, *A Law Dictionary and Glossary for the Use of Students but Adapted also to the Use of Profession at Large* (Callaghan 1893), iii.

of date: 'Obsolescence is an unreliable quality'.[14] No term or text in the history of the common law is ever definitively irrelevant for all conceivable purposes. The tension between conceptual and encyclopaedic approaches to definition is particularly acute. Conceptual distinctions in legal terminology evidently must relate at some level to questions of legal doctrine. Yet an encyclopaedia of law with pretensions to completeness is a huge and complex undertaking. In its encyclopaedic mode, the 'legal' could include both a doctrinal analysis of the questions behind every legal term and an account of every object, process or phenomenon to which law at one time or other has directed its gaze. Pretensions to encyclopaedic coverage can also be resented, in that the overlay of detail and analysis obscures the simple, immediate guidance that a dictionary should offer: 'A Dictionary is not consulted for an essay or treatise on a particular theme, but to answer a sudden doubt, or explain a present difficulty, as to the proper meaning of a certain technicality'.[15]

These are far from ephemeral issues in legal lexicography, as the preface to Cowell's *Interpreter* of 1607 illustrates. The work included 'not onely of words belonging to the art of the lawe, but of any other also, that I thought obscure, of what sort soever; as Fish, Cloth, Spices, Drugs, Furres, and such like'. The lawyer should profess 'true Philosophy' and 'should not be ignorant (if it were possible) of either beastes, foules, or creeping things, nor of the trees from the Cedar in Lebanon, to the Hyssop that springeth out of the wall'.[16] The contrast between the 'linguistic' and the 'encyclopaedic' was stressed by Burrill in his *New Law Dictionary* of 1850. The dictionary was concerned to 'illustrate the *language* of law' and it therefore excluded 'superadded' encyclopeadic summaries of the law relating to a particular entry. It allowed more space for the proper definition of 'law terms' which included 'not only technical terms or "words of art", properly so called', but also 'ordinary words which have been used in technical senses, or which have been made the subjects of judicial or legislative construction or definition'.[17] This reflected the superior lexicographic tradition of his forerunners, Cowell's *Interpreter* and in particular Spelman' *Glossarium Archaiologicum* of 1664.[18] Similarly, Stimson's *Glossary* of 1881 defined its aim as that of 'giving in common English an explanation of the words and phrases, English as well as Saxon, Latin or French, which are of common technical use in the law'. It was purely a work of definition, not 'a compilation of law, like the larger dictionaries'. The definitions were to reflect 'the popular and usual acceptation of each phrase, in much the same

14 Editor's preface, *Glossary: Scottish Legal Terms, Latin Maxims and European Community Legal Terms* (Butterworths/Law Society of Scotland, 1992), 3.

15 John Jane Smith Wharton, *The Law Lexicon or Dictionary of Jurisprudence Explaining All the technical Words and Phrases Employed in the Several Departments of English Law* (M'Kinley & Lescure 1848), iii.

16 John Cowell, *The Interpreter* (John Legate 1607).

17 Alexander Burrell, *A New Law Dictionary and Glossary* [...] (Voorhies 1850), v.

18 Henry Spelman, *Glossarium Archaiologicum: Continens Latino-Barbara, Peregrina, Obsoleta, & Novatae Significationis Vocabula* (2nd edn, Ward 1664).

rough and general shape in which it would stand in the mind of the trained lawyer', adding occasionally 'a hint of its more correct and exact meaning'.[19]

In the preface to the *Dictionary of American and English Law with Definitions of the Terms of the Canon and Civil Laws* of 1888 the editors argued that none of the existing reference works was in the strict sense 'a dictionary of the law'. One was a 'mere glossary', chiefly of interest to the 'antiquarian and philologist'; another contained 'a large amount of matter foreign to its avowed object' and was more a digest of court practice. A third was incomplete, and 'the attempt to embrace the definitions of words and phrases to be found in the reported cases' had been subject to severe criticism. In their view, a practical law dictionary should contain three kinds of information: (1) definitions of technical terms of the Common, Civil and Canon law; (2) Latin maxims with translations; (3) a guide to how the courts have construed words and phrases 'in ordinary use', showing how the law, 'urged on by the necessities of the case', has 'imported meanings more or less different from the vernacular sense'. For the third class of information, the authors had drawn on an unpublished MS prepared by a certain John Brown entitled *Adjudged Words and Phrases*.[20]

*The American and English Encyclopedia of Law* of 1887, consistent with its insistence that it was not a law dictionary, distinguished the legal encyclopaedia, which supplies 'in convenient form the whole body of modern law', from the law dictionary (Merrill 1887).[21] The original *Black's Law Dictionary* of 1891 noted more ambivalently that the work did not 'trench upon the field of the English dictionary', but that however 'vernacular words and phrases, so far as construed by the courts, are not excluded from its pages'.[22] The chief aim of the dictionary was comprehensive coverage.[23] There was in addition an evident need in the United States to knit together the different state jurisdictions and the recording and commenting upon definitions within statutes and case-law was a flourishing genre. The phrase 'adjudged words and phrases' appeared in the title of Winfield's compendium of definitions 'taken from judicial decisions'.[24] *The Judicial Interpretation of Common Words and Phrases* of 1883 was also part of this trend, though it was presented more as a collection where the 'judicial interpretation of common words and phrases' had some 'humorous or curious characteristics in

---

19 Frederic Jesup Stimpson, *Glossary of Technical Terms, Phrases, and Maxims of the Common Law* (Little, Brown 1881), iii.

20 Stewart Rapalje and Lawrence Robert, *Dictionary of American and English Law with Definitions of the Terms of the Canon and Civil Laws* (Linn 1888), iii–iv.

21 John Houston Merrill, *The American and English Encyclopaedia of Law* (Edward Thompson 1887).

22 Henry Campbell Black, *Dictionary of Law Containing of the Terms and Phrases of American and English Jurisprudence Ancient and Modern* (West 1891).

23 Black, *Dictionary of Law*, iii.

24 Charles H. Winfield, *Adjudged Words and Phrases: Being a Collection of Adjudicated Definitions of Terms Used in the Law* (Griffiths 1882), iv.

the light of legal construction'.[25] In 1904 the multi-volume *Judicial and Statutory Definitions of Words and Phrases* appeared.[26]

The creation and maintenance of fundamental conceptual unity was also the underlying aim of *Stroud's The Judicial Dictionary of Words and Phrases Judicially Interpreted* (1890), directed at 'the English-speaking lawyer, not only in the Mother Country, but also in the Colonies and dependencies of the Queen'. It was a 'Dictionary of the English Language [...] so far as that language has received interpretation by the Judges'. The work was very much written with an eye on the empire and the great achievements of the judges who had 'laid down the law for such an expansive and ever-widening civilization as that of the British Empire'. In the second edition (1903) this imperial theme is even more prominent. The idea was not only that the work 'be of frequent practical utility to the English speaking lawyer' but also that it should become 'the authoritative Interpreter of the English of Affairs for the British Empire'. The aim was to forge a 'link in the golden chain of common interest and community of feeling which binds together its various peoples' and also to serve as a 'living entity to business people in the various societies forming the British Empire'.[27]

Questions concerning the scope of the law dictionary remain current. Terms from medicine and finance have proved challenging for legal lexicographers.[28] In the most recent *Black's Law Dictionary* the editor explains how a large number of terms included in the 6th edition have been removed. These were words such as: *botulism*, *bouche* ('mouth'), *bough of a tree*, *bought*, *bouncer*, *bourg*, *boulevard*, *bourgeois*, *Brabant*, *brabanter* and their exclusion followed from the fact of their being insufficiently 'legal'. Whatever appeared in the dictionary 'should be plausibly a law-related term – and *closely* related to the law'. The entire dictionary had been reworked to produce an 'increase in precision and clarity'. An innovation adopted from the 7th edition onwards was the clear separation of 'definitional information' from 'encyclopaedic information'.[29] In one sense, it is evident that *botulism* has no place in a legal dictionary. But this takes us all the way back to the Cowell's *Interpreter*, and the lingering sense that no word or concept is truly foreign to law, and that some non-legal terms do belong in a law dictionary. *Black's* 9th edition after all retains the entry for *vehicle*.

---

25 Irving Browne, *The Judicial Interpretation of Common Words and Phrases* (Sumner, Whitney 1883), vi,

26 Editorial Staff, National Reporter System, *Judicial and Statutory Definitions of Words and Phrases* (West 1904).

27 Frederick Stroud, *The Judicial Dictionary or Words and Phrases Judicially Interpreted to Which has been Added Statutory Definitions* (2nd edn., 2 vols, Sweet & Maxwell 1903), vii–ix.

28 Roy M. Mersky and Jeanne Price, 'The Dictionary and the Man: The Eighth Edition of *Black's Law Dictionary*, Edited by Bryan Garner' (2006) 63 *Washington and Lee Law Review* 719, 727.

29 Bryan Garner, ed., *Black's Law Dictionary* (9th edn, West 2009), xiii–xvii.

## *Vehicle* in Legal Dictionaries

The *OED* has citations in the 'mode of transport' sense dating back to the seventeenth century. Coles dictionary of 'difficult terms' (1676) included entries for *vehicular* and *vehicles*, with the gloss 'any carriages'.[30] In English case-law, *vehicle* starts to appear in its meaning of 'mode of transport' in the 1830s (for example *Sharp v Gray*[31]), but it was not included, for example, in Winfield's *Adjudged Words and Phrases* of 1882.[32] The 1888 *Dictionary of American and English Law*, presumably drawing on Brown's MS., had an entry: *VEHICLE* (a ferry boat is not).[33] The reference was to the Indiana Law Reports and the case of *Duckwall v Albany*.[34] Browne's *The Judicial Interpretation of Common Words and Phrases*[35] entry for *vehicle* also referenced this case:

> A street sprinkling-car is a 'public vehicle', within the meaning of an ordinance imposing a license on public *vehicle*s using the streets for trade or traffic. City of *St. Louis v. Woodref*, 71 Mo. 92. A ferry boat is not a *vehicle*, within a statute for taxing 'carriages and other *vehicle*s used for passengers for hire' in a city. *Duckwall v. City of New Albany*, 25 Ind. 283. The court said: 'Webster states that the word '*vehicle*' is rarely applied to water-craft, and our statute requires us to give the word as used in the act its 'ordinary and usual sense'.

A much more detailed doctrinal entry on *vehicle* can be found in Merrill's *The American and English Encyclopedia of Law* of 1887, in keeping with its insistence that it was not a law dictionary. Entries on non-legal terms are in the form of long notes. The entry on *vehicle* is sub-divided into topics, reviewing judicial debate as to whether a bicycle was a *vehicle* or *carriage*; the status of 'drays'; a case involving 'sprinkler cart'; the ferryboat case *Duckwall v City of New Albany*; and the status of 'street car'. There is no general definition of *vehicle* at the head of the entry.[36] In the revised edition of 1904,[37] a general definition of *vehicle* was added in the main body of the text: 'A *vehicle* is defined to be any carriage moving on land, either on wheels or on runners; a conveyance; that which is used an

---

30 John Coles, *An English Dictionary* (Peter Parker 1676).

31 [1833] 9 BING 457.

32 Charles H. Winfield, *Adjudged Words and Phrases: Being a Collection of Adjudicated Definitions of Terms Used in the Law* (Griffiths 1882).

33 Stewart Rapalje and Lawrence Robert, *Dictionary of American and English Law* (Linn 1888).

34 (1866) 25 Ind 283.

35 Irving Browne, *The Judicial Interpretation of Common Words and Phrases* (Sumner, Whitney 1883).

36 John Houston Merrill, *The American and English Encyclopaedia of Law* (Edward Thompson 1887).

37 David S Garland et al., eds, *The American and English Encyclopaedia of Law* (2nd edn, Edward Thompson 1904).

instrument of conveyance, transmission, or communication'. The digest of the case-law is updated and extended, but also condensed onto a single page of notes, with the sub-headings: '*vehicle*' itself; 'bicycle'; 'canal-boats', 'dray', 'wagons-drays', 'street sprinkler-public *vehicle*', 'ferryboat', 'railroad locomotives and cars', 'street car'.

Stroud's *The Judicial Dictionary of Words and Phrases Judicially Interpreted* has a brief entry for *vehicle*,[38] as does Black's (1891): 'The word "vehicle" includes every description of carriage or other artificial contrivance used, or capable of being used, as a means of transportation on land'. This is taken from a legal source, the Revised Statutes of the United States (1873–74).[39] The definition is repeated in the second edition of 1910.

The multi-volume *Judicial and Statutory Definitions of Words and Phrases* (1904) had an even more elaborate taxonomy for the entry *vehicle* ('bicycle, tricycle, or motor carriage', 'dray or wagon', 'ferryboat', 'locomotives or cars', 'sleigh', 'street car', 'threshing machine'), as well as cross-references to 'carriage', 'motor vehicle', 'public vehicle', and 'wheeled vehicle'. Ballentine's *Law Dictionary* of 1916, which defined its scope as covering 'words, terms, abbreviations and phrases which are peculiar to law and of those which have a peculiar meaning in law', focused on Latin phrases and maxims and did not include an entry for *vehicle*.[40]

The use of the term 'encylopedia' or 'cyclopedia' in the title of a work does not necessarily imply that it deals with mundane non-legal vocabulary that has been the subject of case-law adjudication. For example, *The Cyclopedic Dictionary of Law* (1901) restricted itself to legal terminology narrowly defined.[41] However the third (Rawle's) revision of *Bouvier*, entitled *Bouvier's Law Dictionary and Concise Encyclopedia* (1914), had a short entry for *vehicle*: 'The word includes every description of carriage or other artificial contrivance used or capable of being used as a means of transportation on land'. There follows brief mention of the 'street sprinkler', 'street car' and 'ferry boat' cases.[42]

In the 4th edition of *Black's Law Dictionary*, the entry begins:

38 Frederick Stroud, *The Judicial Dictionary or Words and Phrases Judicially Interpreted to Which has been Added Statutory Definitions* (2nd edn, 2 vols, Sweet & Maxwell 1903).

39 *Revised Statutes of the United States, Passed at the First Session of the Forty-Third Congress 1873–74* (Government Printing Office 1874).

40 James Arthur Ballentine, *A Law Dictionary of Words, Terms, Abbreviations and Phrases which are Peculiar to Law and of Those which have a Peculiar Meaning in Law* [...] (Bobs-Merrill 1916).

41 Walter A. Shumaker and George Longsdorf, *The Cyclopedic Dictionary of Law* (Keefe-Davidson 1901).

42 Francis Rawle, ed., *Bouvier's Law Dictionary and Concise Encyclopedia* (8rd edn, 3rd rev., West 1914).

> That in or on which a person or thing is or may be carried from one place to another, especially along the ground, also through the air; any moving support or container fitted or used for the conveyance of bulky objects; a means of conveyance.[43]

This is followed by a case reference *Moffitt v State Automobile Ins. Assn.*[44] In that decision the court held (revising its previous holding) that a hay grinder was a *trailer* within the exclusion clause of an insurance policy. One point in the judgment was that definitions in non-pertinent statutes could not oust the 'common meanings' of everyday terms. However the definition in the case was itself cited from *Webster's* 2nd edition (1934).[45] The phrase 'also through the air' was added there.[46] In the case-law this definition is sometimes cited as if it originated from *Black's*[47] and sometimes from *Webster's*.[48] This complex interaction between the two streams of lexicography can be further illustrated from entries in *Webster's* which explicitly reference law cases. Here is a striking example from the 1923 edition's entry for *vegetable*:

> There is no well-drawn distinction between vegetables and fruits [...] in the popular sense; but it has been held by the courts that all those which, like potatoes, carrots, peas, celery, lettuce, tomatoes, etc., are eaten (whether cooked or raw) during the principal part of the meal are to be regarded as *vegetables*, while those used only for dessert are *fruits*.

The reference (not given in the dictionary) is to *Nix v Hedden*.[49]

Jumping to the present day, as noted, *Black's Law Dictionary* (9th edition) retains an entry for *vehicle*. It is defined there as follows: '1. An instrument of transportation or conveyance. 2. Any conveyance used in transporting passengers or things by land, water, or air'. The definition does not reference any statute or adjudged meanings. There is also an entry for the National Motor Vehicle Theft Act (or Dyer Act) of 1919,[50] which made it unlawful 'to transport a stolen motor *vehicle* across state lines'. In the online version, one can find via hyperlinks to the texts of this and other statutes and the relevant case-law, including the Supreme

43 *Black's Law Dictionary* (4th edn, West 1968).

44 40 Neb. 578, 300 N.W. 837 (1941), vacating on rehearing, 139 Neb. 512, 297 N.W. 918 (1941).

45 *Supra*, note 2.

46 *Supra*, note 2.

47 *Starr v Starr* 1999 WL 33430058 (Ill.Ct.Cl.), 2.

48 *Conrad v Dillinger* 176 Kan. 296 (1954), 299.

49 149 U.S. 304 (1893).

50 National Motor Vehicle Theft Act (18 USCA para 231).

Court decision in *McBoyle v United States*[51] (see below). Ballentine's 3rd edition of 1969, currently available through Nexus.com, offers a definition from the legal code ('An instrumentality for the carrying of goods or people') and a number of case references, including again the decision in *McBoyle*.[52]

By contrast to *Black's*, the current *Dictionary of Canadian Law*[53] has a complex entry reflecting general English, statutory and case-law definitions, as well as several entries for compound terms ('vehicle identification number', 'vehicle inspection record' and so on) and a large set of cross-references. Its first subentry is a lengthy quotation from *Bennett & White (Calgary) Ltd. v Sugar City (Municipality)*.[54] However there is no possibility of a reference work, even one of 1,411 pages, capturing the full range of issues, definitions and doctrinal questions found in the case-law. An alternative format is found in *Australian Legal Words and Phrases 1900–1996*, which is updated annually. The entries 'reference the legislation that defined the word and/or the case that interpreted it', but no actual definitions are cited.[55]

## A Brief Glimpse of *Vehicle* in the Case Law

Modern industrial civilization, including modern warfare, is built on the rise of particular kinds of vehicles. The key vehicle in the creation of the pre-modern global economy was the ship. Following the industrial revolution, the law relating to vehicles was an enormous growth area. Questions about tolls on particular forms of carriage governed by local Acts (*The Queen v Ruscoe*,[56] *Short v Hudson*,[57] *Eatwell v Richmond*,[58] *Pearson v Tazewell*,[59] *Comley v Carpenter*[60]) gave way to laws relating to national public transport, especially railways. Questions such as whether the pushing of a perambulator along a public footpath was a nuisance (*Regina v Mathias*[61]) and the operator's liability to a passenger for a defect in the manufacture of a coach (*Sharp v Grey* 1833[62]) morphed into the vast modern law of tort. The law of ships and the sea was extended and modified to include the law of the air and airplanes. One of the founding decisions of modern tort law also involved a *vehicle* (a train), though not questions of definition (*Palsgraf v Long*

51 283 US 25 (1931).
52 *Ballentine's Law Dictionary* (3rd edn, Lawyers Co-operative Pub. Co. 1969).
53 Daphne A Dukelow, ed., *Dictionary of Canadian Law* (4th edn, Carswell 2011).
54 [1950] CTC 410, 463.
55 *Australian Legal Words and Phrases* (Butterworths Editorial, 1993-annual updates).
56 [1838] 8 AD & E 386.
57 [1860] 5 H & N 660.
58 [1865] 18 CB (NS) 363.
59 [1865] 19 CB (NS) 383.
60 [1865] 18 CB (N S) 378.
61 [1861] 2 F & F 570.
62 [1833] 9 BING 457.

*Island Railroad Co.*[63]). The rise of the private automobile raised a whole range of issues in constitutional and criminal law (for example the law of burglary[64]), insurance, planning, consumer law, to name but a few. One might make a parallel with partially new or adapted fields of law, such as the law of electricity.[65] A work entitled *The Law of Street Surface Railroads* was published in 1902 and reissued in 1911 as *The Law of Street Railroads*.[66] Charles Babbitt's *The Law Applied to Motor Vehicles* first published in 1911 appeared in a second edition in 1917.[67] Bobbitt insisted that no new legal principles were necessary to deal with the rise of the motor vehicle. The opening sections gave a detailed account of definitional issues relating to *motor vehicle*, *vehicle*, *carriage* and so on. Likewise Davids' *The Law of Motor Vehicles* (1911) devoted its first chapter to questions of definition, including the relation of *motor vehicle* to *carriage*.[68] Vehicles are also a key element in the rise of the registration and licensing regimes and the 'legal seizure' of personal and object identity.[69] The automobile became, in Marshall McLuhen's (1911–80) phrase, one of the key technological 'extensions of man'.[70]

*Carriage*, the traditional term closest to the modern *vehicle*, remained legally relevant, not least because of the persistence of statutes containing the term. In the late nineteenth century, statutes that used the term *carriage* had to be applied to a world with increasing numbers of bicycles. In *Taylor v Goodwin*[71] a conviction for 'furiously' driving a carriage was upheld after an argument as to whether a bicycle was a *carriage* within the meaning of the Highway Act of 1835, s. 78. In *Cannan v Earl of Abingdon*[72] an Act authorizing the collection of a bridge toll on 'every

63 248 NY 339, 162 NE 99 (NY 1928).

64 Jerome C.Latimer, 'Burglary is for Buildings, or is It? Protected Structures and Conveyances under Florida's Present Burglary Statute', 9 *Stetson Law Review* 347.

65 Arthur F Curtis, *The Law of Electricity* (Bender 1915).

66 Andrew Nellis, *The Law of Street Surface Railroads* (Bender 1902); *The Law of Street Railroads* (Bender 1911). See also: Henry Booth, *A Treatise on the Law of Street Railways* (Johnson 1911).

67 Charles J. Babbitt, *The Law Applied to Motor Vehicles, Citing All the Reported Cases Decided During the First Fifteen Years of the Use of Motor Vehicles Upon the Public Thoroughfares* (John Byrne 1911), second edition prepared by Arthur W. Blackmore (John Byrne 1917).

68 Berkeley Reynolds Davids, *The Law of Motor Vehicles* (Edward Thompson 1911); see also De Witt Clinton Blashfield *Cyclopedia of Automobile Law: A Complete Encyclopedic Treatment of the Law of Automobiles* (Vernon Law Book Co. 1927).

69 The phrase is from Jane Caplan, '"This or That Particular Person": Protocols of Identification in Nineteenth Century Europe', in *Documenting Individual Identity. The Development of State Practices in the Modern World* (Jane Caplan and John Torpey, eds, Princeton University Press 2001), 49–66, 54.

70 Marshall McLuhen, *Understanding Media: The Extensions of Man* (MIT 1994), first published 1964.

71 [1879] 4 QBD 228.

72 [1900] 2 QB 66.

coach, chariot, berlin, hearse, chaise, chair, calash, wagon, wain, dray, cart, car, or other carriage' was held to apply to a bicycle. In *Corkery v Carpenter*[73] the point was reargued with the same outcome, on that occasion in relation to the Licensing Act of 1872.[74] The shift in statutory language from *carriage* to *vehicle* still left room for doubt about the law relating to bicycles. In the Canadian case of *Moore v The Queen*[75] a cyclist who went through a red light was held not to have been driving a vehicle, given that the statutory definition: 'a vehicle not run upon rails that is designed to be self-propelled or propelled by electric power obtained from overhead trolley-wires'.[76] Since the cyclist was not driving a vehicle he was thus not required to give his name and address under s. 126. However bicycles were obliged by the statute to obey traffic signals and the court ruled by five to two that the cyclist was guilty of obstructing the police.

An interesting class of cases concerns the stability of the category *vehicle* over time. An object may slip in or out of the category. This might occur at the macro-level of historical time, where categories like *horse* and *airplane* leave or enter the category. This can also happen at the micro-level, in relation to a single object. A non-vehicle might be adapted so as to be used as a vehicle, for example a chicken coop on wheels pulled behind another vehicle (*Garner v Burr*[77]); a vehicle can be altered so to change its class, for example a cycle with auxiliary engine which had been disabled (*Lawrence v Howlett*[78]); and a vehicle can be functionally shifted out of the class all together, for example a caravan trailer being used as a residence and therefore, it was argued, as a building (*Police v McInnes*[79]). It was ruled in *Garner v Burr* that the chicken coop, by virtue of running on the highway on wheels, which lacked the required pneumatic tires, was a vehicle under the Road Traffic Act 1930;[80] in *Lawrence v Howlett* it was held that the cycle with the disabled and partially dismantled engine was no longer a motorcycle, even though it retained some fuel in its tank; in *Police v McInnes* the recorder found that the trailer retained its intrinsic status as a vehicle, since it was still capable of being drawn along the highway, even though the owner intended to occupy it as a (non-mobile) home. In *Macro Auto Leasing Inc. v Canada (Minister of Transport)* the question was whether imported vehicle parts seized by the Canadian Ministry of Transport amounted to a vehicle under

73 [1951] 1 KB 102.

74 s12.

75 [1979] 1RCS 195.

76 Motor-vehicle Act, RSBC 1960, c 253., s 2.

77 [1951] 1 KB 31.

78 [1952] 2 All ER 74.

79 Coventry Sessions, 17th August, 1961, reported in: 'Is a caravan always a trailer' (1926) 26 *Journal of Criminal Law* 21.

80 The 'chicken coop on wheels' case is discussed in Timothy Endicott, 'Law and Language', *The Stanford Encyclopedia of Philosophy* (Fall 2010 Edition), plato.stanford.edu/archives/fall2010/entries/law-language.

s 2 of Motor *Vehicle* Safety Act. The court concluded that a *vehicle* was more than the sum of a sub-set of its parts:[81]

> By no stretch of the imagination can it be said under the present definition of *vehicle* that the body/chassis seized in this case, without the wheels, the tires, the wheel hub adaptors, the differential, the brakes, the rotors, the bearings, the electrical fittings, the steering shaft and column, the battery, the engine, the transmission, the clutch, the driving shaft, the ignition, the carburator, the water pump, the motor mounts, the alternator and the distributor, to name just a few of the missing components of what is to become a Shelby Cobra once assembled, is a *vehicle* within the meaning of the Act.

One important area of 'vehicle law' in the United States relates to the automobile as an 'extension of man' and to the constitutional category of *search.* Put briefly, the Fourth Amendment as understood today requires an officer of the law to obtain a warrant in order to search a dwelling, unless the situation justifies urgent entry ('exigent circumstances'). The authorities must show 'probable cause' in order to obtain the warrant. However *Carroll v United States*[82] set up what came to be known as the 'vehicle exception', under which a vehicle stopped on the highway could be searched without a warrant, if there was probable cause. The vehicle by its very nature could be moved immediately from the scene and escape the jurisdiction. The police had to 'act upon a belief, reasonably arising out of circumstances known to the seizing officer' (*Carroll v United States*[83]). In terms of level of constitutional protection, the dwelling and the vehicle on the highway are at opposite ends of a continuum.

In the case of *California v Carney*[84] the space at issue was a motor home parked in a public parking lot. There was credible evidence gathered on the spot that the occupant was dealing in drugs, including exchanging merchandise for sexual favours, and officers entered the motor home without a warrant. The motor home as a class of object is an awkward legal hybrid. It combines in apparently equal measure qualities of the entities at the extremes of the continuum of protected spaces, of the most protected and the least protected spaces. If we look at the court decisions at the three levels California Court of Appeal, California Supreme Court, US Supreme Court, it is possible to analyse how individual judgments dealt with three fundamental issues. These are: (1) the characterization of the motor home in general, as an abstract type, that is, whether it is more 'residence-like' or 'vehicle-like'; (2) the characterization of the particular motor home, in relation to the facts of the case as essentially a residence or a vehicle. These

81 (2008) CarswellNat 1075, [4].

82 *Carroll v United States* 45 SCt 280 (1925).

83 *Carroll v United States*, 284.

84 *People v Carney* 117 CalApp.3d. 36, 172 CalRptr.430 (1981); *People v Carney* 34 Cal 3d 597 (1983); *California v Carney* 471 US 386, 105 SCt 2066 (1985).

facts might include where it was parked, its condition, the presence of curtains, the arrangement and fittings of the interior and so on; and (3) the preferred jurisprudential framework to be applied to the Fourth Amendment, in relation to balancing the operational needs of policing versus the protection of privacy and the sanctity of the private residence. The table below summarizes the decisions in relation to this issue:

**Table 11.1 The automobile exception and the status of the motor home**

| | **Issue 1** | **Issue 2** | **Issue 3** |
|---|---|---|---|
| Court of Appeal (CA) | | | |
| (majority) | vehicle | vehicle | Automobile exception and factor of inherent mobility gave greater flexibility in defining a reasonable search |
| (dissent) | residence | residence | A residence was a sanctuary |
| Supreme Court (CA) | | | |
| (majority) | residence | residence | A residence was a castle in which there was a high expectation of privacy |
| (dissent) | vehicle | vehicle | Police needed practical guidelines and clear definitional guidance; there was a strong presumption that an immediately moveable motor home was a vehicle |
| Supreme Court (US) | | | |
| (majority) | vehicle | vehicle | Inherent mobility of automobile; automobile is accepted as being subject to high levels of scrutiny and regulation; the mobile home is particularly suitable for carrying out illegal activities |
| (dissent) | residence | residence | There is a strong burden to be met in justifying any exception to warrant rule; each and every domicile, however humble, deserves the same level of constitutional protection |

The search was upheld and the conviction affirmed.[85] When the judges considered the category *motor home* as well as Carney's motor home, they literally did not perceive the same kind of object. The characterization of *motor home* as an abstract category, that of the actual vehicle in the case, the jurisprudential

85 For further analysis of these cases, see Christopher Hutton, *Word Meaning and Legal Interpretation: An Introductory Guide* (Palgrave 2014).

attitude to the Fourth Amendment and the decision itself are all aligned. The 'extension of man' question and the Fourth Amendment were also at issue in *Jones v United States*, where the Supreme Court ruled that evidence obtained by attaching a GPS tracker to a private car was not admissible.[86] The automobile represents the problematic technological extension of the private sphere into the public domain.

The Canadian courts have made a large number of decisions relating in varying degrees of directness to the definition of *vehicle*. These relate overwhelmingly to taxation categories and customs, notably the definition-rich case of *Seaspan International Ltd. v R*.[87] There is case-law as to: whether a vehicle was a public space in relation to solicitation by a prostitute;[88] a government car was a 'public work';[89] a fire started by a gasoline pump mounted on a *vehicle* was 'damage occasioned by a motor vehicle';[90] a missile thrown from a *vehicle* caused injury arising out of the 'use or operation of a vehicle';[91] the definition of 'care and control' of a vehicle;[92] the status of a trailer home in relation to *vehicle*;[93] the boundary between 'mining equipment' and 'vehicle' under ss 21(3.1) and 29(1) of the Excise Tax Act;[94] the boundary between a 'ferry' and a 'passenger cruise ship'.[95]

A more recent typical 'vehicle case' is *The Lecht Ski Co Ltd v The Commissioners for Her Majesty's Revenue & Customs*.[96] The question arose as to whether a ski-lift was a *vehicle* and therefore qualified for zero-rating. The tribunal found that it was not, since it took passengers 'in one direction over a fixed route from one extremity of the device to the other, and not beyond'. It had a 'fixed' location and was 'not capable of independent or relatively independent movement', unlike the categories of 'ship' and 'aircraft' mentioned in the statute.[97] The court made a distinction in terms of design and function between a *vehicle* and the ski-lift.

86 132 S.Ct. 945 (2012).

87 (1993) CarswellNat 960.

88 *Hutt v R* (1978) CarswellBC 555.

89 *The King v Dubois* [1935] SCR 378.

90 *F.W. Argue Ltd. v Howe* (1968) CarswellOnt 95.

91 *Anita Chan v Insurance Corporation of British Columbia* (1996) CanLII 353 (BC CA).

92 *Saunders v The Queen* [1967] SCR. 284; *Mallery v R* (2008) NBCA 18; *R v Burbella* (2002) MBCA 105.

93 *Moore (Township) v Farr* (1978) CarswellOnt 599.

94 *Westar Mining Ltd v R* (1990) CarswellNat 385.

95 *Navigation Madeleine Inc.v The Attorney General of Canada* (2004) CarswellNat 475.

96 [2008] UKVAT V20886.

97 Value Added Tax Act 1994 c 23, schedule 8.

### *Vehicle* in the 'common mind': McBoyle v United States

The most famous vehicle case of all is undoubtedly *McBoyle v United States*.[98] McBoyle was convicted in the District Court (Western District of Oklahoma) of transporting a stolen vehicle, a 'Waco' airplane, across a state line.[99] The relevant wording in the statute defined *motor vehicle* as including: 'an automobile, automobile truck, automobile wagon, motor cycle, or any other self-propelled vehicle not designed for running on rails'. McBoyle argued on appeal that the word *vehicle* only applied to 'conveyances that travel on the ground'; an airplane was not a '*vehicle* but a ship' and, applying the principle of *ejusdem generis*, the phrase 'any other self-propelled vehicle' could not be construed to include an airplane.[100] The majority, in upholding the conviction, cited a range of dictionary definitions and noted that the Latin term *vehiculum* meant 'a ship as well as a carriage'. *Webster's* had the following: 'That in or on which any person or thing is or may be carried, esp. on land, as a coach, wagon, car, bicycle, etc.; a means of conveyance'.[101] The *Corpus Juris* surveyed the statutory definitions of *motor vehicle* and concluded as follows: 'it is generally defined as including all vehicles propelled by any power other than muscular power, except traction engines, road rollers, and such motor vehicles as run only upon rails or tracks'.[102] The court found an airplane was a motor *vehicle* within the meaning of the Act. It was self-propelled by virtue of its gasoline motor; it transported passengers and freight; it ran 'partly on the ground but principally in the air'; it offered 'a rapid means for transportation of persons and comparatively light articles of freight and express'. There was a functional equivalence between an automobile and an airplane. Both served the same purpose and the maxim of *ejusdem generis* had not been violated.[103] In dissent, Judge Cotteral stressed the rule that penal statutes must 'state clearly the persons and acts denounced' (often termed 'the principle of lenity'). Congress could have explicitly mentioned aircraft: 'The omission to definitely mention airplanes requires a construction that they were not included'. The fact that 'vehicles running on rails' were exempted was a clarification; it implied that the statute applied to 'vehicles that run, but not on rails'.[104]

The decision was appealed to the Supreme Court.[105] Writing for a unanimous bench, Justice Oliver Wendell Holmes (1841–1935) conceded that the term *vehicle* could and had been used to include aircraft in some legislation: 'No doubt etymologically

98 283 US 25 (1931).

99 The National Motor Vehicle Theft Act, 1919.

100 *McBoyle v United States* 43 F.2d 273 (1930), [5].

101 *McBoyle v United States* (1930), [6–13], citing *Webster's* 1923 entry (*supra*, note 2).

102 Vol. 42, p. 609, s 1.

103 *McBoyle v United States* 43 F2d 273 (1930), [13].

104 *McBoyle v United States* (1930), [3].

105 *McBoyle v United States* 283 US 25 (1931).

it is possible to use the word to signify a conveyance working on land, water or air, and sometimes legislation extends the use in that direction'. An example was the Tariff Act of 1922;[106] other statutes however defined *vehicle* in a sense restricted to 'a means of transportation on land'.[107] In the Tariff Act of 1930 (c. 497, s. 401(b)) aircraft were expressly excluded from the meaning of the word *vehicle*. In the statute at issue the word was used with its meaning 'in everyday speech'. This called up 'the picture of a thing moving on land'. Congress could have included mention of aircraft had it been minded to do so: 'Airplanes were well known in 1919 when this statute was passed, but it is admitted that they were not mentioned in the reports or in the debates in Congress'.[108] The statutory language carefully listed 'the different forms of motor vehicles' and it was not a possible reading to extend this to aircraft ('a term that usage more and more precisely confines to a different class'). It was 'reasonable that a fair warning should be given to the world in language that the common world will understand, of what the law intends to do if a certain line is passed'.[109] Holmes argued that the rule was laid down 'in words that evoke in the common mind only the picture of vehicles moving on land'. An aircraft was not a motor vehicle; the judgment was reversed. As authority for his interpretative approach Holmes cited *United States v Bhagat Singh Thind*.[110]

The jurisprudential issue in *McBoyle* was framed as a choice between legal English and ordinary English. The Court of Appeals took the statutory definition as defining a class of objects, each with an analogous function. The criteria listed in the statute applied unproblematically to motor *vehicle*s of all kinds, including aircraft. Holmes by contrast chose to read the statutory definition through the lens of 'everyday speech' and the picture evoked, at least according to his intuition, by the word in the 'common mind'.

## Legal and Non-legal Language in Hart's Theory of Adjudication

*McBoyle* was the stimulus for the most influential model of adjudication produced in the twentieth century, the account of the rule 'no vehicles in the park' offered by H.L.A. Hart (1907–92). Schauer calls this 'the most famous hypothetical in the common law world'.[111] This fictitious rule was key to Hart's debates with Lon

106 c. 3567, s 410(b).

107 Rev St s 4 (1) USCA s 4.

108 *McBoyle v United States* 283 US 25 (1931).

109 *McBoyle v United States* (1931), 26–7.

110 261 US 204 (1923).

111 Frederick Schauer 'A Critical Guide to Vehicles in the Park' (2008) 83 *New York University Law Review* 1109, 1109. Just a few examples: Pierre Schlag, 'No Vehicles in the Park' (1999) 23 *Seattle University Law Review* 381; Bernard Bell, '"No Motor Vehicles in the Park": Reviving the Hart-Fuller Debate to Introduce Statutory Construction' (1998) 48 *Journal of Legal Education* 88; Antonin Scalia and Bryan Garner, *Reading Law: The*

Fuller (1902–78) and Ronald Dworkin (1931–).[112] Hart stressed that legal rules use general terms like *animal*, *game*, *person*, *building*, *cruelty*, *negligence*:

> The law must predominantly [...] refer to *classes* of person, and to *classes* of acts, things, and circumstances; and its successful operation over vast areas of social life depends on a widely diffused capacity to recognize particular acts, things, and circumstances as instances of the general classifications which the law makes.[113]

To determine the legal effect of the 'no vehicles in the park' rule, law had to be able to recognize particular acts or incidents 'as instances of general classifications'. Words and phrases had 'a core of settled meaning', but there was always what Hart termed a 'penumbra of doubt' where there was 'interpretation and disagreement'.[114] The categories of language could not be regarded as fully closed in relation to particular facts: 'Natural languages like English are when so used irreducibly open textured'.[115] In 'all fields of experience' there was 'a limit, inherent in the nature of language, to the guidance which general language can provide'.[116] In the case of a legal rule about *vehicle*s, there were 'plain cases constantly recurring in similar contexts to which general expressions are clearly applicable'. A motor car was clearly a *vehicle*, but what about 'bicycles, airplanes, roller skates?'.[117] The rule applies unproblematically where the word *vehicle* in ordinary usage would apply and legal uncertainty arises from uncertainty in the application of the word *vehicle* to the object in question. Hart's organizing metaphor of core and penumbra is a visual one, evoking a two-dimensional plane: it gives us the impression that we can *see* how legal problems look *in general*. Hart pointed out that everyday objects were unable to speak and declare what kind of category they belonged to:

> The toy automobile cannot speak up and say, 'I am a vehicle for the purpose of this legal rule', nor can the roller skates chorus, 'We are not a vehicle'. Fact situations do not await us neatly labeled, creased, and folded, nor is their legal classification written on them to be simply read off by the judge.[118]

*Art of Interpreting Legal Texts* (West 2012), 33–41; see also Michael Dorf, 'A Supreme Court Admiralty Case Sheds Light on a Longstanding Debate', http://verdict.justia.com, accessed 26 October 2012.

112 Lawrence Solan 'Law, Language and Lenity' (1998) 40 *William and Mary Law Review* 57, 81.

113 H.L.A. Hart, *The Concept of Law* (2nd edn, Clarendon 1994), 124.

114 Scott Veitch, Emilios Christodoulidis and Lindsay Farmer, *Jurisprudence: Themes and Concepts* (2nd edn, Routledge 2012), 132.

115 H.L.A. Hart, *The Concept of Law* (2nd edn, Clarendon 1994), 128.

116 Ibid., 126.

117 Ibid., 126.

118 H.L.A. Hart, 'Positivism and the Separation of Law and Morals' (1958) 71 *Harvard Law Review* 593, 607.

On the one hand, Hart implies that the word *vehicle* is just the ordinary English word dropped into the legal rule. Yet this surreal passage indicates that *vehicle* cannot be the ordinary English word, since the classification is 'for the purpose of this legal rule'.

If we take the case of *The Lecht Ski Co Ltd v The Commissioners for Her Majesty's Revenue & Customs*[119] briefly described above, one could view the status of *ski lift* as penumbral within Hart's model, and see the court as plucking a criterion from the unbounded set of possible points of comparison between a ski lift and a normative unproblematic member of the set of *vehicle*s. But was this a 'penumbra case' at all, in Hart's terms? The court might equally have determined that a *vehicle* is a device for transporting people or goods from one location to another, and that the ski lift performed this function. Or was it simply that the ordinary language category *vehicle* did not cover ski-lifts at all? Hart's theory provides no meta-rule, no rule of recognition, by which we can distinguish easy cases from hard; nor could it.

Fuller writes of Hart: 'The most obvious defect of his theory lies in its assumption that problems of interpretation typically turn on the meaning of individual words'.[120] This reading of Hart is disputed by Schauer, who argues that nothing in Hart's wider argument is 'inconsistent with the (correct) view that it is sentences, not individual words, that are the principal carriers of meaning'.[121] But if this is so, then why stop at the sentence? Surely texts are the principal carriers of meaning? Once we go above the individual word the theory loses its relationship to ordinary language, since statutory sentences and legal rules cannot be called 'ordinary English'. And once the link to ordinary English is broken, then legal problems of the application of the language of rules cannot be explained by a discussion of terms like *vehicle* and the core-penumbra model.

What grounds Hart's theory is the highly traditional Western understanding of language as (paradigmatically) a word-object pairing. This goes back to Adam naming the animals in Genesis (2:xix–xx). Instead of the 'natural kinds' we find in Genesis, Hart takes *vehicle* as the paradigm category. *Vehicle*s are technological objects, but their definition is not primarily technological or scientific. *Vehicle* refers to a class of physical objects to which an intuitive core meaning can apparently be ascribed, but which in their variability and multi-functionality are the product of a complex human social order and its myriad forms of interdependency. It is not on the surface an ideologically charged category, since *vehicle*s mediate between places and people, facilitating the circulation of goods and passengers. *Vehicle*s are mundane objects of modern civilization and yet also so profoundly enmeshed with the fabric of law as to represent plausibly the idea of a vast middle ground of

---

119 [2008] UKVAT V20886.

120 Lon Fuller, 'Positivism and Fidelity to Law – A Reply to Professor Hart' (1958) 71 *Harvard Law Review* 630, 662.

121 Frederick Schauer 'A Critical Guide to Vehicles in the Park' (2008) 83 *New York University Law Review* 1109, 1119.

overlap between legal language and 'ordinary language'. The categories of ordinary language are for Hart in effect a mode of perception, in virtue of which we can label most phenomena that we encounter. Yet the toy automobile, even if it could speak, would be unable to say whether it was a *vehicle* for the purpose of the legal rule. Even in a surreal world where objects could speak and declare their essential nature the toy would need to have legal training and be able to 'think like a judge'.

One sting in the tail of *McBoyle* is the authority of *United States v Bhagat Singh Thind* (1923).[122] *Thind* concerned the meaning of the phrase *white person* in the context of the Naturalization Act of 1917.[123] This restricted the class of people eligible for naturalization to 'aliens being free white persons and to aliens of African nativity and to persons of African descent'. The court found that scholarly and scientific accounts of racial categories were too complex and unclear to be applied by the court. In any case it was the original as well as the popular meaning of the phrase *white person* which was the relevant one. Dr Thind (1892–1967), a Sikh, was not, in the generally accepted meaning of the phrase, *white*. In *Thind* the object of law's classificatory gaze, Dr Thind himself, was, unlike Hart's toy automobile, quite able to speak up and declare his status under the legal rule.[124] But this was not deemed legally relevant.

## Constructing Ordinary Language

It has been argued that the meanings of ordinary words 'exist antecedently of any interpretive enterprise in law, and thus a theory of interpretation in law is free to incorporate such ordinary meanings or not'.[125] Textualism treats the 'ordinary-meaning rule' as 'the most fundamental semantic rule of interpretation'.[126] But any attempt to reach out past the judicial frame and appeal to extra-legal linguistic norms can only arise out of and be justified by the prior legal analysis of the case as a factual and jurisprudential nexus. Ordinary language does not exist as a stable extra-legal resource on which law can draw if the particular theory of adjudication and interpretation requires it. The related idea that a dictionary definition offers a neutral characterization of ordinary meaning is not sustainable: 'Generalized focus makes no more semantic sense than private property that belongs to no one'.[127]

---

122 261 US 204 (1923).

123 United States Revised Statutes, s 2169.

124 A website dedicated to Dr Thind declares: 'Thind was clearly Caucasian. Most North Indians are in fact Caucasian', http://www.bhagatsinghthind.com/naturalization_summary.php, accessed November 23, 2012.

125 Michael Moore, 'A Natural Law Theory of Interpretation' (1985) 58 *Southern California Law Review* 277, 288.

126 Scalia and Garner, *Reading Law*, 69, *supra*, note 109.

127 Roy Harris and Christopher Hutton, *Definition in Theory and Practice: Language, Lexicography and the Law* (Continuum 2007), 212.

There is no genuine sense in which the category *vehicle* sets out in advance, on the level of generality suggested by Hart, the set of its unproblematic members. Although 'vehicles and parks are material objects, they are also cultural artifacts defined by their social significance and functions'.[128] Within law the category always comes into question within and in relation to a legal rule. There is no 'ordinary' context in which the category is considered completely in the abstract and to which law can appeal. The notion of 'ordinary language' is fictively outside the boundary of law, but in terms of praxis lies fully within it. It is a category of legal discourse required by the operation of law; but it is also necessary to law's operation that it be imagined fully outside the law. It is the undifferentiated and stable background which law must assume in order to operate; yet the more law needs it to adjudicate, the less stable it turns out to be.[129] Ordinary language is like the mirage of an oasis to which travellers orient as they cross the desert. The closer the travellers get, the more blurred and indistinct the oasis appears. The more you ask of ordinary language, the less it can tell you.

Ordinary language is not a category generally appealed to within linguistics, but it is of central importance within modern Anglo-American philosophy of language.[130] Like law, ordinary language philosophy presumes a neat division of labour between the philosopher and the linguist or lexicographer.[131] In his essay 'Ordinary Language' the philosopher Gilbert Ryle (1900–76) asserted that 'usually we are in no doubt whether a diction does or does not belong to ordinary parlance'.[132] But how would we know whether the wording quoted here from Ryle belongs to ordinary language or not? For the linguistic philosopher J.L. Austin (1911–60), ordinary language was a reservoir of the linguistic habits of a community. These represented the accumulation of wisdom and insight created over many generations:

> Our common stock of words embodies all the distinctions men have found worth drawing, and the connexions they have found worth marketing, in the lifetimes of many generations[.][133]

---

128 Brian Slattery, 'Three Concepts of Law: The Ambiguous Legacy of H.L.A. Hart' (1998) 61 *Saskatchewan Law Review* 323, 331.

129 Christopher Hutton, *Language, Meaning and the Law* (Edinburgh UP 2009), 177–84.

130 Roy Harris, 'Ordinary Language' *Integrationist Notes and Papers* (Authors on Line 2012), 57–64, 59.

131 Roy Harris, 'Murray, Moore and the Myth' *Linguistic Thought in England* (Roy Harris ed, Duckworth 1988), 1–26.

132 Gilbert Ryle, 'Ordinary Language' (1953) 62 *The Philosophical Review* 167, 168; Roy Harris, 'Ordinary Language' *Integrationist Notes and Papers* (Authors on Line 2012), 57–64, 59.

133 J.L. Austin, 'A Plea for Excuses' (1956) 57 *Proceedings of the Aristotelian Society* 1, 8.

Austin saw law as sometimes pushing ordinary language beyond breaking point. A hard case is one to which ordinary language fails to provide an answer:

> In the law a constant stream of actual cases, more novel and more tortuous than the mere imagination could contrive, are brought up for decision – that is, formulae for docketing them must somehow be found. Hence it is necessary first to be careful with, but also to be brutal with, to torture, to fake and to override, ordinary language: we cannot here evade or forget the whole affair.[134]

But this 'ordinary language' becomes a philosophical category, rather than a reflection of 'real usage'.

Put another way, it is law's duty to adhere to the categories and meanings of ordinary language as closely as possible. For the legal theorist Michael Moore, ordinary language meanings 'are the place to start in constructing the meaning of a legal text'; they 'form the conceptual inheritance of all native speakers of the language' and their deployment enhances predictability and transparency.[135] Yet if language is 'the shelter from which we know the world and act in it',[136] then it has a double role. It is both outside of independent of the world (as in Adam's moment of naming the animals) and yet also a mode of action within it. It is a set of standards for measuring and categorizing the world, for telling us whether something is a *vehicle* and some other thing is not. At the same time it is a situated contextual activity implicated within the everyday routines of social life and the pressures, tensions and conflicts that constitute it. Law requires ordinary language to serve simultaneously as an external point of reference and a mode of adjudicative action.

## Benign and Harmful Fictions

Law's application within adjudication of 'what we ordinarily call things' operates as the unstable yet strategic interface between ordinary language and legal language: the category of ordinary language has a gravitational power for legal discourse. It appears to guarantee that legal interpretation is grounded in a social reality outside itself. This offers the reassurance that law, while it may depart in contingent or systematic ways from ordinary language categories, is by default fundamentally aligned with popular modes of perception. One could understand the entry for *vehicle* in *Black's* 9th edition in the same way. After hundreds of case-law decisions which reflect the legal-definitional complexity of *vehicle*, we return

134 Austin, 'A Plea for Excuses' (1956), 12.

135 Michael Moore, 'A Natural Law Theory of Interpretation' (1985) 58 *Southern California Law Review* 277, 288, 321.

136 Marianne Constable, 'Democratic Citizenship and Civil Political Conversation; What's Law Got to Do with it?' (2012) 63 *Mercer Law Review* 877, 877.

to generic definition of the ordinary English word. There is no way to communicate the totality of the adjudicated definitions of *vehicle*, except in their absence, as an unbounded set of both overlapping and contradictory adjudged meanings. What gives the appearance of shape over time is the fictive ordinary (or 'prototype'[137]) meaning at their centre.

The history of legal reference works reflects the uncertainties of the boundary between legal language and ordinary language, at the same time as these boundaries are constantly re-inscribed and re-engineered. When a legal reference work such as Browne's *The Judicial Interpretation of Common Words and Phrases*[138] (see above) summarizes case-law adjudications relating to *vehicle*, and in relation to one of the cases we find a definition from *Webster's* cited by a judge, the ordinary definition of *vehicle* is both external to the legal dictionary and embedded within it. If the dictionary meaning is the relevant meaning for the purpose of the legal rule, and the dictionary meaning represents the ordinary meaning, then this represents the ideal alignment of three interpretative frames: the 'ordinary and usual sense', the dictionary definition and the legally relevant meaning.

What is being argued here is that the category of 'ordinary language' (and its close relations 'plain language', 'plain meaning' and so on) arises out of the interpretive needs of law. It is in effect 'judge-made language'. There is nothing 'ordinary' about it. The notion is problematic sociologically and sociolinguistically, in the sense that if a textualist judge of the Supreme Court were to set out on a walk from the centre of Washington, the sense of what is 'ordinary' or what a 'public meaning' might be would vary dramatically block by block; it is problematic jurisprudentially, in that the role of appeals to ordinary language within the adjudicative culture of law is essentially *ad hoc*; it is problematic methodologically, in that the decision to look for the ordinary meaning arises out of a particular textual and factual nexus where the ordinary meaning is already at stake. Intuition or dictionary definitions are then brought to bear on a problem that has already been framed in a particular way. The 'ordinary' is problematic philosophically, in that what is ordinary is relational and therefore in some sense contextual, so that it is a category without ontological boundaries; it is problematic evidentially, in that there is no agreed method for documenting what counts as ordinary language; it is problematic lexicographically, since, as we have seen, 'ordinary language' and 'legal language' are in practice intertwined. Modern electronic corpora of linguistic usage add a new dimension to the documenting of words and phrases across social domains and genres.[139] Their impact on the linguistic culture of law remains to be seen, but it is arguably not possible to improve our understanding of

137 John R. Taylor, *Linguistic Categorization: Prototypes in Linguistic Theory* (Oxford UP 1995).

138 Irving Browne, *The Judicial Interpretation of Common Words and Phrases* (Sumner, Whitney 1883).

139 Stephen Mouritsen, 'The Dictionary Is Not a Fortress: Definitional Fallacies and a Corpus-Based Approach to Plain Meaning' (2010) *Brigham Young University Law*

what is ordinary by better documenting the massive diversity of language usage. The defamiliarization effect of the corpus may be valuable, however, in that it offers a tool whereby intuitions about meaning and word use may be destabilized. The question is whether reference tools should mimic (or at least hint at) the disorderly life of language or seek to impose a fictive definitional regime with neat boxes and subcategories. A 'realistic' definition of *vehicle* would have to be many hundreds of pages; that of *man* or *woman*, many thousands.

Hart in effect domesticated the language of the law, contextualizing law's struggles with meaning in a mundane setting redolent of modern suburban life. In choosing the category *vehicle*, Hart's model raised the category of ordinary words for mundane objects to a jurisprudential dogma, indirectly and inadvertently entrenching not just *McBoyle* but the authority of *Thind*. The rule in *Thind* is structurally analogous to 'only white people admitted to the park'. Hart could not see the problem that *Thind* poses, not because of his politics (impeccably liberal), but because of his use of *vehicle* to stand as the paradigm category for ordinary language. Once we shift our focus away from reassuringly (but quite misleadingly) humdrum *vehicle* and look at categories of human identity, including *man* and *woman*,[140] Hart's model definitively collapses. It is not that Hart's model works for mundane categories for objects but not for categories of people. Rather the key question that Hart never addresses is the question of 'whose language' ordinary non-legal language really is. It is with this question that the linguistic culture of law, including legal lexicography, meets its most serious and complex challenge.

---

*Review* 1915; 'Hard Cases and Hard Data: Assessing Corpus Linguistics as an Empirical Path to Plain Meaning' (2011) 13 *The Columbia Science & Technology Review* 156.

140 See for example *Bellinger v Bellinger* [2003] UKHL 21.

# Chapter 12

# Establishing Meaning in a Bilingual and Bijural Context: Dictionary Use at the Supreme Court of Canada

Mathieu Devinat*

In Law, dictionaries play an important role and serve as tools that help jurists understand the meaning of words they use or read in legal texts. Although these lexicographical works enjoy no formal legal status, they are often referred to as authorities, particularly when judges and lawyers assess the scope and meaning of statutes. As a consequence, they can constitute both a source of information on the meaning of words or expressions, and a basis for legal arguments. Their double function in law and their frequent use make them an object of interest for legal scholars and practitioners.

The use of dictionaries by judges has attracted scholarly attention and formed the subject of a number of articles. Most of the focus has been placed on their appearance in decisions of the *United States Supreme Court*[1] and of the *World Trade Organization*,[2] the theoretical difficulties raised by this practice[3] and its close relationship with *textualist* approaches to statutory construction[4]. In this chapter, however, I will discuss particular issues that arise from the use of dictionaries by the Supreme Court of Canada (SCC). Because of its official bilingualism and bijural character, Canadian Law is a fertile ground for interesting and original questions, mostly related to judicial reasoning in a context where words and phrases are to be read in two different languages that evolve inside two different legal cultures. For example: when judges refer to bilingual statutes in order to establish the ordinary meaning of a word or expression, do they rely

---

* *Professeur titulaire*, Faculté de droit, Université de Sherbrooke, *Chercheur invité*, Faculté de droit, Université de La Rochelle. The author wishes to thank Sophie Audette-Chapdelaine, Ph.D. student at the Faculté de droit, Université de Sherbrooke, for her enthusiastic assistance in this research project and the editor of this volume for his comments on an earlier draft of this chapter.

1 Weis (1987–88), Rynd (1991), Solan (1993), Randolph (1994), Aprill (1998), Metzmeier (2007), Sullivan (2008: 27–38).

2 Lo (2013), Lo (2010), Pavot (2012), Van Damme (2011).

3 See, in particular: Aprill (1998).

4 Solan (1993).

on a dictionary in one language or on lexicographical sources in both languages? Other questions result from the bijurality of Canadian Law. When engaging in the construction of statutes governed by Civil Law or Common Law, do judges limit their study to relevant 'system bound' legal dictionaries, such as the *Black's' Law Dictionary* for the Common Law or the *Vocabulaire juridique* or the *Private Law Dictionary* for Civil Law?

In order to depict the Canadian approach to these questions, SCC cases in which a reference to a dictionary (whether specialized or not) is made were analysed. We restricted our ambit to decisions published between 2000 and 2012. Our main purpose is not to provide an exhaustive description of the Court's practice, but to study judicial pronouncements to discover to what extent and how the linguistic and legal background of words is considered in the construction of bilingual and bijural legislation.

## The Use of Dictionaries in Interpreting Bilingual Legislation

In order to understand the legal issues involved in dictionary use, it is important to first describe how official bilingualism works in Canada and explain how this policy applies to judicial decisions.

In Canadian Law, both versions of bilingual legislation are deemed to enjoy the same authority.[5] According to this principle, Canadian jurists cannot ignore one version of a statute on the basis that it is merely a translation of the other.[6] The equal authority principle can also lead to the conclusion that a citizen can rely on one version of a statute only, without having to consult the other. Although it may be a good rule of thumb for an ordinary citizen, the same cannot be said for the Courts, as Sullivan rightly points out: '[t]he duty of the courts to read both versions of bilingually enacted legislation is well established and repeatedly emphasized by the courts'.[7]

---

5 The 'equal authority' principle was affirmed in *The King v. Dubois*, [1935] SCR 378 as being derived from Section 133 of the *Constitutional Act of 1867* that states that both versions should be published. The principle has since been expressly provided for in the Canadian *Charter of Rights and Freedom*, at section 18. See also: *R. v. Jarvis*, [2002] 3 SCR 757, par 79; *Att. Gen. of Quebec v. Blaikie et al.* [1979] 2 SCR 1016, 1022.

6 See: *Doré v. Verdun (City)* [1997] 2 SCR 862, par 24, J. Gonthier for the Court: 'This argument was rejected by Baudouin J.A. in the judgment under appeal, partly on the basis that the English version of the Civil Code is [TRANSLATION] "merely a translation of the original French version" (p. 1327). With respect, although what he stated is unfortunately true, it cannot be used to reject the argument made by the appellant. Section 7 of the *Charter of the French language*, R.S.Q., c. C11, provides that the French and English versions of Quebec statutes "are equally authoritative". This is in accordance with s. 133 of the *Constitution Act*, 1867 which requires that the statutes of the legislature of Quebec be enacted in both official languages and that both versions be equally authoritative and have the same status'.

7 Sullivan (2008: 98).

Official bilingualism also applies to judicial decisions. By reason of the *Official Languages Act*, all final decisions, orders or judgments of federal courts are given in one language and translated in the other.[8] Therefore, SCC judgments are made available in both official languages, but with an explicit indication of which version is a translation (the translated *official* version is indicated by the legend 'Version française du jugement de … rendu par'/'English version of the judgment … delivered by'). Leaving aside rare cases where both versions are equally authentic (that is, neither text is a translation of the other),[9] the question whether the French and English versions share the same authority is the subject of much debate although the general consensus is that unlike with legislation, the authentic version of a judgment should prevail over its translation.[10]

Dictionaries are usually referred to by judges when they discuss interpretation issues related to statutes,[11] more precisely when they determine their scope. In most cases, the wording of the Act is the starting point in the interpretation process, followed by a consideration of the context and purpose of the Act.[12] In the absence

8 *Official Languages Act*, R.S.C., 1985, c. 31 (4th Supp.), Section 20.

9 In some cases, mostly involving constitutional issues or languages rights, the reasoning for judgments is delivered by 'The Court/La Cour' with no mention of the language in which the judgment was originally drafted. Both version of the judgment in such cases are understood to share equal authority. On this subject, see Scassa (1994: 174–81).

10 Authors agree that there are no governing rules on this question, but disagree on the principles that should apply. For conflicting points of view, compare: 'il est indéniable que les versions anglaise et française des jugements de la Cour fédérale, de la Cour d'appel fédérale et, surtout, de la Cour suprême du Canada, font pareillement autorité'. (Bastarache et al. (2009: 119–21) with Scassa. 'Nonetheless, it is equally easy to assume that where it is clear that one version is original and the other a translation, in case of discrepancy, the original will prevail' (1994: 181). See also, Solan (2012: 173): 'Both versions of bilingual judgments (which must be published in French and English) should generally be seen as authentic because judgments define and develop the law'. The consequences of conflicting versions of judgments are discussed in Leckey (2007).

11 Dictionaries are also sometimes used to discuss the meaning of previous judgments, see: *R. v. Szczerbaniwicz*, 2010 SCC 15, [2010] 1 SCR 455, JJ. Binnie and Fish, dissenting, par 42; *Canadian Western Bank v. Alberta*, [2007] 2 SCR 3, 2007 SCC 22, JJ. Binnie and Lebel, for the majority, par 52.

12 For an example of the reasoning process: *Canada Trustco Mortgage Co. v. Canada*, 2005 SCC 54, [2005] 2 SCR 601, par 10: 'It has been long established as a matter of statutory interpretation that "the words of an Act are to be read in their entire context and in their grammatical and ordinary sense harmoniously with the scheme of the Act, the object of the Act, and the intention of Parliament": see *65302 British Columbia Ltd. v. Canada*, [1999] 3 SCR 804, par 50'. The wording of an act has an importance that varies from one case to another, as Justice Abella recently framed it: 'The words, if clear, will dominate; if not, they yield to an interpretation that best meets the overriding purpose of the statute' (*Celgene Corp. v. Canada (Attorney General)*, 2011 SCC 1, [2011] 1 SCR 3, par 2).

of legislative definitions,[13] dictionaries are seen as standard tools for determining the *ordinary meaning* of words.[14] When interpreting a bilingual statute, however, the process of determining meaning raises technical but policy-driven issues: when SCC judges refer to a dictionary, like *Le Robert*, in order to describe the ordinary meaning of a French expression, to what extent will they subject the *other* official language to the same inquiry and consider the English 'ordinary meaning'? More fundamentally, is meaning conceived separately in terms of each version of the statute (a form of legal *dualism*[15]) or is meaning the result of both the French and English texts read together (legal *bilingualism*)? In order to get a broad insight into the Court's practice, one needs to extend one's focus beyond the reading of SCC judgments in one language only and compare both the authentic and translated versions. Interestingly, we found that certain translation techniques used by the Court reflect different ways of establishing ordinary meaning in law and different levels of sensitivity towards the linguistic realities of *each* community. Although a single clear pattern of practice in dictionary usage could not be detected, three very different methods seem to be followed and could be described schematically in the following way:

1. Independent assessment of 'two' *ordinary meanings*: a French dictionary is used to describe the meaning of the French version of the statute and an English dictionary is referred to in the other version of the judgment to define the equivalent English wording of the same statute;
2. Simultaneous identification of 'one' *ordinary meaning*: both versions of the judgment refer to both French and English dictionaries to describe the French and English wordings of a statute;
3. Description of a single language *ordinary meaning*: ordinary meaning is established by referring to a single language dictionary in the original version of the judgment, which is simply translated into the other language.

Each of these practices related to the use of dictionaries reveals different conceptions of 'ordinary meaning' in a bilingual context, and it is worth exploring them in greater detail in order to better understand their implications.

## Independent Assessment of 'Two' Ordinary Meanings

Surprisingly, in the absence of a comparison of both versions of the Courts' judgment, this first method may go largely unnoticed. Only when the reader combines both the original and the translated versions of the judges' opinions can he/she realize that in

---

13 The absence of a relevant legislative definition is generally seen as a prerequisite before consulting a dictionary.

14 We agree with Sullivan (2008: 27–8) that 'ordinary meaning' and 'dictionary meaning' are conceptually distinct.

15 Dualism being 'the practice of two legal unilingualisms' (Macdonald, 2007: 154).

numerous cases, the 'translated' version of the judgment does not refer to the same dictionary as the original, nor does it contain a definition of the same words.

For example, it is not uncommon to find that the English version of a judge's opinion refers to the *Oxford English Dictionary* in order to establish the ordinary meaning of the English version of a statute, while in the French translated version of his opinion, reference will be made to the *Nouveau Petit Robert* to establish the meaning of the French version of the statute (the reverse holds true where the French version is the original). In *R. v. Tran*, Justice Charron wrote:

> The general meaning of the noun 'insult' as defined in the *Shorter Oxford English Dictionary on Historical Principles* (6th ed. 2007), vol. 1, at p. 1400, is '[a]n act or the action of attacking; (an) attack, (an) assault'. Likewise, the action of insulting means to '[s]how arrogance or scorn; boast, exult, esp. insolently or contemptuously. ... Treat with scornful abuse; subject to indignity; ... offend the modesty or self-respect of'.

This was translated as:

> Premièrement, on voit mal comment la conduite de Mme Duong et de M. An Tran pourrait constituer une insulte au sens usuel du terme. Le *Nouveau Petit Robert: Dictionnaire alphabétique et analogique de la langue française* (2010) définit l' « insulte » comme suit à la p. 1347: « Acte ou parole qui vise à outrager ou constitue un outrage ». De même, l'action d' « insulter » s'entend de celle d' « attaquer (qqn) par des propos ou des actes outrageants ».[16]

In this scenario, judges establish meaning in parallel by taking into consideration different dictionaries with specific definitions for each linguistic version of the statute.

This practice of establishing ordinary meaning of both linguistic versions independently is found in many cases. One such typical case is *Society of Composers, Authors and Music Publishers of Canada v. Canadian Assn. of Internet Providers*, where Justice Binnie wrote:

> The word 'communicate' is an ordinary English word that means to 'impart' or 'transmit' (*Shorter Oxford English Dictionary on Historical Principles* (5th ed. 2002), vol. 1, at p. 463).

Which opinion was translated:

> Dans son sens ordinaire, le mot 'communiquer' signifie 'faire connaître' 'transmettre' (*Le Nouveau Petit Robert* (2003), p. 485).[17]

---

16 2010 SCC 58, [2010] 3 SCR 350, par 44.

17 *Society of Composers, Authors and Music Publishers of Canada v. Canadian Assn. of Internet Providers* [2004] 2 SCR 427, 2004 SCC 45, par 45.

In keeping with this approach, we found a fair number of SCC cases where the judges refer to different dictionaries in both versions of their judgments.[18] As we can see from the previous quotes, this practice has the benefit of using lexicographical tools that are relevant to each linguistic community. Although one may question the value of relying on the Oxford English Dictionary or the American Merriam-Webster Dictionary when similar works describe Canadian linguistic usages, the decision to prefer those established dictionaries is justifiable on the basis of the greater prestige they enjoy.[19] This translation practice does, however, raise issues regarding the official bilingualism policies in Canada.

Firstly, under this practice the French and English versions of judgment cannot be viewed as exact equivalents:[20] the entries and definitions in *Le Robert* are not the same and sometimes differ from those of *Oxford*'s.[21] In a context where the quality and reliability of translations are prerequisites for ensuring access to justice in both languages, this practice is open to criticism. It could, in fact, give rise to unnecessary divergences between both versions of the judgment, with the

---

18 For examples, see: *Entertainment Software Association v. Society of Composers, Authors and Music Publishers of Canada*, 2012 SCC 34, [2012] 2 SCR 231, Rothstein, dissenting, par 72; *Opitz v. Wrzesnewskyj*, 2012 SCC 55, [2012] 3 SCR 76, C.J. McLachlin, at 147; *Masterpiece Inc. v. Alavida Lifestyles Inc.*, 2011 SCC 27, [2011] 2 SCR 387, J. Rothstein, for the Court; Veuve *Clicquot Ponsardin v. Boutiques Cliquot Ltée* [2006] 1 SCR 824, 2006 SCC 23, par 23, J. Binnie, for the Court; *R. v. Clark* [2005] 1 SCR 6, 2005 SCC 2, par 13, J. Fish for the Court; *R. v. Woods* [2005] 2 SCR 205, 2005 SCC 42, par 13, J. Fish, for the Court; *R. v. Hamilton* [2005] 2 SCR 432, 2005 SCC 47, par 21, J. Fish, for the Court; CCH *Canadian Ltd. v. Law Society of Upper Canada* [2004] 1 SCR 339, 2004 SCC 13, par 38, Justice McLachlin, for the Court, par 18; *United Taxi Drivers' Fellowship of Southern Alberta v. Calgary (City)* [2004] 1 SCR 485, 2004 SCC 19, Bastarache, for the Court par 13; Cartaway *Resources Corp. (Re)* [2004] 1 SCR 672, 2004 SCC 26, par 61, Lebel, for the Court.

19 As Sullivan (2008: 34) pointed out, in her review of the selection process behind dictionary use: 'in Canada [...] there is no official or standard dictionary for the languages in which legislation is drafted. Although there are a number of dictionaries based on Canadian usage, the courts generally rely on dictionaries published in England or the United States for English words and on dictionaries published in France for French words'.

20 In *R. v. C.D.; R. v. C.D.K.* [2005] 3 S.C.R. 668, 2005 SCC 78, par. 29, for example, reference is made the *Oxford English Dictionary* (2nd ed. 1989) to establish the 'ordinary meaning', while the French translation refers to Cornu's *Vocabulaire juridique*.

21 For example, in *Opitz v. Wrzesnewskyj*, 2012 SCC 55 [2012] 3 SCR 76, at 147: 'Suivant son sens ordinaire, l'adjectif "irrégulier" évoque ce qui "n'est pas conforme à la règle établie, **à l'usage commun**, ..."' (*Le Grand Robert de la langue française, version* électronique). / 'In the ordinary sense of the word, something is "irregular" when it is "[n]ot in conformity with rule or principle"' (*The Oxford English Dictionary* (2nd ed. 1989), vol. VIII, at p. 93) [emphasis added]. *United Taxi Drivers' Fellowship of Southern Alberta v. Calgary (City)*, [2004] 1 SCR 485, 2004 SCC 19, par 1: 'Le terme "réglementer", selon *Le Nouveau Petit Robert* (2003), p. 2218, signifie "[a]ssujettir à un règlement"'. / 'To "regulate", as defined in the *Oxford English Dictionary* (2nd ed. 1989), vol. XIII, is "subject to ... **restrictions**"' [emphasis added].

translated version most at risk of being seen as of doubtful authority.[22] On the other hand, the translation process at the SCC does contain some safeguards that can mitigate this risk, namely its expertise in this area and in the fact that the author of the judgment is consulted during the process and must agree on the final text. She or he is accordingly in a position to compare the content of each version in order to confirm that they communicate the same message. In order to further appreciate the practical impact of this technique, an extensive comparative study of the definitions involved would be necessary.

This translation method raises legal issues related to the construction of bilingual legislation. By assessing *ordinary meaning* in one language without referring to the other version of a statute, the Court implicitly acts as if each version can independently 'stand on its own'. One can argue, on the contrary, that the determination of *ordinary meaning* should systematically be made by comparing and taking into consideration both versions of a statute *at the same time*. As Sullivan points out, '[in] drawing inference [on the legislatures' intent] interpreters are obliged to take both language versions into account'.[23] In the same manner, both versions of a statute 'should be read together', or at least consulted, when determining its scope.[24] Although the compounded French and English *meaning*, when found, should not be seen as being conclusive; it remains, in our view, an essential element to be considered in the interpretation process. It seems, then, that this first judicial method of establishing ordinary meaning reflects the widespread practice of not engaging in a systematic reading or comparison of both versions of a bilingual statute, particularly when there are no alleged discrepancies between them.[25]

Even though this way of determining ordinary meaning seems to stem from an accepted translation technique,[26] it raises issues that go beyond technical

---

22 For a similar argument, related to the translation of a quote of a bilingual enactment, see Leckey (2007: 591): 'When a judge quotes the version of a bilingual enactment corresponding to the language in which she is writing, should the translation of that judgment systematically quote the corresponding version of the destination language? [...] The best answer is likely that the judge, in the original set of reasons and the translation, should quote both language versions of the enactment'. We agree with Leckey.

23 Sullivan (2008: 120).

24 In *R. v. Jarvis*, [2002] 3 SCR 757, par 79, JJ. Iacobucci and Major wrote for the Court: 'As several of this Court's recent cases have illustrated, the words employed in the English and French versions of a federal statute are equally authoritative and should be read together in order to ascertain the proper meaning of the terms'.

25 The practice seems contrary to the requirement that parties reproduce both versions of a statute in their factums, see: *Rules of the Supreme Court of Canada*, SOR/2002–156, section 42 (2) (g). On the importance of consulting both versions of a statute, see: *R. v. Mac*, [2002] 1 SCR 856, 2002 SCC 24.

26 One argument in favour of this translation technique is that it leads to a target text that is independent from the source text and that the reader of the translated version is in the same 'communicative situation' as the reader of the original version. Our opinion is that

considerations of correspondence or equivalence between both versions of judgments. A basic flaw in this approach is that it sets aside a comparative analysis of the French and English wording of legislation and deprives judicial reasoning of insights that could enrich our understanding of statutes, as the following approach illustrates.

## Simultaneous Identification of 'One' Ordinary Meaning

This next method shows how ordinary meaning can be established by considering both versions of statutes at the same time. In numerous cases, we found that judges referred in the original judgment to both the English and French wording of a statute by providing a dictionary definition of each word or term.[27] As Justice Fish stated in R. v. Steele, 'the ordinary meaning of "use" (or "utilise", in the corresponding French version of a statute) can be discerned from its dictionary definitions in both languages'.[28] Although it is difficult to determine why judges sometimes prefer this method of determining ordinary meaning to the first method set out above, it can be observed that this methodology is generally found when both linguistic versions confirm the judges' interpretation.

For example, in *Monsanto Canada Inc. v. Schmeiser*, Justices McLachlin and Fish discuss the meaning of 'use'/'*exploiter*' in the following way:

> Determining the meaning of 'use' under s. 42 is essentially a matter of statutory construction. The starting point is the plain meaning of the word, in this case 'use' or '*exploiter*'. *The Concise Oxford Dictionary* defines 'use' as 'cause to act or serve for a purpose; bring into service; avail oneself of': *The Concise Oxford Dictionary of Current English* (9th ed. 1995), at p. 1545. This denotes utilization for a purpose. **The French word '*exploiter*' is even clearer**. It denotes utilization with a view to production or advantage: '*tirer parti de (une chose), en vue d'une production ou dans un but lucratif. [...] Utiliser d'une manière avantageuse*': *Le Nouveau Petit Robert* (2003), at p. 1004.[29]

---

the translated version of the judgement should faithfully reproduce the judges' reasoning, which this translation technique does not seem to do (that is, she or he presumably did not refer to the other language dictionaries).

27 For example, in *R. v. Audet* [1996] 2 SCR 171, Justice La Forest wrote: 'In the absence of statutory definitions, the process of interpretation must begin with a consideration of the ordinary meaning of the words used by Parliament. Le *Grand Robert de la langue française* (2nd ed. 1986) defines the French word "autorité" as [...] [and] *The Oxford English Dictionary* (2nd ed. 1989) suggests similar definitions for the English word "authority"' [at par. 34.].

28 *R. v. Steele* [2007] 3 SCR 3, 2007 SCC 36, J. Fish, for the Court, par 31.

29 *Monsanto Canada Inc. v. Schmeiser* [2004] 1 SCR 902, 2004 SCC 34, C.J. McLachlin and Fish, par 31, for the majority [emphasis added].

Recourse to the dictionary definition of the French word 'exploiter' seems to lend some added weight to the ordinary meaning argument.[30] More recently, in R. v. Venneri, the Court had to decide if the fact of buying drugs on a regular basis from members of an organized crime gang, with a view to selling them to one's own clients, could be considered as membership of a 'criminal organization'. The Court's answer was negative, partly by virtue of the wording of the statute and the meaning of the terms 'organize' and 'organization'. As we can see in this excerpt, Justice Fish examines both the French and English expressions:

> Qualifying 'organized' in s. 467.1 by 'however' cannot, as a matter of language or logic, be taken to signify that no element of organization is required at all. 'Organized' necessarily connotes *some form* of structure and co-ordination, as appears from the definition of 'organized' in the *Shorter Oxford English Dictionary on Historical Principles* (6th ed. 2007), vol. 2: Formed into a whole with *interdependent* parts; *coordinated* so as to form an orderly *structure*; systematically arranged. [Emphasis added: p. 2023] **In French, the definitions in *Le Grand Robert de la langue française* (electronic version) are consistent with this**: it defines the noun '*organisation*' as the [TRANSLATION] '[a]ction of organizing (something); the result of such an action' and the verb '*organiser*' as '[t]o give a specific *structure* or composition, order, or method of functioning or administration to'.[31]

In these cases and in a number of others, the French and English versions are expressly consulted in the determination of ordinary meaning, and dictionaries in both languages are referred to.[32] Even if this technique, like any argument based on a dictionary definition, can be said to further rhetorical objectives,[33] it has

---

30 This method of determining ordinary meaning derives from the 'shared meaning rule' that applies to bilingual legislation. As Sullivan points out, 'the effect of relying on both versions is to lend further weight to the presumption in favour or ordinary meaning' (2007: 102).

31 *R. v. Venneri*, 2012 SCC 33 [2012] 2 SCR 211, J. Fish, for the Court, par 30 [emphasis added].

32 *Canada (Information Commissioner) v. Canada (Minister of National Defence)*, 2011 SCC 25 [2011] 2 SCR 306, Justice Charron, par 48; *Canada Post Corp. v. Lépine* [2009] 1 SCR 549, 2009 SCC 16, par 54; *R. v. Steele* [2007] 3 SCR 3, 2007 SCC 36, J. Fish, for the Court, par 31; *Reference re Employment Insurance Act (Can.), ss. 22 and 23* [2005] 2 SCR 669, 2005 SCC 56, par 61; *Martineau v. M.N.R.* [2004] 3 SCR 737, 2004 SCC 81, par 75; *I.A.T.S.E., Stage Local 56 v. Société de la Place des Arts de Montréal* [2004] 1 SCR 43, 2004 SCC 2, par 25, Justice Gonthier, for the Court; *Martineau v. M.N.R.* [2004] 3 SCR 737, 2004 SCC 81, par 75–78; *R. v. Daoust*, [2004] 1 SCR 217, 2004 SCC 6, J. Bastarache, for the Court, par 50; *Harvard College v. Canada (Commissioner of Patents)* [2002] 4 SCR 45, 2002 SCC 76, par 45, 162–3.

33 Sullivan suggests, correctly in our view, that the 'effect of relying on both versions is to lend further weight to the presumption in favour of ordinary meaning' (2008: 33–5).

the advantage of reminding the reader of the French and English versions of the judgment that there are two different linguistic realities involved in the reading of bilingual statutes.

By engaging in a comparative study of both versions, this method of establishing ordinary meaning is, in our view, closer to the spirit of the *equal authority* principle. It also respects the importance that the SCC attributes to the "common" or "shared" meaning of both versions.[34] In order to arrive at this common ordinary meaning, it is necessary to refer to, and hopefully compare the different meanings conveyed in the English and French texts.[35] Another advantage of this approach over the preceding approach is that the simultaneous study of both versions leads to a superior quality of the translated judgment. When judges study both versions by referring to different dictionaries, translators give a literal rendering of the original judgment, therefore improving the reliability of the translation.

## Unilateral Description of a Single Ordinary Meaning

One last, but relatively uncommon method discovered is the practice of simply referring to a single dictionary when establishing the ordinary meaning of a bilingual act. This usage results in a situation where the ordinary meaning of the other official version of the statute is not specifically examined. In discussing only one version of the statute, they generally do so without offering an explanation as to why the other version is not formally considered.

In *Chieu v. Canada (Minister of Citizenship and Immigration)*, Justice Iacobbuci had to determine if the wording of the *Immigration Act*[36] could allow the court to consider potential hardship that could be suffered in a foreign country in deciding whether to uphold an order to remove an individual from Canada. More precisely, the question was whether this potential hardship could be covered by the expression 'having regard to all the circumstances of the case'. Only the English wording of the act is examined:

> The second factor favouring a broad reading of s. 70(1)(b) is the grammatical sense of the phrase 'all the circumstances of the case'. The word 'all' is defined by the *Concise Oxford Dictionary* (8th ed. 1990), at p. 29, as 'entire number

---

34 It is important to remember that this shared meaning does not prevent the courts from taking into consideration the context and purpose of the act. The SCC has, however, sometimes expressed a stronger view of the authority of the shared meaning (see *R. v. Mac* [2002] 1 SCR 856, 2002 SCC 24; *R. v. Daoust* [2004] 1 S.C.R. 217, 2004 SCC 6, par 44). For a critical appraisal of a 'strong' version of this principle, see: Sullivan (2011–12).

35 It could be argued that if the Court was consistent in its application of the 'shared meaning rule', it would systematically refer to both versions of bilingual statutes in each version of its judgment.

36 Section 70(1)(b), *Immigration Act*, R.S.C. 1985, c. I-2.

> of' or 'greatest possible'. In this context, it would therefore mean considering the greatest possible number of factors relevant to the removal of a permanent resident from Canada. It is evident that one such factor is the conditions an individual would face upon removal.[37]

Although an examination of the French version of the statute ('aux circonstances particulières de l'espèce') would also support this conclusion, it is not discussed in the translated version of the judgment:

> Le deuxième facteur favorisant l'interprétation large de l'al. 70(1)b) est le sens grammatical de l'expression 'all the circumstances of the case' dans la version anglaise. Le mot 'all', selon le *Concise Oxford Dictionary* (8e éd. 1990), p. 29, signifie [TRADUCTION] 'le nombre total de' 'le plus possible'. Dans ce contexte, cela veut dire qu'il faut examiner le plus grand nombre possible de facteurs intervenant dans la décision de renvoyer un résident permanent du Canada. Il est évident que l'un de ces facteurs est la situation dans laquelle il se trouverait après son renvoi.[38]

We found no explanation as to why the French wording is not explicitly referenced, but this method leads one to conclude that it has not been taken into consideration (probably because it did not add further weight to the argument). Another (more dubious) illustration of this practice is found in *Society of Composers, Authors and Music Publishers of Canada v. Canadian Assn. of Internet Providers*.[39] Justice Binnie states that:

> The words of s. 2.4(1)(b) [of the *Copyright Act*] must be read in their ordinary and grammatical sense in the proper context. 'Necessary' is a word whose meaning varies somewhat with the context. The word, according to *Black's Law Dictionary*, may mean something which in the accomplishment of a given object cannot be dispensed with, or it may mean something reasonably useful and proper, and of greater or lesser benefit or convenience, and its force and meaning must be determined with relation to the particular object sought. (*Black's Law Dictionary* (6th ed. 1990), at p. 1029).

In the French version of the decision, he does not refer to a French dictionary in order to establish the ordinary meaning of 'nécessaire'. In fact, the translation reads:

---

37 *Chieu v. Canada (Minister of Citizenship and Immigration)* [2002] 1 SCR 84, 2002 SCC 3, J. Iacobucci, for the Court, par 30.

38 *Chieu v. Canada (Minister of Citizenship and Immigration)* [2002] 1 SCR 84, 2002 SCC 3, J. Iacobucci, for the Court, par 30.

39 [2004] 2 SCR 427, 2004 SCC 45. See also: *R. v. Sharpe* [2001] 1 SCR 45, 2001 SCC 2, C.J. McLachlin, for the majority, par 45.

> Il faut interpréter les termes employés à l'al. 2.4(1)b) dans leur sens ordinaire et grammatical, selon le contexte. La signification du mot 'nécessaire' ('necessary', en anglais) varie en quelque sorte en fonction du contexte. Voici la définition qu'en donne le *Black's Law Dictionary*: [traduction] [S]e dit de ce dont on ne peut faire l'économie pour accomplir quelque chose, ou de ce qui est raisonnablement utile et approprié et présente un avantage plus ou moins grand, la force et le sens de ce mot devant être déterminés eu égard à la fin recherchée. [Je souligne.] (*Black's Law Dictionary* (6e éd. 1990), p. 1029).

This method of determining 'ordinary meaning' is problematic for a number of reasons. Firstly, it seems to give unequal weight to one version of a statute, in a way that is contrary to the principles of equal authority.[40] This concern was voiced in Pharmascience Inc. v. Binet, by Justice Lebel who, after having studied at length the French version, wrote, for the majority:

> If there were any concern that the significance given to this common meaning might give disproportionate weight to the French version, contrary to the principles of interpretation of bilingual statutes, it should be noted that the ordinary sense of the English version of s. 122, which provides that '[t]he syndic and assistant syndics may … require that they be provided with any information or document', is equally supportive of the appellants' position.[41]

As this quote illustrates, attributing too much weight to one version over the other can be viewed as a violation of the principles of equal authenticity.

Secondly, and more importantly, the method of assessing ordinary meaning by referring to a single version can be seen as a form of linguistic selection that conceals the possible discrepancies between the two versions of the statute. In the case *Society of Composers, Authors and Music Publishers of Canada v. Canadian Assn. of Internet Providers*, the ordinary meaning of '*nécessaire*', whether in law or in ordinary usage, does not extend – in French – to conditions that would be 'reasonably' useful as stated in *Black's Law Dictionary.*[42] The assertion that 'La signification du mot "nécessaire" ("necessary", en anglais) varie en quelque sorte

40 This comment does not extend to English unilingual statutes. In these case, we noted that judges referred only to English dictionaries; see, for example: *Alberta Union of Provincial Employees v. Lethbridge Community College* [2004] 1 SCR 727, 2004 SCC 28, J. Iacobucci, par 30; *Krangle (Guardian ad litem of) v. Brisco* [2002] 1 SCR 205, 2002 SCC 9, par 34.

41 [2006] 2 SCR 513, 2006 SCC 48, par 31.

42 See for example: in Cornu (2003) 'nécessaire': 'adj. – Lat. necessarius: inéluctable, indispensable, nécessaire. 1. Exigé (en droit), requis, obligatoire (not. pour l'accomplissement d'un acte)'; in Reid (2010) 'Nécessaire': '1. Se dit d'une condition, d'un moyen que la loi impose pour la validité d'un acte. Ex. Le consentement nécessaire du conjoint pour la vente de la résidence familiale. Comp. Impératif 2. Indispensable, dont on ne peut se passer'.

en fonction du contexte', would seem to contain the dubious suggestion that the French and English words are identical and therefore interchangeable. In our view, it would be preferable to address the difficulty raised by the divergences between both versions and to engage in a comprehensive study of the whole of the act.

As we can see, dictionary use by the SCC raises a number of methodological issues, some of which are directly related to the policy of official bilingualism in Canada. The method by which judges establish 'ordinary meaning', through the use of dictionaries, reflects a certain approach to the reading of bilingual statutes. It may point to the importance that is given to ordinary meaning when constructing statutes. Dictionaries are only a means to an end, as Justice Iacobucci wrote:

> … statutory interpretation in the context of constitutional review is not an exact science. While reference to common parlance and standard dictionary definitions are often of assistance in interpreting legislative provisions, regard must be had not only to the ordinary and natural meaning of the words, but also to the context in which they are used and the purpose of the provision as a whole: *R. v. Lewis* [1996] 1 S.C.R. 921. The most significant element of this analysis is the determination of legislative intent.[43]

Another interesting dimension of dictionary use in Canadian Law is its relationship with the two existing different legal systems, the Common Law and the Civil Law. How judges actually take into consideration variations in meaning within these two legal systems will now be examined.

## The Use of Legal Dictionaries in a Bijural Legal System

Although legal and general dictionaries both describe meaning, legal dictionaries are inspired by ambiguous lexicographical principles that make them at the same time descriptive (of legal discourse) and prescriptive (of what words should mean in law).[44] Because of their prescriptive function, legal dictionaries define legal meaning by referring to national legal systems (for example *Dictionary of Canadian Law*) or, in a more general way, to legal traditions (for example Common Law for the *Blacks' Law Dictionary* and Civil Law for the *Vocabulaire juridique*).[45] In this way, legal dictionaries can be said to be 'system bound' or intrinsically related to a specific legal culture. When a statute is governed by Civil Law or Common

43 *R. v. Monney*, [1999] 1 SCR 652, par 26.

44 On this subject, see: Garner (2003), Cornu (2003: preface, 1992). For an appraisal of the civilian lexicographical approach, see Devinat (2005).

45 This is a very superficial presentation of their content. Both dictionaries have historically been based on national systems (American and English Law for *Black's*, French Law for *Cornu*) and both take into consideration some *foreign* vocabulary, like feudal law, Roman Law and Spanish Law (See the eighth edition of *Black's* for example).

Law, to what extent will judges effectively take into consideration this background when referring to a legal dictionary? Surprisingly, our study shows that no such differentiation is made, at least not explicitly. In fact, legal dictionaries seem to be treated like general language dictionaries. Before describing this judicial approach to law dictionaries, it is useful to give an overview of their use by the SCC.

Legal dictionaries are referred to less frequently than their general counterparts: in the period analysed, we found only 48 references in 33 judgments. Compare with the 77 references in 61 judgments to general dictionaries. Another significant feature is the overwhelming use of the *Black's Law Dictionary* (22 decisions), with Reid's *Dictionnaire de droit québécois et canadien avec table des abréviations et lexique anglaisfrançais* (10 decisions) as the most cited reference work. The following works also feature, though less prominently: Cornu's *Vocabulaire juridique* (6 decisions), Dukelows' *Dictionary of Canadian Law* (5 decisions) and Crépeau's *Dictionnaire de droit privé et Lexiques bilingues* (4 decisions).[46] Compared to *foreign* legal dictionaries, such as the *Vocabulaire juridique* or *Black's Law Dictionary*, Canadian lexicographical tools are less cited in SCC judgments.[47]

The most striking feature of legal dictionaries is that they are frequently used to determine 'plain' or 'ordinary' meaning. In fact, the idea that they might convey some distinctive or technical 'legal' meaning is rarely[48] mentioned in judgments. As a consequence, SCC judges use them to describe the 'ordinary and grammatical sense',[49] the 'ordinary and accepted meaning'[50] and generally simply to describe

46 If we take into consideration both editions of this dictionary: the 2nd, Crépeau (1991) and the 3rd, Crépeau (2003).

47 This conclusion extends to all works of Canadian lexicography, whether specialised in law or not. Between 1990 and 2012, we found a meagre 33 references to Canadian works of lexicography, compared to 204 references for non-Canadian material.

48 We found one quote: *R. v. Ulybel Enterprises Ltd.* [2001] 2 S.C.R. 867, 2001 SCC 56, Justice Iacobucci, par 44: 'Furthermore, the legal definition of "forfeiture" is "a divestiture of specific property without compensation": see *Black's Law Dictionary* (6th ed. 1990), at p. 650'.

49 *Society of Composers, Authors and Music Publishers of Canada v. Canadian Assn. of Internet Providers* [2004] 2 SCR 427, 2004 SCC 45, par 45: 'The words of s. 2.4(1)(b) [of the *Copyright Act*] must be read in their ordinary and grammatical sense in the proper context. "Necessary" is a word whose meaning varies somewhat with the context. The word, according to *Black's Law Dictionary:* may mean something which in the accomplishment of a given object cannot be dispensed with [...]'. See also, *R. v. C.D.; R. v. C.D.K.* [2005] 3 S.C.R. 668, 2005 SCC 78, par 29; *Markevich v. Canada* [2003] 1 S.C.R. 94, 2003 SCC 9, par 24.

50 *R. v. Steele* [2007] 3 S.C.R. 3, 2007 SCC 36, par. 31: 'These observations are entirely consistent with the ordinary and accepted meaning of "use". And the Court has recognized that the ordinary meaning of "use" (or "*utilise*", in the corresponding French version of a statute) can be discerned from its dictionary definitions in both languages. [...] Likewise, according to *Black's Law Dictionary* (6th ed. 1990), "use" means "make use of; to convert to one's service; to employ; to avail oneself of; to utilize; to carry out a purpose or action by means of; *to put into action or service, especially to attain an end*" (emphasis added)'.

'meaning'[51] in the same way they would refer to any other language dictionary. For example, Justice Bastarache refers indistinctively to general and legal dictionaries to describe 'the ordinary meaning' of the word 'transfer/*transfert* that is':

> [TRANSLATION] '[a]ct whereby a person transmits a right to another': *Le Nouveau Petit Robert* (2002); [TRANSLATION] '[t]ransmission of a right from one holder to another': Gérard Cornu, ed., *Vocabulaire juridique* (8th ed. 2000); '[a]ny mode of disposing of or parting with an asset or an interest in an asset': *Black's Law Dictionary* (7th ed. 1999).[52]

This approach also seems to extend to the translation process described above: the Court having at least once translated an Oxford English Dictionary definition by its equivalent in Cornu's Vocabulaire juridique.[53] In sum, legal dictionaries are generally seen and treated as ordinary language dictionaries.

Although legal dictionaries describe meaning conveyed within a particular legal tradition, they are used as language dictionaries, without considering the legal background of the statute. The practice does not seem to raise particular difficulties for the Court: *Black's Law Dictionary* was used to describe the meaning of an English expression in the *Quebec Civil Code*[54] and conversely Cornu's *Vocabulaire juridique* has been called upon to help define a French expression in a federal statute governed by Common Law.[55] Moreover, no mention is made of the 'foreign' legal origins on which are based these favoured dictionaries. Even if *Black's Law Dictionary* is principally based on American legal material, it is used to interpret Canadian legislation. A solitary critical note was struck by Justice McLachlin in a dissenting opinion:

---

51 Judges sometimes do not even use the word's 'meaning' at all: *Canada (Information Commissioner) v. Canada (Commissioner of the Royal Canadian Mounted Police)* [2003] 1 S.C.R. 66, 2003 SCC 8, Gonthier, for the Court, par. 25.

52 *R. v. Daoust* [2004] 1 S.C.R. 217, 2004 SCC 6, par 49.

53 *R. v. C.D.K.* [2005] 3 S.C.R. 668, 2005 SCC 78, par 29. This case is interesting because in the English version, Cornu's *Vocabulaire* is also referred to, but in another part of the judgement (par 68 and 85) when Justice Bastarache studies the expression 'violence' found in the French version of the *Youth Criminal Justice Act*. The same expression is studied at par 29, but in English he quotes the *Oxford English Dictionary*.

54 In *Canada Post Corp. v. Lépine*, 2009 SCC 16 [2009] 1 S.C.R. 549, Justice Lebel, par 54: 'The term "dispute" has a broad meaning that encompasses all types of legal proceedings (see *Black's Law Dictionary* (8th ed. 2004), at p. 505; see also, regarding the term *litige* used in the French version of art. 3155(4), H. Reid, *Dictionnaire de droit québécois et canadien* (3rd ed. 2004), at p. 355; *Le Grand Robert de la langue française* (2nd ed. enl. 2001), vol. 4, at p. 864'.

55 In the following case, the term 'violent' found in the federal *Youth Criminal Justice Act: R. v. C.D.K.* [2005] 3 S.C.R. 668, 2005 SCC 78, par. 29 and 85. See also: *R. v. Daoust* [2004] 1 S.C.R. 217, 2004 SCC 6, par 49.

> The majority, at para. 34, relies on the definition of '*bona fide*' in *Black's Law Dictionary* (8th ed. 2004), at p. 186. It might be suggested that an American law dictionary is not the most authoritative source of a term that has over the decades assumed a special juridical meaning in Canadian human rights law.[56]

When dealing with Civil Law issues however, we did notice that greater attention was given to 'civilian' dictionaries. This is particularly true when the Court discussed terminological questions that are specific to Quebec Civil Law. For example, in *Bruker v. Marcovitz*,[57] the Court described particular Civil Law concepts by referring extensively to the Private Law Dictionary (Crépeau (2003)). In Caisse populaire Desjardins de Val-Brillant v. Blouin, Justice Gonthier described the meaning of the term 'title' by quoting Quebec dictionaries, both in the French and English versions of his judgements.[58] Other cases illustrate this same tendency to take into consideration the distinct character of Quebec Civil Law when describing its terminology.[59]

Apart from these examples, the use of legal dictionaries at the SCC does not seem to be guided by explicit methodological principles as to their relevancy or authority. The general practice seems to rest on the assumption that these dictionaries are to be referred to in the same manner as any other language dictionary.

This approach to legal dictionaries can be criticized on the basis that it does not seem to take into account the following considerations. Even if their content and methodology vary, legal dictionaries overwhelmingly rely on legal sources to establish their definitions. In this sense, they do not intend to describe meaning as it is understood in common parlance. Their usefulness rests on the fact that they describe different usages or meaning found in legal literature, whether it be legislation, case-law or legal scholarship. It is possible that in certain circumstances meaning conveyed in a general dictionaries and legal dictionaries overlap or correspond,[60] but to use a legal dictionary in order to establish 'ordinary meaning' unnecessarily 'blur[s] the distinction between legal and ordinary meanings'.[61] If

56 *New Brunswick (Human Rights Commission) v. Potash Corporation of Saskatchewan Inc.* [2008] 2 S.C.R. 604, 2008 SCC 45, J. McLachlin, diss.

57 [2007] 3 S.C.R. 607, 2007 SCC 54, par 49: 'The civil law of Quebec recognizes three kinds of obligations: moral, civil (or legal) and natural. Only the first two are engaged in this case. They are defined in *Private Law Dictionary and Bilingual Lexicons: Obligations* (2003)'.

58 [2003] 1 S.C.R. 666, 2003 SCC 31, paras 3–4.

59 *Caisse populaire Desjardins de l'Est de Drummond v. Canada*, 2009 SCC 29 [2009] 2 S.C.R. 94, Justice Deschamps, dissent, par 88–98.

60 Especially when legal dictionaries reproduce judicial pronouncements in which we find reference to a language dictionary, on the fluctuating boundaries between legal and ordinary meaning. (For more, see Chris Hutton, Chapter 11 in this volume.)

61 Sullivan (2008: 61).

'ordinary meaning' is to be sought in a credible way, then it should be found in dictionaries that describe everyday usages, that is, in non-legal corpora.[62]

More questionable is the practice of referring to legal dictionaries that are not related to the legal tradition on which is based the legislation. When judges refer to *Black's Law Dictionary* when reading the *Civil Code of Quebec*, they refer to a dictionary that has no ambition of describing Civilian legal parlance; the same can be said regarding Gérard Cornu's *Vocabulaire juridique* and the French version of the *Criminal Code*. This practice goes against one of the principles that should logically apply to dictionary use: the interpreter should prefer dictionaries that reflect the linguistic usages to which the legislation refers to at a certain time period.[63] In some circumstances, judges have rightly refrained from using French language dictionaries – made in France – because they did not take into consideration the Quebec particular usage in French.[64] A stronger argument can be made against using a civilian dictionary when reading a statute governed by Common Law, even if both of them are written in French.

The Court's use of legal dictionaries as general language dictionaries should come under even closer scrutiny when dealing with federal legislation related to private law. Civil Law and Common Law have been recognized as the sources of general law (*droit commun*) for federal statutes that refer to private law.[65] They are presumed – under certain conditions[66] – to act as suppletive law for their application.[67] The complementarity of provincial private law with federal law also extends to terminology used in federal statutes. As it is stated in Section 8.2 of the *Interpretation Act*:

---

62 The distinction between 'legal' and 'ordinary' meaning is of course a difficult question that is not discussed here.

63 Côté (2009: 302).

64 Côté (2009: 302); *Dubuc v. Cité de Rouyn* [1973] C.A. 1128.

65 Section 8.1 of the *Interpretation Act* (R.S.C., 1985, c. I-21): '*Both the common law and the civil law are equally authoritative and recognized sources of the law of property and civil rights in Canada* and, unless otherwise provided by law, if in interpreting an enactment it is necessary to refer to a province's rules, principles or concepts forming part of the law of property and civil rights, reference must be made to the rules, principles and concepts in force in the province at the time the enactment is being applied/ *Le droit civil et la common law font pareillement autorité et sont tous deux sources de droit en matière de propriété et de droits civils au Canada* et, s'il est nécessaire de recourir à des règles, principes ou notions appartenant au domaine de la propriété et des droits civils en vue d'assurer l'application d'un texte dans une province, il faut, sauf règle de droit s'y opposant, avoir recours aux règles, principes et notions en vigueur dans cette province au moment de l'application du texte' [emphasis added].

66 These conditions are referred to in section 8.1 of the *Interpretation Act* (R.S.C., 1985, c. I-21): '*unless otherwise provided by law*' and if '*it is necessary* to refer to a province's rules, principles or concepts'.

67 There is a debate as to when the interpreter should refer to this suppletive law, see: Sullivan (2004: 1027–54).

> *Unless otherwise provided by law*, when an enactment contains both civil law and common law terminology, *or terminology that has a different meaning in the civil law and the common law*, the civil law terminology or meaning is to be adopted in the Province of Quebec and the common law terminology or meaning is to be adopted in the other provinces. / *Sauf règle de droit s'y opposant, est entendu dans un sens compatible avec le système juridique de la province d'application le texte* qui emploie à la fois des termes propres au droit civil de la province de Québec et des termes propres à la common law des autres provinces, ou qui emploie des termes qui ont un sens différent dans l'un et l'autre de ces systèmes [emphasis added].[68]

The conditions related to the application of this article are unclear.[69] It's wording, however, draws a distinction between two different 'meanings', one related to civil law, the other to Common Law. The expression 'terminology/termes' designates words whose usage is limited to a particular legal or scientific community (for example 'emphyteusis' in civil law); it can also extend to those who are used in everyday language but have a technical or particular meaning within this same community (for example 'possession' or 'to deliver') (Cornu, 2003: IX, Mattila, 2012: 178–9). Particularly in presence of everyday words that are related to private law (like 'take', 'distribute', 'enjoy', 'person' and so on), the question as to whether they constitute 'terminology that has a different meaning in the civil law and the common law' should be answered by engaging in a comparative study of legal meaning within each legal system, and not by simply discussing their ordinary meaning. The fact that legal dictionaries are used to describe ordinary meaning seems to sidestep the whole process of assessing the

68 *Interpretation Act*, R.S.C., 1985, c. I-21.

69 Sullivan (2008: 128–30) limits its application to specific federal legislative drafting techniques of generic terms that are used to refer to both Common Law and Civil Law concepts. The underlying concern in the debate on the scope of Section 8 is the applicability of provincial rules when applying federal legislation that refers to private law. For Sullivan, provincial law should not be referred to and section 8.2 does not apply when: 1)'the drafter uses terminology from a single legal system in both language versions or creates a concept that is *sui* generis' (Sullivan, 2008: 133), or 2) when a statute contains words with no specific legal meaning: '[w]hen interpreting bijural federal legislation, the first task is to decide whether the language to be interpreted is ordinary i.e. draws on the conventions of language shared by the general community – or is legal – i.e. refers to specialized legal concepts, institutions or principles' (2004: 1047). France Allard describes a similar approach that is based on a somewhat less rigid opposition between words that should be interpreted by reference to provincial law and others that should not (2009: 309): 'plus un terme a une charge technique, plus on aura tendance à s'en remettre aux règles provinciales pour déterminer son régime juridique […] Par ailleurs, lorsqu'un terme a un potentiel polysémique ou lorsqu'il est assez générique pour prendre un sens en fonction du contexte d'application, un sens propre au contexte fédéral peut-être découvert'.

differences, if any, between the meanings conveyed in the two legal systems in presence, and the possible application of Section 8 (2).[70]

Leaving aside the matter of the bijurality of Canadian Law, the use of legal dictionaries as general language dictionaries could be understood positively as a reflection of their limited scope: the information they contain conveys '(legal) meaning' of words, not 'rules'. The fact that they are seldom used to assess substantive law should then be applauded, because they are not legal treatises. The line between lexicographical works in law and legal textbooks is sometimes thin, but SCC use of legal dictionaries in terms of treating them as language dictionaries respects them for what they essentially are: sources of information on meaning. On the other hand, we are of the view that they should be used in a way that is consistent with their purpose and content, that is to describe *legal* (as opposed to *ordinary*) meaning, in a particular legal system, tradition or community.

## Conclusion

Although it was not directly discussed in this paper, dictionary use by the SCC also raises interesting issues regarding the process by which 'meaning' is established by judges. As Sullivan rightly stated, 'ordinary meaning of a text is judicially noticed' (2008: 29) and therefore, judges are not 'obliged' to justify why and how they reach their conclusions on these subjects. The fact that they regularly refer to dictionaries can be understood as reflecting their status and authority inside the legal community.[71] The paradox in some instances is that unprincipled use of dictionaries may detract rather than enhance their authority. One author (April, 1998) has described the practice of dictionary shopping at the United States' Supreme Court; it would be a shame if the same could be said of Canadian Law.

As Sullivan indicated, dictionary use has its pitfalls when used to interpret statutes (2008). Like any other work of scholarship, legal dictionaries also have their own limitations. Nonetheless, they are very valuable and useful resources and can enlighten legal reasoning. A way to avoid criticism when doing so would be to take into consideration the purposes for which they were written and the corpora on which they are based. It might be that Cornu's definition of *violence* conveys the same meaning intended by the federal legislator when it adopted

70 For a similar concern, see Denault (2008: 101–10).

71 See, for example, the impact of dictionary definitions on interpretation in the following opinion: *Charlebois v. Saint John (City)* [2005] 3 S.C.R. 563, 2005 SCC 74, Bastarache, dissenting, par 54: 'Another important factor is that the terms "pleadings" and "process" are clearly defined in dictionaries (see H. Reid, *Dictionnaire de droit québécois et canadien* (3e éd. 2004), at p. 433 ("*plaidoirie*"); *Black's Law Dictionary* (8th ed. 2004), at pp. 1191 and 1241–42) and case law (*MacDonald v. Montreal (City)*, [1986] 1 S.C.R. 460, at p. 514 (Wilson J., in dissent, but on a different point)). *Any intention to depart from these definitions would have to be clearly expressed'* [emphasis added].

the *Youth Criminal Justice Act* or that the definition in *Black's Law Dictionary* echoes the meaning of the English version of the *Québec Civil Code*. But it is more probably just a coincidence. Dictionary use by Courts, like any other authority referred to in the course of legal reasoning, cannot escape the mockery of sceptics (or of realists!), but at the same time courts could strike a happy balance between dictionary use as a basis for a legal arguments and as a principled approach to determining the different meanings of words.

## References

Note (anonymous). 1994. Looking it up: Dictionaries and Statutory Interpretation. *Harvard Law Review*, 107, 1437.

Allard, F. 2009. La disposition préliminaire du *Code civil du Québec*, l'idée du droit commun et le rôle du code en droit fédéral. *Canadian Bar Review*, 88, 277.

April, E.P. 1998. The Law of the Word: Dictionary Shopping in the Supreme Court. *Arizona State Law Journal*, 30, 275.

Bastarache, M. et al. 2009. *Le droit de l'interprétation bilingue*. Montréal: Lexis Nexis.

Cornu, G. (ed.). 2003. *Vocabulaire juridique*, 4th Edition. Paris: Presses Universitaires de France.

Cornu, G. 1992. Rapport de synthèse, *Archives de philosophie du droit et de philosophie sociale*, 48, 81.

Côté, P.-A. 2004. Bilingual Interpretation of Enactments in Canada: Principles v. Practice. *Brooklyn Journal of International Law*, 29, 1067.

Crépeau, P.-A. et al. 1991. *Dictionnaire de droit privé et lexiques bilingues*, 2nd Edition. Cowansville: Yvon Blais.

Crépeau, P.-A. et al. 2003. *Dictionnaire de droit privé et lexiques bilingues: les obligations*, 2nd Edition. Cowansville: Yvon Blais.

Denault, P. 2008. *La recherche d'unité dans l'interprétation du droit privé fédéral: cadre juridique et fragments du discours judiciaire*. Montreal: Thémis.

Devinat, M. 2005. Réflexion autour des dictionnaires de droit civil, in *Jurilinguistique: entre langues et droits/Jurilinguistics: Between Law and Language*, J.C. Gémar and N. Kasirer, Montréal: Thémis, 321–38.

Dukelow, D.A. ed., 2011. *Dictionary of Canadian Law*, 4th Edition. Toronto: Carswell.

Forget, P. and Devinat, M. 2011. *La rhétorique du code complet: unir pour exclure, in À l'avant-garde de la dualité – Mélanges en l'honneur de Michel Bastarache / At the Forefront of Duality – Essays in honour of Michel Bastarache*, N. Lambert, Cowansville: Yvon Blais, 251–81.

Garner, B.A. 2003. Legal lexicography: A view from the front lines. Notes on the compilation of a classic dictionary of law. *English Today*, 19, 33.

Hutton, C., 2013 Defining ordinary words for mundane objects: legal lexicography, ordinary language and the word vehicle, 177–200 herein.

Kasirer, N. 1990. The Annotated Criminal Code en Version Québécoise: Signs of Territoriality in Canadian Criminal Law. *Dalhousie Law Journal*, 13, 520.

Leckey, R. 2007. Prescribed by Law/Une Règle de Droit. *Osgoode Hall Law Journal*, 45, 3, 571.

L'Heureux-Dubé, C. 2001–02. Bijuralism: A Supreme Court of Canada Justice's Perspective. *Louisiana Law Review*, 62, 2, 449.

Lo, C.F. 2013. A Clearer Rule for Dictionary Use Will Not Affect Holistic Approach and Flexibility of Treaty Interpretation – A Rejoinder to Dr Isabelle Van Damme. *Journal of International Dispute Settlement*, 3, 89–94.

Lo, C.F. 2010. Good Faith Use of Dictionary in the Search of Ordinary Meaning under the WTO Dispute Settlement Understanding. *Journal of International Dispute Settlement*, 1, 431.

Macdonald, R.A. 1997. Legal Bilingualism. *McGill Law Journal*, 42, 119.

Metzmeier, K.X. 2007. You Can Look it Up: The Use of Dictionaries in Interpreting Statutes. [online: Louisville Bar Briefs, 14–15, July 2007, University of Louisville School of Law Legal Studies Research Paper Series No. 2008–25] Available at http://ssrn.com/abstract=1005653 [accessed: 4 September 2013].

Pavot, D. 2012. The Use of Dictionary by the WTO Appellate Body – Beyond the Search of Ordinary Meaning. *Journal of International Dispute Settlement*, 1.

Randolph, R.A. 1994. Dictionaries, Plain Meaning, and Context in Statutory Interpretation. *Harvard Journal of Law and Public Policy*, 71.

Reid, H. 2010. *Dictionnaire de droit québécois et canadien*. 4th Edition, Montréal: Wilson & Lafleur.

Rynd, A. 1991. Dictionaries and the Interpretations of Words: A Summary of Difficulties. *Alberta Law Review*, 29, 712.

Scassa, T. 1994. Language of Judgement and the Supreme Court of Canada. *University of New Brunswick Law Journal*, 43, 167.

Slovenko, R. 1996. Dictionary Use by Judge and Jury. *Journal of Psychiatry and Law*, 24, 125.

Solan, L. 2012. *The Oxford Handbook of Language and Law*. Oxford: Oxford University Press.

Solan, L. 1993. When Judges Use Dictionaries. *American Speech*, 68, 50.

Sullivan, R. 2008. *Sullivan on the Construction of Statutes*, 5th Edition. Toronto: Lexis.

Sullivan, R. 2011–12. Some Problems with the Shared Meaning Rule as Formulated in R v. Daoust and the Law of Bilingual Interpretation. *Ottawa Law Review*, 42, 1, 71.

Van Damme, I. 2011. On Good Faith Use of Dictionary in the Search of Ordinary Meaning under the WTO Dispute Settlement Understanding – A Reply to Professor Chang-Fa Lo. *Journal of International Dispute Settlement*, 2, 231.

Weis, J.L. 1987–88. Jurisprudence by Webster's: The Role of the Dictionary in Legal Thought. *Mercer Law Review*, 39, 961.

Winchester, S. 2003. *The Meaning of Everything: The Story of the Oxford English Dictionary*. Oxford: Oxford University Press.

# Chapter 13

# La phraséologie chez des jurilexicographes: les exemples linguistiques dans la deuxième édition du *Dictionnaire de droit privé et lexiques bilingues**

Patrick Forget

In this article the linguistic examples of the second edition of the *Dictionnaire de droit privé et lexiques bilingues* published by the Paul-André Crépeau Centre for Private and Comparative Law in 1991 are analysed. Those linguistic examples which, according to the author, are made up of phraseological units are provided by the team of lexicographers as an illustration of the correct usage of the headwords. In the first part of this article, a broad definition of the concept of phraseological units in specialized languages is offered, a definition which is founded on idiomaticity and ultimately what constitutes a phraseological unit in a given context is left to the determination of specialists in the given field. The analysis of the 754 linguistic examples identified in this reference work is preceded by a critical review of the Centre's lexicographic output. This article, which is primarily aimed at lawyers, is part of a larger research project which seeks to determine to what extent and how a more systematic study of legal language could further our knowledge of the law.

La phraséologie, qui s'intéresse aux « séquences lexicales perçues comme préconstruites » (Legallois et Tutin 2013: 3), connaît un engouement depuis plus d'une vingtaine d'années (Tutin 2010a: 7–13). Le développement de programmes informatiques capables de filtrer de grands corpus de textes pour en

---

* Nous tenons à remercier la direction du Centre Paul-André Crépeau de droit privé et comparé d'avoir accepté de mettre à notre disposition la banque de données constituée des versions électroniques des dictionnaires de droit privé préparés par le Centre avant même que cette banque de données ne soit disponible au public. Nous exprimons notre profonde gratitude à l'endroit du directeur du Centre, le professeur Lionel Smith, ainsi qu'à l'endroit de la directrice adjointe d'alors, Me Régine Tremblay, pour cette faveur. Nous tenons à remercier Mme Manon Berthiaume pour l'aide précieuse qu'elle nous a apportée dans l'interrogation de la banque de données. Ce texte a profité du travail de recherche de Me Nadia Chammas à qui nous exprimons de sincères remerciements. Nous portons entièrement la responsabilité des erreurs ou omissions que ce texte contient sans doute.

extraire les contextes des mots analysés permet de nourrir la quête de précision et d'exhaustivité dans la description et le traitement lexicographique de la combinatoire des mots (Delagneau 2010; Archer 2009: 23–4; L'Homme 2004: 18). Cette quête a mené à l'élaboration d'ouvrages lexicographiques, en particulier à des dictionnaires consignant les collocations de la langue générale (Tutin 2010b; Béjoint 2007: 19–20; Tutin 2005).

L'engouement pour la phraséologie a rapidement traversé le champ de la langue générale pour atteindre celui des langues de spécialité (L'Homme et Meynard 1998; Clas 1994; Picht 1987). Il faut dire que l'intérêt de la phraséologie pour affiner la description des termes dans les dictionnaires de langue de spécialité tient presque de l'évidence (L'Homme 2004: 32–45 et 111–14; Pesant et Thibault 1997; Picht 1987).

Lorsqu'il consulte un dictionnaire de droit privé en français sous la vedette *responsabilité civile*, l'usager, en particulier le juriste débutant ou le juriste non francophone, tirerait avantage à ce qu'on lui dise qu'une *personne engage* sa responsabilité civile (typiquement lorsqu'elle commet une faute dommageable) – il est moins idiomatique de dire qu'une *personne entraîne* sa responsabilité civile lorsqu'elle commet une faute dommageable. En revanche, on peut tout aussi bien dire qu'une *conduite fautive engage* ou *entraîne* la responsabilité civile de la personne qui s'y est livrée. Ce sont là des exemples de contraintes d'ordre phraséologique, qui agissent sur la combinatoire du terme *responsabilité civile*, et que les jurilexicographes peuvent utilement consigner dans leurs ouvrages (voir Heid et Freibott 1991).

Malgré l'intérêt des linguistes et des terminologues pour la description de la combinatoire des termes en langue de spécialité, malgré l'intérêt de l'information d'ordre phraséologique, en particulier pour les apprenants du domaine de la spécialité (ou d'une langue du domaine), les traducteurs ainsi que les rédacteurs techniques, encore peu de dictionnaires spécialisés offrent un traitement du fonctionnement des termes susceptible d'aider les usagers à produire un texte idiomatique. Plusieurs auteurs font le constat que les ouvrages consacrés à la description des langues de spécialité favorisent encore nettement le recensement d'informations d'ordre conceptuel et encyclopédique (Preite 2012; L'Homme 2010; Collet 2004).

Dans un article précédent, nous avons tenté de montrer l'importance pour les apprenants de la langue juridique d'acquérir non seulement les rouages de la terminologie du droit, mais aussi ceux de sa phraséologie (Forget 2011). Dans une recherche documentaire menée à l'occasion de cet article, nous avons constaté qu'aucun ouvrage de lexicographie juridique en français juridique ne s'est donné comme objectif de dresser un portrait relativement complet de la combinatoire des termes d'un sous-domaine du droit. Certains ouvrages de nature lexicographique mettent l'accent sur la combinatoire des termes, sans passer près, toutefois, de couvrir un sous-domaine en entier (voir, pour le droit québécois ou canadien, Picotte 2012; Mailhot 2009; Beaudoin et Mailhot 2005; Centre de traduction et de documentation juridiques 1995; pour le droit français, voir Lerat 2007; Bissardon et Burel 2005).

Dans le présent article, nous analyserons la rubrique *exemple linguistique* de l'article de la deuxième édition du *Dictionnaire de droit privé et lexiques bilingues* (*Crépeau et al.* 1991, ci-après *Dictionnaire de privé* ou *dictionnaire*). L'exemple linguistique est « formé d'une suite de mots » qui représente « un segment type du discours juridique » (*Crépeau et al.* 1991: xxx). Selon nous, l'analyse de l'information consignée dans ces rubriques offre un éclairage privilégié sur ce que des juristes, experts du droit privé, perçoivent intuitivement comme des illustrations de la phraséologie juridique.

Cet article se divise en trois parties. Dans la première partie, nous défendrons une conception large des unités phraséologiques (UP) en langue de spécialité qui repose sur un critère d'idiomaticité contrôlé, en définitive, par les experts du domaine. Dans la seconde partie, nous ferons une présentation critique du *Dictionnaire de droit privé*. Dans la troisième partie, nous analyserons les 754 exemples linguistiques dénombrés dans la deuxième édition française du *Dictionnaire de droit privé*.

Cet article s'inscrit dans une recherche visant à explorer l'apport potentiel des concepts et des cadres d'analyse élaborés par les sciences du langage à la connaissance du droit; ce faisant, cet article s'adresse, en premier lieu, aux juristes intéressés par les rapports entre la langue et le droit. Cette recherche repose sur un certain nombre de postulats, présentés ailleurs (Forget 2014; Forget 2011). Ces postulats ont trait au rôle primordial joué par la langue et la parole en droit, au rapport entre la langue générale et les langues de spécialité ainsi qu'à l'intérêt des travaux portant sur une langue spécialisée réalisée par des chercheurs qui, malgré leur expertise dans le domaine de spécialité concerné, demeurent des linguistes amateurs (voir, sur la notion de linguiste amateur, Paveau 2008).

## 1. Les unités phraséologiques (UP) en langue de spécialité

La phraséologie, suivant la perspective de Cowie, s'est donné pour mission d'étudier « the structure, meaning and use of word combinations » (Cowie 1994: 3168, cité par Granger et Paquot 2008: 1). La phraséologie s'attache à étudier les conditions d'emplois des mots d'une langue dans leur contexte immédiat et se focalise sur « les tournures typiques d'une langue, soit par leur fréquence, soit par leur caractère idiomatique » (*Trésor de la langue française informatisé*; voir aussi Dubreil 2008).

La phraséologie part d'au moins deux constats. Premièrement, les mots s'emploient rarement seuls. Ce qu'un mot isolé, même fortement sémantisé, peut exprimer reste, en général, limité. Le plus souvent le locuteur est appelé à combiner les composantes de la langue pour encoder sa pensée, première étape de la communication. Les discours et leur intelligibilité passent donc par l'enchaînement raisonné des diverses composantes de la langue ou parties du discours: verbe, nom, adjectif, adverbe, etc.

Deuxièmement: non seulement les mots s'emploient-ils rarement seuls, mais on remarque aussi qu'ils existent entre ceux-ci un jeu d'affinités et de répulsions, que les règles de la syntaxe et de la sémantique peinent à rendre compte et à expliquer.

La langue contraint le locuteur à choisir certaines combinaisons de mots et en à exclure d'autres. Le locuteur compétent doit notamment connaître les combinaisons syntaxiquement permises (p. ex., *on se souvient de qqch*; mais *on se rappelle qqch*), mais aussi celles sémantiquement permises (p. ex. *noir* au sens de macabre se combine avec *humour* et *pensée: un humour noir*, *une pensée noire*, mais pas, du moins pas aussi naturellement, avec *plan* ou *rêve*: ?*un plan noir*, ?*un rêve noir*)[1].

L'unité phraséologique (UP) peut se définir comme une suite privilégiée de deux ou plusieurs mots ou encore, avec Legallois et Tutin, comme une séquence lexicale perçue comme préconstruite (Legallois et Tutin 2013: 3). Ainsi définie, l'UP forme une catégorie qui se compose d'éléments disparates (p. ex. *qui a bu boira*, *défense de stationner*, *prendre peur* et *fruit de mer*). La description et la modélisation des UP représentent un défi pour les linguistes, notamment en raison de cette hétérogénéité.

La plupart des descriptions et modélisations partent de l'idée que les UP sont le reflet de liens privilégiés, d'affinités entre les mots d'une langue (Silva *et al.* 2004; Tutin et Grossman 2002; Larivière 1998: 178), affinités qu'on observe aussi bien dans la langue générale que dans les langues de spécialité (L'Homme 1998). Prises du revers, ces affinités peuvent être comprises comme autant de contraintes, de restrictions ou de « non-libertés » qui agissent sur les mots impliqués au point, peut-on faire valoir, d'en faire partie (Polguère 2008: 40–41; Mel'čuk 2003). Par exemple, d'une personne qui a subi une blessure importante au plan physique, on dira qu'elle est *grièvement* ou *gravement blessée* et non qu'elle est *très* ou *grandement blessée*. On peut donc faire valoir qu'une caractéristique du mot *blessé* (entendu au sens de *blessé physiquement*) consiste à favoriser nettement *grièvement* et *gravement* lorsqu'il vient de temps de lui associer un intensificateur.

Ces observations soulèvent la question des critères permettant de distinguer les combinaisons qui révèlent une affinité « véritable » en langue de celles qui n'en révèlent pas. Encore une fois, prises du revers, ces observations soulèvent la question des critères qui permettent de distinguer les combinaisons plus ou moins phraséologisées (ou plus ou moins contraintes, ou plus ou moins figées) des combinaisons libres, du moins des combinaisons considérées comme libres. Car un mot ne se combine pas jamais totalement librement. Un mot est contraint syntaxiquement par sa nature (p. ex. *on téléphone à qqn*; *on ne téléphone pas qqn*), mais il est contraint aussi par ses composantes sémantiques (p. ex. *on téléphone à qqn*; *on ne téléphone pas à qqch*) (Pecman 2004; Prandi 1998: 39–41).

---

1 Il convient de noter que la frontière entre ce qui est permis et ce qui ne l'est pas ou encore ce qui est correct et ce qui l'est moins reste toutefois poreuse. En particulier, l'usage phraséologique évolue (Polguère 2011a; Blumenthal 2007: 26–7) et même en synchronie, cet usage peut varier d'un individu à l'autre ou d'un groupe d'individus à un autre (Polguère 2003: 16).

Puisque les langues de spécialité se caractérisent en premier lieu par l'usage de terminologies spécifiques et que les termes qui composent ces terminologies peuvent être considérés comme autant d'unités lexicales, nous concentrerons notre étude sur la combinatoire lexicale des mots[2]. Plusieurs critères, qui mettent en jeu notamment la fréquence, la notion de prédictibilité ou encore le principe de compositionnalité sémantique, ont été proposés pour distinguer, en langue générale, sur le plan lexical, les combinaisons non libres (ou UP) des combinaisons libres.

Cette première partie présente certains des critères, parmi les plus fréquemment convoqués en langue générale, pour décrire les combinaisons non libres. Nous montrerons que ces critères ne sont pas en mesure de rendre compte des UP dans les langues de spécialité, en général, et dans la langue du droit, en particulier. L'une des raisons de cet état de fait tient, selon nous, à l'existence, en langue de spécialité, de deux grandes catégories d'UP que nous nommerons, provisoirement, *collocation conceptuelle* et *collocation lexicale*[3] (Bertrand 1998a; Bertrand 1998b).

À défaut de trouver en langue générale de critérium opérationnel pour distinguer les combinaisons phraséologisées des combinaisons libres, nous nous croyons justifié de nous en remettre, afin de caractériser l'UP en langue de spécialité, à un critère d'idiomaticité fondé, en définitive, sur la validation par des experts du domaine.

## 1.1. Certains critères des UP en langue générale appliqués à la langue spécialisée

La phraséologie tente de déterminer les critères qui distinguent les combinaisons non libres, idiomatiquement marquées, même *a minima* (p. ex. *passer un examen*), de celles qui sont considérées comme libres (p. ex. *corriger la réponse d'un étudiant*) (Pecman 2004). Au sujet de cet objectif de la phraséologie, deux précisions doivent être faites avant d'examiner à tour de rôle les critères fondés sur la fréquence, le principe de compositionnalité sémantique et la prédictibilité.

Premièrement, pour les linguistes, la question de la distinction entre les combinaisons non libres et les combinaisons libres est indissociable de la question de la catégorisation des combinaisons considérées comme non libres. Par conséquent, les critères qui servent à définir le caractère non libre ou phraséologisé d'une combinaison libre servent souvent à distinguer les classes d'UP entre elles. Rappelons que les UP forment un groupe hétérogène d'expressions polylexicales.

---

2 Entendue par opposition à la combinatoire syntaxique des mots (voir, à ce sujet, dans la langue scientifique, Gledhill 1997).

3 Nous préférons les termes *UP conceptuelle* et *UP lexicale* afin de distancer ces concepts des collocations de la langue générale. Nous utiliserons les termes *UP conceptuelle* et *UP lexicale* lors de l'analyse des exemples linguistiques du dictionnaire, dans la troisième partie du présent texte.

Deuxièmement, si les linguistes ne s'entendent pas sur les critères de détermination et de classement des UP, les modèles proposés admettent, le plus souvent, la présence d'un continuum entre les combinaisons totalement figées et les combinaisons libres (Legellois et Tutin 2013: 3 Polguère 2011a: 2; Pecman 2004: 142–3). Entre les UP totalement phraséologisées et les combinaisons libres, les modèles attestent de l'existence d'une ou plusieurs catégories intermédiaires d'UP. On peut postuler que ce sont ces catégories intermédiaires, en particulier celles qui restent le près du degré zéro de la phraséologisation, qui permettent d'inférer le ou les critères susceptibles de distinguer les UP des combinaisons libres. Ces combinaisons partiellement contraintes (p. ex. *passer un examen*; *tirer un chèque*; *humour noir*) sont souvent désignées, en langue générale, et même en langue de spécialité, sous le nom de *collocation.*

### 1.1.1. Les UP sont des combinaisons dont la fréquence dans un corpus est statistiquement significative.

Selon une approche statistique fondée sur la linguistique de corpus, les UP sont des combinaisons dont la fréquence est considérée comme statistiquement significative. À la différence d'autres critères de détermination des UP qui sont fondés, en tout ou en partie, sur une propriété en langue, le critère statistique repose sur l'usage et envisage l'UP comme un phénomène lié au contexte d'énonciation, en particulier à l'importance de la répétition dans un texte (Macko 2011: 68).

Selon une approche statistique, le statut d'UP est directement lié au nombre d'occurrences d'une combinaison de deux ou plusieurs mots (à l'intérieur d'une fenêtre de X mots prédéfinie) dans un corpus donné. Afin d'attester du caractère significatif du nombre d'occurrences de la combinaison, on applique un ou plusieurs tests statistiques qui comparent la probabilité que les unités lexicales constitutives de la combinaison apparaissent ensemble plutôt que séparément dans le corpus en question (Evert 2004: 21).

L'approche statistique fondée sur l'extraction d'UP dans un corpus constitue certes une voie d'accès privilégiée aux UP d'une langue, qu'il s'agisse de la langue générale ou d'une langue spécialisée. En contrepartie, cette méthode reste dépendante de l'extension du corpus. Il se peut, par exemple, que l'adage *En fait de meubles, la possession vaut titre*, en raison de son emploi relativement peu fréquent, ne se trouve pas dans un corpus de textes juridiques. On peut soutenir, pourtant, que cet adage constitue une combinaison de mots typique de la langue du droit.

Qui plus est, peu importe les tests statistiques appliqués pour établir la fréquence et le caractère statistiquement significatif d'une séquence polylexicale, ces tests ne se suffisent pas à eux-mêmes de sorte que « l'intervention manuelle du lexicographe ou du linguiste reste [ … ] indispensable » pour écarter les bruits et, éventuellement, les faux positifs (Tutin 2010a: 126–7). Par exemple, en droit québécois, l'usage fréquent des expressions *nouveau Code* ou *nouveau*

*Code civil* dans les textes de droit privé pour désigner le *Code civil du Québec* relève, selon nous, davantage du phénomène de réduction anaphorique que du phénomène phraséologique à proprement dit (voir, sur le phénomène de réduction, Collet 2004).

La fréquence d'une combinaison de mots dans un corpus et le caractère statistiquement significatif de cette combinaison sont certes des indices de premier ordre de la présence d'une UP. Mais ces indices appellent toujours une validation sur la base d'autres modèles, notamment de modèles lexico-syntaxiques[4].

### 1.1.2. Les UP sont des combinaisons qui ne sont pas compositionnelles.

Selon plusieurs auteurs, les UP sont des combinaisons qui ne respectent pas, en tout ou en partie, le principe de compositionnalité (Pecman 2004: 138–9).

Selon le principe de compositionnalité, du moins selon une certaine conception du principe de compositionalité (voir Legallois et Tutin 2013: 6–7), une combinaison de mots est dite compositionnelle s'il est possible d'en interpréter le sens à partir du sens de chacun de ses constituants (Polguère 2003: 57). En gros, le sens d'un énoncé comme *Le livre est sur la table* se calcule à partir du sens de chacun de ses constituants, c'est-à-dire LE + LIVRE + ÊTRE + SUR + LA + TABLE. Dans une combinaison qui respecte le principe de compositionnalité, le sens de la combinaison égale la somme des sens de ses constituants.

Une combinaison sera dite non compositionnelle si le sens de la combinaison n'intègre aucun de sens de ses constituants. Par exemple, un fruit de mer n'est pas un fruit qui pousse dans la mer, bien qu'on comprenne le patron métaphorique sur lequel cette locution a été formée (Polguère 2008: 55–7).

Une combinaison de deux mots peut être dite semi-compositionnelle si l'un des mots, appelé *base*, conserve son sens usuel ou l'un de ses sens usuels, et si l'autre, appelé collocatif, prend un sens particulier (L'Homme 1998: 516; L'Homme et Meynard 1998: 202–3), un sens que le mot réserve à cette base ou à certaines bases seulement. Auprès de cette base, le collocatif prendra un sens qui peut être considéré comme figuré (p. ex. la *flambée* des prix) ou encore un sens qui peut être considéré comme très général, presque vide (p. ex. *porter* attention), mais, dans tous les cas, le sens du collocatif est déterminé par celui de sa base. À un niveau plus fondamental, on peut dire que le collocatif est sélectionné en fonction de la base précisément pour révéler un élément de la combinatoire sémantique de cette dernière (p. ex. si l'on veut dire que les prix ont connu une augmentation importante et soudaine, on parlera de *la flambée des prix* ou encore on dira que *les prix flambent*).

4 D'ailleurs, des chercheurs qui s'intéressent aux phénomènes de cooccurrences dans la perspective de linguistique de corpus établissent une distinction entre le phénomène de cooccurrence des mots dans un corpus, lequel peut entièrement être appréhendé au moyen de statistiques, et le phénomène phraséologique à proprement dit, lequel ne peut pas l'être (voir Evert 2004: 17–18).

Selon le critère de compositionnalité, tel que présenté ci-dessus, le jeu d'affinité entre les mots d'UP se constate par l'effet qu'il produit sur le sens d'un ou de chacun de ses constituants. Dans le cas des UP non compositionnelles, le sens des constituants disparaît complètement, ce qui force le locuteur à prendre l'UP comme un tout et à l'apprendre comme s'il s'agissait d'un mot.

Dans le cas des UP semi-compositionnelles, la non-liberté ne réside pas la disparition des sens de ses constituants; elle est plutôt le résultat du jeu de la combinatoire du mot appelé *base* au sein de la combinaison. Lorsqu'une base donnée s'associe à un autre mot ou à d'autres mots pour exprimer un sens que son sémantisme rend possible, mais qu'elle n'est pas en mesure d'exprimer seule et qu'elle privilégie, pour ce faire, un certain mot ou un certain groupe de mots pour exprimer ce sens, il se produit, *de facto*, une contrainte sur la sélection de sa combinatoire, qui n'est pas, en général, sans effet sur le sens que prend le collocatif dans la combinaison. Le sens du collocatif se démarque alors par rapport à son sens usuel ou à l'un de ses sens usuels et peut se qualifier, selon de la perspective, de *figuré*, de *général*, voire de *vide*.

Une auteure a tenté d'importer le critère de compositionnalité dans son analyse d'une catégorie d'UP en langue de spécialité, soit des UP semi-figées formées sur un verbe (Larivière 1998: 176). Cette tentative a fait long feu: l'auteure, elle-même, au terme de son étude, a remis en question le critère de compositionnalité pour rendre compte des combinaisons perçues privilégiées en langue de spécialité (Larivière 1998: 191). Les terminologues semblent convenir que le critère de compositionnalité est difficilement applicable dans le contexte des langues de spécialité, faisant valoir que nombre de combinaisons considérées comme typiques par les spécialistes d'un domaine sont entièrement compositionnelles (L'Homme 2000: 97; L'Homme 1998: 516–17; L'Homme et Meynard 1998: 205). Ainsi est-il, par exemple, en langue du droit, de l'expression *exonérer (telle partie du contrat) de sa responsabilité civile* qui se calcule à partir de la combinaison de ses constituants lexicaux: *exonérer*, *partie (au contrat)* et *responsabilité civile.*

### 1.1.3. Les UP sont des combinaisons non prédictibles

Le critère de prédictibilité se rapproche du critère de compositionnalité en ce qu'il repose aussi sur une mise en rapport des éléments constitutifs de la combinaison et la combinaison prise comme un tout. En application du critère de prédictibilité, cette mise en rapport fait intervenir cependant la personne de l'apprenant étranger (Tutin 2010a: 36; Hausmann 1989: 1010). En ce sens, le critère de prédictibilité est un critère qui intervient au niveau de la parole plutôt qu'au niveau de la langue.

En application du critère de non-prédictibilité sera une combinaison non libre, la combinaison qui n'est pas prédictible pour l'apprenant étranger. Cette absence de prédictibilité ne se manifeste pas au moment du décodage de l'UP. Pour nombre d'UP, l'apprenant étranger sera en mesure d'en interpréter le sens, évidemment dans l'hypothèse où il connaît les mots qui forment la combinaison. Cette absence de prédictibilité se manifeste plutôt en production. Une UP est une combinaison que l'apprenant étranger « ne saura pas automatiquement reproduire » (Hausmann 1989: 1010).

Le critère de prédictibilité des UP met en scène un locuteur imaginaire, soit l'apprenant étranger, ce qui soulève un certain nombre de problèmes méthodologiques. Sauf à tester un éventail d'UP hypothétiques sur un échantillon représentatif d'apprenants étrangers, il est difficile de se faire une représentation juste, suivant ce critère, des UP d'une langue. En outre, ce qu'un apprenant étranger pourra automatiquement reproduire dépend de la comparaison entre la langue maternelle de ce locuteur et la langue seconde à laquelle il est initié. Les résultats produits par l'application du critère de prédictibilité pourront varier en fonction de la langue maternelle de l'apprenant. Ce qui fait dire à Williams que le critère de prédictibilité (aussi appelé, par certains, dont Williams, le critère d'arbitrarité) est « un critère de traduction qui peut seulement être jugé entre les couples de langues »(Williams 2001: 4).

De toute manière, en ce qui concerne les UP en langues de spécialité, le critère de prédictibilité achoppe pour les mêmes raisons que le critère de compositionnalité. Nombre de combinaisons qui sont perçues par les spécialistes du domaine comme des UP peuvent être reproduites par des apprenants étrangers, pour peu qu'ils maîtrisent la terminologie du domaine de spécialité. Nombre d'UP en langue de spécialité sont parfaitement prédictibles en ce qu'ils sont la réunion de deux termes (p. ex. *abandonner son immeuble*).

D'autres critères que ceux fondés sur la fréquence, le principe de compositionnalité sémantique et la prédictibilité sont avancés pour identifier les UP en langue générale et, en particulier, les collocations (voir Tutin 2010a: 34–59; Dubreil 2008; Pecman 2004). Aucun des critères ainsi proposés pour statuer sur l'existence d'une UP et, ainsi, pour marquer le degré zéro de la phraséologisation ne semble faire consensus chez les linguistes.

Tous les critères se heurtent à des difficultés qui minent leur capacité à rendre compte du phénomène phraséologique dans son entier, à supposer qu'il soit possible de rendre compte globalement de ce phénomène (voir Tutin 2013: 61). Même le critère fondé sur le principe de compositionnalité ne va sans soulever de problèmes en langue générale (Legallois et Tutin 2013: 6–7; Pecman 2004: 139), bien que nous ayons omis d'en traiter, nous contentant de montrer que ce critère ne pouvait expliquer le phénomène phraséologique en langue de spécialité.

Selon nous, une raison expliquant que les critères fondés sur le principe de compositionnalité et sur la prédictibilité de la combinaison ne peuvent caractériser les UP dans les langues de spécialité tient à la présence, dans ces langues, de collocations qui peuvent être qualifiées de conceptuelles.

### 1.2. Les collocations conceptuelles et les collocations lexicales en langue de spécialité

Les langues de spécialité comprennent des UP qui ressemblent aux collocations de la langue générale (L'Homme 1998: 514). On peut postuler qu'au sein des langues spécialisées, les collocations spécialisées sont la forme la plus élémentaire d'UP, en ce qu'il s'agit de combinaisons qui s'envisagent comme des touts, sans pour autant former des UP entièrement figés. L'étude de ces collocations permet aussi d'offrir un éclairage plus immédiat sur le phénomène de phraséologisation en langue de spécialité.

À la différence de la langue générale, sinon, à tout le moins, d'une manière plus évidente que dans la langue générale (voir Tutin et Grossmann 2002: 22–3), les langues de spécialité comprennent deux grandes catégories de collocations spécialisées, ce que nous désignerons provisoirement sous le nom de *collocation conceptuelle* et de *collocation lexicale* (Bertrand 1998a; Bertrand 1998b). À notre avis, la présence de collocations conceptuelles permet d'expliquer que les critères de compositionnalité et de prédictibilité, notamment, sont peu opérationnels dans les langues de spécialité et qu'ils ne permettent pas de rendre compte d'UP pourtant perçues comme typiques par les spécialistes du domaine.

D'entrée de jeu, il convient de mentionner que la plupart des terminologues qui distinguent les collocations conceptuelles et les collocations lexicales fondent la distinction sur la productivité des cooccurrents (L'Homme 2000: 98–101; Bertrand 1998a: 34 et s.; Bertrand 1998b; L'Homme 1998: 518; Heid 1994: 237–40). Dans le cas des collocations conceptuelles, le cooccurrent, c'est-à-dire le mot en position de collocatif, peut s'associer à de nombreux termes du domaine de spécialité (p. ex., dans la langue du droit, *stipuler* peut s'associer à *clause*, *condition*, *servitude* (dans un acte de transfert de propriété) ou *communauté de biens* (dans un contrat de mariage)). En revanche, dans le cas des collocations dites lexicales, le cooccurrent ne peut s'attacher qu'à un terme. Les UP lexicales seraient rares (Bertrand 1998a), une observation qui tend à réduire la valeur de la distinction. Malgré cela, cette distinction met en lumière le fait qu'un cooccurrent donné, en particulier un cooccurrent verbal (L'Homme 1998: 518–19), aura tendance à se combiner avec des termes appartenant à une même classe conceptuelle.

À la suite de Sylva *et al.* (2004: 352), nous proposons plutôt de distinguer les collocations conceptuelles des collocations lexicales en langue de spécialité sur un autre critère que celui de la productivité du cooccurrent. Pour nous, la collocation conceptuelle est une combinaison typique partiellement phraséologisée qui met en rapport des termes du domaine de spécialité. Par exemple, *exonérer une partie au contrat de sa responsabilité civile* met en rapport trois termes juridiques *exonérer*, *partie (au contrat)* et *responsabilité civile.*

En revanche, la collocation lexicale est une combinaison typique partiellement phraséologisée qui intègre une unité lexicale non terminologique. Par exemple, dans *rechercher en responsabilité civile*, le verbe *rechercher* n'est pas un terme juridique. On peut arguer que le verbe *rechercher* dans l'UP *rechercher en responsabilité civile* conserve un sens proche de celui qu'il a en langue générale et, surtout, il ne lui est associé aucun concept juridique comme en témoigne le fait que l'expression *rechercher en responsabilité civile* ne se nominalise pas: **recherche en responsabilité civile.*

Dans une perspective proche de celle de Dechamps, on peut dire que l'UP lexicale « représente une charnière » entre la langue générale et la langue de spécialité (Dechamps 2004: 364). Nous convenons que la distinction entre la collocation conceptuelle et la collocation lexicale ou, plus généralement, entre l'UP conceptuelle et l'UP lexicale doit reposer sur une définition opérationnelle du terme, qui reste peut-être toujours à trouver (Petit 2001). En ce qui a trait aux UP formés sur un verbe, en particulier, il peut être difficile de distinguer les verbes terminologiques des verbes non terminologiques (L'Homme 2012).

Les difficultés inhérentes à la mise en œuvre de la distinction entre collocation conceptuelle et collocation lexicale n'altèrent pas de manière rédhibitoire son pouvoir explicatif. Entre autres, cette distinction reste capable d'expliquer pourquoi les critères fondés sur le principe de compositionnalité et sur la prédictibilité ne permettent pas de rendre compte de combinaisons que des juristes percevraient comme typiques du domaine du droit. À la différence des collocations lexicales, les collocations conceptuelles sont compositionnelles et, pour peu qu'on maîtrise les termes d'un système juridique donné, elles sont tout à fait prédictibles.

Au fond, les collocations conceptuelles sont le reflet de relations que le réseau conceptuel du domaine de spécialité rend possible. La maîtrise des concepts juridiques permet d'expliquer, par exemple, qu'on peut s'exonérer de sa responsabilité civile, mais qu'on ne peut abandonner sa responsabilité civile. L'exonération se rapporte à une obligation de l'agent; en contrepartie, l'abandon porte sur un droit de l'agent.

### 1.3. Le critère des UP en langues spécialisés: l'idiomaticité

À défaut de pouvoir importer en langue de spécialité un critérium reconnu pour distinguer les UP des combinaisons libres en langue générale, nous proposons, afin de caractériser les UP en langue de spécialité, d'appliquer un critère d'idiomaticité. Le critère d'idiomaticité est compris à la fois comme le reflet des habitudes langagières des spécialistes d'un domaine et l'écart existant entre la langue de spécialité du domaine en question et la langue générale (Pesant et Thibault 1998).

En première analyse, puisque les langues de spécialité se caractérisent d'abord par leur terminologie, on peut arguer que toutes les combinaisons typiques, qui intègrent une ou plusieurs unités terminologiques, satisferont potentiellement au critère d'idiomaticité et, par conséquent, se classeront au rang des UP du domaine. À notre avis, Meynard et L'Homme en appellent à un semblable critère lorsqu'elles écrivent: « Il appert que les questions d'usage au sein d'un domaine aient préséance sur la notion de «mutation sémantique » pour retenir une séquence lexicale dans un répertoire voué à la description des usages lexicaux d'un domaine. Tous les mots ayant, d'une manière ou d'une autre, un statut particulier dans un domaine et se combinant typiquement avec d'autres sont retenus » ((1998: 206); voir aussi Tryuk 2000: 67–8).

Dans l'application du critère d'idiomaticité, les terminologues pourront profiter du filtrage de grands corpus de textes du domaine de spécialité afin d'extraire les combinaisons types du domaine et d'établir leur fréquence ainsi que leur caractère statistiquement significatif. Dans le cas des UP conceptuelles, au sens où nous les avons définies ci-dessus, la démonstration du fait que chacun des constituants lexicaux de la combinaison dénote un concept du domaine et que la relation exprimée au moyen de cette UP participe du domaine servira aussi à asseoir sa qualification en tant qu'UP.

Dans les cas où surgit un doute quant à la caractérisation d'une combinaison, la décision de recenser ou non une combinaison en tant qu'UP doit revenir au spécialiste du domaine ou, mieux, à un groupe de spécialistes du domaine. Une combinaison sera considérée, selon nous, comme idiomatique si elle est perçue comme telle par les experts du domaine. En cela, la détermination de l'idiomaticité d'une combinaison ne se distingue pas outre mesure de la détermination du statut de terme.

En effet, quelle que soit l'approche terminographique privilégiée, la détermination du statut de terme se réalise en fonction d'un domaine de spécialité (L'Homme 2004: 53). Plus précisément, si l'on accepte de mettre de côté le travail néologique, un terme candidat se voit conférer le statut de terme s'il est le reflet d'un concept dans le domaine de spécialité et si l'usage du terme candidat, dans la langue de spécialité, est suffisamment stable.

En tant que vecteurs de connaissances spécialisées, les termes supposent donc, relativement à un domaine de spécialité donné, l'existence d'une ou plusieurs communautés de spécialistes. Et ce sont les spécialistes constituant ces communautés qui, dans leurs activités quotidiennes, développent, précisent et mettent en discours, au moyen de termes, les concepts de leur domaine. De cet état de fait, il est facile d'en tirer un argument pour soutenir que les spécialistes du domaine sont les personnes les mieux placées pour déterminer si un terme candidat dénote un concept compris dans les limites de leur domaine de spécialité et si le terme fait partie du lexique du domaine (voir L'Homme 2005: 1122–3; L'Homme 2000: 73).

L'affinement des technologies destinées à l'extraction des termes au sein de volumineux corpus, voire l'identification des relations qui unissent les concepts que les termes dénotent, n'a pas rendu caduc le recours aux spécialistes du domaine pour valider les informations recueillies. « [T]oute analyse linguistique, qui plus est lorsqu'il s'agit de discours spécialisés, doit systématiquement être pensée comme une co-construction interprétative entre le terminologue et l'expert. Le linguiste se sert d'indices linguistiques à sa disposition pour construire et proposer une théorie autour des phénomènes langagiers relevés tandis que l'expert joue un rôle de partenaire, en validant et éventuellement en complétant les structures préétablies » (Gormezano et Peraldi 2012: 259 (références omises).

Dans les langues de spécialité, la détermination du caractère terminologique d'une unité tout autant que la détermination du caractère idiomatique d'une combinaison incluant une telle unité exigent une connaissance approfondie du domaine, qui reste, en ce qui nous concerne, l'apanage de l'expert. Partant de cela, les UP en langue de spécialité peuvent être, à notre avis, définies comme des séquences polylexicales que des experts perçoivent comme typiques de la langue de leur domaine de spécialité.

Cette posture ne doit pas être compris comme une remise en cause de l'apport nécessaire des terminologues et linguistes dans la description des langues spécialisées, qui, seuls, ont les connaissances pour ne pas faire systématiquement passer les savoirs spécialisés avant les mots de la spécialité. Cette posture n'exclut pas, selon nous, au demeurant, la possibilité qu'un terminologue ou un linguiste acquière une expertise dans le domaine à force de travailler à la description de sa terminologie ou de sa langue. En ce qui nous concerne, nous faisons reposer sur cette posture l'intérêt que nous voyons à analyser les éléments de combinatoire recensés par un groupe d'experts d'un domaine de spécialité, sans formation linguistique particulière, comme c'est le cas des exemples linguistiques recensés dans la deuxième édition du *Dictionnaire de droit privé.*

## 2. Le Dictionnaire de droit privé

Dans cette partie, qui commence par une présentation générale *du Dictionnaire de droit privé*, puis qui examine la structure de l'article type dictionnaire, nous souhaitons mettre en évidence un fait particulier, à savoir que le *Dictionnaire de droit privé* recense presque exclusivement des éléments d'information qui aident l'usager à améliorer sa connaissance des termes juridiques et, partant, à interpréter les textes juridiques.

En ce sens, et ce, à l'instar de la quasi-totalité des dictionnaires de droit monolingue français que nous avons répertoriés, le *Dictionnaire de droit privé* est un dictionnaire de décodage plutôt que d'encodage (voir, sur cette distinction, Preite 2012; Polguère 2008: 232; Verlinde *et al.* 2006). Le dictionnaire renferme très peu d'informations susceptibles d'aider l'usager à encoder idiomatiquement sa pensée dans la langue du droit.

### 2.1. Le projet du Dictionnaire de droit privé

Le *Dictionnaire de droit privé* est un projet phare du Centre Paul-André Crépeau de droit privé et comparé. Le *Dictionnaire de droit privé* a pour objectif de décrire, en français et en anglais, le droit privé applicable au Québec. La première édition du dictionnaire en français est parue en 1985 (Crépeau *et al.* 1985; Crépeau *et al.* 1988) et la deuxième édition, dans ses versions française et anglaise, en 1991 (Crépeau *et al.* 1991; Kouri *et al.* 1991).

Une partie du travail réalisé en vue de la publication de la troisième édition, qui doit comprendre plus 10 000 termes juridiques (Kasirer 1999: XXII), est déjà accessible dans trois publications, lesquelles portent sur le vocabulaire du droit de la famille (Crépeau *et al.* 1999), du droit des obligations (Crépeau *et al.* 2003) et du droit des biens (Allard *et al.* 2012). Il convient de mentionner, ici, que, de 2001 à 2007, nous avons occupé diverses fonctions au Centre Paul-André Crépeau de droit privé et comparé (qui se nommait alors *Centre de recherche en droit privé et comparé du Québec*) et que nous avons participé à la préparation d'articles de la troisième édition du dictionnaire.

Par rapport aux trois publications plus récentes, les éditions de 1985 et 1991 du *Dictionnaire de droit privé* peuvent être dites générales. Ces deux éditions ont, en effet, vocation à couvrir, dans la perspective du système juridique québécois, tous, sinon la plupart des domaines du droit privé fondamental. Bien que générale dans son approche, même l'édition de 1991 reste incomplète dans la nomenclature qu'elle dresse du vocabulaire de droit privé québécois. L'édition de 1991 compte 3 549 vedettes (en excluant 10 doublets fonctionnels: p. ex. v° à terme et v° terme (à) n'est compté qu'une fois) et 4 059 termes (en excluant les mêmes 10 doublets fonctionnels)[5].

Sur le plan du contenu, le dictionnaire sert « la double fonction de préciser le sens d'un terme juridique et donner son équivalent » dans l'autre langue officielle du Canada (Crépeau *et al.* 1991: XXI). Si l'on exclut les lexiques français-anglais et anglais-français, nous verrons qu'aucune rubrique du *Dictionnaire de droit privé* ne fournit *systématiquement* à l'usager d'informations sur la manière d'employer les termes définis. En particulier, pour chacun des termes, le dictionnaire n'apporte pas, sauf exception, de solutions aux difficultés que ces termes peuvent soulever en contexte de production.

5 Pour connaître le nombre de mots vedettes du dictionnaire, nous avons réalisé deux dénombrements manuels. Pour connaître le nombre de termes dans le dictionnaire, nous avons profité du transfert (manuel) du manuscrit de la deuxième édition du *Dictionnaire de droit privé* dans une base de données informatique. Après avoir extrait automatiquement tous les termes de la version électronique de la deuxième édition, nous avons vérifié deux fois la concordance entre la version papier et la version électronique. La version électronique contient plus de termes que la version papier, essentiellement parce qu'un groupe de termes en droit des successions a été versé au manuscrit après sa publication en 1991. Les résultats présentés dans le présent texte ne tiennent compte que des éléments d'information contenus dans la version papier de la deuxième édition du dictionnaire.

## 2.2. La structure de l'article du Dictionnaire de droit privé

Vu l'objet du présent article, nous nous focaliserons sur le contenu des rubriques de l'article du *Dictionnaire de droit privé*. Nous ne présenterons pas la méthode présidant à l'élaboration du dictionnaire en général ainsi qu'à la détermination du contenu de chacune des rubriques en particulier, sauf en ce qui a trait à la rubrique à l'étude, soit l'exemple linguistique, la seule qui, dans le dictionnaire, est destinée à contenir des informations utiles à la production d'énoncés idiomatiques en langue du droit.

L'analyse des exemples linguistiques proposée dans la troisième partie du présent texte est basée sur la deuxième édition du dictionnaire, soit celle de 1991. Cette édition, malgré le fait qu'elle fût publiée il y a plus de 20 ans, profite, encore aujourd'hui, d'une autorité certaine auprès des juristes québécois comme en fait foi le fait qu'elle soit une référence régulièrement citée par les tribunaux. L'analyse des exemples linguistiques se fonde sur la deuxième édition afin de profiter du spectre plus large de sa nomenclature.

La présentation de l'article du dictionnaire qui suit se fera, par conséquent, principalement dans la perspective de la version française du *Dictionnaire de droit privé* et, en particulier, de l'édition parue en 1991. Notons que les rubriques types n'ont pas subi, au fil des éditions, de changements majeurs. Depuis la première édition, l'article du *Dictionnaire de droit privé* se structure en six blocs, qui se présentent toujours dans l'ordre suivant: le bloc-entrée, le bloc-définition, le bloc-occurrence, le bloc-remarque, le bloc-renvoi et le bloc-lexique. Les rubriques des deux premiers blocs, soit le bloc-entrée et le bloc-définition, nous intéressent davantage. Nous exposerons d'abord brièvement le contenu des quatre derniers blocs.

### 2.2.1. Le bloc-occurrence, le bloc-remarque, le bloc-renvoi et le bloc-lexique

Le bloc-occurrence ne contient qu'une rubrique, annoncée par l'abréviation **Occ.** Cette rubrique présente des sources législatives, par exemple des articles de loi, où le terme défini apparaît, soit au singulier, soit au pluriel. Une désignation paraphrastique du concept ne constitue pas une occurrence du terme. Par exemple, l'article 1591 du *Code civil du Québec* (ci-après C.c.Q.) où l'on retrouve le syntagme *lorsque sa créance est exigible* n'est pas recensé comme une occurrence du terme *créance exigible* (Crépeau *et al.* 2003: v° créance exigible). Le bloc-occurrence a pour objectif de témoigner de l'usage que le législateur fait du terme sur le plan normatif; le texte législatif n'y est pas cité.

Le bloc-remarque aussi ne contient qu'une rubrique, annoncée par l'abréviation **Rem.** La majorité, voire la très grande majorité des remarques sont d'ordre conceptuel ou encyclopédique. Les remarques conceptuelles types informent l'usager sur la situation du terme dans le réseau conceptuel du sous-domaine auquel il appartient (p. ex.: « On doit distinguer le jurisconsulte[2] du juriste, car ce dernier ne donne pas toujours des consultations juridiques. » (Crépeau *et al.* 1991: v° jurisconsulte)). Les remarques d'ordre encyclopédique types informent l'usager sur des éléments du régime juridique afférent au terme (p. ex.: « L'adoption crée un lien de parenté à l'égard de la famille adoptive et rompt le lien de parenté à l'égard de la famille d'origine (art. 627 C. civ. Q.) [art. 577 C.c.Q.]. » (Crépeau *et al.* 1991: v° parenté)). Les remarques linguistiques parmi les plus fréquentes se rapportent à l'étymologie du terme. Les remarques fournissent très rarement des informations sur la combinatoire du terme (pour un contre-exemple, Crépeau *et al.* 1991: v° compensation[1]).

Le bloc-renvoi permet d'attester deux types de renvoi, les renvois synonymiques précédés par Syn. et les renvois analogiques et notionnels précédés par V.a. Les renvois synonymiques attestent l'existence de termes qui dénotent le même concept (p. ex. les termes *illégal*[2] et *illicite* sont considérés comme synonymes (Crépeau *et al.* 1991: v° illégal[2] et illicite)). Le phénomène synonymique ouvre la voie à la définition par renvoi, type de définition dont nous traiterons dans la prochaine sous-section. Les renvois analogiques présentent des termes avec lesquels le terme recensé entretient un rapport conceptuel que ce soit un rapport de causalité, d'ingrédience, de complémentarité, de réciprocité ou d'antonymie. Il convient de mentionner que les deux premières éditions des dictionnaires connaissaient le renvoi d'opposition, noté **Opp.**, désormais compris dans les renvois analogiques et notionnels. Le renvoi d'opposition visait les rapports d'antonymie, de complémentarité et de réciprocité (Crépeau *et al.* 1991: xxxi).

L'article du dictionnaire se termine sur le bloc-lexique, noté **Angl.** dans les dictionnaires en français. Ce bloc à rubrique unique présente les équivalents du terme dans l'autre langue officielle du Canada. Dans le dictionnaire en français, le bloc-lexique fournit une assistance à l'usager qui souhaite exprimer le concept en anglais.

### 2.2.2. Le bloc-entrée et le bloc-définition

Le bloc-entrée comprend le mot vedette, sa catégorie grammaticale et, lorsque le mot vedette est formé d'au moins un vocable provenant d'une autre langue que le français, la mention de la langue d'origine (p. ex., Crépeau *et al.* 1991: v° obligation *in solidum*). Le mot vedette peut être simple (p. ex., Crépeau *et al.* 1991: v° dette) ou complexe (p. ex., Crépeau *et al.* 1991: v° dette solidaire). Les mots vedettes complexes ne sont pas regroupés sous leur base; ils apparaissent au long. La catégorie grammaticale des mots vedettes complexes n'est pas précisée, à moins qu'il ne s'agisse, de l'avis du Comité de rédaction du dictionnaire, d'une locution.

En cas de polysémie, les termes sont regroupés sous leur dénomination commune. Les termes polysémiques partagent donc le même bloc-entrée, y compris la même vedette. Il en est ainsi du contrat en tant que *négotium* et du contrat en tant qu'*instrumentum*. Les autres blocs de l'article des termes polysémiques sont distincts. Mentionnons, enfin, au sujet du bloc-entrée, que le *Dictionnaire de droit privé* de 1991 recense, à côté des substantifs (3206), nettement majoritaires, des verbes ou locutions verbales (196), des adjectifs ou locutions adjectivales (575), des adverbes ou locutions adverbiales (78) ainsi que des locutions prépositives (4). Ce déséquilibre entre les différentes parties du discours y décrites s'aligne sur la tendance générale observée dans les dictionnaires de langue de spécialité (L'Homme 2012: 94).

De son côté, le bloc-définition peut comprendre jusqu'à sept rubriques: le numéro d'acception, le domaine d'emploi, la mention d'usage, la définition, l'illustration juridique, la citation et l'exemple linguistique.

Le numéro d'acception sert à distinguer les différents sens des termes polysémiques. Dans la première et la deuxième édition des dictionnaires, une distinction était établie entre la polysémie très fine et, disons, aux fins de la présentation, la polysémie ordinaire (Crépeau *et al.* 1991: XXVI). Lorsque la distinction de sens entre deux termes était jugée *très fine*, le classement des acceptions se faisait au moyen de lettres (voir, p. ex., contrat en tant que *negotium* (Crépeau *et al.* 1991: v° contratA) vs le contrat en tant qu'*instrumentum* (Crépeau *et al.* 1991: v° contratB)). Lorsque la polysémie n'était pas jugée *très fine*, le classement se faisait au moyen de chiffres (voir, p. ex., illégal au sens de contraire à la loi (Crépeau *et al.* 1991: v° illégal$^1$) et illégal au sens d'illicite (Crépeau *et al.* 1991: v° illégal$^2$)). Cette distinction entre polysémie très fine et polysémie ordinaire a été abandonnée dans la troisième édition; les acceptions des vocables polysémiques sont désormais toutes ordonnées au moyen de chiffres. Le dictionnaire ne précisait d'ailleurs pas sur quel critère on jugeait du caractère « très fin » d'une distinction de sens.

Après le numéro d'acception, on précise, entre parenthèses, le ou les domaines du droit auquel ou auxquels on considère, généralement, que le concept dénoté par le terme appartient. Le domaine d'emploi est une rubrique propre aux dictionnaires généraux. Les dictionnaires qui ne portent que sur un domaine du droit omettent cette rubrique. Les dictionnaires généraux omettent aussi cette rubrique si le terme, par sa généralité, sinon sa transversalité, ne s'identifie à aucun domaine du droit en particulier ou encore s'il s'identifie à plus de deux domaines du droit.

La troisième rubrique du bloc-définition est la mention d'usage. À côté des mentions d'usage qui peuvent se passer d'explications: *Vieilli*, *Rare* et *Néol.*, il y a le (Q), qui désigne un emploi propre au droit privé québécois, inconnu des autres communautés juridiques de droit civil de langue française, et le (X), qui désigne un emploi à proscrire. Les mentions d'usage (Q) et (X) sont disparues dans la troisième édition des dictionnaires, remplacées, dans certains cas, par une remarque qui présente les enjeux que l'utilisation d'un terme soulève, par exemple les critiques qui peuvent lui être adressées (comparer Crépeau *et al.* 1991: v° *considération*$^2$ et *droit de premier refus* et Crépeau *et al.* 2003: v° *considération*$^3$ et *droit de premier refus*).

On peut soutenir que les dictionnaires connaissent deux types de définition: les définitions analytiques par genre prochain et différence(s) spécifique(s) ainsi que la définition-renvoi. Les définitions analytiques situent le concept dénoté par le terme dans son réseau conceptuel en identifiant le concept superordonné et les traits spécifiques de ce concept par rapport aux concepts voisins. On peut arguer que certaines définitions dites analytiques, en particulier celles des acteurs d'un régime juridique ainsi que, dans certains cas, celles des adjectifs, des verbes et des adverbes, opèrent par renvoi implicite à la définition analytique du concept-clé auquel le concept qu'elles définissent peut être rattaché. Par exemple, la définition de créancier – titulaire d'un droit personnel – renvoie, comme on peut le constater, au concept de droit personnel (Crépeau *et al.* 1991: v° créancier et droit personnel).

Les définitions-renvoi proprement dites sont de deux espèces. Il y a d'abord les définitions synonymiques. Parmi les termes considérés comme synonymes, le Comité de rédaction identifie un synonyme principal auquel il est attaché préférentiellement la définition, l'illustration juridique, les remarques et le réseau des renvois. Les synonymes dits secondaires renvoient au synonyme principal. Deuxièmement, il y a les définitions qui renvoient l'usager vers un ou plusieurs autres termes du dictionnaire dont l'article est susceptible d'apporter un éclairage au sujet du « terme » attesté, mais non défini. Ces définitions, qui, au fond, n'en sont pas du tout, sont précédées par l'abréviation V. Le *Dictionnaire de droit privé* de 1991 compte 447 de ces « termes » attestés, mais non définis qui renvoient à un ou à plusieurs termes.

À la suite de la définition, il peut être présenté une ou plusieurs illustrations juridiques du concept dénoté par le terme. Ce sont des cas de figure ou des exemples du concept défini. Les rapports qui s'inscrivent entre l'exemple et le concept défini varient d'un terme à l'autre si bien qu'il serait intéressant de faire une étude plus approfondie de cette rubrique[6].

La sixième et avant-dernière rubrique du bloc-définition est la citation. Un effort particulier est fait par les rédacteurs des dictionnaires pour trouver des citations qui permettent de « mettre en contexte le terme défini, que ce soit sur le plan juridique ou linguistique » (Allard *et al.* 2012: XXIV). La préférence accordée aux citations qui communiquent des informations de nature conceptuelle ou encyclopédique transparaît de la présentation qui est faite de cette rubrique: « La citation peut reprendre la définition en d'autres mots ou en préciser certains aspects. Parfois, elle énonce certaines règles qui gouvernent l'application de la notion, critique une distinction doctrinale ou, encore, annonce une classification

---

6 Dans certains cas, l'exemple juridique est un concept hyponyme par rapport au concept défini (p. ex. l'hypothèque est donnée comme exemple à *droit réel accessoire* (Crépeau *et al.* 1991: v° droit réel accessoire)). Dans d'autres cas, l'exemple juridique traduit une situation type couverte par le concept défini, c'est-à-dire une situation qui appelle, en droit, une qualification au moyen du concept en question (p. ex. une vente qui camoufle une donation est donné comme exemple à *acte apparent* (Crépeau *et al.* 1991: v° acte apparent)). Enfin, l'exemple peut être d'ordre référentiel (p. ex. la doctrine d'Aubry et Rau sur la notion de patrimoine est donnée comme exemple à *doctrine* (Crépeau *et al.* 1991: v° doctrine²)).

à l'intérieur de la notion définie. » (Allard *et al.* 2012: xxiv; comparer Crépeau *et al.* 1991: xxix).

L'exemple linguistique (EL) forme la septième et dernière rubrique du bloc-définition. L'EL est formé « d'une suite de mots qui reproduit un segment type du discours juridique ». Dans une perspective monolingue, l'exemple linguistique est la seule rubrique qui a vocation à attester d'éléments de la combinatoire conceptuelle ou lexicale du terme recensé. Parmi les rubriques formant l'article type du *Dictionnaire de droit privé*, cette rubrique apparaît donc comme une anomalie, en tous les cas, elle fait figure d'exception. Dans la troisième partie du texte, nous examinerons cette rubrique et analyserons les exemples proposés dans cette rubrique dans la deuxième édition du *Dictionnaire de droit privé*.

Pour l'heure, force est de constater que les rubriques de l'article des dictionnaires privilégient nettement, pour ne pas dire presque exclusivement, la consignation de renseignements d'ordre conceptuel ou encyclopédique et, en général, ils ne contiennent pas, sinon peu d'informations susceptibles d'aider l'usager à produire un discours juridique idiomatique en droit privé québécois. À l'analyse des articles du dictionnaire et de ses rubriques, nous pouvons soutenir que le dictionnaire s'adresse, en premier lieu, à un usager qui consulte le dictionnaire pour se familiariser avec un terme qu'il ne connaît pas ou avec un terme qu'il maîtrise mal, et ce, en vue de poursuivre plus efficacement sa lecture.

## 3. La phraséologie dans le Dictionnaire de droit privé: le cas des exemples linguistiques

Dans un premier temps, nous décrirons le contenu de la rubrique désignée sous le nom d'*exemple linguistique* (EL) ainsi que la méthode qui préside à la détermination de son contenu. Tous les exemples linguistiques recensés dans le *Dictionnaire de droit privé* peuvent se qualifier, selon nous, d'unités phraséologiques (UP), du moins selon la conception que nous défendons de l'UP en langue de spécialité. Tous ces EL sont des suites typiques ou idiomatiques de deux ou plusieurs mots, étant entendu que la détermination du caractère typique ou idiomatique d'une suite de mots dans une langue de spécialité reste sous l'autorité ultime des experts du domaine, ce que sont les juristes formant le Comité de rédaction du dictionnaire.

Dans un second temps, nous analyserons les EL de la deuxième édition du *Dictionnaire de droit privé*, à la lumière des deux hypothèses suivantes: 1. La majorité des EL consignés dans le *Dictionnaire de droit privé* sont des structures verbales (par opposition à des structures sans verbe); 2. Parmi les EL comprenant un verbe, la majorité des EL consignés sont des collocations lexicales (par opposition aux collocations conceptuelles).

### 3.1. La rubrique exemple linguistique: contenu et méthode

Mis à part la rubrique unique du bloc-lexique, l'EL est la seule rubrique qui a vocation de fournir une information susceptible d'aider l'usager dans la production d'un discours juridique. Dans le *Dictionnaire de droit privé*, la rubrique unique du bloc-lexique consigne le ou les termes qui dénotent le même concept en langue anglaise. De son côté, la rubrique formée de l'exemple linguistique est la seule qui soit destinée à consigner une information juridique pertinente quant à l'encodage du terme en contexte monolingue.

Le texte de présentation des dictionnaires décrit l'EL comme « une suite de mots qui reproduit un segment type du discours juridique », qui « place le terme défini en contexte, fournit un modèle du bon usage et renseigne sur les tournures propres au style juridique » (Allard *et al.* 2012: xxv; Crépeau *et al.* 2003: xxvii)[7]. Par exemple, dans l'article du terme *adoption* du dictionnaire de 1991, les quatre EL suivants sont recensés: *prononcer l'adoption*, *faire l'objet d'une adoption*, *une demande d'adoption* et *un jugement d'adoption.*

Les exemples linguistiques doivent être compris pour ce qu'ils sont, à savoir des exemples. La rubrique EL n'a jamais eu pour objectif de décrire exhaustivement la combinatoire des termes recensés. La rubrique EL n'étant pas une rubrique obligatoire, cette rubrique peut même, pour un terme donné, rester vide. Et la rubrique EL reste vide la plupart du temps. La deuxième édition du *Dictionnaire de droit privé* comprend 4 059 termes. Or, moins de 10% des termes recensés consignent un EL ou plus, soit 400 termes[8]. En comparaison, 417 termes sur 4 059 contiennent au moins une illustration juridique et 1342 termes sur 4 059 contiennent au moins une remarque[9].

Parmi les 400 articles qui consignent de l'information dans la rubrique EL, 178 articles proposent un seul EL. Trente-six termes sur les 222 restants consignent quatre EL ou plus. Voici ces 36 termes avec, pour chacun, le nombre d'EL indiqué entre parenthèses à sa suite: adoption (4), caution[1] (4), condition[5] (7), congé(4), contracter[1] (5), devis (4), discernement (4), disposition[2] (6), dissolution (4),

7 Dans la présentation de la deuxième édition du dictionnaire, on précisait que l'exemple linguistique était un « segment non figé » (Crépeau *et al.* 1991: xxx) et, dans la présentation de la première et de la deuxième édition, on précisait que « la spécificité de la langue juridique justifie qu'on s'intéresse aussi, dans un dictionnaire de droit, à l'aspect syntaxique » (Crépeau *et al.* 1985: x; Crépeau *et al.* 1991: xxx). La référence à l'aspect syntaxique de la langue du droit est disparue dans le *Dictionnaire de droit privé de la famille* (Crépeau *et al.* 1999: xxxiv-xxxv). La référence au caractère non figé des segments répertoriés est disparue dans le dictionnaire suivant, portant sur le droit des obligations (Crépeau *et al.* 2003: xxvii).

8 Le dénombrement des exemples linguistiques a été réalisé suivant une méthode analogue à celle appliquée pour dénombrer les termes du dictionnaire, voir note vi ci-dessus.

9 Le dénombrement des illustrations juridiques et des remarques a été réalisé suivant une méthode analogue à celle appliquée pour dénombrer les termes du dictionnaire, voir note vi ci-dessus.

exécution (4), fait[3] (5), hypothécairement (4), hypothèque (4), interdiction[1] (5), irrévocable (5), judiciaire[3]A (5), jurisprudence[2] (4), légitime[1] (4), mainlevée (5), mandat[1] (4), nul (4), nullité (6), partie (5), plan (4), possession[1] (7), prescription (7), qualification[1] (4), radiation (4), réparation (5), répéter (4), responsabilité[2] (6), révocation[1] (7), révoquer (4), sûreté[1] (4), temporaire (4), terme[2] (4).

Sur le plan de la méthode, tant la décision de consigner ou non un EL pour un terme donné que le choix de l'EL à consigner pour un terme donné ne se basent sur aucun critère exprès. Si un tel cadre décisionnel existait, on peut présumer que le texte de présentation du dictionnaire en ferait mention. Bien que la description de la rubrique EL ait varié depuis la première édition du dictionnaire, aucune des descriptions proposées n'a fourni de réponse à la question suivante: comment choisit-on les « segments types du discours juridique » qui sont consignés dans le dictionnaire?

L'absence de critérium relativement aux choix des EL se reflète dans la proportion somme toute minime de termes pour lesquels un ou plusieurs EL sont consignés. L'existence et l'application de critères exprès auraient certainement éveillé les chercheurs travaillant au projet ainsi que les membres du Comité de rédaction aux éléments de phraséologie des termes recensés, tout au moins des termes simples recensés. Car il est évident, par exemple, qu'un dictionnaire de droit n'a pas à reprendre la combinatoire du terme *action* pour chaque terme qui dénote un type d'action. Ainsi, si on intente une action à (ou contre) quelqu'un, on peut prédire qu'on intentera une action en déclaration de simulation à (ou contre) quelqu'un ou encore qu'on intentera une action en désaveu de paternité à (ou contre) quelqu'un. Cela rejoint l'observation faite par les terminologues selon laquelle, en langue de spécialité, des cooccurrents peuvent souvent se combiner avec les termes appartenant à une même classe conceptuelle (L'Homme 1998: 517). Mais même en ne considérant que les termes simples du dictionnaire (1772), seuls 367 d'entre eux sont munis d'au moins un EL, soit à peine plus d'un sur cinq.

L'absence de ce critérium se reflète aussi dans le choix des termes qui, sur le plan phraséologique, se voit éclairer ou non par un ou plusieurs EL. Pourquoi des termes comme *acceptation*, *accomplissement*, *acheter*, *acquisition* et *avocat*, pour ne s'en tenir qu'à la lettre A, consignent-ils un ou plusieurs EL alors que des termes comme *abornement*, *acquit*, *adjonction*, *affidavit*, *alluvion*, *anatocisme*, *animus*, *antichrèse*, *atterrissement*, *ayant cause* et *ayant droit* n'en consignent aucun? Pourtant, tous conviendront que, par rapport aux termes de la première liste, les termes de la seconde sont plus difficiles à actualiser en discours, en particulier pour l'usager type à qui s'adresse le dictionnaire. Notons que si les termes de la seconde liste sont plus difficiles à manier en discours, c'est vraisemblablement parce que ces termes ne profitent pas, eux, d'un vocable d'emploi courant dans la langue générale afin d'en éclairer le sens *et* la phraséologie.

Pour avoir siégé au Comité de rédaction du dictionnaire, nous savons qu'on s'y fie à l'expérience et à l'intuition en langue du droit des chercheurs qui travaillent sur les versions préliminaires des articles du dictionnaire ainsi qu'à l'expérience et à l'intuition des membres du Comité de rédaction pour choisir les EL. D'un point de vue lexicographique, le recours à l'expérience et à l'intuition seules, sans autre critère, pour statuer si la rubrique EL d'un terme restera vide ou non et, le cas échéant, pour déterminer le ou les EL recensés tient de l'arbitraire.

Dans la première partie de ce texte, nous avons soutenu que l'expertise dans un domaine de spécialité est essentielle pour juger, en définitive, si un segment est idiomatique dans la langue de ce domaine. Il reste néanmoins que cette expertise, qui se fonde, pour une bonne part, sur l'expérience dans le domaine, mais, pour une part aussi, sur l'intuition, doit être balisée afin de pouvoir justifier les choix qui sont faits en son nom. *A posteriori*, le groupe d'experts, en ce qui nous concerne le Comité de rédaction du dictionnaire, doit être en mesure d'affirmer que leur expérience et leur intuition, qui sous-tendent leur expertise, ont été sollicitées, pour tous les termes recensés, d'une manière comparable. En particulier, le groupe d'experts doit être en mesure d'affirmer que leur expérience et leur intuition ont profité d'une recherche phraséologique préalable comparable. Ce qui n'est pas le cas.

Du point du vue du Comité de rédaction du dictionnaire, les exemples linguistiques doivent être compris pour ce qu'ils sont, à savoir des exemples de l'usage en droit, rien de plus. Du point de vue de l'analyste, les EL du dictionnaire restent le résultat de décisions arbitraires, fondées sur l'expérience et l'intuition de juristes, qui ne sont pas des experts en langue. Pour l'analyste, ces EL peuvent, malgré les tares qui les minent à l'échelle individuelle, constituer collectivement un matériau d'analyse intéressant. À défaut de fournir une information qui repose sur des bases méthodologiques solides, les données recensées dans la rubrique EL, prises comme un tout, révèlent peut-être la conception intuitive des structures sémantico-syntaxiques les plus typiques de la langue du droit, celles qui seraient, selon un groupe d'experts du domaine, les plus pertinentes dans la production d'un discours en langue du droit. En tout cas, c'est le postulat sur lequel reposent nos deux hypothèses de recherche.

### 3.2. Les EL de la deuxième édition du Dictionnaire de droit privé

Dans un premier temps, nous présenterons et expliquerons nos hypothèses de recherche, qui visent à mettre en lumière ce qui, pour un groupe de juristes non-linguistes, constitue « un segment type du discours juridique » (Crépeau *et al.* 1991: xxx). Dans un deuxième temps, nous analyserons les EL de la deuxième édition du *Dictionnaire de droit privé* et, entre autres choses, vérifierons si les résultats confirment nos hypothèses. Afin d'éviter toute confusion sur la nature de notre étude, nous nous permettrons de faire remarquer la dimension largement heuristique des hypothèses présentées: la valeur de ces dernières tient (beaucoup) moins à leur véracité ou à leur fausseté qu'à ce qu'elles nous permettent de dire (ou de ne pas dire) au sujet des EL choisis par un groupe de juristes non-linguistes qui élaborent un dictionnaire juridique.

### 3.2.1. La présentation des hypothèses de recherche au sujet des EL de la deuxième édition du Dictionnaire de droit privé

Selon nous, l'une difficulté première lorsqu'on veut communiquer dans une langue, fût-elle spécialisée, est de connaître les verbes qui se combinent avec les mots (Ramos 1998) et, en langue de spécialité, avec les termes du domaine, lesquels sont, la plupart du temps, des noms. Par conséquent, pour actualiser en discours un terme nominal, il faut savoir, en premier lieu, le « conjuguer », c'est-à-dire le combiner correctement avec ses verbes cooccurrents.

Nous postulons que les juristes comprennent intuitivement l'importance des verbes dans la communication en langue du droit. Si cette intuition s'avère, elle devrait se refléter dans le choix des EL. Nous posons l'hypothèse que les membres du Comité de rédaction du *Dictionnaire de droit privé* ont favorisé majoritairement, au titre d'EL, des segments qui comprennent un terme associé à un verbe cooccurrent.

Notre deuxième hypothèse se rapporte à la distinction entre collocations conceptuelles (ci-après renommées *UP conceptuelles*) et collocations lexicales (ci-après renommées *UP lexicales*) que nous avons présentée dans la première partie du texte. Pour rappel, les UP conceptuelles sont, pour nous, des combinaisons dans lesquelles chacune des unités lexicales est un terme. Les UP conceptuelles sont entièrement décomposables: le sens de l'UP est compris comme la somme des termes qui la compose. Dans une UP lexicale, l'une des unités lexicales combinées n'est pas un terme juridique.

Nous postulons que, dans l'esprit des juristes, les UP lexicales paraissent plus idiomatiques parce qu'elles ne sont pas décomposables terme par terme. Elles doivent, à l'instar des locutions et des collocations types de la langue générale, être apprises comme un tout pour pouvoir être mobilisées en discours, ce qui renforce leur caractère d'idiomaticité. Nous croyons que les juristes comprennent intuitivement cette réalité. Si cette intuition s'avère, elle devrait se refléter dans le choix des EL. Nous posons l'hypothèse que, parmi les EL comportant un verbe, le verbe sera, dans la majorité des cas, un verbe non terminologique.

Nous appliquerons le test à deux volets suivant pour déterminer si un verbe est terminologique ou non: 1. Le verbe, dans le sens qu'il porte dans l'EL à l'étude, est-il recensé dans le *Dictionnaire de droit privé* ou dans le *Vocabulaire juridique* (Cornu 2011), un dictionnaire de droit français comprenant une nomenclature de plus de 10 000 termes? 2. Le dérivé nominal du verbe en question, toujours au regard du sens dont le verbe est porteur dans l'EL à l'étude, constitue-t-il un terme attesté dans l'un ou l'autre de ces deux ouvrages de lexicographie juridique? Si le verbe satisfait à l'un *ou* l'autre des volets de ce test, il sera considéré comme terminologique, autrement il sera considéré comme non terminologique et comme participant à la construction d'une UP lexicale.

### 3.2.2. Les EL du Dictionnaire de droit privé

Dans un premier temps, nous classerons les EL de la deuxième édition du *Dictionnaire de droit privé* et, dans un deuxième temps, nous analyserons les EL recensés à l'aune des hypothèses que nous avons formulées.

#### 3.2.2.1. Les structures sémantico-syntaxiques des EL du Dictionnaire de droit privé

Faute d'espace, nous ne pouvons reproduire la liste des 754 EL que nous avons dénombrés dans la deuxième édition du *Dictionnaire de droit privé*, après avoir soustrait les doublets et les deux faux positifs: grands-parents (Crépeau et al. 1991: v° parent, ente) et des porte-fort (Crépeau et al. 1991: v° porte-fort)[10].

En premier lieu, nous avons tenté, au meilleur de nos connaissances linguistiques, de classer ces 754 EL en fonction de leur structure syntaxique, comme souvent le font les dictionnaires qui consignent la combinatoire des unités qu'ils recensent, du moins en langue générale (Tutin 2010b: 1083; voir aussi Resche 1997). À cette fin, nous avons distingué les structures formées sur des locutions prépositive, adjectivale, adverbiale ou conjonctive, les structures verbales et les structures sans verbe. Nous avons classé à part les EL qui sont l'expression totale ou partielle d'un adage ou d'une règle de droit.

Voici les neuf EL qui reproduisent totalement ou partiellement un adage ou une règle de droit, suivie du ou des termes où ces EL sont consignés:

1. L'accessoire suit le principal. (v° accessoire)
2. Les versements d'une rente s'arréragent. (v° arrérager (s'))
3. Les choses de genre ne périssent pas. (v° chose de genre)
4. La loi ne dispose que pour l'avenir (v° disposer[2]; loi[1])
5. Le paiement s'impute sur le capital. (v° imputer[3])
6. La faute s'apprécie *in abstracto*. (v° *in abstracto*)
7. Possession vaut titre. (v° possession[1]; titre[1])
8. Une faute dommageable ouvre droit à réparation. (v° réparation)
9. Le mort saisit le vif. (v° vif)

Nous avons recensé 21 EL formés sur des locutions prépositive, adjectivale, adverbiale ou conjonctive, dont les cinq suivants:

1. Sous peine de déchéance (v° déchéance[1])

---

10 Ces deux mots composés ne remplissent pas, selon nous, les critères définitionnels de l'exemple linguistique parce qu'ils ne sont pas formés d'une suite d'au moins deux mots, ce qui suppose dans le contexte en cause, à notre avis, que ces deux mots soient séparés par un blanc (voir Crépeau *et al.* 1991: xxx).

2. À moins que le contrat n'en dispose autrement (v° disposer[2])
3. En bonne et due forme (v° forme[1])
4. Faute d'avoir satisfait une obligation (v° faute de)
5. En bon père de famille (v° père)

Parmi les EL qui possèdent une structure verbale, nous avons distingué entre sept sous-structures. De loin la plus représentée est celle qui peut se généraliser en V (+ PRÉP.) + N (+ PRÉP. + N) ou (+ ADV.), où les éléments placés entre parenthèses sont facultatifs. Dans cette structure, l'un sinon les deux « N » sont des termes juridiques nominaux, lesquels peuvent consister en des termes simples ou complexes. Nous avons répertorié 223 de ces EL dont les huit suivants:

1. Consentir un nantissement (v° nantissement[2])
2. Donner en nantissement (v° nantissement[2])
3. Convoler en justes noces (v° noces)
4. Se destiner au notariat (v° notariat[1])
5. Donner notification (v° notification)
6. Recevoir notification (v° notification)
7. Emporter nullité (v° nullité)
8. Entraîner la nullité (v° nullité)

Parmi les six autres structures verbales, il y a d'abord la structure N + PRÉP., qui ne compte qu'un représentant, à savoir *se dessaisir de ...* (v° dessaisir (se)). Notons qu'il suffirait de compléter la proposition (ce que, du reste, les trois points incitent à faire) pour intégrer cet EL au groupe précédent.

La structure N + V (+ X), où X peut être un nom, un adverbe, voire une proposition, compte 11 candidats (p. ex. *Le contrat stipule que ...* (v° stipuler)). Nous avons inclus la structure impersonnelle *Il est de principe que* dans cette catégorie. Nous avons, par contre, exclu de cette catégorie les huit EL de type N + VERBE À L'INFINITIF, lesquels nous semblent à mi-chemin entre des unités terminologiques et phraséologiques (p. ex. *mode de contracter* (v° contracter[1]), *intention de frauder* (v° frauder) et *promesse de vendre* (v° vendre)). Notons aussi que la structure V + (+ PRÉP.) + VERBE À L'INFINITIF compte un candidat: *citer à comparaître* (v° comparaître).

Enfin, il y a les structures où le verbe s'accompagne d'un adverbe ou encore, ce qui est rare, d'un adjectif. Le *Dictionnaire de droit privé* compte 10 EL qui prennent la forme V + ADV (p. ex. *agir hypothécairement* (v° hypothécairement) et *qualifier* lege fori (v° qualifier)). L'EL *être tenu civilement responsable* (v° responsable), le seul de son espèce, a été classé dans la structure verbale de type V + ADJ puisque l'EL contient expressément le verbe *être* et qu'il peut s'analyser comme la forme passive de Y tient X civilement responsable (comparer avec *frappé de nullité* (v° nullité) considéré comme formé sur une structure sans verbe).

Parmi les structures non verbales, nous avons distingué entre 10 structures, parmi lesquels la plus productive est N (+ PRÉP.) + N (+ MOD.) où la structure modificatrice (MOD.) est le plus souvent un complément du nom. Dans cette structure, l'un sinon les deux « N » sont des termes juridiques nominaux, lesquels peuvent consister en des termes simples ou complexes. Le *Dictionnaire de droit privé* compte 216 EL de ce type, parmi lesquels les cinq suivants:

1. Vente d'un immeuble avec la maison et ses dépendances (v° dépendances)
2. Compensation du préjudice (v° compensation[1])
3. Violation des formes (v° forme[1])
4. Opposition au mariage (v° mariage[1])
5. Respect de l'ordre public (v° ordre public)

Proches de la structure ci-devant, il y a la structure N + CONJ. + N, qui ne compte qu'un représentant, soit l'EL *plan et devis* (vo devis; plan), ainsi que la structure ADJ. + N + (+ PRÉP.) + N, qui ne compte elle aussi qu'un représentant: *bon père de famille* (v° famille[5]).

La structure N + ADJ. OU PART. PASSÉ est la deuxième structure non verbale la plus représentée, avec 211 occurrences. Dans cette structure, le « N » peut consister en un terme simple ou complexe, tout comme l'adjectif d'ailleurs.

1. Prescription décennale (v° prescription)
2. Mur privatif (v° privatif, ive)
3. Propriété privative (v° privatif, ive)
4. Prix courant (v° prix)
5. Procureur *ad litem* (v° procureur)
6. Délai prorogé (v° proroger)
7. Obligation légale *lato sensu* (v° *lato sensu*)
8. Responsabilité légale *lato sensu* (v° *lato sensu*)

Ont été inclus dans cette structure, l'EL unique qui a pour patron: N + ADJ. + CONJ. + ADJ. (*biens présents et à venir* (v° bien à venir; bien présent)), l'EL unique qui a pour patron N + ADJ. + ADV. + PART. PASSÉ (*intérêt légitime juridiquement protégé* (v° légitime[3])) ainsi que l'EL unique qui a pour patron N + PART. PASSÉ + ADJ. (p. ex. *mariage déclaré nul* (v° nul, nulle)).

Nous avons répertorié 22 EL formés *grosso modo* sur la structure N (+ PRÉP. + N) + ADJ. ou PART. PASSÉ (+ PRÉP.) + N. Nous avons divisé ces EL en deux sous-catégories selon qu'il soit possible ou non d'insérer « qui est » / « qui sont » entre la base nominale de l'EL et l'adjectif ou, selon le cas, le participe passé.

1. Les conditions [qui sont] prescrites par tel article (v° condition[5])
2. Les conditions [qui sont] fixées par tel article (v° condition[5])
3. Les conditions [qui sont] énoncées par tel article (v° condition[5])
4. Les conditions de tel article, [qui sont] prévues par telle loi (v° condition[5])
5. Une obligation [qui est] contractée sous telle condition (v° condition[1])
6. Consentement [qui est] entaché d'erreur ou de dol (v° consentement[1])

7. Contrat [qui est] entaché de dol (v° dol[1])
8. Règles [qui sont] exorbitantes du droit commun (v° droit commun[1])
9. Fait [qui est] générateur de responsabilité (v° fait[2])
10. Comportement [qui est] entaché de faute (v° faute[1])
11. *Exercice [qui est] fautif d'un droit (v° fautif, ive)
12. Acte [qui est] accompagné de formalités (v° formalité)
13. *Exercice [qui est] illégal d'une charge (v° illégal, ale[1])
14. *Cause [qui est] légitime de préférence (v° légitime[1])
15. Prix [qui est] payable par mensualités (v° mensualité)
16. *Direction [qui est] morale de la famille (v° moral, ale[3])
17. *Possession [qui est] constante d'état (v° possession d'état)
18. *Contenu [qui est] réel d'un contrat (v° réel, elle[1])
19. Rente [qui est] créée en perpétuel (v° rente[1])
20. Rente [qui est] créée en viager (v° rente[1])
21. Un bail [qui est] résilié pour le défaut d'une partie d'exécuter ses obligations (v° résilier[2])
22. Bien [qui est] consomptible par le premier usage (v° usage[2])

Il reste enfin, pour achever le portrait, quatre structures non verbales, lesquelles sont d'occurrence relativement marginale: N + ADV. (2 représentants), N + ADJ OU PART. PASSÉ + ADV. (2 représentants), ADJ OU PART. PASSÉ (+ PRÉP.) + N (8 représentants) et ADJ. OU PART. PASSÉ + ADV. (6 représentants). Voici, dans l'ordre, un exemple d'EL pour chacune de ces quatre structures.

1. Appréciation *in concreto* (v° *in concreto*)
2. Prix payable à terme (v° terme(à))
3. Frappé de nullité (v° nullité)
4. Attaché à perpétuelle demeure (v° perpétuelle demeure (à))

Dans un deuxième temps, nous avons analysé les 255 EL formés sur une structure verbale pour distinguer celles qui, au regard du test à deux volets présenté ci-dessus, forment des UP conceptuelles de celles qui forment des UP lexicales. Deux verbes ont posé des problèmes de classement plus épineux, soit *donner* et *recevoir*.

Dans le cas des combinaisons formées sur *donner*, nous avons considéré comme des UP conceptuelles les combinaisons dans lesquelles la base terminologique nominale dénotait un concept clairement associé au droit de propriété ou à un droit réel (voir Cornu 2011: v° donner (1) et (2)). C'est pourquoi *donner en échange* est classé comme une UP conceptuelle, mais que *donner à bail*, *donner en garantie* et *donner (une) sûreté* sont plutôt classés comme des UP lexicales. (En droit civil, on considère que le bail n'est pas constitutif de droit réel et la garantie ou la sûreté donnée peut être aussi bien personnelle que réelle.) Toutes les combinaisons formées sur *recevoir* ont été considérées comme des UP conceptuelles (voir Cornu 2011: v° réception (1)), sauf *recevoir congé* (où *recevoir* signifie *être l'objet de*) et *recevoir mandat* (où *recevoir* signifie *se voir conférer*).

Voici deux listes présentant les résultats obtenus. La première liste recense les 83 EL à structure verbale qui, selon le test pratiqué, se qualifient d'UP lexicales, la seconde recense tous les EL à structure verbale qui se qualifient d'UP conceptuelles.

**Liste des UP lexicales**

1. Donner un acte de notoriété (v° acte de notoriété)
2. Faire l'objet d'une adoption (v° adoption)
3. Tenir en antichrèse (v° antichrèse[2])
4. Servir des arrérages (v° arrérages)
5. Rendre un arrêt (v° arrêtA)
6. Donner à bail (v° bailA)
7. Prendre à bail (v° bailA)
8. Se destiner au barreau (v° barreau[1])
9. Poser des bornes (v° borne)
10. Donner (une) caution (v° caution[1])
11. Fournir (une) caution (v° caution[1])
12. Se porter caution (v° caution[1])
13. Se rendre caution (v° caution[1])
14. Fournir un cautionnement (v° cautionnement[1])
15. Toucher une commission (v° commission[1])
16. Le paiement se fait comptant (v° comptant)
17. Avoir compétence (v° compétence[1])
18. Faire des conditions de paiement (v° condition de paiement)
19. Donner congé (v° congé)
20. Recevoir congé (v° congé)
21. Faire une consignation (v° consignation)
22. Faire crédit (v° crédit[1])
23. Avoir du crédit (v° crédit[1])
24. Obtenir du crédit (v° crédit[2])
24. Faire crédit (v° crédit[3])
26. Donner décharge (v° déchargeA)
27. Prendre un décret (v° décret[1])
28. Donner un devis (v° devis)
29. Faire un devis (v° devis)
30. Éprouver un dommage (v° dommage)
31. Faire un don (v° don[1])
32. Venir à échéance (v° échéance[1])
33. Fonder une famille (v° famille[5])
34. Être en faute (v° faute[2])
35. Donner en garantie (v° garantie[2])
36. Fournir (une) garantie (v° garantie[2])

37. Avoir sous sa garde (vº garde$^{3}$)
38. Faire acte d'héritier (vº héritier, ière)
39. Faire appel à un homme de loi (vº homme de loi)
40. Être dans l'indivision (vº indivision$^{1}$)
41. Demeurer dans l'indivision (vº indivision$^{1}$)
42. Sortir de l'indivision (indivision$^{1}$)
43. Le contrat comportant un *intuitus personae* (vº *intuitus personae*)
44. Rendre (un) jugement (vº jugementA)
45. Rendre justice (vº justice$^{3}$)
46. Faire une libéralité (vº libéralité$^{1}$)
47. Changer la localisation (vº localisation)
48. Donner mainlevée (vº mainlevée)
49. Donner mandat de (vº mandat$^{1}$)
50. Avoir mandat (vº mandat$^{2}$)
51. Donner mandat de (vº mandat$^{2}$)
52. Recevoir mandat (vº mandat$^{2}$)
53. Convoler en justes noces (vº noces)
54. Se destiner au notariat (vº notariat$^{1}$)
55. Donner notification (vº notification)
56. Emporter nullité (vº nullité)
57. Entraîner la nullité (vº nullité)
58. Remplir ses obligations (vº obligation$^{3}$)
59. Rentrer en possession (vº possession)
60. Reprendre possession (vº possession)
61. Invitation à entrer en pourparlers (vº pourparlers)
62. La prescription court à compter de … (vº prescription)
63. Il est de principe que … (vº principe)
64. Donner quittance (vº quittance)
65. Donner quitus (vº quitus)
66. Faire un règlement (vº règlement$^{1}$)
67. Prendre un règlement (vº règlement$^{1}$)
68. Servir une rente (vº rente$^{2}$)
69. Former une requête (vº requête)
70. Présenter une requête (vº requête)
71. Dégager sa responsabilité (vº responsabilité$^{2}$)
72. Rechercher en responsabilité (vº responsabilité$^{2}$)
73. Être tenu civilement responsable (vº responsable)
74. Emporter révocation (vº révocation$^{1}$)
75. Entraîner la révocation (vº révocation$^{1}$)
76. Valoir révocation (vº révocation$^{1}$)
77. Pratiquer une saisie (vº saisie)
78. Pratiquer une saisie-exécution (vº saisie-exécution)
79. Fournir des services (vº service$^{1}$)
80. Recueillir une succession (vº succession$^{2}$)

81. Fournir (une) sûreté (v° sûreté[1])
82. Donner (une) sûreté (v° sûreté[1])
83. Fournir titres (v° titre[2]B)

**Liste des UP conceptuelles**

1. Promesse d'acheter (v° acheter)
2. Acquérir force de loi (v° acquérir)
3. Acquérir force de chose jugée (v° acquérir)
4. Acquitter une dette (v° acquitter)
5. Défendre à une action (v° action[2])
6. Intenter une action (à, contre) quelqu'un (v° action[2])
7. Prononcer l'adoption (v° adoption)
8. Annuler un contrat (v° annuler)
9. Annuler une renonciation (v° annuler)
10. Constituer en antichrèse (v° antichrèse[2])
11. Remettre en antichrèse (v° antichrèse[2])
12. Interjeter appel (v° appel)
13. Stipuler des arrhes (v° arrhes)
14. Arriérer un paiement (v° arriérer)
15. Être admis au barreau (v° barreau[1])
16. Délivrer un bref (v° bref)
17. Délivrer un certificat de coutume (v° certificat de coutume)
18. Percevoir une commission (v° commission[1])
19. Citer à comparaître (v° comparaître)
20. Comparaître en justice (v° comparaître)
21. Défaut de comparaître (v° comparaître)
22. Opposer la compensation (v° compensation[3])
23. Accorder une indemnité en compensation de la perte subie (v° compensation[1])
24. Payer comptant (v° comptant)
25. Confirmer un contrat (v° confirmer)
26. Signifier congé (v° congé)
27. Convoquer un conseil de famille (v° conseil de famille)
28. Recevoir une consignation (v° consignation)
29. Contracter mariage (v° contracter[1])
30. Mode de contracter (v° contracter[1])
31. Offre de contracter (v° contracter[1]; offre)
32. Contracter une assurance (v° contracter[1])
33. Contracter par-devant notaire (v° contracter[1])
34. Contracter une dette (v° contracter[2])
35. Contracter une obligation (v° contracter[2])
36. Conclure un contrat (v° contratA)
37. Négocier un contrat (v° contratA)

38. Passer contrat (v° contratA)
39. Consentir du crédit (v° crédit[2])
40. Faculté de se dédire (v° dédire (se))
41. La condition défaille ou se réalise. (v° défaillir)
42. Déguerpir un fonds (v° déguerpir[1])
43. Déguerpir un héritage (v° déguerpir[1])
44. Commettre un délit (v° délit)
45. Constituer le débiteur en demeure (v° demeure[1])
46. Être en demeure (v° demeure[1])
47. Mettre le débiteur en demeure (v° demeure[1])
48. Se dessaisir de … (v° dessaisir (se))
49. Détenir pour autrui (v° détenir)
50. Détenir pour soi (v° détenir)
51. Établir un devis (v° devis)
52. Discuter le débiteur principal dans ses biens (v° discuter)
53. Disposer d'un bien (v° disposer[1] A)
54. La loi dispose que … (v° disposer[2])
55. Réparer un dommage (v° dommage)
56. Recevoir un don (v° don[2])
57. Dire le droit (v° droit[1])
58. Donner en échange (v° échange)
59. Recevoir en échange (v° échange)
60. Le terme échoit le 15 mars. (v° échoir)
61. Légitimer un enfant naturel (v° enfant naturel)
62. Juger en équité (v° équité[2])
63. Traiter avec équité (v° équité[2])
64. Évincer quelqu'un de quelque chose (v° évincer)
65. Commettre une faute (v° faute[1])
66. Établir une filiation (v° filiation[1])
67. Contester une filiation (v° filiation[1])
68. Construire à forfait (v° forfait)
69. Frauder ses créanciers (v° frauder)
70. Intention de frauder (v° frauder)
71. Frauder la loi (v° frauder)
72. Soustraire frauduleusement (v° frauduleusement)
73. Donner en gage (v° gage[2])
74. Mettre en gage (v° gage[2])
75. Transporter en garantie (v° garantie[2])
76. Attribuer la garde (v° garde[1])
77. Recevoir un héritage (v° héritage[3])
78. Acquérir par héritage (v° héritage[2])
79. Transmettre par héritage (v° héritage[2])
80. Consulter un homme de loi (v° homme de loi)
81. Agir hypothécairement (v° hypothécairement)

82. Constituer une hypothèque (v° hypothèque)
83. Purger un bien d'une hypothèque (v° hypothèque)
84. Commettre une illégalité (v° illégalité[2])
85. Vivre dans l'illégalité (v° illégalité[2])
86. Imputer le paiement sur le capital (v° imputer[3])
87. Indemniser le dommage (v° indemniser[2])
88. Indemniser la victime (v° indemniser[1])
89. Indexer un emprunt sur l'indice du coût de la vie (v° indexer)
90. Agir en interdiction (v° interdiction)
91. Prononcer l'interdiction (v° interdiction)
92. Déclarer l'interdiction (v° interdiction)
93. Lever l'interdiction (v° interdiction)
94. Contracter intuitu personae (v° intuitu personae)
95. La jurisprudence est fixée (v° jurisprudence[2])
96. Exercer la justice avec rigueur (v° justice[3])
97. Agir dans les limites de la légalité (v° légalité[2])
98. Consentir une libéralité (v° libéralité[1])
99. Libérer le débiteur (v° libérer)
100. Libérer un fonds d'une charge (v° libérer)
101. Recevoir en location (v° location)
102. Voter une loi (v° loi[2])
103. Louer à quelqu'un (v° louer[1])
104. Accorder mainlevée (v° mainlevée)
105. Ordonner mainlevée (v° mainlevée)
106. Confier un mandat (v° mandat[1])
107. Le mandant révoque le mandat. (v° mandat[1])
108. Le mandataire renonce au mandat. (v° mandat[1])
109. Acquérir la mitoyenneté (v° mitoyenneté)
110. Consentir un nantissement (v° nantissement[2])
111. Donner en nantissement (v° nantissement[2])
112. Recevoir notification (v° notification)
113. S'acquitter de ses obligations (v° obligation[3])
114. Satisfaire ses obligations (v° obligation[3])
115. Être partie à un contrat (v° partie)
116. Invoquer la péremption (v° péremption)
117. Dresser un plan (v° plan)
118. Posséder pour autrui (v° posséder)
119. Posséder pour soi (v° posséder)
120. Entrer en possession (v° possession)
121. Prendre possession (v° possession)
122. Causer (un) préjudice (v° préjudice)
123. Réparer un préjudice (v° préjudice)
124. Acquérir la prescription (v° prescription)
125. Interrompre la prescription (v° prescription)

126. Suspendre la prescription (v° prescription)
127. Renoncer à la prescription acquise (v° prescription)
128. Prescrire contre son titre (v° prescrire)
129. Prescrire la propriété d'un bien (v° prescrire)
130. Exécuter une prestation (v° prestation)
131. Intenter un procès (v° procès)
132. Désavouer un procureur (v° procureur)
133. Proroger un bail (v° proroger)
134. Proroger une échéance (v° proroger)
135. Qualifier *lege fori* (v° qualifier)
136. Qualifier *lege causae* (v° qualifier)
137. Recevoir des travaux (v° recevoir)
138. Exercer un recours collectif (v° recours collectif)
139. Édicter un règlement (v° règlement[1])
140. Régler en espèces (v° régler[1])
141. Régler une succession (v° régler[2])
142. Verser une rente (v° rente[2])
143. Appliquer le renvoi (v° renvoi)
144. Refuser le renvoi (v° renvoi)
145. Demander réparation (v° réparation)
146. Exiger réparation (v° réparation)
147. Répéter les dommages-intérêts (v° répéter)
148. Répéter les frais (v° répéter)
149. Répéter l'indu (v° répéter)
150. Répéter une chose (v° répéter)
151. Rescinder un contrat (v° rescinder)
152. Résilier un bail à durée indéterminée (v° résilier[1])
153. Résilier une vente (v° résilier[1])
154. Demander la résolution du contrat (v° résolution[1])
155. Encourir une responsabilité (v° responsabilité[2])
156. Engager sa responsabilité (v° responsabilité[2])
157. Exonérer de responsabilité (v° responsabilité[2])
158. Poursuivre en responsabilité (v° responsabilité[2])
159. Retraire un immeuble (v° retraire)
160. Révoquer une donation (v° révoquer)
161. Révoquer un mandat (v° révoquer)
162. Révoquer une offre (v° révoquer)
163. Révoquer un testament (v° révoquer)
164. Établir une servitude (v° servitude réelle)
165. Le contrat stipule que … (v° stipuler[1])
166. Subroger le prêteur dans les droits du créancier (v° subroger)
167. Être appelé à une succession (v° succession[1])
168. Venir à une succession (v° succession[1])
169. Constituer une sûreté (v° sûreté[1])

170. Produire titres (v° titre²B)
171. Usacaper la propriété (v° usucaper)
172. Promesse de vendre (v° vendre)

### 3.2.2.2. Analyse des résultats et vérification des hypothèses

À la lumière des résultats obtenus, force est de constater que ni l'une ni l'autre de nos hypothèses ne s'est avérée.

En ce qui concerne la première hypothèse, le Comité de rédaction n'a pas spontanément privilégié, dans la préparation du *Dictionnaire de droit privé*, des EL construites sur un verbe, malgré l'importance des UP verbales pour actualiser en discours les termes juridiques. Les EL à structure verbale comptent pour 255 des 754 EL du dictionnaire. Si on ajoute à ces 255 EL les neuf EL reproduisant totalement ou partiellement des adages ou des règles de droit (lesquels contiennent tous un verbe) ainsi que les trois EL formés sur les locutions qui contiennent un verbe, on compte 267 EL sur 754 qui contiennent un verbe, soit un peu plus de 35%.

Nous pourrions trouver matière à consolation dans le fait que le patron syntaxique le mieux représenté dans le dictionnaire reste une structure verbale, soit V (+ PRÉP.) + N (+ PRÉP. + N) ou (+ ADV.) avec 223 occurrences. Cette affirmation masquerait cependant une observation plus importante encore, soit que les trois structures suivantes [1.] V (+ PRÉP.) + N (+ PRÉP. + N) ou (+ ADV.), [2.] N (+ PRÉP.) + N (+ MOD.) et [3.] N + ADJ. OU PART. PASSÉ, sont à peu près également représentées ([1.] 223 occurrences, [2.] 216 occurrences et [3.] 211 occurrences) et qu'elles comptent ensemble pour 650 des 754 EL consignés, soit plus de 85%.

À l'analyse, on se rend compte que les EL empruntant les patrons N (+ PRÉP.) + N (+ MOD.) et N + ADJ. OU PART. PASSÉ soulèvent une délicate question de frontière qui pourrait se formuler ainsi: où s'arrête l'unité terminologique et où commence l'unité phraséologique (voir Resche 1997)?

En langue de spécialité, on reconnaît qu'il est difficile de distinguer les termes complexes des UP lorsque les combinaisons empruntent des patrons syntaxiques du type N (+ PRÉP.) + N (+ MOD.) et N + ADJ. OU PART. PASSÉ. (L'Homme 1998: 515). On pourrait se demander, pour chacun EL modelé sur ces patrons, s'il s'agit de termes complexes ou d'UP. Ou bien, afin de rester plus près de la description de l'EL du dictionnaire, on pourrait demander si tous ces EL ne font pas que « place[r] le terme défini en contexte » et « renseigne[r] sur les tournures propres au style juridique » (Crépeau et *al.* 1991: XXX), ou s'ils ne sont pas carrément des termes juridiques qui devraient faire l'objet d'un article à part entière dans le *Dictionnaire de droit privé*.

Par exemple, les 20 EL suivants sont-ils des unités terminologiques ou des unités phraséologiques?

| | |
|---|---|
| 1. Assiette de la servitude (v° assiette) | 1. Acte illicite (v° acte1) |
| 2. École du Barreau (v° barreau1) | 2. Désignation cadastrale (v° cadastral, ale) |
| 3. Délai de congé (v° congé) | 3. Numéro cadastral (v° cadastral, ale) |
| 4. Pays de coutume (v° coutume2) | 4. Mort civile (v° civil, ile7) |
| 5. Acte introductif d'instance (v° instance) | 5. Institution contractuelle (v° contractuel, elle) |
| 6. L'intention du législateur (v° législateur) | 6. Convention matrimoniale (v° convention) |
| 7. Congé de maternité (v° maternité1) | 7. Fiction juridique (v° fiction) |
| 8. Réception des travaux (v° réception) | 8. Taxe foncière (v° foncier, ère) |
| 9. Mise sous séquestre (v° séquestre1) | 9. Prêt hypothécaire (v° hypothécaire2) |
| 10. Vente par shérif (v° shérif) | 10. Procureur ad litem (v° procureur) |

Se pourrait-il, par ailleurs, que ces 20 unités soient à la fois terminologiques et phraséologiques? Ces 20 unités ne seraient-elles pas terminologiques dans la perspective du *domaine du droit* en ce que chacune d'elles, peut-on soutenir, dénote un concept juridique distinct? mais que ces 20 unités soient aussi phraséologiques dans la perspective de la *langue du droit* en ce que chacune d'elles, peut-on soutenir, constitue une suite de mots typique ou idiomatique qui, n'étant pas figée au point d'en faire une locution à part entière, peut s'analyser compositionnellement en fonction de sa base terminologique?

En ce qui concerne la deuxième hypothèse, le Comité de rédaction du dictionnaire n'a pas intuitivement privilégié, parmi les EL à structure verbale, des UP lexicales par rapport aux UP conceptuelles, et ce, contrairement à l'hypothèse que nous avons posée. Le *Dictionnaire de droit privé* compte 83 UP lexicales contre 172 UP conceptuelles. Moins du tiers des 255 EL à structure verbale du dictionnaire sont des UP lexicales.

À l'analyse des EL à structure verbale, nous nous sommes rendu compte à quel point le droit a tendance à terminologiser des unités lexicales dont le sens ou bien se distingue difficilement du sens de l'un de ses pendants en langue générale (voir dans Cornu 2011, le sens général d'*accorder*, d'*admission*, d'*agissements*, d'*attribution*, de *construction*, de *réception*, de *constitution*, d'*établir* et d'*établissement*, d'*exercice*, de *dressé, ée*, de *refus*, de *soustraction* et de *traitement*) ou bien dont le rôle d'actualisateur est clairement reconnu (voir, dans Cornu 2011, le sens général de *levée* et, en particulier, celui de *mise*, qui est ainsi défini: « Terme neutre désignant dans les expressions qui suivent toutes sortes d'actes juridiques ou matériels (décision, mesure, sanction, remise, etc.) »).

De fait, on peut s'interroger à savoir si chacun de ces 16 « termes » juridiques, pourtant recensés et définis dans un dictionnaire de renom, le *Vocabulaire juridique*, dénote un concept dans le domaine du droit, sinon s'ils dénotent des concepts juridiques de même nature que ne le font des termes comme *contrat*, *déguerpir*, *faute*, *gage* ou *illégal*. Force est d'admettre que des UP comme *être admis au barreau* ou *recevoir notification* se décomposent moins naturellement terme par terme que *confirmer un contrat* ou *déguerpir un fonds / un héritage*.

En ce qui a trait aux EL de la deuxième édition du *Dictionnaire de droit privé*, vingt-deux des 255 EL à structure verbale ont profité de ces termes dénotant des concepts, au mieux, flous pour se qualifier d'UP conceptuelles. Ces observations remettent certes en question le test à deux volets utilisé pour distinguer les UP conceptuelles des UP lexicales. Plus fondamentalement, ces observations exigent de remettre en question la distinction entre UP conceptuelle et UP lexicale, du moins en langue du droit et, peut-être davantage encore, de s'interroger sur la question de l'identité, qui sait plurielle, du terme juridique et de ses rapports avec les mots de la langue générale (sur cette question, voir L'Homme et Polguère 2008).

Cette étude portait sur la phraséologie dans la deuxième édition du *Dictionnaire de droit privé*, ouvrage élaboré par des juristes qui n'ont pas d'expertise particulière en terminologie ou en linguistique. Nous avons montré que l'article du dictionnaire fait peu de place aux éléments d'ordre phraséologique. À l'instar de la plupart des dictionnaires spécialisés, le *Dictionnaire de droit privé* est au service de l'interprète; il est destiné à transmettre une connaissance fondamentale sur le droit privé afin d'aider l'usager à décoder des énoncés juridiques.

En dépit de son inclination conceptuelle et encyclopédique, le *Dictionnaire de droit privé* contient une rubrique qui consigne (il faut le dire: inégalement à travers ses articles) des marques de la spécificité de la phraséologie de droit privé. Nous avons répertorié 754 exemples linguistiques différents qui sont autant d'unités phraséologiques en langue de spécialité, selon la définition que nous avons défendue, à savoir des séquences polylexicales que des experts perçoivent comme typiques de la langue de leur domaine de spécialité.

Nous avons cru que, dans la rubrique EL, le Comité de rédaction du dictionnaire aurait naturellement été porté à consigner des UP verbales, lesquelles sont essentielles pour mettre en discours les termes juridiques, très majoritairement nominaux. Nous avons cru aussi que le Comité de rédaction du dictionnaire aurait été naturellement porté à opter pour des UP lexicales, lesquelles comprennent une unité lexicale non terminologique, ce qui est de nature à renforcer leur idiomaticité. Dans les deux cas, l'analyse des EL a montré que nous avions tort, quoiqu'il faille reconnaître que les EL à structure verbale (ou UP verbales) et les UP lexicales forment des minorités bien représentées parmi les 754 EL du dictionnaire.

En dépit de leur fausseté, ces hypothèses ont été l'occasion pour nous de classer et d'analyser les 754 EL de la deuxième édition du *Dictionnaire de droit privé*. Ce travail nous a, en outre, convaincu de trois choses. Afin d'enrichir les dictionnaires de droit, il est nécessaire de pouvoir décrire et analyser correctement les éléments qui, dans la langue du droit, relèvent de la terminologie juridique *et* ceux qui relèvent de la phraséologie juridique. Afin de transmettre plus efficacement la connaissance au sujet du droit, il est nécessaire de poursuivre l'examen des rapports qui s'établissent entre le vocabulaire juridique et la langue générale et, ainsi, de mieux comprendre l'utilisation que la langue du droit fait des ressources lexicales de la langue générale. Enfin, les juristes qui travaillent en jurilinguistique ou en jurilexicographie doivent s'adjoindre l'expertise de spécialistes de la langue.

Pour le *Dictionnaire de droit privé,* la mise en place d'une telle collaboration lui permettrait de remonter vers sa source première, qui, à sa tête, comptait des juristes et des experts de la langue. Le regretté professeur Crépeau n'écrivait-il pas, en 1985, dans l'avant-propos de la première édition du dictionnaire que « le *Dictionnaire de droit privé* a été conçu essentiellement comme une œuvre de collaboration entre juristes et linguistes » et qu'il s'agissait là du gage de son originalité (Crépeau *et al.* 1985: I)[11]?

## Références

Allard, France et al. 2012. *Dictionnaire de droit privé – les biens et lexiques bilingues/Private Law Dictionary – Property and Bilingual Lexicons.* Cowansville (Qc): Éd. Yvon Blais.

Archer, Vincent 2009. *Graphes linguistiques multiniveau pour l'extraction de connaissances: l'exemple des collocations.* Thèse de doctorat en informatique. Université Joseph Fourier: Grenoble 1, http://tel.archives-ouvertes.fr/docs/00/42/65/17/PDF/Archer-These.pdf (consulté le 29 juillet 2013).

Beaudoin, Louis et Mailhot, Madeleine 2005. *Expressions juridiques en un clin d'oeil*, 3e éd. Cowansville (Qc): Éd. Yvon Blais.

Béjoint, Henri 2007. Informatique et lexicographie de corpus: les nouveaux dictionnaires. *Revue française de linguistique appliquée* XII(1): 7–23.

Bertrand, Claudine 1998a. *Étude comparative des combinaisons lexicales spécialisées dans deux domaines de spécialité: collocations lexicales et collocations conceptuelles en aéronautique et en philosophie.* Mémoire présenté en vue de l'obtention du grade de Maître ès arts (M.A.) en traduction. Montréal: Université de Montréal.

Bertrand, Claudine 1998b. Étude comparative des combinaisons lexicales spécialisées dans deux domaines du savoir (aéronautique et philosophie) et opposition entre les collocations lexicales et conceptuelles. *TTR: Traduction, terminologie, rédaction* 11(1): 229–49.

Bissardon, Sébastien et Burel, Raphaële 2005. *Guide du langage juridique: vocabulaire – pièges et difficultés*, 2e éd. Paris: Litec.

Blumenthal, Peter (2007). Sciences de l'Homme vs sciences exactes: combinatoires des mots dans la vulgarisation scientifique. *Revue française de linguistique appliquée* XII(2): 15–28.

Centre de Traduction et Documentation Juridiques 1995. *Lexique législatif de droit pénal = Criminal law legislation lexicon.* Vanier (Ont.): Centre franco-ontarien de ressources pédagogiques.

11 Parmi les collaborateurs de la deuxième édition du Dictionnaire de droit privé, on ne comptait plus de linguiste ou de terminologue (Crépeau *et al.* 1991: V).

Clas, André 1994. Collocations et langues de spécialité. *Meta: journal des traducteurs / Meta: Translators' Journal* 39(4): 576–80.

Collet, Tanja 2004. Esquisse d'une nouvelle microstructure de dictionnaire spécialisé reflétant la variation en discours du terme syntagmatique. *Meta: journal des traducteurs / Meta: Translators' Journal* 49(2): 247–63.

Cornu, Gérard (dir.) 2011. *Vocabulaire juridique*, 9e éd. Paris: PUF (Quadrige).

Cowie, Anthony P. (1994). Phraseology. In *The Encyclopedia of Language and Linguistics*, Asher, R.E. (dir.), 3168–71. Oxford: Oxford University Press.

Crépeau, Paul-André et al. 1985. *Dictionnaire de droit privé.* Centre de recherche en droit privé et comparé du Québec: Université McGill.

Crépeau, Paul-André et al. 1988. *Lexique de droit privé français-anglais – anglais-français* (Supplément au *Dictionnaire de droit privé* (1985)). Centre de recherche en droit privé et comparé du Québec: Université McGill.

Crépeau, Paul-André et al. 1991. *Dictionnaire de droit privé et lexiques bilingues.* Cowansville (Qc): Éd. Yvon Blais.

Crépeau, Paul-André et al. 1999. *Dictionnaire de droit privé de la famille et lexiques bilingues / Private Law Dictionary of the Family and Bilingual Lexicons.* Cowansville (Qc): Éd. Yvon Blais.

Crépeau, Paul-André et al. 2003. *Dictionnaire de droit privé – les obligations et lexiques bilingues / Private Law Dictionary of Obligations and Bilingual Lexicons.* Cowansville (Qc): Éd. Yvon Blais.

Dechamps, Christina 2004. Enseignement/apprentissage des collocations d'une langue de spécialité à un public allophone: l'exemple de la langue juridique. *Études de linguistique appliquée* 135(3): 361–70.

Delagneau, Jean-Marc 2010. Analyse assistée par ordinateur de discours spécialisés et élaboration de dictionnaires de combinatoire. R*echerche et pratiques pédagogiques en langues de spécialité* XXIX(1): 83–97.

Dubreil, Estelle 2008. Collocations: définitions et problématique. Texto! T*extes et Cultures* XIII(1) http://www.revue-texto.net/docannexe/file/126/dubreil_collocations.pdf (consulté le 30 juillet 2013).

Evert, Stefan 2004. *The Statistics of Word Cooccurrences: Word Pairs and Collocations.* PhD Thesis, University of Stuttgart. http://www.stefan-evert.de/PUB/Evert2004phd.pdf (consulté le 30 juillet 2013).

Forget, Patrick 2011. L'enseignement de la phraséologie juridique au baccalauréat: la méthode et les postulats d'un projet pilote lancé à la Faculté de droit de l'Université de Moncton. *Revue de la common law en français.* (2010–2011) 12: 5–53.

Forget, Patrick 2014 (à paraître). Les phraséologismes verbaux en droit: une étude de cas à partir du terme responsabilité civile. In *Decision-Making in Translation, Interpretation and Speech Act – Cultural Mediation Techniques*, Semiotica Special Issue, Wagner, Anne et Gémar, Jean-Claude (dir.), Berlin/New York: De Gruyter.

Gledhill, Chris 1997. Les collocations et la construction du savoir scientifique. *La Revue du GERAS* ASp 15–18: 85–104.

Gormezano, Nathalie et Peraldi, Sandrine 2012. Terminologies et nouvelles technologies. *Meta: journal des traducteurs / Meta: Translators' Journal* 57(1): 248–63.

Granger, Sylviane and Paquot, Magali 2008. Disentangling the phraseological web. In *Phraseology. An interdisciplinary perspective*, Granger, Sylviane and Meunier, Fanny (dir.) 27–50. Amsterdam: John Benjamins.

Hausmann, Franz Joseph 1989. Le dictionnaire de collocations. In *Wörterbücher: ein internationales Handbuch zur Lexicographie. Dictionaries. Dictionnaires*, Hausmann, Franz Joseph et al. (dir.), 1010–19. Berlin, New-York: De Gruyter.

Heid, Ulrich 1994. On the Way Words Work Together – Topics in Lexical Combinatorics. In Proceedings of the VIth Euralex, Martin, Willy et al. (dir.), 226–57. Amsterdam, http://www.euralex.org/elx_proceedings/Euralex1994/ (consulté le 31 juillet 2013).

Heid, Ulrick et Freibott, Gerhard (1991). Collocations dans une base de données terminologique et lexicale. *Meta: journal des traducteurs / Meta: Translators' Journal* 36(1): 77–91.

Kasirer, Nicholas 1999. Note introductive. In *Dictionnaire de droit privé de la famille et lexiques bilingues / Private Law Dictionary of the Family and Bilingual Lexicons*, Crépeau Paul-André et al. (dir.), XV-XXIII. Cowansville (Qc): Éd. Yvon Blais.

Kouri, Robert P. et al. 1999. *Private Law Dictionary and Bilingual Lexicons*. Cowansville (Qc): Éd. Yvon Blais.

Larivière, Louise 1998. Valeur sémantique du verbe dans les collocations verbales spécialisées. *TTR: traduction, terminologie, rédactio*n 11(1): 173197.

Legallois, Dominique et Tutin, Agnès 2013. Vers une extension du domaine de la phraséologie. *Langages* 189(1): 3–25.

Lerat, Pierre 2007. *Vocabulaire du juriste débutant*. Paris: Ellipses.

L'homme, Marie-Claude et Meynard, Isabelle 1998. Le point d'accès aux combinaisons lexicales spécialisées: présentation de deux modèles informatiques. *TTR: traduction, terminologie, rédaction* 11(1): 199–227.

L'homme, Marie-Claude 1998. Caractérisation des combinaisons lexicales spécialisées par rapport aux collocations de langue générale. In *Proceedings EURALEX'98*, Fontenelle, Thierry et al. (dir.), 513–22. Université de Liège: Liège, 4–8 août 1998.

L'homme, Marie-Claude et Bertrand, Claudine 2000. Specialized Lexical Combinations: Should they be Described as Collocations or in Terms of Selectional Restrictions. In *The Proceedings of the Ninth Euralex International Congress*, 497–506. Stuttgart, Germany, Stuttgart University.

L'homme, Marie-Claude 2000. Understanding Specialized Lexical Combinations. *Terminology* 6(1): 89–110.

L'homme, Marie-Claude 2004. *La terminologie: principes et techniques*. Montréal: Les Presses de l'Université de Montréal.

L'homme, Marie-Claude 2005. Sur la notion de « terme ». *Meta: journal des traducteurs / Meta: Translators' Journal* 50(4): 1112–32.

L'homme, Marie-Claude et Polguère, Alain 2008. Mettre en bons termes les dictionnaires spécialisés et les dictionnaires de langue générale. In *Lexicographie et terminologie: histoire de mots. Hommage à Henri Béjoint*, Maniez, François et al. (dir.), 191–206. Lyon: Presses de l'Université de Lyon.

L'homme, Marie-Claude 2010. Designing Terminological Dictionaries for Learners based on Lexical Semantics: The representation of actants. In *Specialised Dictionaries for Learners*, Fuertes-Olivera, P. (dir.), 141–53. Berlin/New York: De Gruyter, http://gendocs.ru/docs/15/14876/conv_1/file1.pdf#page=152 (consulté le 31 juillet 2013).

L'homme, Marie-Claude 2012. Le verbe terminologique: un portrait des travaux récents. *3e Congrès Mondial de Linguistique Française*. 1: 93–107, http://www.shs-conferences.org/articles/shsconf/pdf/2012/01/shsconf_cmlf12_000340.pdf (consulté le 30 juillet 2013).

Macko, Daiva 2011. Typical Collocations in the Judgments on Appeal of the European Court of Justice. Santalka: *Filologija Edukologija* 19: 67–80. http://www.cpe.vgtu.lt/index.php/cpe/article/viewFile/cpe.2011.08/pdf_1 (consulté le 30 juillet 2013).

Mailhot, Madelaine 2009. *Les bons mots du civil et du pénal: dictionnaire français-anglais des expressions juridiques*, 3e éd. Montréal: Wilson & Lafleur.

Mel'cuk, Igor 2003. Collocations dans le dictionnaire. In *Les écarts culturels dans les dictionnaires bilingues*, Szende, Thomas (dir.), 19–63. Paris: Honoré Champion, olst.ling.umontreal.ca/pdf/MelcukColloc2003.pdf (consulté le 31 juillet 2013).

Paveau, Marie-Anne 2008. Les non-linguistes font-ils de la linguistique? Une approche anti-éliminativiste des théories folk. *Pratiques* 139–40: 93–109, http://halshs.archives-ouvertes.fr/hal-00516247/ (consulté le 31 juillet 2013).

Pecman, Mojca 2004. L'enjeu de la classification en phraséologie. EUROPHRAS 2004, 26–9 août 2004. Université de Bâle, Suisse. http://www.initerm.net/public/langues%20de%20sp%C3%A9cialit%C3%A9/terminologie/l_enjeu_de_la_classification_en_phras_ologie.pdf (consulté le 30 juillet 2013).

Pesant, Ghislaine et Thibault, Estelle 1998. Pour une combinatoire de la publicité des droits. *Meta: journal des traducteurs / Meta: Translators' Journal* 43(2): 328–31.

Petit, Gérard 2001. L'introuvable identité du terme technique. *Revue française de linguistique appliquée* VI: 63–79.

Picht, Heribert 1987. Terms and their LSP Environment – LSP Phraseology. *Meta: journal des traducteurs / Meta: Translators' Journal* 32(2): 149–55.

Picotte, Jacques 2012. Juridictionnaire. Recueil des difficultés et des ressources du français juridique, actualisé au 30 mai 2012, en ligne: Centre de traduction et de terminologie juridiques <www.cttj.ca>.

Polguère, Alain 2003. Collocations et fonctions lexicales: pour un modèle d'apprentissage. In *Les collocations: analyse et traitement, Travaux et recherches en linguistique appliquée*, Grossmann, Francis et Tutin, Agnès (dir.) 23–44. Amsterdam: Éditions de Werelt, olst.ling.umontreal.ca/pdf/PolguereCollocations2003.pdf (consulté le 31 octobre 2012).

Polguère, Alain 2008. *Lexicologie et sémantique lexicale. Notions fondamentales*, 2e éd. Montréal: Les Presses de l'Université de Montréal.

Polguère Alain 2011a. Figement et ellipse dans une perspective lexicographique: le cas de dé à jouer et dé à coudre. In *Le figement linguistique: la parole entravée*, Anscombre, Jean-Claude et Mejri, Salah (dir.) 363–73. Paris: Champion.

Polguère, Alain 2011b. Perspective épistémologique sur l'approche linguistique Sens-Texte. In L'architecture des théories linguistiques, les modules et leurs interfaces. Mémoires de la Société de Linguistique de Paris XX, 79–114. Peeters Publishers: Leuven, http://hal.archives-ouvertes.fr/hal-00686461/ (consulté le 31 juillet 2013).

Prandi, Michele 1998. Contraintes conceptuelles sur la distribution: réflexions sur la notion de classe d'objets. *Langages* 32: 34–44.

Preite, Chira 2012. *Exemples de lexicographie juridique à orientation pédagogique en France: le Vocabulaire du juriste débutant et le Guide du langage juridique.* In *Proceedings of the 15th EURALEX International Congress* – Sprakradet Oslo (NOR), 570–77, http://www.euralex.org/elx_proceedings/Euralex2012/pp570–577%20Preite.pdf (consulté le 31 juillet 2013).

Ramos, Margarita Alonso 1998. Étude sémantico-syntaxique des constructions à verbe support. Thèse présentée à la Faculté des études supérieures en vue de l'obtention du grade de Philosophiae Doctor (Ph.D.) en linguistique, Montréal: Université de Montréal.

Resche, Catherine 1997. Prolégomènes à la phraséologie comparée en langue de spécialité: exemple de l'anglais et du français de la finance. *Le Revue du GERAS* ASp 15–18: 407–503.

Silva, Raquel, Costa, Rute et Ferreira, Fátima 2004. Entre langue générale et langue de spécialité une question de collocations. *Études de linguistique appliquée* 135(3): 347–58.

Trésor de la langue française informatisé. Analyse et Traitement Informatique de la Langue Française., http://atilf.atilf.fr/ (consulté le 30 juillet 2013).

Tryuk, Malgorzata 2000. La phraséologie en terminologie. Quelques problèmes de traduction. *Babel – Revue internationale de la traduction* 46(1): 66–76.

Tutin, Agnès et Grossmann, Francis 2002. Collocations régulières et irrégulières: esquisse de typologie du phénomène collocatif. *Revue française de linguistique appliquée* VII-1: 7–25

Tutin, Agnès, 2005. Le dictionnaire de collocations est-il indispensable? *Revue française de linguistique appliquée* X-2: 31–48.

Tutin, Agnès 2010a. Sens et combinatoire lexicale: de la langue au discours. Dossier non publié en vue de l'habilitation à diriger des recherches, vol. 1: synthèse, Université Stendhal Grenoble 3, w3.u-grenoble3.fr/lidilem/labo/file/HDR_Tutin.pdf (consulté le 31 juillet 2013).

Tutin, Agnès 2010b. Le traitement des collocations dans les dictionnaires monolingues de collocations du français et de l'anglais. Actes du CMLF 2010, 2e

Congrès mondial de linguistique française, 12 juillet 2010, Neveu, Franck et al. (dir.), pp. 1075–90, http://dx.doi.org/10.1051/cmlf/2010141 (consulté le 29 juillet 2013).
Tutin, Agnès 2013. Les collocations lexicales: une relation essentiellement binaire définie par la relation prédicat-argument. *Langages* 189(1): 47–63.
Verlinde, Serge et al. 2006. Corpus, collocations et dictionnaires d'apprentissage. *Langue française* 150: 84–98.
Williams, Geoffrey 2001. *Sur les caractéristiques de la collocation.* Tutoriel, Tome 2, Actes de TALN (Conférence sur le traitement automatique des langues naturelles), Tours 2–5 juillet 2001.

# Chapter 14
# Inconsistencies in the Sources and Use of Irish Legal Terminology

Malachy O'Rourke

A brief look at the state of legal terminology in Irish might indicate a fairly satisfactory situation with a vast amount of terms now available on the Focal.ie website. Unfortunately such an impression would be an illusion. Since the foundation of the state only one collection of legal terms purporting to be authoritative and authentic has been published and that was *Téarmaí Dlí* (*TD*) in 1957. It was a slight tome and it has long been out of print. It was never re-issued, amended, expanded, supplemented or treasured. It purported to lay the foundations for a systematic attempt to provide an exhaustive list of core legal terms in Irish. An Irish Legal Terms Act was enacted in 1945 to provide legal certainty as regards the interpretation of certain 'technical' words and terms.[1] Ten orders were published between then and 1956 covering a broad range of areas of law after a fashion, with the exception ironically of constitutional law. That may have been deemed to be too hot a political potato. These terms were then compiled and published as *Téarmaí Dlí*. Under the Act, the representative of the *Rannóg* convenes the committee and acts as its joint secretary. It is, however, a very unbalanced committee largely composed of legal experts when the obvious requirement is for linguistic experts. In the same year (1957) an Official Standard was published (*an Caighdeán Oifigiúil* – *CO*) which purported to provide guidance on all matters, linguistic and orthographical, but what began as an attempt to standardize spelling seems to have become an authority on grammatical matters as well.

When the Irish state was founded in 1922 and when it was decided rather audaciously to translate all legislation into Irish, the assumption might have been that Irish as a language was a coherent, well-formed entity. Nothing could have been further from the truth. One of the reasons why Irish floundered from the seventeenth century onwards was that the language was split. The classical

1 A committee was envisaged to be convened by the Príomh-Aistritheoir and of which he would be secretary, made up of representatives of all branches of the legal profession, empowered to replicate what was achieved in *TD*. New terms devised in the context of legislation could have been approved by this committee and made available to the public. The committee was convened on a regular basis in the sixties and seventies but nothing was communicated to the public. Apparently a new Irish Legal Terms Advisory Committee has been established as of 16 November 2011.

language was dying on the bed of its own rigidity and the colloquial language of the people was not sufficiently healthy to resist the political attacks made on it. At the end of the nineteenth century when the Irish revival took root this dichotomy was still unresolved. To the extent that a compromise was reached it mainly reflected the structure of the classical language. This had the added advantage of being based on the Latin paradigm.

The first Dáil translators did what they could with the weapons at their disposal. Little by little they were establishing their own conventions and consistency. But when the 1937 constitution had to be translated they were overlooked. The appointed translators duly came up with terms which were at variance with what was already in existence. When the constitution conferred the primacy of interpretation on the Irish version this created a new layer of division, terminological this time. Thus began a new chapter in the story of the diverging language. With the publication of the *CO* at roughly the same time as the publication of the *TD* it might be supposed that some sort of unity had been achieved between the two alternative and conflicting forms of the language. But the *CO* was neither fish nor fowl. It provided clarity on spelling but its contributions on what could be called matters of grammar was unremarkable. Offering it as a source of grammatical coherence was like giving a mechanic a box of tools and expecting him to build a computer.

There are two related problems. First, the provision of the terms, while indispensable, is not sufficient in itself. The concept 'legal term' refers ordinarily to a 'word', 'lexeme' or 'term' which has a specific legal meaning, the precise significance of which is understood in all its ramifications by legal practitioners and about which there should be no inherent ambiguity. English legal terminology had been established authoritatively in court judgments over centuries of jurisprudence. *TD* was an effort to provide (artificially) similar legal certainty with regard to terms in Irish. Second, it must be possible to use such terms with the utmost precision in such a way that there is no underlying ambiguity, either grammatical or orthographical. *TD* was intended as a first step in the provision of certain terms but it turned out to be a first and a last step.

Two further general questions arise: was the failure to build on this an indication of an implicit, indeed an explicit, reluctance on the part of practitioners of Irish to be bound by authoritative terminology, or was it an unspoken acknowledgement that such authentic terms were not necessary because there was no desire to initiate litigation through Irish. In either case, it is axiomatic that if legal terms are not available, they cannot be used. What follows is an analysis of the validity of these assertions. A further preliminary remark that could be made is that, on the basis of this modest collection, only a very limited form of litigation could be envisaged through the medium of Irish.

Legal terms normally involve at least three complementary phases: provision, dissemination and use. The story of legal terms in Irish is one of missed opportunities. If terms are devised but not used they lapse. For instance there was a Terminology Committee (Coiste Téarmaíochta, CT) in existence in the thirties which published two anthologies, *Foclóir Staire is Tír-eóluíochta* (1929) and

*Téarmaí Staire* (1934). The current CT published *Téarmaí Staire* in 1996 and it is interesting to compare how certain key terms have changed, for example 'democracy' was rendered as *coitchiantacht* and 'authority' as *cumhachtóir*. Terms can be assessed on the basis of their passive vitality (they are familiar to people) or their active vitality (people use them) but in the case of Irish it is doubtful if passive knowledge of most of the terms would have exceeded 50 per cent and the active knowledge might have been as low as 10–15 per cent.

Nevertheless it could have been a belated beginning to a new consistent approach to Irish legal terminology had a number of factors not militated against it, some external and others internal, one of which had immediate effect and the others which had implications in the longer term, all of them an adumbration of the fragility of the language and the fretfulness of its users. Firstly, the existence of this collection of terms should have been promulgated and the importance of adhering to its recommendations needed to be underlined from the outset, and it should have been updated and expanded regularly. In fact it has never been re-issued. Secondly, the terms should have featured prominently in the new English-Irish Dictionary which was being prepared. Even though a comprehensive English-Irish dictionary[2] had been published in 1935 (and reprinted in 1948) to supplement the other comprehensive dictionary[3] already available, these were not deemed to be 'modern' enough, so a third dictionary appeared in 1959 (EID).[4] This made an enormous contribution to the provision of modern terminology in Irish but surprisingly did not contain all the terms made official in *Téarmaí Dlí*. Another Irish-English dictionary (*FGB*) was also in preparation but would not appear until 1978.[5] Ideally the new official terms should have been included in both dictionaries with a special indication that they were authenticated legal terms. Some are indeed included but without any particular reference to their provenance, while other terms are ignored and an alternative proposed.

The number of examples of alternatives or omissions is perhaps less important than the fact that no particular status is given to the specific terms from *Téarmaí Dlí* to the effect that they are the only terms that will be recognized by the courts. In EID *Jur.* is listed among the abbreviations on page xi on a par with *Bill* (billiards) or *euph.* (euphemistically). If the terms given in *TD* were to be accepted and used it was critical that they be incorporated into the standard English-Irish dictionary, otherwise these 'authenticated' terms would be seen as having nothing to do with modern vocabulary, much less modern terminology. This is another example of the existence of two strands in the language, one of them traditional and to be fostered, the other an unwelcome stranger to be tolerated.

---

2 *Foclóir Béarla agus Gaedhilge (English-Irish Dictionary),* L McCionnaith, S.J., 1935.

3 *Larger English-Irish Dictionary (Foclóir Béarla-Gaedhilge)*, T. O'Neilll Lane, 1921.

4 *English-Irish Dictionary*, edited by Tomás de Bhaldraithe, 1959.

5 *Foclóir Gaeilge-Béarla* (Irish-English Dictionary), Niall Ó Dónaill, 1977 (but published in 1978).

To give a few examples: in *TD briogadh* is given for 'provocation' but in EID four alternative terms are proposed. EID gives a number of terms for 'accident' whereas for *TD* there is only one *tionóisc*. *Tadhlach* is in *TD* for 'adjoining' but does not appear in EID. A 'negative search' is rendered *cuardach atrialach* but does not appear in EID (or in *FGB*). In EID we also find *mórghadaíocht* for 'aggravated larceny' accompanied by *Jur.*, whereas in *TD* we have *goid* for 'larceny' and *tromionsaí* for 'aggravated assault' (*FGB* distinguishes between *gadaíocht, 'stealing, theft'* and *goid*, theft, larceny, but without any *Jur.*). In *TD* there is *tionscnaím imeachtaí* (I bring proceedings) and *tionscnamh imeachtaí* (institution of proceedings) whereas in EID there is *dlí a chur ar dhuine/duine a thabhairt chun dlí* (to take/institute proceedings against s.o.) – not even one common element is present in the rendering of this term in the two collections. Similarly, though *tarmligean* is given for 'delegation (of powers)' EID suggests three alternatives. *TD* gives *meabhlaireacht* for 'deceit' but in EID there are four possibilities, given without context viz. *cealg, calaois, meabhal, camastaíl*. *Foriarratas* is given in *TD* for 'motion' but EID gives *iarratas*, while adding the key, *jur*, even though in *TD iarratas* is 'application'. Both concur as regards 'executory' in one case. In *TD* 'executory consideration/contract' is rendered *comaoin/conradh le comhlíonadh* and EID has (*breithiúntas*) *le comhlíonadh*. However *TD* also has *eastát/iontaobhas/leas cinniúnach* for 'executory estate/ trust/interest. This is utterly confusing. It is not helpful either where only the plural form is given as in *sliochtaigh* (descendants). There are also slight divergences as regards spelling. *TD* has *duine éagóraithe* for 'aggrieved person' whereas it is spelt *duine éagóirithe* in EID (and returns to *duine éagóraithe* in *FGB*). While there are many instances where EID has followed *TD*: *mísc* (mischief), their irregularity suggests such convergence is as much coincidental as intentional.

But it was not only EID which was showing scant respect for the terms in *TD*. As Micheál Ó Cearúil points out,[6] 'the terms found in *Téarmaí Dlí* are not always adhered to in translating the Acts'. The phrase *leas an phobail* seems to be favoured over *Téarmaí Dlí*'s *an mhaitheas phoiblí* (while *FGB* has *an mhaith choiteann*). *Téarmaí Dlí*[7] purported not only to be a very significant addition to the limited corpus of terminology available in Irish but it contained the only

6 *Bunreacht na* hÉireann, A study of the Irish text, Dublin, 1999, p. 23, footnote 75.

7 A minor anomaly that is worth adverting to is in the title itself. In the Irish Legal Terms Act of 1945 and in the subsequent orders 'legal terms' was rendered 'téarmaí dlíthiúla' yet in the compilation it is rendered 'téarmaí dlí'. This change of mind illustrates a number of the difficulties bedevilling the core of the language and which will be addressed in more detail later. Suffice to say at this point that the preference for the genitive of the noun over the adjective is justified in this case because it is a collection of terms which are not 'legal' as opposed to 'illegal' but 'pertaining to the law'. Among the entries we find entries which endorse this distinction: *ceist dlí* (question of law), *sócmhainní dlí* (legal assets) but *argóint dhlíthiúil* (legal argument). Other anomalies flow from this. *Dlíthiúil* is the adjectival form for 'legal' and *dleathach* for 'lawful' yet *neamhdhleathach* is the only version given for 'illegal' and also for 'unlawful'.

terms acceptable to the courts. For this reason it had the potential to transform the language as it constituted the first step on the way towards the goal of 'imposing' terminological consistency but it needed to be supported by all other agencies. Containing or controlling the grammatical and colloquial variations or simplifying the spelling, which was the aim of the *CO*, was indeed laudable. Though relatively successful in the short term it was akin to herding the proverbial mice. The mind of the (native) Irish speaker has an inbuilt resistance to continuity or consistency and to any form of linguistic authority even where failure to conform is undermining the very language whose preservation is sought. Legal terms with a judicial imprimatur and allowing of no alternative was a new concept and could have been the catalyst for a reinvigorated language because the courts would have insisted on total accuracy and consistency in every detail. Even punctuation errors as well as spelling mistakes can lead to a case being dismissed. The need to abide by these 'official' terms would have imposed a discipline which appears to elude practitioners of the language. Might it have been found acceptable if properly presented? Unfortunately, we will never know since *TD* turned out to be a damp squib, a flying star which appeared briefly in the firmament before imploding and disappearing without trace.

However, if we look at the contents of *TD* it has to be said that it is not a very satisfactory compilation. While many of the terms are clearly 'legal' in a technical sense there are just as many which are either very general or for which there is really no alternative. Terms like *ceapachán* (appointment), *gníomhaire ginearálta* (general agent), *íocaíocht sheachtainiúil* (weekly payment) *monarcha* (factory) whereas *fostaíocht leanúnach* (continuous employment) or *polasaí uileghabhálach* (comprehensive policy) would not necessarily be the only translation for those particular terms. (Such general terms dilute the value of *TD* especially when one thinks of the properly legal terms which could have been included from the legislation over the previous 30 years.) It was important to establish that *dearbhú* and *toiliú* were the sole correct legal terms for 'declaration' and 'consent', even though they would not necessarily be the consistently preferred choice, even today, and that *locht* is the correct term for 'defect' even if *éalang teidil* is given for 'defect of title'. Other terms are largely self-explanatory but *TD* has the merit of establishing the required form for certain terms, for example *coirpeach* (criminal) – but no term for 'crime' or 'criminality' in a general sense – *cosantóir* (defendant), *creidiúnaí* (creditor), *cúisí* (accused), *cúlpháirtí* (accessory), *díthiomnóir* (intestate), *féichiúnaí* (debtor), *iarratasóir* (applicant) *teisteoir* (deponent), to mention but a few.

There are other serious shortcomings of a more general kind, particularly in relation to semantic ambiguity and ease of use. There is needless ambiguity in some headwords. This is a reflection of a prevalent attitude in Irish that it is enough to apply strict so-called grammatical rules to achieve clarity. But language structures do not exist independently of the meanings they have to carry. The use of the verbal noun in the genitive form when it can be mistaken for a verbal adjective is the most obvious example, for example *earbadh in aisce* (gratuitous bailment). Side by side, for example, are *caiteachas adhlactha* (funeral expenses) and *teach troscánaithe* (furnished house). There is also *iontaobhas forghníomhaithe* (executed trust) and *ordú forghníomhaithe* (execution order) – thus no clarification as to the apparent inaccuracy in the Irish. *Fiach neamhleachtaithe* (unliquidated debt) and *foraithne neamhnithe (phósta)* (decree of nullity (of marriage)) and *clásal fianaithe* (attestation clause) (a similar ambiguity occurs in the Succession Act 1965 where *an fhoirm fhianaithe* is the translation of 'form of attestation'[8]) provide further examples of this confusion. Strangely enough, though *cothromasach* is given for 'equitable', in all the examples of 'equitable + noun' *cothromais* is used for example 'equitable assets' is *sócmhainní cothromais* and 'equitable estate' is *eastát cothromais* and so on.

This evokes the other major weakness in *TD* which is that no practical grammatical information is provided. Looking only at legal terms in Irish is not to miss the bigger picture, it's to miss the picture entirely. The only information provided to the user is the reference to the order in which each entry first appeared. This is mere insider information and was probably never of much relevance to the ordinary user. Whatever relevance it had originally, it has none now. In its stead there was need for details on syntactic properties, principles of sentence formation and interpretation, whether the word is a verb or a noun, what verb is required by what noun, whether a particular verb is transitive or intransitive, which active verb can be used passively or causatively, the gender and declension of the nouns and what preposition is associated with the noun or verb, what are now referred to as 'selectional restrictions'. The lexicon should provide an explicit phonological, morphological, syntactic and semantic analysis of each vocabulary item; and it should state the general constraints which the language imposes on the phonological, morphological, syntactic and perhaps semantic structure of the word.

There is a clear demarcation between syntactic and semantic knowledge. If a sentence sounds ill-formed we should be able to identify where exactly the deviance lies: to say whether it violates syntactic rules, semantic rules or some non-linguistic principles. It would also be useful to know whether *praghas iomlán ceannaigh* (total purchase price) can be treated as a phrase noun and so immutable when governed by a compound preposition or a preceding noun. Similarly, with *fios collaí neamhdhleathach* (unlawful carnal knowledge), there is no indication as to whether the phrase might lose its legal integrity if unrecognizable forms emerge in the genitive. Is it always self-evidently the same semantic construction we find in a phrase to which the current inflectional rules have been applied as in the term given in *TD*? The rationale behind this failure to elucidate these rather obvious difficulties is hard to fathom. At best it indicates that the English term is so clear that the only requirement for the Irish term is agreement that it corresponds precisely to the English term. The fact that it places overwhelming pressure on the conventional grammatical rules is simply ignored. Particular lexical words

8 Article 78.2, p. 92.

which are translation equivalents in the two languages do not always belong in the same class of noun. In other words, words which are semantically similar in the two languages do not necessarily function syntactically in the same way, and vice versa. Certain hidden assumptions about the comparability of the two languages have yet to be examined to ascertain whether there is ever or sometimes or never equivalence of meaning.

It was stated in the course of the contemporary Dáil debate: 'There is no difficulty about finding Irish translations for technical terms, but, on account of the very nature of technical terms, a dispute may arise as to whether any particular translation conveys the technical meaning assigned to the original English term'.[9] This statement would be valid if the grammatical properties of English and Irish were identical and that every variation of case and number preserved the exact meaning of the basic term. But the two languages are dissimilar. Does *barántas forghníomhaithe* mean 'a warrant of execution' or 'an executed warrant', or *mionnscríbhinn fhorghníomhaiathe chuí* 'a duly executed affidavit' or 'an affidavit of due execution'? Another question relates to the situation which arises where a 'term' is qualified in such a way that a genitive could be expected. If before *árachas dliteanais fhostóra* (employer's liability insurance) there is a qualifier (noun, compound preposition), the only guarantee of legal certainty being preserved is if the term is left unchanged. See *fógra glactha choinníollaigh* which apparently means 'notice of qualified acceptance' though this is far from obvious. Is it obvious that *comhaontú athraithe* means 'variation agreement', or *meabhrán comhaontaithe* 'a memorandum of agreement', or *comhaontú fuascailte* 'a redemption agreement', or *deimhniú corpraithe* 'a certificate of incorporation', especially as in the previous entry *cuideachta chorpraithe* is 'an incorporated company'? Another over-precise grammatical application occurs in *inniúlacht chonraithe* (capacity to contract). How would one decide? Would reference to the term in *TD* always suffice? There are signs of awareness of the semantic difficulty because we have *dearbhú dílseacháin* (vesting declaration) and *dlínse maidir le pósadh* for 'matrimonial jurisdiction'. *Dlínse phósta* would indeed have been a caricature. Then we find *conradh iarphósta* (post-nuptial contract) where a selectional restriction clearly applies. (In EID there is *bainisiúil* for 'nuptial' but the word does not appear in FGB.) While *caiteachais adhlactha* (funeral expenses) is completely unintelligible, it is less of a caricature than *adhlacóir adhlactha* for 'funeral undertaker'. *TD* offers no guidance on such matters even though earlier grammars provide a pertinent suggestion: 'A noun followed by a genitive (*not having the force of an adjective)* is in most cases treated as a compound or phrase-noun, and is hence *invariable*' (italics in text).[10] The same point is made by O'Nolan: 'The Genitive form is not used in phrase nouns'.[11] The application

9 *Dáil Éireann*, Parliamentary Debates, Vol. xcvi, col. 1892.

10 *Irish Composition*, The Irish Christian Brothers, 1921.

11 *Studies in Modern Irish*, Gerald O'Nolan, 1919, p. 144.

of this principle to every term listed in *TD* would help to eliminate the risk of uncertainty and ambiguity.

Paradoxically, such guidance could have been provided in the official standard for spelling and accidence[12] known as *CO*, but it concerned itself mainly with the superficial features of the language, orthographical and phonological. It was everything but an analysis of the grammatical properties of the language. Alan Bliss forecast that it would one day be seen 'as an old-fashioned eccentricity',[13] yet a new version of the 'eccentricity' was produced in 2012 as if no linguistic advances had been made in the meantime. Irish was still predominantly seen in a diachronic and deductive context. The *CO* has all the properties of a medical textbook. It is a primer for pedants and purists but modern linguists are looking for grammatical rules which will enable us to recognize and produce correct sentences. This joint effort in the fifties will be remembered for the golden opportunity that was missed, when relevant and intelligible grammatical guidelines could have been constructed and *TD* (and future collections) would have been provided with the explicitness and semantic transparency required to make it fully exploitable. If languages like English or French feel the need to use prepositions where syntactic considerations tend to overshadow semantic relations, why not Irish? 'Shelf for books' is more explicit than 'bookshelf'.

The period between then and the publication of *FGB* in 1977 was understandably but unfortunately a period of intense inactivity. Obviously *FGB* was in gestation but there was little enough coordination as regards legal terms. Interestingly enough there are examples from the legislation of that period which not only endorse the terms in *TD* but place them in a context. *TD* could have been the foundation stone for a consolidation of Irish as a modern language or at least a significant stepping stone along the way. However, as we have already noted, its contents were hardly endorsed in EID. It was neglected even more blatantly in the new comprehensive grammar (GG) which was published in 1960.[14] While many examples of usage were concocted to demonstrate grammatical rules, no illustrations of a legal kind were provided which might enlighten a user of *TD* (nor indeed are there any examples in the most recent edition published in 1999).

The most telling fact which undermined whatever hopes or ambitions *TD* might have generated was the complete absence of litigation through Irish. Who needed legal terms in Irish if these were not to be tested in court? This is still the position according to the Irish Language Commissioner.[15] The real negligence derives from the fact that no effort was made to update or supplement *TD* so that citizens would be encouraged to use Irish for litigation purposes even though legislation was being produced on a regular basis which not only used 'legal' terminology but

12 *Gramadach na Gaeilge agus Litriú na Gaeilge – An Caighdeán Oifigiúil*, 1958.

13 *The Crane Bag*, 1982, p. 82.

14 *Graiméar Gaeilge na mBráithre Críostaí*, Dublin, 1960.

15 'Ó Mhám Trasna go Doire an Fhéich: an Ghaeilge sna Cúirteanna', Article in *Comhar*, Eanáir 2013, 10–11.

indicated how it might be used within the constraints of traditional grammatical rules without losing its specific character.

Herewith are a limited number of examples. In *TD* there is no entry for 'deceive' but for 'deceit' there is *meabhlaireacht* and for 'innocent' there is *neamhchiontach*. An interesting statement appears in a 1960 Act:[16] 'not proved to have been made innocently or without intent to deceive' which is translated *nach gcruthófar gur go neamhurchóideach agus gan rún meabhlaíochta a tugadh*. (We will turn our attention later to this typical and slightly deviant use of the future.) Another example[17] highlights the shortcomings of *TD*. 'The wrong may be a tort, breach of contract or breach of trust or any combination of them' is translated *féadfaidh an éagóir bheith ina thort, ina shárú conartha nó ina shárú iontaobhais nó ina chumasc ar bith díobh*. In *TD* 'combination' is given as *cuallaíocht* (which in *FGB* is given as 'companionship, society'). Clearly the correct option was followed in the legislation but the point is that *TD* fails to clarify the precise context in which *neamhchiontach* corresponds to 'innocent' and *cuallaíocht* to 'combination'. Two interesting examples[18] illustrate the inconsistencies which are prevalent from the outset. The first 'because the court negatives contributory negligence' is rendered *mar gheall ar an gcúirt d'obadh d'fhaillí rannpháirteach*. In *TD* only one meaning is given for *obadh*, namely 'dishonour (that is, cheque) (with the highly ambivalent example *fógra obtha* (notice of dishonour) – with no regard for other conceivable examples such as *seic obtha*); according to EID 'negative' in this context is best rendered by *cuir gníomh ar neamhní* or *fág gníomh gan éifeacht*. The second 'because he obtains judgment by default' is rendered *mar gheall ar é d'fháil breithiúnais mhainneachtana* though *TD* has two versions: *trí mhainneachtain*(by default) and *breithiúnas mainneachtana* (judgment by default). *Finné mainneachtana* is the ordinary translation for 'defaulting witness' which represents an entirely different grammatical relationship. *FGB* has the adjectival form *mainneachtnach*. One other example[19] would certainly contribute to any compilation of legal terms: 'that that person is in need of housing on medical, compassionate or other similar grounds' is translated *go bhfuil tithíocht ag teastáil (uaidh) ar chúiseanna liachta, atruacha nó cúiseanna eile dá short*. In EID there is *truach, truachroíoch* ar 'compassionate'. The real dilemma pertains to 'medical' which has been translated and continues to be translated in various ways. EID opts for *leighis*[20] but elsewhere we find *míochaine* and *liachta* used seemingly interchangeably. The courts have never been called upon to adjudicate.

While all legislative texts might be expected to provide unprecedented legal terms there were a number of documents in the sixties which were dealing with specifically judicial matters: The District Court Rules were published as a

16 Rent Restrictions Act, No 42, 1960, Article 12.6, p. 38.

17 Civil Liability Act, No 41, 1961, Article 11.2,b, p. 22.

18 Ibid. Article 38.12,a.

19 Housing Act, No 21, 1966, Article 16.2,b, p. 40.

20 *Leigheas* is more usefully reserved for 'remedy'.

Statutory Instrument in 1962 and expressly stated that 'defaulter' was no longer *faillitheoir* but *mainnitheoir*, and 'levy' was *tobhach* not *cruinniú*. There was the Courts (Supplemental Provisions) Act,[21] the Civil Liability Act,[22] the Trade Marks Act,[23] the Copyright Act,[24] the Patents Act,[25] the Succession Act,[26] the Landlord and Tenant (Ground Rents) Act,[27] not to mention the massive Income Tax Act[28] which runs to 1,115 pages. None of the terms in these acts were ever catalogued for public use, much less analysed for relevance and coherence or disseminated. Nor are they always faithful to *TD*. There 'execution order' is *ordú forghníomhaithe* (which is ambiguous) while we find *an tOrdú Feidhmiúcháin* for 'the Execution Order'.[29] Perhaps the most significant translation provided was Act No 33, the Companies Act in 1963, that is, six years after the publication of *TD*. This is an excellent example of how *TD* was used by the translator and how many new terms appear which could have been included in a new edition of *TD* and thus brought to the attention of the general public.

It was noted earlier that *tionóisc* was the only term in *TD* for 'accident'. Here we have the statement 'either accidental or due to inadvertence or some other sufficient cause' which is rendered *gur de thionóisc nó de neamhaire nó ar chúis leormhaith éigin eile*.[30] It sometimes ignores the genitive constraint in the interests of clarity: *i gcás aon fhiach, oibleagáid nó conradh faoina ndeachaigh sé*.[31] This is a regular source of confusion even within the same document. In the Income Tax Act 1967, we find *i gcás aon bhliain mheasúnachta* (for any year of assessment)[32] and *de dheasca éalainge aigne nó coirp* (through infirmity of mind or body).[33] The use of the genitive can be positively confusing as in *i gcoinne seachanta dlíthiúla* (against legal avoidance).[34] A similar aberration occurs in the Patents Act 1964 where we find *i modh séanta nó ceartaithe* (by way of disclaimer or correction).[35] In the Succession Act 1965 *riarachán a dheonú i leith eastát duine éagtha* (to grant administration for the estate of a deceased person)[36] and *i leith gach cúis*

21 No 39, 1961.
22 No 41, 1961.
23 No 9, 1963.
24 No 10, 1963.
25 No 12, 1964.
26 No 27, 1965.
27 No 2, 1967.
28 No 6, 1967.
29 District Court Rules, Statutory Instrument, No 8, 1962, Article 19.1, p. 12.
30 Companies Act, No 33, 1963, Article 34.2.
31 Article 20.1, p. 78.
32 Article 104.2,b, p. 244.
33 Article 235.3,b, p. 452.
34 Annex xx, p. 1026.
35 Article 55.3, p. 108.
36 Article 20.1, p. 32.

*caingne* (in respect of all causes of action).[37] The use of a genitive instead of a simple adjective can lead to something like *úinéir ionchais cóipchirt* (prospective owner of copyright)[38] which could be translated in several different ways. There are many other interesting examples which unfortunately remain hidden away, for example *cibé acu a agraíodh na héagóiritheoirí sin go feadh breithiúnais nó nár eagraíodh* (whether such wrongdoers have been sued to judgment or not). In EID 'wrong-doer' is rendered *aimhleastóir, drochdhuine, coirpeach, ciontóir*. Neither *aimhleastóir* nor *éagóiritheoir* appear in *FGB*.

By the time *FGB* appeared in 1977, 20 years had elapsed since the publication of *Téarmaí Dlí*, and it is no exaggeration to describe them as lost years in terms of developing, clarifying and expanding a corpus of legal terms. The terms which feature in the legislation are locked away in the Dail archives. The hope was that FGB would endorse what was contained in *TD* and include some of the new terms from the legislation. Surely whatever terms of interest which existed in the Dáil archives would have been communicated to Niall Ó Dónaill? A few examples suggest that either he opted to ignore such terms or they were not brought to his attention or he did not regard them as being part of the same language: *dídhílsiú aon mhaoine* (divesting of any property),[39] *comhleanúntais* (incidents),[40] *mífhaisnéisigh* (misrepresent as a verb),[41] *follasghnéitheacht an tsáraithe* (flagrancy of infringement),[42] *intochsail* (distrainable),[43] *eiseachtain* (ejectment),[44] *fógra athshuímh* (reinstatement notice),[45] *spreagluaíochtaí* (incentives)[46] are not included. In the case of 'prototype houses', rendered *tithe freamhshamplacha*,[47] *FGB* has *freamhshamhail* (prototype). We find *iarratas suaibhreosach cráiteach* (frivolous, vexatious application),[48] but *FGB* gives 'ridiculous, contemptible' under *suaibhreosach* while there is no entry for *cráiteach*. These examples illustrate the fact that the parallel sources of legal terms continues under *FGB*, with consequent questions as to authenticity and coherence. It will be seen later that while *FGB* includes a significant number of what can be described as legal terms, these are not necessarily accessible to the normal reader and are not authenticated.

The more important question is how many of the entries in *Téarmaí Dlí* are endorsed in *FGB*. A cursory comparison shows that the following do not appear in *FGB*: *agarcheisteanna* (interrogatories), *ar meisce agus mí-iomprach*

---

37 Article 48, p. 56.
38 Article 25.10, p. 90.
39 Courts (Supplemental Provisions) Act, 1961, No 39, Article 59.3,g, p. 98.
40 Trade Marks Act, 1963, No 9, Article 29.1,b, p. 44.
41 Ibid., Article 36.7,c (ii), p. 62.
42 Copyright Act, 1963, No 10, Article 22.4,a, p. 82.
43 Income Tax Act, 1967, No 6, Article 494.1, p. 860.
44 Courts Act, 1971, No 36, Article 7,a(ii), p. 8.
45 Housing Act, 1969, No 16, Article 5.1, p. 16.
46 Ibid., Article 113, p. 20.
47 Ibid., Article 20.1.
48 Income Tax Act, 1967, No 6, Article 241.8, p. 480.

(drunk and disorderly), *athchomhshó* (reconversion), *bantiomnóir* (testatrix), *barrógaíocht* (embracery), *bothaíocht* (stallage), *both-thionóntacht* (cottier tenancy), *céadghinteacht* (primogeniture), *ceannach éigeantach* (compulsory purchase), *cianúlas* (remoteness), *cíosmhuirear* (rent-charge), *claonchasadh* (embezzlement), *claonchothú* (maintenance), *comhoidhrseach* (coparcener), *cros-fhoraithne* (cross-decree), *diomailt fhaillíoch* (permissive waste), *dlúth-thóir* (fresh pursuit), éalang teidil (defect of title), *eascaire aisig* (writ of restitution), *éigeantas* (duress), *faisnéisí príobháideach* (common informer), *faoiseamh cothromais* (equitable relief – which is not listed under either *cothromas* or *faoiseamh*), *féichiúnaí éalaitheach* (absconding debtor), *foraithne thráthchoda* (instalment decree), *foriarratas iar bhfógra* (motion on notice), *gnáthchaitheamh agus gnáthchumailt* (fair wear and tear), *imthosca maolaitheacha* (extenuating circumstances), *inchúlghairthe* (revocable), *indíotáilte* (indictable), *iontaobhas cinniúnach* (executory trust), *ionsaí agus slacairt* (assault and battery), *ollchumasc* (hotchpot), *seachshásamh* (ademption), *toimhde infhrisnéise* (rebuttable presumption) – while *comaoin/conradh le comhlíonadh* is given for 'executory consideration/contract', *an phléadáil chonlaithe* (the rolled-up plea), *seilbh chodarsna* (adverse possession).

Then there are the terms which are reproduced but with an amended spelling: *foghail-bhrabúis* in *TD* reads *foghailbhrabúis* (mesne profits) in *FGB*, *bruach-úinéir* reads *bruachúinéir* (riparian owner), *easaontacht fhianaise* reads *easaontas fianaise, gníomhas aonpháirtí* reads *gníomhas aon pháirtí, iombualadh* becomes *imbhualadh, meabhair-éalangach* becomes *meabhairéalangach*, *nasc-thionónta* becomes *nascthionónta*, sítheoilte becomes *síothóilt*.

Finally, there are those where no reference is made to their legal standing or to the fact that they appear in *TD*: *ainbhreitheach* (perverse), *fianaise/doiciméad a thabhairt ar aird* (to adduce/produce a document), *ballbhasc* (maim), *baránta feiliúnachta* (warranty of fitness), *bintiúrach* (debenture-holder), *blianachtóir* (annuitant), *cabhrú agus neartú le duine* (aid and abet), *cáilmheas* (good will), *cealú* (rescission, cancellation), *cogairsigh* (marshall), *coigistigh* (confiscate), *coimhthigh* (alienate), *coir mhaireachtála* (means of subsistence), *coirloscadh* (arson), *comhéigean* (coercion), *comhthacaíocht* (corroboration), *cúbláil* (defalcation), *diansir* (importune), *dlíthí* (litigant), *dlíthíocht* ('litigation' in *TD* but 'litigiousness' in *FGB*), *faillí rannpháirteach* (contributory negligence), *fianaise dhochloíte* ('conclusive' in *TD* but 'irrefutable' in FGB), *eadóirseacht* (naturalization), *eistíreachas* (exterritoriality), *forléasadh* (demise), *geallearbóir* (pawnbroker), *tionchar míchuí* (undue influence), *mórfhaillí* (gross negligence), *rithim (brionnú)* (I utter a forgery), *teasargaim as coimeád dleathach* (I rescue from lawful custody), *trochlú* (dilapidation), *tugaim ar aghaidh* (I prosecute (appeal, proceedings)), *uacht dhual/neamhdhual* (officious/inofficious will), *urbhac ar fhoras iompair* estoppel by conduct).

It is quite clear from these samples that *FGB* did not choose the entries from *TD* at random but exercised considerable discretion as to which entries would be included and which would be omitted. What is significant is the lack of coordination between the various agencies, highlighting again the fact that Irish is operating on two parallel tracks to the detriment of both. This is not to say that FGB did not include a considerable number of what could be called 'legal terms' which did not appear in *TD*, some of which are accompanied by the sign *jur*. We have no knowledge as to the reasons behind these choices or on what basis some entries were deemed to be worthy of the *jur.* endorsement. We do know that as they were not produced within the remit of the Advisory Committee they would have no particular standing in court proceedings. (A supplement to EID[49] was published at the same time but it included no new terms with the mention *jur.*) There are approximately 50,000 headwords in *FGB* of which as many as a third are non-entries, simply offering an alternative spelling to another headword. The rough average per page of 45 headwords includes only 7 with examples, 25 with explanation only and 16 which are alternative spellings. Yet in a rough total of 50,000 headwords as many as 4,000 are legal terms, either indicated by a *jur.* or suitable for use in a legal context. There are no explanatory notes which reflect the work produced over a 50-year period by the Dáil translation service. *FGB* is essentially a dictionary which highlights the metaphorical and figurative range of the language. This is evident from the space accorded to prepositions (including prepositional verbs), body parts (*aghaidh, bun, ceann, cos, cúl, lámh, leath*) and common verbs (*bain, caith, cuir, fág, gabh, glan, leag, rith*) and conjunctions (*ach, agus, mar*), while the 'irregular' verbs occupy an apparently disproportionate area but which reflects the unusual focus of the language.

The following list is just a representative selection of such 'legal' words in *FGB* which do not appear in *TD* or anywhere else, have a certain legal connotation and are grouped under five roughly common headings:

general legal relevance:
**accomplice**: *cionpháirtí*, **accused (person)**: *lítheach*, **accuser**: *coiritheoir*, *cúiseoir*, **bigamy**: *biogamacht*, (*biogamaíocht* in EID), *déchéileachas* (*déphósadh* in TD), **boycott**: *eascoiteannú*, **common good**: *an mhaith choiteann*, **counterplea**: *frithagra*, **criminality**: *coiriúlacht*, **criminologist**: *coireolaí*, **culpable negligence**: *cionfhaillí*, **defrauding**: *séitéireacht*, **disrepute**: *táirmheas*, **embezzlement**: *cúigleáil*, **guiltiness**: *ciontacht*, *coireacht*, *coiriúlacht*, **law (rule of)**: *smacht reachta*, **malefactor**: *coirpeach*, *meirleach*, **malevolence**: *anchroí*, *cealgrún*, *naimhdeas*, **misdemeanant**: *oilghníomhaí*, **misjudgment**: *míbhreithiúnas*, **non-fulfilment**: *díchomhall*, *éagomhall*, *neamhchomhall*, *neamhchomhlíonadh*, **oppression**: *ainneart*, *aintreise*, *anfhorlann*, *antrom*, *leatrom*, **order (law and)**: *riail agus reacht*, **pilferer**: *mionbhradaí*, *scealpaire*, *síntealach*, **pilfering**: *mionbhradaíl*, *mionfhoghail*, *mionghadaíocht*, *scealpaireacht*, **practice (of law)**: *dlíodóireacht*, **presumptive evidence**: *fianaise dhóchúil*, **rebutal**: *frisnéis*, **satisfaction for injury**: *eineachlann*, **slander**: *béadán*, *ithiomrá*, *spíd*, *tuaileas*,

49 *English-Irish Dictionary*, Terminological Additions and Corrections, 1978.

**statute of limitations**: *reacht na bhfoirceann* (*reacht na dtréimhsí* in TD), **transgression**: *cion, coir, iomarbhas, míriail, tairmtheacht, targhabháil*
physical or mental health:
**deficiency (mental):** *éalang mheabhrach*, **derangement**: *íorthacht*, **disabled**: *daorbhacach*, **disablement**: *cróilí*, **helplessness**: *dímrí*, **idiocy**: *dímheabhair*, **lamed (severely)**: *daorbhacach*, **limping gait (person with):** *leisíneach*, **mad (person)**: *íorthachán*, **mental aberration**: *iomrall céille*, **mental aberration:** *saochan céill*, **mental confusion**: *réaltóireacht*, **mental deficiency**: *éalang mheabhrach*, **mental illness**: *meabhairghalar*, **mentally retarded**: *mallintinneach*, **retarded (mentally)**: *mallintinneach*

popular language:
**certain knowledge**: *oireas*, **certainty (legal)**: *deimhneacht dlí*, **clerical error**: *dearmad pinn*, **concealment**: *ceal, ceileantas, coigilt, díchealt, dílsiú*, **court (in open)**: *idir barra is binse*, **detente**: *éideannas*, **empty words**: *fuighle fáis*, **error (of judgment)**: *iomrall breithiúnais*, **evacuation**: *aslonnú*, **excommunication**: *eascoiteannú*, **grave injustice**: *dígeann*, **hyperbole**: *urtheilgean*, **idea**: *tuaileas*, **identity (mistaken)**: *iomrall aithne, mearaithne*, **incompatibility**: éaguibhreannas, **occult knowledge**: *fiosaíocht*, **officialese**: *meamraiméis*, **open court (in)**: i gcúirt phoiblí, idir barra is binse, **outsider**: *tuilí*, **perception**: *léirstean*, **period (nine-day)**: *naomhaí*, **period (three-month)**: *ráithe*, **period for settlement of debt**: *téarmaíocht*, **practice of attending funerals**: *comhairíochas*, **privileged person**: *neimheadh*, **procrastination**: *sínteoireacht aimsire*, **pursuit (in hot)**: *ar teaintiví*, **roguery**: *scealpaireacht*, **secrecy**: *ceileantas, ceilteanas, dearraide*, táidhe, *discréid*, **secret**: *dearraid*, díchealta, *folaitheach*, **separation (from bed and board)**: *dealú ó chuibhreann agus ó chaidreamh*, **trafficking (in commodities)**: *ceannaíocht (in) earraí*, **treachery**: *anbhrath, cealg, fealltacht, tréatúireacht*, **truism**: *léireasc*

verbs:
**abuse, revile**: *díbligh*, **accommodate**: *déan oiriúntas* (le), **adjourn**: *atráthaigh*, **attaint**: *eisreachtaigh*, **censure**: *milleánaigh, táinsigh, tathaoir, conceal, tearmannaigh, dílsigh, dícheil*, **encroach**: *cúngaigh*, **make allegations against**: *coirigh ar*, **ostracize**: *eascoiteannaigh*, **outlaw**: *eisreachtaigh*, **recriminate**: *comhchoirigh*

adjectives:
**actionable**: *caingneach*, **assignable**: *inainmnithe*, **implausible**: *mídhealraitheach*, **inconclusive**: *neamhchonclúideach*, **inconsistent**: *neamhréireach*, **indefeasible**: *dochealaithe*, **indefinable**: *dotheoranta*, **indescribable**: *dofhaisnéise*, **indisputable**: *doshéanta*, **ineffacable**: *doscriosta*, **irrational**: *aingiallta*, **irreconcilable**: *doréitithe*, **irreformable**: *doleasaithe*, **irrefutable**: *dobhréagnaithe, dochloíte*, **paradoxical**: *saobhchiallda*, **permutable**: *iniomalartaithe*, **questioning**: *imchomharcach*, **uncontentious**: *neamhspairneach*, **undisciplined**: *ainrialta*,

**undiscriminating**: *maolbhreithiúnach*, **unjust**: *aincheart*, *ainfhíréanta*, éagórach, *neamhchóir*, **unreasoning**: *aingiallta*, *feillbhéasach*, *neamhiontaofa*, *neamh-mhuiníneach*, **untrustworthy**: *míchreidiúnach*, *neamhiontaofa*, *neamh-mhuiníneach*, **vandalism**: *mínós*, **villainy**: *meirleachas*, **vindictiveness**: *díchúis*

The discrepancy or the gap between what was to be found in the main dictionaries and what was current in the legislation spills over into another area. The need for terms with legal certainty is not confined to strictly legal terms but is relevant with regard to terms describing social welfare situations, particularly as regards physical and mental health. The Social Welfare (Consolidation) Act, 1981 was a huge document of 584 pages in which many technical definitions are set out. Among them are the following important descriptive states which are rendered in Irish as follows:

Bodily or mental disablement: *míchumas coirp nó meabhrach*,[50] though *sochar míchumais* (disability benefit)[51] and *sochar míthreorach* (disablement benefit)[52] suggest a crossing of wires, but then TD does not distinguish between 'disability' and 'disablement'. *Máchailiú* translates 'disfigurement'[53] and, what is a slightly less relevant but interesting entry in this context, for 'misconduct, skylarking, negligence' there is *mí-iompar, ábhaillí, faillí*[54] *Lá éagumais chun oibre* translates 'day of incapacity for work',[55] *agus cailleadh cumais choirp* translates 'loss of physical faculty'.[56] *Éalang ó bhroinn* translates 'congenital defect',[57] *agus pinsean easláine* 'invalidity pension'.[58] As regards 'incapable' or 'incapacitated' there is *éagumasach ar é féin a chothabháil* (incapable of self-support),[59] *buan-éagumasach chun oibre* (permanently incapable of work)[60] and *chomh héagumasach* (so incapacitated)[61] and *go mbeidh sé faoi éagumas* (he shall remain incapable).[62]

There are further refinements where we find *éiglíocht éigin coirp nó meabhrach* which translates 'some physical or mental infirmity'[63] and *duine faoi mhíchumas coirp* (physically disabled person) and *duine faoi mhóréislinn meabhrach* (severely

50 Social Welfare (Consolidation) Act, 1981, No 11, Article 2.1,c, p. 56.
51 Ibid., Article 18, p. 90.
52 Ibid., Article 17.1,d, p. 88.
53 Ibid., Article 36.2, p. 120.
54 Ibid., Article 39.2,b(i), p. 126.
55 Ibid. Article 18.1, p. 90.
56 Ibid. Article 36.2, p. 120.
57 Ibid. Article 43.3,b(i), p. 134.
58 Ibid. Article 56.2, p. 160.
59 Ibid. Article 81.1,b, p. 200.
60 Ibid. Article 81.1,a, p. 200.
61 Ibid. Article 81.3(i), p. 200.
62 Ibid. Article 223.1,b(iii), p. 418.
63 Ibid. Article 50.6, p. 148.

mentally handicapped person) in another act,[64] and *daoine corp-éislinneacha* (physically handicapped persons) in a different act.[65] In yet another act there is *duine mímheabhrach* (a person of unsound mind)[66] and in the same year *daoine meabhairéislinneacha* (mentally handicapped persons).[67]

These are very precise terms with specific concomitant social (and legal) entitlements. They can be summarized as follows: *éiglíocht* (infirmity), *míchumas* (disability), *míthreoir* (disablement), *éagumas* (incapacity), *éalang* (defect), *easláine* (invalidity), *éislinneach* (handicapped) and *meabhairéislinneach* and *corp-éislinneach, mímheabhrach* (of unsound mind). While their legal standing was uncertain since they were not approved by the Special Advisory Committee these were terms which were not interchangeable because they referred to a unique medical or social condition. They were not newly devised but they were identified with a specific state and they all had to fall within the ambit of social welfare provisions. Unfortunately they were never brought to public attention. How do they fare in *FGB*? *Éiglíocht* appears as *téiglíocht* (faintness, languidness), *míchumas* (inability, incapacity, disablement, and *jur.* disability), *míthreoir* (misguidance; upset, confusion, confusion, shiftlessness, feebleness), *éagumas* (incapability, inability; impotence), *éalang* (flaw, defect; weakness …), *easláine* (unhealthiness, morbidity), *éislinneach* (insecure, unsafe; vulnerable; unsound, defective) and *meabhairéislinneach* (no entry, though *meabhairéalangach* is as in *TD*) and *corp-éislinneach* (no entry), *mímheabhrach* (of unsound mind).

In light of the previous remarks it is interesting to note how a particular phrase 'any impairment of a person's physical or mental condition' has been translated over the years: any impairment of a person's physical or mental condition, *aon dochar do staid choirp nó mheabhrach duine,*[68] *aon dochrú ar staid fhisiciúil nó intinne duine*,[69] *aon mháchail ar staid coirp nó meabhrach duine*,[70] *aon lagú ar staid coirp nó meabhrach duine,*[71] *aon mháchail ar a staid coirp nó meabhrach,*[72] *aon lagú ar staid coirp nó meabhrach duine.*[73] When such slippage occurs within the otherwise highly consistent adherence to precedent in the *Rannóg* it gives a clear idea of the vast gap that exists between provision and use, and illustrates the grammatical and terminological confusion which obtains. A further difficulty arises from the fact that of the four terms used to translate 'impairment', *dochar,*

64 Housing (Miscellaneous Provisions) Act, 1979, No 27, Article 15.2, p. 32.
65 Local Government (Toll Roads) Act, 1979, No 34, Article 3.3, p. 8.
66 Fisheries Act, 1981, No 1, Article 43.6,a, p. 116.
67 Restrictive Practices Act, 1981, No 7, Article 26.1, p. 81.
68 Civil Liability Act, 1961, No 41, Article 2.1, p. 12.
69 Courts Act, 1981, No 11, Article 22.3, p. 32.
70 Animals Act, 1985, No 11, Article 1.1, p. 4.
71 Health Act, 1986, No 10, Article 1, p. 4.
72 Control of Dogs Act 1986, No 32, Article 1, p. 8.
73 Courts Act, 1988, No 14, Article 1.7, p. 8.

*dochrú*, *máchail*, *lagú*, none are translated 'impairment' in *FGB* and only *lagú* translates 'impairment' in EID.

On the other hand it has to be said that *FGB* provides a wide range of 'legal terms', some of which carry the *jur.* symbol though it is not always clear what the basis for that is. And, of course, the indication is erroneous if it implies that they are authenticated terms. Moreover, their usefulness is limited by the fact that they are difficult to locate. The following are a brief selection of terms to be found in the Dáil legislative texts which do not appear in *FGB*: *ánracht* (fellowship), *bunadh* (source), *cineál-cheadaithe* (type-approved), *cinedhíothú* (genocide), *eisiomlú* (representation), *foclaigh* (to word), *leordhóthanach* (sufficient), *leormhaith* (adequate), *margántaíocht* (bargaining), *neamhfheidhmiúlacht* (unfitness), *oirtheoir gáis* (gas-fitter), *postvótálaí* (postal voter), *roghchoiste* (select committee), *scartáil* (demolish), *urbhang* (veto); the following appear in European legislation (the version of the Treaties published in 1974) but not in *FGB*: *comhbheartas* (common policy), *comhchuibhiú* (harmonization), *duine dlítheanach* (legal person), *treoirphraghas* (guide price), *ualú* (weighting); and the number of terms in EID which are not reproduced in *FGB* is limitless.

In a paper entitled 'a Model and an Hypothesis for language structure' delivered on 13 November 1959, Victor H. Yngve said that 'one of the outstanding characteristics of language is its wealth of complexity, particularly on the level of sentence structure'.[74] This signalled the beginning of a trend to attach importance to the knowledge of individual words as well as the syntactic relations between them. A lexicon was not merely a list of words but it also associated each word with its syntactic properties. It would be unfair to expect the authors of *TD* to be aware of the major developments which were taking place in linguistics in the fifties, much less what was going to happen in the sixties and seventies. While an explosion was occurring in the science of linguistics and totally new forms of linguistic analysis were being elaborated, Irish was in a state of conceptual stasis. Had the provisions of the Act been adhered to, a new committee on legal terms would have been functioning, could have taken account of new trends and the first edition of *TD* could have been revised and supplemented, and even FGB might have been different. Not only did this not happen, but the actual first edition has been so long out of print that most modern readers would be unaware that it ever existed and the reason for its existence.

The situation when Ireland became a member of the European Communities in 1972 could not be anything other than confused. Apart from the inherent inconsistency noted in all aspects of Irish legal terminology at this point, the infrequency of the demands for translation into Irish meant that Community translations into Irish display more than usual terminological inconsistency. Otherwise positive developments were taking shape. A new Terminology Committee (CT) was established in 1968 and had become increasingly active in the eighties. It produced a series of sectoral dictionaries which were comprehensive

74 Proceedings of the American Philosophical Society, Vol. 104, No 5, October 1960.

in every sense of the word. However, most of its work was done in the abstract and it took some time before the urgent need for clarification and simplification of the grammatical rules manifested itself so that the terms could be used intelligibly. Besides, the CT frequently found itself devising terms which, unknown to it, already featured in existing legislative documents and thus had a certain pre-eminence. Maintaining consistency from one glossary to another was also a recurring problem which would only be resolved when all lists were computerized in the late nineties. It was only then that it became clear how frequently different terms in Irish had been proposed for the same term in English. It still remains one of the weaknesses of the lists in *Focal.ie* that while a context is often provided there is no way of knowing which term is preferable, or whether a new one will be added tomorrow.

The CT did not provide legal terms as such. A comprehensive list of legal terms was submitted to it for consideration in the nineties but the committee was informed that legal terminology was the exclusive preserve of the *Rannóg*. It was assured that the matter was in hand and that a re-issue or a new edition of *TD* was imminent. As a result the list was published in due course without being scrutinized by anyone.[75] But it is in the public domain and that alone confers an authority because it has the merit of filling a gap in essential terminology.

Legal/linguistic experts throughout the European Union are working towards an 'effective multilingualism'[76] because of the realization that discrepancies undermine the uniform application of Community law and the hope is that such discrepancy can be avoided by appropriate methods of legal drafting. They understand that 'the relationship between concepts and words is not the same in all legal languages'.[77] The work done in *Focal.ie* is helping to clarify this aspect of the problem. There is also in existence a Legal Taxonomy Syllabus which is seeking ways of obviating unnecessary obscurities in legal language between the official languages of the Union. If Irish is to participate meaningfully in this programme it will have to address the problem of the inconsistencies of expression and understanding in its own legal terms. Legal terms can be translated but their meaning cannot be divorced from their relation to a legal system. A beginning could be made by identifying existing terminological variants, translation errors and material inconsistencies.

The way forward has already been set out in a recent publication from Fiontar, DCU, the originators and promoters of the *Focal.ie* website.[78] In a comprehensive review of the current situation in the European Union as a whole, with particular

75 *Focal sa Chúirt*, Leachlainn S. Ó Catháin, Coiscéim, 2001.

76 'Language and Terminology', Gerhard Dannemann, Silvia Ferreri and Michele Graziadei, in *The Cambridge Companion to European Private Law*, Christian Twigg-Flesner (Editor), 2010.

77 Ibid., p. 76.

78 *Terminology for the European Union* – the Irish Experience: the GA IATE Project, Úna Bhreathnach, Fionnuala Cloke, Caoilfhionn Nic Pháidín, Dublin, 2013.

reference to the languages of countries which joined the Union in the last ten years, they attempt to identify the challenges which will have to be overcome in the road ahead. They refer to the fact that they are obliged to 'park' certain issues 'because of uncertain grammar rules and lack of clarity regarding grammatical rules in multi-word terms' and that their work is progressing 'despite the uncertainty regarding grammar rules and the inconsistency in Irish-language terminology resources'.[79]

Which brings us back to the problem which could have been resolved in the fifties but was perpetuated instead. Two major offerings were published, the *CO* and *TD*: one of which was so detailed and rule-heavy it could have been the income tax code, the other so devoid of detail it could have been a bus timetable. In retrospect they jointly contrived to deprive countless students of the right to feel they had a mastery of the language and to consign countless writers and translators to a feeling of helplessness. The *CO* claimed to present a coherent set of grammatical and orthographical rules but it was a basically dishonest intellectual exercise. There were irregular verbs as there were in Latin, and five declensions as there were in Latin. No reference was made to the fact that there are many verbs which are more irregular than the supposedly irregular ones and that the most irregular aspect of most verbs was the formation of the verbal noun. The five declensions, each with a supposedly foolproof algorithm, were in fact a cover for at least 30 effective paradigms. What was proposed was in fact a psychological impossibility for the vast majority of learners (and teachers).

This is not the place for detailed comment on this question but a few remarks are called for as a background to the suggestions to follow on specific grammatical points. Language is a process and we have to explore it. Irish has not been successfully regenerated over the last 300 years. In the fifties grammatical rules were virtually synonymous with syntactic rules and so grammar and meaning were kept apart. Following the path of traditional grammars is no longer an option particularly as the ancient paradigms suggested reflect a psychological condition which is no longer relevant. So we need to clarify features of the language and so identify the basic templates which are proper to the language. These will enable us to establish rules which account for as many features as possible and reduce exceptions to the minimum. Grammar now includes not only syntactic rules for generating the sentences but also semantic rules for assigning meaning to those sentences.

As regards specific suggestions, the following are to be understood in the context of legal proceedings where accuracy of expression and interpretation are paramount. In this context it is important to remember how much linguistic analysis has been carried out on the English language over the last 50 years and how much remains to be done whereas Irish has been the subject of practically no analysis.

I will refer briefly to just two: the adjective under a number of guises and the verb (tense in particular).

79 Ibid., p. 82.

The easiest concept to grasp is perhaps what we know as the adjective. We all think we know what an adjective is and that in Irish nouns can also be adjectives. The adjective was the most unpretentious part of speech and was largely defined in terms of the various ways it could qualify a noun. This is no longer seen as an adequate description. In Irish grammars the adjective was required to follow the same modifications as the noun it qualified. It was believed that the full description or explanation of the syntactic construction of an adjective simply meant calling it attributive or predicative. In Irish it was treated with disdain without a clear status, whereas its value can be crucial to understanding. But such intelligibility requires a modicum of reflection.

There are three general areas of confusion:

- where the genitive of the noun is used as an adjective: *tráchtála*, *trádála*, *oiliúna miotaseolaíocht*, *cógaseolaíocht*, *eacnamaíocht*, *múinteoireacht*, *cráifeacht*, *oideachas*, *tiomáint*, *fealsúnacht*. This amounts to neutering the adjective because in this form it is incapable of distinguishing singular from plural. These 'adjectives' cannot be turned into adverbs, nor used in a predicative position. There are also other 'ordinary' adjectives which cannot be turned into adverbs, for example *fliuch*, *insilteach*, *suntasach*;
- where the selectional rules about which words can co-occur come into play and where there is an obvious adjectival form. The obvious distinction is between *teach an phobail* and *teach poiblí*. Compare also *ceant poiblí* with *sláinte an phobail*, *cearta an duine* with *meon daonna*, *duine polaitiúil* with *aidhmeanna na polaitíochta*, *pobal na hÉireann agus tréith Éireannach*, *oíche cheolmhar agus scrúdú ceoil*, *riachtanais an chultúir* with *riachtanais chultúrtha*;
- where the genitive of the verbal noun (the verbal adjective) is used as a noun and where the semantic element is completely obscured: is *cóip dheimhnithe* 'a certified copy' or 'a copy of a certificate', *foraithne neamhnithe* 'a decree of nullity' or 'an annulled decree'; this construction can run into multiples and then becomes totally opaque when qualified *de bhun ordaithe cothabhála nó ordaithe astaithe tuillimh* which *can* mean 'pursuant to a maintenance order or an attachment of earnings order' apparently. It should be noted here that the phonological element is overlooked completely because no aural distinction can be made between *ordaithe* and *orduithe*; is *deimhniú diúltaithe* 'a certificate of refusal' or a 'refused certificate' and *deimhniú iniúchta* 'a certificate of inspection' or 'an inspected certificate'? We saw in *TD* that *comhaontú fuascailte* is 'a redemption agreement' but it can also come in a different guise: *meabhrán fuascailte* 'a memorandum of vacate' and we find *meabhrachán sannta breithiúnais* as 'a memorial of assigment of a judgement' when its more immediate meaning would appear to be 'an assigned memorial of judgement'. If *na critéir ghlactha* translates 'the acceptance criteria' and *an critéar diúltaithe* 'the rejection criterion', how would 'the accepted acceptance criteria' be translated? Not

> to mention a phrase like 'as amended by the amended amendment slip'? This particular problem highlights the extent to which terms based on this usage are entirely unintelligible orally and thus the divergence between oral and written comprehension is brought into sharp focus.

There are 'ascriptive' adjectives (involving a close identification in meaning between the noun and the adjective) and 'associative' (where they are not really connected), and we know that the relationship between an attributive adjective and its noun is not the same as that between a predicative adjective and its noun. This kind of semantic subtlety casts doubt on the usefulness of the present inflectional system.

The most difficult to translate is what is called the post nominal attributive position (noun phrase + (be) + verbal adjective): *the crime alleged* where the 'adjective' is translated in all sorts of ways, frequently being rendered by a different tense verb: 'a training programme organised with the approval of B' is rendered *clár oiliúna a eagrófar le ceadú B*, 'traffic sign authorised by B' as sín tráchta *a údaraíodh le B* and 'workers employed by B' as *oibrithe atá fostaithe ag B*. So we have three different interpretative tenses in Irish.

This leads on to the problems associated with tense. Tenses in every case in Irish do not correspond to tenses in English but there seems to be a particular problem with the future tense. The template for Irish usage was probably set by Tomás Ó Rathile's remark: 'To be noted is the use of the future in a subordinate verb when the principal verb is in the future'.[80] This is a very interesting approach and is largely followed in the significant grammars produced in the first half of the twentieth century. But identity of name does not imply identity of function and Irish has a peculiar set of time notions, the implications of which for the Irish understanding of time and the passage of time have yet to be studied. The particular form taken by the grammatical system of language is closely related to the social and personal needs that language is required to serve. In *TD* the phrase '*cúramaí géillte a breithníodh ina gheilt ag ionchoisne nó le hordú na cúirte*' is given to mean 'committee of a lunatic so found by inquisition or by order of the court'. The verb is tense-less in English but in Irish it is too emphatically in the past. But the efforts to apply this rule to legal texts can lead to some incomprehensible situations.

This could lead sometimes to political problems as in this example: '(these) shall apply to a national of Greece who is coming to the State to take up or pursue an activity ... or who is in employment ..., only if the employment is in accordance with a permit granted by B' is rendered '*beidh feidhm le ... maidir le náisiúnach den Ghréig a bheidh ag teacht go dtí an Stát chun dul i mbun gníomhaíochta ... nó a bheidh fostaithe sa Stát, ... ach amháin i gcás go mbeidh an fhostaíocht de réir cheada (sic) arna dheonú ag B*'. The dilemma derives from the fact that there is no certainty as to the actual location of this person at a given moment. How does Irish cope with the following alternatives: (a) there is a person coming to the

80 *Desiderius*, Dublin, 1965.

door; (b) there is a person coming to the door tomorrow; (c) I see a person who is coming to the door in my dreams; (d) if you see a person coming to the door. If English states: 'you will say to the person who is coming to the State …' both verbs are referring to the same period.

It is not clear, however, what period is being referred to when you have 'existing workers who have already completed 5 years' service who do not offer themselves …' rendered as '*na hoibrithe láithreacha a mbeidh 5 bliana seirbhíse críochnaithe cheana féin acu ach nach dtairgeann iad féin …*', or 'workers who have completed their 5th year …' as '*oibrithe a bhfuil a 5ú bliain seirbhíse críochnaithe go acu …*' Translating 'goods which are hazardous, inflammable, objectionable or fragile' as '*earraí a bheidh contúirteach, inlasta, inlochtaithe nó sobhriste*' raises the question as to when the danger becomes a reality which would clearly have implications in a court case.

Several problems crop up in a sentence like the following: 'in the case of a vehicle registered in … (unless) there is in force a certificate issued … showing that the vehicle has passed a roadworthiness test complying with the provisions …' which is rendered '*i gcás feithicle a cláraíodh i ... mura rud é go mbeidh deimhniú i bhfeidhm arna eisiúint ... ina dtaispeántar gur éirigh leis an bhfeithicil i dtástáil ród-acmhainneachta a chomhlíonann forálacha …*' where four different tenses are used in Irish.

Such elasticity would obviously be very ambiguous in a context such as the following: 'where a person whose name and address is demanded refuses or fails to give his name and address … or gives a name which is false or misleading he shall be guilty of an offence' rendered '*i gcás go ndiúltóidh nó go bhfailleoidh duine, a n-éileofar a ainm agus a sheoladh air, a ainm agus a sheoladh a thabhairt nó go dtabharfaidh sé ainm atá bréagach nó míthreorach beidh sé ciontach i gcion*' when looked at alongside a sentence such as 'a member of the Garda Síochána may arrest without warrant a person who refuses or fails to produce a certificate … demanded under …' rendered as '*féadfaidh comhalta den Gharda Síochána duine a ghabháil gan bharántas ar duine é a dhiúltaíonn nó a fhaillíonn deimhniú ... a éilítear faoi ... a thabhairt ar aird …*' When did the events occur?

One last point needs to be made to illustrate the prevalent confusion between the use of the passive verb and the verb 'to be' plus the verbal adjective. In 'any area described' can be rendered '*aon limistéar a thuairiscítear*' when '*atá tuairiscithe*' would be preferable. This very subtle distinction appears to have been discarded in modern Irish. In the example '*aon fhocal atá scríofa ar phár*' there is no doubt that the act is complete, whereas in '*aon fhocal a scríobhtar ar phár*' it could be referring to any action past, present or future. In a sentence such as 'in any proceedings in which it is alleged that the defendant contravened … that the animal in relation to which the offence is alleged to have been committed was moved' there are two instances of 'alleged'. Is it a solution to put one in the present and the other in the future (along with three verbs in the past tense) as: '*in aon imeachtaí ina líomhnófar gur sháraigh an cosantóir ... go ndearnadh an t-ainmhí ar ina leith a líomhnaítear go ndearnadh an cion a aistriú*'?

As a general rule reference to a text or an article should be in static form: *foráil atá luaite in Airteagal*. See the confusion between 'in respect of any portion of the tax specified in this paragraph' rendered a- *'i leith aon choda den cháin a shonraítear sa mhír seo'* alongside 'the tax specified in this paragraph' rendered as *an cháin atá sonraithe sa mhír seo*. This has become so widespread that it appears to have become acceptable. It is no less confusing, perhaps even deviant. This would be a pity because Irish is not so well equipped with subtle semantic features that it can afford to dispense with any. Equally pertinent is the misuse of the present habitual. It almost seems reckless to use the present habitual in cases such as 'if he is unmarried when he ceased to be a contributing member' rendered '*má bhíonn sé gan pósadh ar scor dó de bheith ina chomhalta ranníocach*' or 'if the pensioner **becomes** incapable of giving a receipt' – '*má bhíonn an pinsinéir* éagumasach *ar admháil a thabhairt*'.

One final example to illustrate a plethora of aimless tense definitions: see how many tenses are used in the Irish version of 'unless there has been produced by the purchaser or the party to whom the apparatus is to be otherwise supplied … a licence granted under the Act of 1926 which was issued to the purchaser or the party so supplied' – '*mura mbeidh ceadúnas a bheidh arna dheonú faoi Acht 1926 tugtha ar aird ag an gceannaitheoir nó ag an bpáirtí a mbeidh an gaireas le soláthar ar shlí eile dó … ar ceadúnas é a bheidh eisithe chuig an gceannaitheoir nó chuig an bpáirtí dá solathrófar amhlaidh é*'. The verb 'issue' seems to cause particular problems as we can see from these further examples: 'a certificate issued by a competent officer' becomes '*deimhniú* ***arna eisiúint*** *ag oifigeach infheidhme*' whereas 'funding bonds issued in respect of interest on certain debts' is '*bannaí cistiúcháin* ***a eisíodh*** *maidir le hús ar fhiacha* áirithe' and 'shares deemed to be issued for public subscription' is translated '*scaireanna* ***a meastar a bheith eisithe*** *le haghaidh a suibscríofa ag an bpobal*' while 'which does not hold any stock, share or security issued by a company …' is rendered '***nach dteachtann*** *aon stoc, scair ná urrús* ***a d'eisigh*** *cuideachta* **…**' that is, four different tenses for what appears like the same temporal situation.

These considerations reflect some of the problems in relation to legal terms and their use, problems which would undoubtedly raise eyebrows in a court of law. It is possible to say that the appropriate legal terms exist but they are not always easy to find. The matter of how to use them within the current grammatical constraints presents much more intractable difficulties. Irish has to become self-explanatory as distinct from using English as a semantic crutch so that we can begin to understand the real grammatical structure of the language. This requirement is relevant both for the learner and the practitioner because if our knowledge of the language is both incomplete and inaccurate it cannot be taught. The language has to be subjected to more rigorous analysis so that legal terms can be used in accordance with the objectives of the European legal project. I have not addressed the complex issue of titles of agreements and so on, but in fact a solution to that problem will not be possible until other more mundane grammatical concerns are clarified.

Chapter 15

# The Struggle for Civic Space Between a Minority Legal Language and a Dominant Legal Language: The Case of Māori* and English

Māmari Stephens and Mary Boyce

## Introduction

Our experience in creating a bilingual Māori-English legal dictionary (*He Papakupu Reo Ture: A Dictionary of Māori Legal Terms*, LexisNexis 2013) has shown us that legal lexicography offers fascinating insights into the relationship between the legal language for special purposes (LSP) of a dominant language such as English, and the legal LSP of a minority language such as Māori (see also Bergenholtz and Tarp 1995). Our experience may be instructive for lexicographers or other lexicographical projects that may want to pay special attention to the legal LSPs that may have emerged from threatened or endangered indigenous languages.[1]

This chapter will demonstrate three particular insights.

a. *A diachronic corpus comprising texts of a threatened indigenous language will yield rich and useful data, but may not provide true comparability between texts*. A diachronic corpus can be critical in the development of a dictionary of legal terms. This kind of corpus enables the development of a profile of lexical change over time. However, the nature of the colonization and urbanization of the indigenous population (in the New Zealand experience) has meant that our diachronic corpus struggles to achieve comparability between texts over time. This observation suggests

---

* Māori is an East Polynesian language belonging to the indigenous Māori inhabitants of Aotearoa, New Zealand. The 2006 census data showed that there were 565,329 people who identified with the Māori ethnic group, and 643,977 people who were of Māori descent. The results of the 2013 census were not available at the time of publication

1 We at the Legal Māori Project are grateful to the Ministry of Business, Innovation and Employment for investing in the Legal Māori Project. Thanks are also due to Victoria University of Wellington for providing initial funds from the University Research Fund and the Library Contestable Fund.

it may be necessary to value richness and depth of lexical data over direct comparability.

b. *Investigation into how borrowings from the dominant language can change in usage over time yields potentially useful insights into lexical change in a diachronic corpus.* Unsurprisingly, borrowings from English legal language are common in Māori legal language. The presence and importance of such borrowings are not static, and their change in usage can provide useful insights into the struggles faced by any indigenous language group fighting to regenerate and revitalise all domains of a language, including legal language. In particular the profile of borrowings offers significant insight into the nature of lexical change over time, particularly in regard to the extent to which legal terms derived from English have maintained their original meanings or have changed in their use in Māori.
c. *Paying particular attention to customary legal terms will yield insights into how an indigenous language absorbs and expresses Western legal concepts.* The third insight presented in this chapter is that we learned early on during the compilation of our corpus that Māori customary legal concepts proved extremely important in identifying modern legal vocabulary, because a level of consonance may be seen to exist between the legal concepts at the heart of Western legal thinking, and the legal concepts at the heart of Māori legal thinking. It may be possible that this focus on traditional legal concepts may bear similar fruit for legal lexicography in other similar jurisdictions.

In order to further explore these insights, some background of the Legal Māori Project and our dictionary is necessary. Although the fact is very rarely acknowledged, the legal history of New Zealand is bilingual. From the earliest missionary-led translations of the New Testament in the early nineteenth century the Māori language has been used to communicate Western legal ideas. Further, Māori legal language has adapted and adopted those Western legal ideas, and the result is the existence of a significant legal vocabulary in Māori that has much to teach scholars of law and language in New Zealand about Māori legal thinking. This vocabulary also provides important insights into the development of the Māori lexicon that could be used to help facilitate effective language planning than can enable Māori to reclaim its rightful place within the New Zealand civic sphere.

The Legal Māori Project/He Kaupapa Reo ā-Ture based at the School of Law at Victoria University of Wellington set out in 2008 to collate, identify and describe, as far as possible, that vocabulary. Our final Project output: *He Papakupu Reo Ture – a Dictionary of Māori Legal Terms* (LexisNexis 2013) describes a representative portion of this legal vocabulary.

## Creating a Corpus

One of the first things to note is that this dictionary is corpus-based. We compiled a corpus of approximately eight million tokens or words of running text from thousands of pages of printed Māori language legal source documents dating from as early as 1828 and as recent as the end of 2009. We have not 'created' any terms for this dictionary; we have relied instead upon words already used by the authors of the texts in the Legal Māori Corpus to express legal concepts.[2] To qualify as a source document each lexical item had to meet the criteria necessary to comprise what we termed a 'legal Māori text'.

For a document to be classified as a legal Māori text for our purposes it had to meet the following criteria by being:

1. a text printed in Māori;[3]
2. dated from 1828–2009;
3. created *to be read or distributed* to 3 or more Māori speakers; and
4. created with the *communicative function* of explaining, clarifying, challenging and enacting Western Law.

These cumulative criteria have meant that the resulting corpus is very broad in its nature. It deals with Māori engagement with Western Law, as well as Crown and *Pākehā* (European) engagement with Māori within that context.[4] To deal appropriately with this breadth, we identified a number of different types of documents that, taken altogether, would provide a representative picture of Māori legal language and vocabulary. By ensuring we collated enough documents within each type (or 'category') no one category of documents is over-represented at the expense of other source documents. In this way the Legal Māori Corpus accurately represents the kinds of sources we found, and the resulting language is as representative as possible of printed legal Māori from 1828 until 2009. Each source document was assigned to one of the following categories of texts:

- *Category One: Official Crown language.* Such documents include *Kāhiti* (the official Māori language Gazette) notices, press-releases, policy documents, speeches in House and correspondence from Crown officials to Māori communities.

---

2 The sole exception to this rule is a small number of Māori language titles of organizations which do not appear in the corpus have been included to ensure the information provided is useful and current.

3 The prohibitive costs of digitizing handwritten sources meant that we restricted our sources to printed texts.

4 The term Pākehā refers to New Zealand settlers or inhabitants of European or Caucasian descent.

- *Category Two: Māori community generated language.* Texts in this category were directed primarily to the Crown and/or the wider community by Māori about legal matters, for example, Māori language petitions and submissions.
- *Category Three: Statutory language.* This category comprised bills and Acts, translated for, and disseminated amongst, Māori communities.
- *Category Four: Language of agreement.* This category included Māori language versions and translations of deeds and Crown/Māori agreements, modern Treaty settlement agreements, and other similar documents.
- *Category Five: Court and tribunal language.* These texts included (mainly) Native/Māori Land Court documents, transcripts, regulations and forms; as well as Waitangi Tribunal documentation. Also included here were some Māori language newspaper accounts of high profile trials from the nineteenth century.
- *Category Six: Quasi-legal language.* Texts included in this category comprised documents from predominantly Māori organizations that could not create legal consequences in the general legal system, but nevertheless provide an important source of Māori legal discourse. Examples include proceedings and documents of the Kotahitanga Parliaments, and Māori Anglican Synod and Native church board proceedings. The Kotahitanga Parliaments were established by the Kotahitanga pan-tribal movements of the 1880s and 1890s (Kawharu 1992: 221–40).

Table 15.1 gives the proportions of each category of text in the Legal Māori Corpus:

**Table 15.1 The complete Legal Māori Corpus by text category (numbers rounded)**

| Category of language | | No. of Tokens | No. of Documents | Time span |
|---|---|---|---|---|
| 01 | Crown language | 4,635,015 | 571 | 1840–2010 |
| 02 | Māori community language | 501,076 | 162 | 1939–2009 |
| 03 | Statutory language | 954,277 | 142 | 1845–2008 |
| 04 | Agreement and obligation | 600,445 | 34 | 1828–2009 |
| 05 | Courts and tribunals | 680,605 | 145 | 1856–2009 |
| 06 | Māori governing bodies | 505,277 | 34 | 1861–2008 |
| | Totals: | 7,876,695* | 1088 | |

* This figure refers to the total number of word tokens *excluding* numerals. 'Tokens' comprise all occurrences of any given word that appears in the Legal Māori Corpus.

Once the Corpus was compiled we interrogated the data in various ways to identify and research the vocabulary of the legal domain in Māori. The Legal Māori Project uses a customised version of the Freelex/Te Mātāpuna software as its dictionary writing system; this software was originally developed on open source protocols by Dave Moskowitz for Te Taura Whiri i te Reo Māori – the Māori Language Commission.[5] We also use WordSmith Tools v. 5 for certain types of analysis (Scott 2008).

There are a few notable and deliberate absences from this collection of texts. We excluded the Māori language translation of the *Bible*, despite its obvious importance to Māori language scholarship. While it contains legal language, and much of the vocabulary we identified does appear in the *Bible*, it is not in itself a legal text (as defined above), and, as a very large text, it would have skewed the balance and representative nature of the Corpus. For this reason we also did not include the entire texts of the Māori newspapers, also a very large and rich source of Māori language data. We did include a series of 11 trial accounts from seven of the newspapers, but otherwise excluded the Māori newspapers from inclusion in the corpus. Instead we included the Māori language *Kāhiti* (Gazette), a very large and important source of Māori legal language and vocabulary, that was published and disseminated to Māori communities from 1865–1933 (Parkinson and Griffith 2004). This was the official government gazette for disseminating official information to Māori, including public notices, appointments and proclamations, explanations of statutes, regulations and Native Land Court hearing notices, among other things. A massive source, in its entirety, we sampled it by including material from 10 yearly intervals to ensure that this one source did not skew the representative nature of the Corpus.

A large number of documents are what might be considered 'highly legal' in the language used, as they create and enact legal consequences. So, for example, there are several hundred land deeds and settlement agreements in the corpus. Other documents, however, reveal a vocabulary that is less formal. One very rich source comes to us from the pages of the *Appendices to the Journals of the House of Representatives*: hundreds of petitions, or summaries of those petitions, from Māori from the mid-nineteenth century well into the middle of the twentieth century, alongside Māori language submissions to Parliament in the latter years of the Corpus. While the language used in these petitions and submissions is less formal and structured, it still provides an invaluable source to determine how Māori viewed, and continue to view, the New Zealand legal system and its effect on Māori life. Similarly instructive are the speeches of Māori MPs from 1867 until 2009. Once again, such speeches alone do not create legal consequences and are influenced by the rules and procedures of Parliament, but they do provide a window into how the Māori language has been used to debate and communicate information about the major legal issues affecting Māori across that time period.

5 Further information about the Freelex/Mātāpuna system is available at http://dave.moskovitz.co.nz

While a majority of the sources texts do derive from the Crown in some way, we made a sustained effort to ensure that the language of Māori communities and groups has been represented in the corpus as much as possible. There will always be more sources that we could have included, and we look forward to adding further sources to the Corpus as time goes by.[6]

## The Challenge of Collating a Diachronic Corpus of Māori

A diachronic corpus comprising texts of a threatened indigenous language will yield rich and useful data, but may not provide true comparability between texts.

To create a diachronic corpus; that is, a corpus that could be used to analyse lexical change in the Māori language in the expression of legal concepts across time, the whole Corpus was divided into three sub-corpora:

- Collection 1: texts from 1828–1909;
- Collection 2: texts from 1910–69;
- Collection 3: texts from 1970–2009.

These date ranges reflected the fact that the range of sources tended to fall into three baskets. The set of 'historical texts', or texts sources available up until 1909, were generated across a period of time when the Crown sporadically enforced its own policy to use Māori to disseminate matters of legal importance. Collations of legislation translated into Māori, speeches in Parliament, official notices and collated, reprinted land deeds were all products of this policy. This was also a very textually complex time as Māori engaged with the power of print and the Crown, as well as with concepts of government and governance (Jones and Jenkins 2011; Parkinson 2001a). In turn, the Crown engaged with Māori in Māori, despite having no long-term plan to retain Māori as a civil language of the New Zealand state. Indeed, while Māori engagement with the Crown in Māori did not cease by 1909 the Crown policy for disseminating official information to Māori in Māori was dying by then. With this gradual policy death, Māori language sources that derive from Government disappear with a couple of exceptions (the *Kāhiti* and Native Affairs Committee reports, discussed below[7]).

The middle period of the Corpus (1910–69) therefore provides stark contrast with the historical period. From more than 5 million words from several hundred

6 We look forward, in particular, to including more oral sources. Although there are some oral transcripts (mainly from court proceedings) in the corpus, they do not constitute a structured representative sub-corpus of oral Māori legal language. To create such a corpus would be an important goal and would enhance our knowledge of Māori legal language significantly.

7 The *Kāhiti* continued until 1933; the Native Affairs Committee's bilingual reports until 1962.

documents up to 1909, the mid-period provides only 97 documents, and just over 813,000 words. There are simply far fewer texts available for analysis, mainly because the Crown had stopped producing many of them, and Māori also appear to have largely turned away from the use of Māori in engaging with the Crown in civic or legal matters.

By contrast again, the contemporary files of the Corpus (1970–2009) reflect changes in Crown policy, with a marked rise in the number of available sources from 1986, with nearly two million word tokens across more than 500 documents. This significant increase in Corpus texts after 1986 reflects a couple of significant changes in the language landscape. In the first instance there were changes in the Standing Orders in Parliament in 1986 that allowed Members of Parliament to speak Māori as of right.[8] This Standing Order was reinforced and confirmed in 1997 by a Speaker's Ruling (*NZPD* 1997, Vol. 562, 3192). By that stage the Standing Order had been in operation since 1985.

Secondly, the Māori Language Act 1987 ascribed official language status to Māori and provided a very circumscribed right only to speak Māori within most courts and tribunals. Both the status and the rights have been very under-developed in the succeeding 25 years since its enactment. Nevertheless the Crown began, as it had done in the nineteenth century to disseminate, or make available Māori language sources, such as pamphlets explaining, for example, individuals' tax obligations and statutory entitlements to legal aid, and the like, although the usefulness of these resources has never really been scrutinised.

Nevertheless use of Māori in Parliament greatly expanded in 1997, and again in 2005 with the introduction of new Māori MPs more willing to speak Māori and thereby utilise the new Standing Orders to their fullest extent (Stephens and Monk 2013). These policy changes also saw a rapid increase after 2004 of corporate documents being tabled in Parliament by Crown agencies and ministry units such as Te Puni Kōkiri (The Ministry of Māori Development) and Te Taura Whiri i te Reo Māori (the Māori Language Commission).[9] The same period witnessed enormous growth in the use of the Waitangi Tribunal as a forum for Māori claims against the Crown for breaches of the Treaty of Waitangi. Use by claimants of Māori in Waitangi Tribunal proceedings has been significant and provides an important vehicle for the Māori community voice in a discourse so often dominated by Crown imperatives.

So the Corpus clearly captures change in the use and prevalence of Māori in legal contexts. However, for the purpose of lexical analysis, the Corpus poses significant problems.

---

8 The House debated Standing Order 151 (later to be known as Standing Order 150, currently known as Standing Order 104) that established that Members of the House could elect to speak either Māori or English.

9 Te Taura Whiri i te Reo Māori (The Māori Language Commission) was set up under the Māori Language Act 1987 to promote the use of Māori as an ordinary means of communication.

*Problems of Comparability*

The Corpus certainly captures change in the kinds of source texts that in turn provided us with the Māori lexicon used to discuss or impart legal information. However, ensuring comparability of usage in the various periods covered by the corpus proved problematic. In other words, we wanted to ensure that we could compare 'like with like' across the spread of texts. This comparability would ensure that any comparison of identified vocabulary over time would be robust. The major obstacle we faced in achieving that comparability of texts was the lack of any source that survived through the Corpus decades, and through the three main corpus eras. There is no doubt of the marvellous richness of much of the Corpus texts, but there were only three sets of texts that were published for long periods of time that might have provided useful comparability across that period:

*The Kāhiti Published Between 1867 and 1933*

This was the official government gazette for disseminating official information to Māori, including public notices, appointments and proclamations, explanations of statutes and regulations and land court hearing notices, among other things. We included all *Kāhiti* issued in the course of one year produced every 10 years. There is arguably some comparability between the texts gathered at those intervals, as the same body issued these texts, with the same purpose across the entire time. But another argument can be made that the sheer variety of content (which precluded applying a consistent 'constructed sample' across any of the target years) may well undermine any argument of direct comparability.

*Native Affairs Committee/Māori Affairs Committee Reports Published from 1876–1962*

This publication contained, *inter alia*, brief summaries of the subjects of petitions to Parliament by Māori, and the Committees' responses to those petitions. These reports were tabled in the *Appendices to the Journals of the House of Representatives*. Established in 1872 one of the primary tasks of the Native Affairs Committee of the House of Representatives was to hear and report to the Government on all petitions formally submitted by Māori to the Crown (Ward 1995). While these texts are certainly comparable over the time of publication, which is useful, they do not provide as strong a basis for comparison as later select committee reports in Māori that feature in the corpus mainly from 2004 onwards.[10] At the end of 2008, bilingual printing and publication of reports into petitions submitted to the

10 Ten petitions have been reported on by the Māori Affairs Select Committee since 2005. Four of these have been reported on in te reo Māori. These petitions and all other select committee documentation are available at http.www.parliament.nz/en-NZ/PB/SC/Documents/Reports/

Committee for consideration were reintroduced, however these are significantly less voluminous. The majority of Māori language reports issued by the Committee are now very different in content, and the purpose of the documents are usually very different, with those latter documents mainly comprising explanatory notes regarding Bills before the House of Representatives.

*Speeches of Māori Members of Parliament*

These have been published in more than one format. One collection of such speeches comprises *Ngā Kōrero Pāremete,* which were bound collections of parliamentary speeches written in Māori for dissemination among Māori communities from 1881–1906. These records were Māori language translations of the English language translations of the Māori MPs' speeches originally delivered in Māori. These records were not, therefore, transcripts of the original speeches. Some speeches were also, on rare occasions, recorded in the *New Zealand Parliamentary Debates (Hansard)* after *Ngā Kōrero Pāremete* ceased but this was not common practice until the late twentieth century. Contemporary Māori MPs' speeches only began to appear regularly in *Hansard* after 1986. None of these sources provides continuity between the pre-1910 texts of the corpus and the post-1970 texts. There are some obvious similarities that can be drawn between the Māori MPs' recorded speeches post 1986, and the speeches translated in *Ngā Kōrero Pāremete*; the environment is effectively the same, the purpose for which the speeches are given is also largely the same (Stephens and Monk 2013). Nevertheless, the organ of publication is different, and the mode of language collection is different. *Ngā Kōrero Pāremete* were collations of speeches gathered for the purpose of dissemination to Māori communities. This is in contrast with *Hansard* which is a general record of the proceedings of New Zealand's House of Representatives. Further, the fact that there is a great gap in the record between 1906 and 1986 also makes it difficult to regard the later set of texts as a direct successor of the earlier set. Notwithstanding these factors, it is possible to argue that there is some level of comparability between the source texts, and the very richness of the texts obviously justifies their inclusion in the corpus.

Given the difficulty of creating a corpus comprising a set of comparable texts across the full 181 years, or even half of that time, it is not possible to claim that we have created a diachronic corpus of truly comparable texts (Macalister 2006). However, there is no doubting the richness of the texts contained in the corpus, and the structure of the corpus does enable some comparison of the incidence of words between the three main corpus eras.

Table 15.2 (below) shows the top 20 content words of a series of Legal Māori Corpus texts. Content words are those words that contain substantive meaning and do not merely perform some kind of grammatical function (such as definite articles *te* or *ngā* ('the' – singular and plural, respectively).

As can be seen below, Table 15.2 contains five columns. Column 1 contains the top 20 content words of parliamentary speeches as published in *Ngā Kōrero*

*Pāremete.* Column 2 contains the top 20 content words of the contemporary speeches by Māori MPs as reported in *Hansard.* Columns 3 and 4 provide similar data with two different sets of texts. Column 3 provides the top 20 content words for the nineteenth-century land deeds. Column 4 reveals the top 20 content words of the texts of contemporary Treaty of Waitangi settlement deeds entered into between various tribes and the Crown.

By way of comparison with a non-legal reference corpus, the top 20 content words of the Māori Broadcast Corpus ('MBC'), a structured corpus of oral Māori broadcast in the public domain and recorded in 1995/1996, have also been included (Boyce 2006).

**Table 15.2 Comparison of top 20 content words in selected texts of the Legal Māori Corpus and the MBC**

| 1. Historical Parliamentary speeches | 2. Contemporary Parliamentary speeches | 3. Historical Land Deeds (pre 1900) | 4. Settlements (post-2000) | 5. MBC |
|---|---|---|---|---|
| *Maori* | *Maori* | *whenua* ** | *whenua*** | *kōrero* |
| *whenua (land)* | *iwi* | *pukapuka (deed, agreement)* | *karauna (crown)* | *mea* |
| *mea (say (v) property (n))* | *korero* | *ingoa (name)* | *awa*** | *mahi* |
| *pire (Bill)* | *kaupapa (issue, claim, topic)* | *kuini (queen)* | *tau*** | *haere* |
| *mema (member of Parliament)* | *mahi* | *tohu (signature, sign)* | *iwi* | *hoki* |
| *kawanatanga (government)* | *hapū (tribe, sub-tribe)* | wahi (section, partition, subdivide, place) | *mahi* | *Māori* |
| *mahi (activity, work)* | *mea* | *Moni* | *hoki (return)* | *wā* |
| *whare (house, chamber)* | *tikanga* | *rau (hundred)* | *mana (authority, authorise, enact)* | *iwi* |
| *tangata (person, people)* | *tau* | *rohe (boundary, territory)* | *ture* | *kaupapa* |
| *ture (statute, law)* | *whare* | *tangata*** | *mea* | *tau* |
| *tikanga (provision, clause, method)* | *whenua (land)* | *awa** (river)* | *tangata*** | *reo* |
| *korero (address, speak)* | *wa (time, term)* | *pauna (pound)* | *noho* | *whakaaro (thought)* |
| *tika (correct, interest, valid)* | *pire* | *utu (pay, price, consideration)* | *tikanga*** | *noho* |

| **1. Historical Parliamentary speeches** | **2. Contemporary Parliamentary speeches** | **3. Historical Land Deeds (pre 1900)** | **4. Settlements (post-2000)** | **5. MBC** |
|---|---|---|---|---|
| *take (claim, interest)* | *noho (settle, live)* | *tau*** | *uri (descendant)* | *whare* |
| *iwi (people, tribe)* | *reo (language, voice)* | *tuku (alienate, lodge, sell, grant)* | *Māori* | *whenua* |
| *moni (money)* | *tangata* | taha (side) | nui | tū |
| tau (settle, grant, vest, year) | wāhi (section, place) | rere (fly – used in determining land boundaries) | tiriti (treaty) | mohio (know, knowledge) |
| nui (big, many, large) | nui | riro (acquire, receive, transfer) | haere (go) | tekau |
| kupu (statement, address, word) | tautoko (support, endorse) | kingi (king) | take | ora |
| pai (good) | whakaae (agree) | tikanga** | tae (arrive) | pai |

Columns 1 to 4 show the top 20 highest frequency content words from selected sources from the Legal Māori Corpus. Column 5 shows the top 20 highest frequency content words from the Māori Broadcast Corpus. *Highlighted* words are all words that appear in Column 1 and in *at least* one other column. Words with ** are words in common between Columns 3 and 4. Note: not all ** words are underlined, as not all words in common between Columns Three and Four are also featured in Column 1. The English glosses are indicative only. Words in Columns 1 and 3 are not macronised, as no macrons were used in the relevant historical source texts.

Columns 1 and 2 – the words in Column 1 serve to provide the primary list of words for comparison with the words in Columns 2, 3, 4 and 5. Note that modern Māori uses macrons to denote length, and that macronised words feature in Column 5, while Columns 1 to 4 feature mainly non-macronised words as most texts in the corpus were printed before the widespread use of macrons (See Lüpke in Austin and J Sallabank 2011). Only five of the high frequency words in Column 1 do NOT appear in any other column. Columns 1 and 2 show, respectively, the 20 highest frequency content words that feature in the texts that comprise *Ngā Kōrero Pāremete* and the 20 highest frequency content words that comprise contemporary parliamentary speeches by Māori MPs. The data above reveals that 12 of the 20 highest frequency words are common between those two sets of texts. Even separated by at least 70 years, this suggests a reasonable amount of similarity between both Column 1 and Column 2, as might be expected when the environment is similar, and the purpose of the texts, the recording of parliamentary speeches in Māori, is also similar. This characteristic may make these two sets of texts somewhat more comparable than other sets of texts in Table 15.1.

Columns 3 and 4 – Column 3 enables a comparison to be made between that the words of Column 1 and the same query made of another important set of texts in the corpus: land deeds. This source is quite specialised and technical; many of the deeds follow a very similar format, even across many decades, and they are functional legal documents that enact a contractual relationship between parties in regard to land. Unsurprisingly *fewer* words are shared between the high frequency content words of the parliamentary speeches of Column 1 and the land deeds of Column 3. Only five of the 20 highest frequency content words in those texts in Column 3 are shared with the words of Column 1.

Similarly to Column 3, Column 4 also contains texts that might be said, at first glance, to be comparable with the texts of Column 3. Column 4 contains words frequent in the texts of contemporary (post-1995) Deeds of Settlement entered into between the Crown and Māori pursuant to the settlement of (mainly historical and land-based) grievances. However, as can be seen by entries marked with **, only five words appear in common between these two sets of texts separated by so much time and context. While both sets of texts reflect *agreements*, the purposes of each set of texts is quite different: the sale and purchase of land (Column 3), and excerpts from an agreement about the nature of the wrongs committed and redress to be provided for such wrongs, in the case of the settlement texts (Column 4). In addition, while the texts of Column 3 enacted legal consequences, the texts of Column 4 do not, as all the substantive and operative clauses of those settlement agreements were only enacted in legislative form in English. This possible decline in specialization and functionality for the texts of Column 4 may be reflected by the fact that Column 4 shares 11 of its high frequency content words with Column 1, and 9 with Column 5 (the reference Māori Broadcast Corpus).

So although the *topic* of each set of agreement texts is often similar (the sale and purchase of land), the different purposes and content from which these documents derive make direct comparison between the texts from Column 3 and Column 4 very problematic.

### *The Māori Broadcast Corpus and a Comment on Comparability*

As further comparison with a general set of texts outside a legal context, the Māori Broadcast Corpus (Column 5) shares nine of its highest frequency content words with the words in Column 1 (historical parliamentary texts), and with Column 4 (settlement texts) (Boyce 2006). Column 5 also shares 12 words in common with Column 2 (contemporary parliamentary speeches). By comparison, Column 3 and Column 5 only share *two* words in common. This data serves to strengthen the impression that the texts of Column 3 are the most specialised set of texts in this collection. Conversely this data also makes it possible to suggest that the texts of the sets of parliamentary speeches and settlement texts are somewhat *less* specialised or technical, as shown by the fact that Columns 1, 2 and 4 share significantly more words with Column 5.

Some argument can be made for limited comparability for at least two significant sets of texts in the Corpus (as shown by Columns 1 and 2 above). But the data in Columns 3 and 4 also shows the difficulty of finding comparability in other sets of texts. Some texts (such as land deeds) are highly specialised and technical, while later documents (settlement texts) that might appear broadly comparable have been stripped of their legal functionality and therefore, arguably, of at least some specialization and technicality of vocabulary. The frequency lists of the parliamentary speeches and the settlement texts appear to show more general Māori vocabulary, as indicated by comparison with the frequency list of the Māori Broadcast Corpus. This variability in specialization and technicality also make comparability between sets of texts, separated by many decades, difficult.

These observations preclude any conclusion that the texts across all three eras of the corpus are easily comparable. However, this data (limited though it is) offers a representative picture of the nature of legal discourse in printed Māori across those eras. For that reason we consider the richness of the texts to be of a very high value; and comparability, while still of great worth where it can be found, is necessarily of secondary importance.

As also discussed below, the frequency of the terms in *He Papakupu Reo Ture: A Dictionary of Māori Legal Terms* wax and wane across the three corpus periods. This changeability reflects the changing nature of the source texts from whence the entries derive. This changeability also reflects the nature of legal discourse, and the real history of the people, as they also change across those three identifiable eras.

### *From Corpus to Dictionary: The Making of a Lexicon*

The Legal Māori Corpus provided approximately 58,315 word types (individual words that appeared at least once in the corpus) (Boyce and Stephens 2013).[11] With such a large number of word types it became very important to identify a method of selecting terms that could form the basis of the dictionary. We did not have the capacity to read all documents in order to identify all potential legal Māori terms that might be included in the dictionary. However we wanted to create a lexicon, or list of words and phrases, that ought to comprise good candidates for inclusion in the dictionary. To be able to create such a lexicon from such a massive amount of data, in the first instance it was important to have a common understanding of words and phrases that would be 'legal enough' for inclusion in the dictionary. We utilised the following definition of a legal Māori term:

> A word or phrase that has *at least* one meaning where that meaning is ***closely*** *related* to Western legal concepts.

11 Research is currently underway to determine rates of error within corpus texts and to identify the primary causes of such error. Once completed it is expected that a number of these word types will be found to be errors. The research is to be completed by the end of 2013.

In our view, legal terms in Māori are those terms used by fluent speakers of Māori for professional communication in Western legal contexts. These legal Māori terms form part of the specialised language used in the legal domain. It is important to note that we did not focus on technical terms alone. Such technical terms are complemented with more common words also often used in the legal domain, words that are typical of and occur more frequently in legal contexts than in the language in general. This vocabulary is also useful for those who use Māori to express legal meaning.

With our definition of a legal Māori term in mind we designed three main methods to collate a lexicon of legal Māori terms. From this lexicon we would derive our final set of dictionary entries. The three methods included:

1. undertaking a pilot project of sample corpus texts;
2. reader lists; and
3. utilizing existing dictionaries.

Further description of our work on this phase is set out below.

*The Pilot Project*

In 2008–09 we carried out a pilot project to test out our processes, procedures and identification of legal Māori terminology (Stephens 2008). To pilot our identification processes we created three small pilot outputs: a small Pilot Corpus consisting of a very small number of selected texts from the texts gathered for the main corpus:

1. Māori language speeches recorded in *Ngā Kōrero Paremete* from 1902 to 1903; and
2. Māori language speeches recorded in *Hansard* between 2006 and 2008.

These texts met the criteria of being legal Māori texts. These pilot texts were comparable in type, and separated by roughly a century. These texts were marked up to exclude all proper names and non-Māori words from analysis.

From this small corpus we identified a list of terms (the Pilot Lexicon) that met the criteria of being identifiably legal Māori terminology. This pilot lexicon was intended to help us to determine if we were able to accurately and consistently identify legal Māori terminology.

From this Pilot Lexicon we created a pilot, or sample, dictionary.[12] We took terms from the Pilot Lexicon and tested how those terms feature within the Legal Māori Corpus, which had been collated by that stage (following Chung 2004). We spent some time identifying the extent of the legal meanings of the terms from the

12 The sample dictionary is available for download from http://www.victoria.ac.nz/law/research/research-projects/past-research-projects/legal-maori/dictionary

pilot lexicon as they now appeared in the larger corpus. We also crafted dictionary entries based on usage examples derived from the complete Corpus.

This process was successful insofar as it proved a useful testing ground for our notion of a 'legal Māori term'. The sample dictionary also profiled a number of the entries that included substantial references to customary Māori legal concepts. This information we pursued further, as will be described shortly.

*Reader lists* We had seven Māori-speaking lawyers or Māori-speaking law graduates employed as researchers at this stage of the Legal Māori Project. Using their language skills and their abilities to identify Western legal concepts at work in Māori language texts we selected a broad range of Corpus documents from across the corpus text categories and across most of the time periods covered by the corpus (1828–2009) for a reading programme. In this step, seven researchers were given a selection of texts from each category of the Legal Māori Corpus.

*Category One*: readers for this category read a selection of contemporary official publications such as Legal Services Agency booklets, and contemporary MPs' speeches.

*Category Two*: readers for this category read through the all available texts of the letters sent by Māori to Native Minister Donald Mclean in 1839, as well as selected trial-related from nineteenth-century Māori newspapers such as *Te Wānanga*, *Te Karere Māori* and *Te Waka Māori o Niu Tīreni*.

*Category Three*: readers for this category read Government Acts and Bills from the years 1892, 1893, 1897, 1898, 1899, 1905, and 1908. In addition readers gathered Māori language terms used in recent/current legislation.

*Category Four*: readers for this category identified appropriate terms in land deeds from the years 1873 and 1879, and in selected modern documents such as the Taupō Joint Management Agreement.

*Category Five*: readers for this category identified terms from transcripts of post-1975 Māori Land Court proceedings and selected Waitangi Tribunal evidence and hearings.

*Category Six*: the reader for this category identified terms gathered from a selection of the Anglican Synod proceedings as well as from a set of Māori Parliament proceedings.

From these texts each researcher identified a list of possible words and phrases that they considered communicated Western legal concepts.

### *Dictionaries and Wordlists*

In this step we sought to use the expertise of lexicographers who had already identified Māori words and phrases used to denote Western legal meaning. During this stage our researchers consulted a collection of dictionaries, wordlists and compendia in order to identify existing Māori terms with identifiable legal meaning that had already been identified as such by the makers of those dictionaries and wordlists.

In addition to these three methods we checked the high frequency words of the Corpus as a check to ensure that we were not inadvertently omitting potentially important high-frequency words and phrases that had not already been identified at the lexicon stage.

All terms identified by these methods were recorded in a spreadsheet with appropriate glosses; the list was subsequently checked for duplications, spelling variants and the like. This output was the Legal Māori Lexicon, and at the end of 2010 stood at 2,614 words and phrases.[13] Over the following two years as we commenced work on the dictionary itself we discovered many more terms and the Lexicon itself grew to more than 5000 words and phrases, all of which could potentially have been included in the dictionary.

One way of ensuring the quality of dictionary entries was to apply certain thresholds for the inclusion of words and phrasal entries. One threshold, applied in respect of most entries, with the exception of titles, was that each entry must appear at least three times in the Corpus. Further, as a high number of entries in this lexicon included phrases incorporating two or more words we also wanted to ensure, as far as possible, that phrases included in the dictionary were 'salient' – that they had sufficient 'glue' holding them together so that the phrase itself ought to be considered to have its own lexical identity; a state otherwise known as 'lexicalisation' (Lipka, Handl and Falkner 2004; Bauer 1983). In other words, we wanted to include only those words and phrases communicating meaning as a single lexical unit, with specific content through frequent use. We wanted to ensure we avoided including a large number of words and phrases that may be merely 'descriptive' or 'stylistic' and not strictly terms.

As noted above the Legal Māori Corpus shows a great deal of change in the nature of its texts, making comparability difficult. One important consequence of this characteristic of the Corpus is that many terms of *He Papakupu Reo Ture* wax and wane in their frequency within the Corpus texts across a time period of 181 years. To some degree this changeability is reflected in the dictionary. Of 2,114 entries in the dictionary only 716 appear throughout the entire time covered by Corpus texts (1828–2009): 1208 entries *only* appear after 1970, and 710 entries *only* appear before 1910 whilst 1,168 entries do not feature *at all* between 1910 and 1970. This aspect indicates that most legal vocabulary we identified is not shared across the Corpus, and this observation reflects the issues about comparability between texts in the Legal Māori Corpus, but also reflects possible change in usage over time as well. One fruitful avenue for exploring lexical change over time is to explore the patterns associated with borrowings from English and how those borrowings are expressed in Māori.

---

13 Available for download at http://nzetc.victoria.ac.nz/tm/scholarly/tei-legalMaoriCorpus.html#legal_maori_lexicon

## Legal Terms Derived from English

Investigation into how borrowings from the dominant language can change in usage over time yields potentially useful insights into lexical change in a diachronic corpus.

Just as the texts of the Legal Māori Corpus reflect enormous change faced by the Māori language community, the nature and extent of borrowings from English are also changeable. How this change occurs offers significant insight into the broader nature of lexical change in legal Māori vocabulary over time, particularly in regard to the extent to which the legal terms derived from English have maintained their original meanings or have changed in their use in Māori.

One effect of the colonization of Aotearoa and the forming of New Zealand was the introduction of Western legal systems and practices. With these came the need for new words and expressions in Māori. Some of these new meanings were achieved by new uses of existing terms, for example through gaining new word senses. Many new words in the legal domain, as in the language as a whole, were acquired by assimilating the phonology of an English legal term into the phonological system of Māori – these are commonly referred to as 'transliterations'. Thus the English word 'court' became *kooti* in Māori.[14] Such borrowings are common in the legal domain, and especially so in the pre-1910 texts (see also Moorfield and Ka'ai 2011). In contemporary times there has been some avoidance of transliteration as a strategy, and preference given to other ways of acquiring new vocabulary.

In the recent texts there is evidence that neologisms with legal meanings have been coined by drawing on the resources of the Māori language. Some of the terms used in contemporary times include words that may have fallen out of use, being revived to replace the original borrowings from English (see below for the example of Māori words for 'claim').

In addition to the continuing research pertaining to such neologisms, words derived from English are also being examined within the Corpus to learn more about their frequencies, their collocations, the phrases or multi-word units they occur in, and their use over time. This work is on-going and large in scale. We report here on the early phase of this work.

### *Frequent Words Derived from English in the Legal Māori Corpus*

For this research, the complete Legal Māori Corpus was run through WordSmith Tools v. 5 to generate a wordlist, and this wordlist was then scanned manually to identify words derived from English or languages other than Māori. The rank, frequency and range across texts of these 'borrowed' items were then recorded.

14 Kooti occurs with the spelling kōti in more contemporary texts, though the original spelling is still to be found.

Their frequency across the three time periods of the corpus was also plotted by running each of the period 'chunks' or sub-corpora through WordSmith separately.

Table 15.3 shows the top ten borrowed legal terms from each time period with simple English glosses to aid those readers who do not speak Māori. The table also shows that just three items appeared in the top ten across all three time periods: *ture, kooti/kōti* and *kawanatanga/kāwanatanga* (law, court and government). A further two, *komiti* and *moni* (committee and money), appear in the top ten items in both the historical and the middle period.

**Table 15.3 The top ten 'borrowed' legal terms from each time period, with indicative glosses. Time period indicated by H – historical, M – mid-period, C – contemporary**

| Type | Indicative gloss | Time period |
|---|---|---|
| Karauna | Crown (as in 'the Crown') | C |
| kawana | governor, government | H |
| kawanatanga, kāwanatanga | government | H, M, C |
| komiti | committee | H, M |
| kooti, kōti | court | H, M, C |
| Kura | school | C |
| mema | member (of Parliament) | H |
| moni | money | H, M |
| Nama | debt, bill | M |
| pire | bill (of Parliament) | H |
| pitihana | petition | M |
| poraka | block (of land) | H |
| Pōti | election, vote | C |
| pukapuka | letter, document, book | H |
| ripoata | report | M |
| Tari | department, ministry | C |
| tekiona | section (of legislation) | M |
| Tiriti | treaty | C |
| ture* | law, statute | H, M, C |

* It is to be noted that the word 'ture' is not derived from English, but is from the Hebrew word 'torah'. All other borrowed terms here derive from English.

Table 15.4 shows the rank frequency of the ten most common of those 'borrowed' terms from each time period. Of course the non-appearance of a given item in these lists of the ten most frequent borrowed legal words does not mean that the word is not used at all in a specific time period; this is merely a list of the top items.

**Table 15.4 The top ten 'borrowed' legal terms across time in rank frequency per sub-corpus**

| pre-1910 | | 1910–1969 | | 1970–2010 | |
|---|---|---|---|---|---|
| *rank* | *type* | *rank* | *type* | *rank* | *type* |
| 33 | ture | 21 | ture | 44 | ture |
| 42 | moni | 26 | pitihana | 72 | karauna |
| 54 | kooti | 30 | nama | 82 | kāwanatanga |
| 56 | kawanatanga | 36 | komiti | 98 | tiriti |
| 58 | pire | 39 | ripoata | 110 | tari |
| 67 | pukapuka | 42 | poraka | 132 | moni |
| 76 | mema | 43 | moni | 151 | kōti |
| 82 | komiti | 49 | tekiona | 175 | pōti |
| 113 | kawana | 56 | kawanatanga | 202 | kura |
| 114 | poraka | 57 | kooti | 227 | kooti |

It is interesting to consider the possible reasons for a term falling into disuse over time or being eventually replaced by another. One useful example of such an exploration arises with the term *moni* (money). *Moni* appears in the historic and mid periods in the top ten list, but *not* in the contemporary period. Money is a fundamental medium of exchange and was so across all three time periods in the corpus, therefore exploring the reasons behind the decline in frequency of this term could well be useful.

*Expressing 'money'*

A preliminary look at the distribution of the word *moni* in the Legal Māori Corpus indicated that it might be less frequent in the contemporary legal domain than in the two earlier periods. It ranked at 42 and 43 in the historical and mid periods respectively, and appeared in each of their top ten lists. It did not appear in the top ten list in the contemporary period.

We first examined the frequency rank of *moni* across the Legal Māori Corpus as a whole, and compared this with its presence in the three time periods of the corpus, and with the Māori Broadcast Corpus, as shown in Table 15.5. The column to the right shows the percentage of the texts in the corpus or sub-corpus that *moni* occurred in.

**Table 15.5 A comparison of the distribution of *moni* across the Legal Māori Corpus and Māori Broadcast Corpus**

| MONI | Rank | Freq. | % of all texts |
|---|---|---|---|
| Legal Māori Corpus overall | 49 | 24,756 | 50.46 |
| Historical Period | 42 | 19,712 | 67.06 |
| Mid-Period | 43 | 2995 | 79.59 |
| Contemporary Period | 131 | 1958 | 32.93 |
| Māori Broadcast Corpus | 213 | 532 | 58.97 |

We can see that while the word *moni* is among the 50 most frequent words of the complete Legal Māori Corpus, it 'slips' to a rank of 131 in the contemporary sub-corpus. It occurs in about a third of the texts of the contemporary sub-corpus, whereas it occurs in two-thirds or more of the texts in the other two sub-corpora. This shows a tendency to be less frequent in modern legal texts.

We decided that money is no less important or relevant in the domain nowadays, and wondered if the transliteration *moni*, from English money, was being replaced with *another* word. We decided to look at the word *pūtea*, to see how it was distributed in the corpus.

*Pūtea* is listed in *Te Matatiki*, a dictionary of neologisms, with the following glosses: finance, financial, bank account, fund (Te Taura Whiri i te Reo Māori 1996). *Te Matatiki* indicates that these are based on the listing in the Williams dictionary (Williams 1971: 317):

> **Pūtē, pūtea,** n. Bag or basket of fine woven flax, for clothes, etc. A wetenga iho taku pūtē rei (M. 323). Tō pūtea te āta take i runga i tō ringaringa (M. 40).

There is no word given under 'money' in *Te Matatiki*. This strongly suggests that the common word *moni* was still in use, hence there was no impetus for the creation of a neologism. In the 4th edition of the Ryan dictionary, 'budget' is an additional gloss. (Ryan 1995) Similar glosses associated with money and finance are found in the Ngata dictionary. *He Papakupu Reo Ture* glosses *pūtea* primarily as 'fund' (Stephens and Boyce 2013: 61).

In the Māori Broadcast Corpus *moni* ranks at 213; it occurred 532 times, and ranged across 58.97 per cent of the texts in that corpus. *Pūtea* ranks at 231, occurs 485 times, across 58.24 per cent of the texts in that corpus. These two words are roughly equivalent in frequency and range.

If we now look at *pūtea* in the Legal Māori Corpus, we see a different picture. First we need to identify the various spellings for *pūtea*. It has a single spelling, *putea*, in the historical and mid-periods. In the contemporary period there are several spellings as shown on Table 15.6:

**Table 15.6 Spellings of *pūtea***

| Word | Freq. |
|---|---|
| Putea | 251 |
| Pūtea | 2,722 |
| Pūteā | 1 |
| Pūtēa | 1 |
| Puutea | 4 |
| Puūtea | 1 |

For our purposes, we will consider only those spellings that occurred more than 50 times: *putea* and *pūtea*. These are presented separately and aggregated in Table 15.6. We can further look at representing the rank frequency of an aggregate of the two most prominent forms of *pūtea* in the complete corpus, as shown in Table 15.7. In the complete Corpus, the form *putea* occurred 251 times, *pūtea* occurred 2,722 times, a total of 2973. This places *pūtea* within the top 300 words overall. It is a high-frequency item.

**Table 15.7 A comparison of the distribution of *pūtea* and *putea* across the Legal Māori Corpus and Māori Broadcast Corpus**

| Pūtea and putea | Rank | Freq. | % of all texts |
|---|---|---|---|
| Legal Māori Corpus overall | | | |
| putea | 1,392 | 251 | 6.38 |
| pūtea | 308 | 2,722 | 12.66 |
| aggregated putea and pūtea | 293 | 2,973 | – |
| Historical Period | 10,781 | 4 | 0.48 |
| Mid-Period | 779 | 45 | 8.16 |
| Contemporary Period | | | |
| putea | 766 | 184 | 10.40 |
| pūtea | 95 | 2,722 | 24.09 |
| aggregated putea and pūtea | 88 | 2,906 | – |
| Māori Broadcast Corpus | 231 | 485 | 58.24 |

*Pūtea* occurred only four times in the historical period, and just 45 times in the mid-period. There is a clear increase in its use over time in legal settings. This is best seen by looking at its occurrences in words per million, as shown in Table 15.8.

**Table 15.8 Relative presence per million words of *pūtea* in the Legal Māori Corpus and the Māori Broadcast Corpus**

| Pūtea | Most frequent forms of pūtea | Frequency of those forms | Occurrences per million words |
|---|---|---|---|
| 1828–1909<br>5.243 million words | Putea | 4 | 0.76 |
| 1910–69<br>0.759 million words | Putea | 45 | 59.28 |
| 1970–2009<br>1.857 million words | putea and pūtea | 2906 | 1564.89 |
| Māori Broadcast Corpus<br>(1 million words) | Pūtea | 485 | 485.00 |

While the figures in Table 15.7 show an increase in the use of the word *pūtea* across time, these 'raw' counts are not adequate on their own to determine the presence of certain meanings of a word. As we saw above, the original meaning of *pūtea* (as given in the Williams dictionary) was for a finely woven flax bag to hold clothing. Is this meaning relevant in a legal context? To investigate this it was necessary to look at each occurrence of the word in its surrounding context to determine meanings.

When a concordance was prepared for the four occurrences of *pūtea* in the historical sub-corpus, it was found that none of the four was being used with the financial meaning. Three were a personal name – Hera Putea – and one was part of a place name – Tihi-o-Putea. So, *pūtea* was not used at all for financial meanings in the historical period.

In contrast, in the middle period the 45 uses of *pūtea* all occurred with financial meanings. When we scanned the concordance lines it was clear that *pūtea* was often used with *moni* in close proximity, both to the left and to the right. To the left, *moni reti* ('rent money'), occurred four times, and *moni whiwhi* ('acquired money'), occurred four times. Including these, *moni* appeared 20 times on the left in close proximity. In addition it was noted that specific sums of money sometimes appeared to the left, and words like *wariu* (value), and *nama* (debt), and *wira* (will) also occurred. The expression *putea moni* (fund of money) occurred 16 times, *putea karahipi* (*scholarship fund*) occurred three times.

Table 15.9 shows the 'patterns' tab output from WordSmith for *pūtea* in the mid-period. It shows the most frequent items in positions to the left and right of the target word. So, *moni* is the most frequent item in the third position to the left, and in the first position to the right of *pūtea.*

**Table 15.9 Patterns of occurrence around *pūtea* in the Legal Māori Corpus mid-period**

| N | L5 | L4 | L3 | L2 | L1 | Centre | R1 | R2 | R3 | R4 | R5 |
|---|---|---|---|---|---|---|---|---|---|---|---|
| 1 | | NGA | MONI | O | TE | PUTEA | MONI | NGA | NGA | | O |
| 2 | | | | KI | TAUA | | MO | MO | TE | | MAORI |
| 3 | | | | I | HEI | | | | | | |

To summarise, it can be seen that the use of *pūtea* with financial meanings increased from no use in the historical period to 59.28 uses per million words in the mid period and 1564.89 uses per million in the contemporary period.

As matters stand it is not possible to state conclusively that the transliteration *moni* is being 'replaced' by the Māori derived word *pūtea* with its newly evolved financial meanings. For one thing *moni* has remained in use, and is reasonably frequent, as it is still to be found in the contemporary period in the top 150 most frequent words. For another, there may be other words with financial meanings that may also have contributed to the relative decline of *moni.* Other candidates include *hua* which is glossed in Williams as fruit, egg and produce. This term has also become increasingly used with financial meanings. Both *He Papakupu Reo Ture* and *Te Matatiki* have glossed *hua* as [financial] asset, and it appears in the Legal Māori Corpus in collocation with other words to communicate financial senses. Such phrases include *hua wātea* (current asset), *hua pūmau* (permanent asset, interest) *hua itareti* (interest).

Nevertheless the *pūtea* data is interesting and points the way to further research into the role of transliterations, such as *moni*, over time in Māori.

### *How is Lexical Change Over Time Reflected in He Papakupu Reo Ture: A Dictionary of Māori Legal Terms?*

For *He Papakupu Reo Ture* this change in the use of terms over time is important to capture, where possible, within the dictionary article. In our case temporal usage of terms is marked by identifying the corpus eras the terms appear in (at least three times). Terms that appear before 1910 are marked <HIST>, terms that appear in the middle era are marked <MID> and terms that appear from 1970 on are marked <CONT>. If the term appears across all periods, there is no marker of temporal usage. The attention paid to the waxing and waning of certain terms prompted us to create two categories of terms that are easily identifiable and offer more information about lexical change over time within the dictionary entries.

Some terms have been included that may not have much life in the Māori-speaking world beyond their inclusion in this dictionary. We have offered them, in part, to assist users who may come across them in texts and not know what they mean. They have also been included to provide some idea as to how legal usage has changed over time. For example, there are a number of old transliterations that may have no further role to play in the development of the Māori lexicon. Such examples might include *pikami* – bigamy, *mū* – move (a motion or amendment), and *tipenetua* – debenture. Their presence, however, is warranted as evidence of the important role of borrowings from English in the legal terminology of earlier decades. In addition, these transliterations appear in some of the usage examples of other entries, so are required to ensure the usage example is fully understandable to the user. These transliterations are distinctive because they have no usage example, and are italicised.

There is another group of terms that only appears in Corpus documents post-1990. These terms (like the now obsolete transliterations) will often be very limited in range, appearing frequently, but confined to a few documents. Many who have worked with documents in modern Māori will attest to the opacity and complexity of the vocabulary used in some of these documents. The simplicity and clarity of pre-1970 documents, notwithstanding the presence of transliterations, is startling when compared with many (although certainly not all) of the modern source texts. Some of the modern terms we have included may prove to have a life in years to come, others will, rightfully, fall by the lexical wayside for want of use.

Both kinds of terms are recognisable in this dictionary: in the case of the obsolete transliterations they are distinguished by their lack of usage example and the latter class of terms are usually marked ‘LD’ for having low distribution.

The final insight we offer in this chapter to legal lexicographers is the necessity of paying attention to the importance of the customary legal concepts of the minority language when constructing a dictionary of legal terms. As our experience demonstrated, this focus not only gave richness to many of our entries, it also provided us with our primary principle for organizing our dictionary.

## Māori Customary Law – a Primary Organizing Principle for a Dictionary

*Paying particular attention to customary legal terms will yield insights into how an indigenous language absorbs and expresses Western legal concepts.*

*He Papakupu Reo Ture: A Dictionary of Māori Legal Terms* presents words and phrases used to express Western legal ideas. It is not a dictionary of Māori customary law terms. However Māori customary law terms have a very significant presence within the Corpus. This observation became very clear to us when undertaking our pilot study. The final set of dictionary entries necessarily has as its core a set of Māori customary law terms that have themselves developed Western legal senses and applications.

In our view, as a result of our experience, the starting point for the development of a legal lexicon at least in the case of the Māori, and likely for others, is traditional legal concepts of the language community. Such concepts include notions of exchange, obligation, correct process, offence against community values, harm to individuals and groups, rights of property and rights of use; it would be difficult to conceive of any functioning culture for which such ideas have no meaning. Consequently a great deal of what we have been identifying as Māori legal terminology has, at its heart, a robust and distinctive customary idea as manifested in practice. The numerous senses of the word *utu* in *He Papakupu Reo Ture* provide illustration of the congruence between two sets of legal ideas. The distance travelled from *utu* being used to communicate the concept of 'reciprocity in exchange' in Māori traditional legal thinking to its use to then describe, communicate and adapt the Western legal notion of 'consideration' is not a long one.

Although recognizing that customary legal terms were going to be vitally important in the organization of the dictionary we still had to decide *which* Māori law terms would serve as this customary core, which would get special attention in the layout of the dictionary. To find our 'core' we turned to the research undertaken by Te Mātāhauariki Research Institute at the University of Waikato. Te Mātāhauariki itself was an entity designed to: 'explore the possibilities for the evolution of laws and institutions in New Zealand to reflect the best of the values and concepts of both founding peoples of the state, Māori and European'. That institute's important resource (Benton, Frame and Meredith 2013) *Te Mātāpunenga, a Compendium of References to the Concepts and Institutions of Māori Customary Law* ('Te Mātāpunenga') provided researchers at the Legal Māori Project with an alphabetical compendium of concepts and institutions of Māori customary law that the institute found to be in use in historical and contemporary Māori discourse, both written and oral. The terms of this compendium came to serve as our core of customary legal Māori terms.

As a result of our focus on *Mātāpunenga* terms we now had an ability to prioritise our completion of dictionary entries. The Legal Māori Project has limited resources for creating the final dictionary and we needed to create a robust and principled system for deciding which terms to include (once identified) and which to exclude. This system would, intentionally or otherwise, reveal our preferences for certain types of legal Māori vocabulary and should be open to scrutiny. In fact, our system for prioritizing which terms would be included in the final product identifies the following types of terms, in descending order of importance:

1. terms that belong to the identified core of customary Māori legal terms;
2. terms comprising a phrasal variation using one of the terms in (1);
3. a 'born Māori' term, with at least one highly legal meaning;
4. a 'born English' term; a loanword with at least one highly legal meaning;
5. a title from a relevant legal context;
6. 'general legal language', non-technical vocabulary that has a high frequency in legal Māori texts.

Our researchers thereafter were allocated entries to complete according to this prioritization. One researcher was given the primary task of identifying how *Mātāpunenga* terms appeared in the Corpus. We had already identified most of these terms as a part of the process of building the lexicon, but this phase involved identifying the customary concept at work in a given *Mātāpunenga* term, and then identifying within the Corpus how that term was used to express Western legal ideas. We also identified phrases that included those customary terms within them. Of particular interest is the fact that out of a total of 2,114 entries, 894 entries, or 42 per cent of all entries fall into level (1) or (2) above.

The corpus clearly revealed that Māori customary legal ideas as expressed in terms such as *utu* and the like have generated a wealth of senses and phrases that, in addition to highlighting Māori law ideas, now also reflect and communicate Western legal notions. So while this dictionary does not purport to explicate intricate layers of Māori law, it does recognise a set of Māori legal ideas that reside at the heart of modern Māori legal language. To understand the interface between Māori law principles and the New Zealand legal system, as revealed by written documents, this resultant terminology is critically important.

*Reflecting the Primacy of Customary Terms in the Dictionary Format*

The next important question to settle was how to design the dictionary article to reflect customary legal ideas at the heart of so many of our entries. Another Māori language dictionary provided us with one suggested route to acknowledge the pre-eminence of customary thinking in the dictionary format. In the monolingual Māori dictionary *He Pātaka Kupu* brief definitions are employed, rather than glosses. One very interesting feature of the entry, unique to *He Pātaka Kupu*, as set out below is the 'atua category'. *Atua* refers to supernatural beings, or gods. Each headword is assigned to the sphere of a relevant atua that reflects the focus of the word, thereby reflecting a Māori worldview in the dictionary format that pays due respect to the sacredness of words as derived from the gods. (Te Taura Whiri i te Reo 2008, ix) In the entry below for *aituā* (note: the *atua* is shown in square brackets):

**aituā**

1. tanga [Whiro] āhua. E waitohu ana tērā tonu pea ka pā he mate, he āhuatanga kino. E ai ki ētahi, ki te hou mai he tīrairaka ki roto i tō whare, he tohu aituā tērā.

2. tanga [Whiro] ing, mahp, āhua. He āhuatanga kino ka tūpono te pā ki te tangata. He aituā waka te takenga mai o tana hauātanga. {kaupapa (kaupapa whiti), maiki, maikiroa}

3. tanga [Whiro] He āhuatanga kino rawa atu ka ohorere te pā, e matemate ai te tangata, e kino katoa ai te whenua, te aha atu rānei. He aituā nui te hū o Tarawera. {inati, maiki, maikiroa, matenga}

In this example, the *atua* referred to using the '*atua* category' is 'Whiro', defined in Williams (1971) as the personification of evil, and of darkness and death.

Ultimately we decided against using an *atua* category similar to that utilised in *He Pātaka Kupu.* While the *atua* category would serve to alert the user to the existence and importance of a Māori worldview, it was not clear to us how this category would, in the case of a dictionary of legal terms, enhance users' understanding of the relationship between customary and Western legal ideas. Further, allocating terms to the sphere of a particular *atua* would require certainly a high level of expertise and time that we lacked, at least for the first edition. The *atua* category on its own, in our view, would not necessarily further understanding for many of the users of our dictionary without further explanation and explication of the method than is currently publicly available. Until the method is explained in more detail there is little incentive for other Māori dictionary makers to utilise this innovative tool. We determined that we would mark the importance of the Māori worldview in a different way.

We decided that we did need to provide some visual cue to users that alerted them to important customary law information. Further, we also wanted to provide some substantive, albeit limited, information that would serve to colour users' understanding of the relevant terms. The following entry illustrates our different use of format to communicate the importance of customary legal concepts:

**aituā** (-tia)
This term customarily denotes a misfortune or disaster. An aituā is sometimes caused by a violation of tapu or by mākutu, but it can also be the result of a random set of circumstances or some disturbance to the natural order. TM

1. accident

Ko ngā pūtea moni e whakahuaina ake nei mō ngā aituā i pā ohorere ki te tangata i muri mai o te 1 o ngā rā o Aperira 1983. ATL-87b <MID/CONT>

2. injustice

He aituā kino rawa i pā ki te iwi Māori i raro i ngā tikanga o te Ture Kōti Whenua Māori 1865. S241886 <HIST/MID>

▸ This sense is most often used in relation to the negative consequences for Māori that result from the enactment of certain laws.

see also ***hē, kino***

3. accidental

Ka tonoa atu hoki kia āta whiriwhiria e koutou he ture … hei whakarite utu hoki mō ngā kaimahi e mate aituā ana. S241900 <HIST/MID>

As can clearly be seen, the paragraph at the top of the entry (and at the top of all similar entries) informs the user that the entire entry is affected by the fact that the term has a traditional or customary law meaning. *Te Mātāpunenga* (as indicated by the use of 'TM' in the entry above) is the obvious source for full information, but this box alerts the reader to the important customary legal concept at work. The Western legal context can be seen in the glossing of *aituā* as 'accident', 'injustice' and 'accidental', each illustrated by a usage example. For the first sense, the noun 'accident', the usage example is taken from a pamphlet explaining claimants' rights to accident compensation pursuant to New Zealand's no-fault accident compensation scheme (known as ACC) which replaced the Common Law right to sue for personal injury in New Zealand in the early 1970s. By including the shaded box at the head of the entry the user is in no doubt as to why *aituā* has been chosen to refer to accidents for the purpose of Accident Compensation legislation; a no-fault system that compensates for injury caused by a discrete and identifiable *accident* often the result of a random set of circumstances, or disturbance of the natural order. There is a clear relationship between the traditional usage and the modern Western legal notion of a legally defined 'accident' event pursuant to ACC legislation.

Interestingly, it can also be seen in this entry that this modern legal notion of a definable accident causing injury *that can be compensated* appears only in the MID and CONT eras of the Corpus. The notion of events as mere unfortunate accidents, or events *occurring* accidentally is an old one, as can be seen by the fact that sense three ('accidental') appears in the historic (1828–1909) and middle corpus era (1910–69). Rather, it is the conceptualization of a severable and identifiable accident 'event' with legal consequences (the availability of compensation) that appears to be new. This makes sense, upon further investigation. The handful of corpus examples of *aituā*, 'accident', from the middle corpus era (1910–1969) refer to payments given to widows whose husbands had died due to suffering an accident under the Social Security Act 1938, and appears also in reference to the Workers Compensation Act 1950 which was replaced by ACC legislation in 1972. The Corpus can show, therefore, the evolution of a new Western legal sense developing out of a traditional customary legal term.

Sense 2 of this entry is also interesting. This sense is glossed as 'injustice' and the usage example refers to the injustices suffered by the Māori as a result of the imposition of the Native Lands Act 1865, during a period of terrible civil unrest in New Zealand, known as the New Zealand Wars. It was not sufficient to gloss this sense as merely 'unlucky' or 'ill-omened' because sufficient examples could be identified, like the one used here, that added another layer of meaning; of disaster that *unjustly* imposed burdens upon Māori at the hands of Pākehā. This 'injustice' sense disappears from Corpus texts by 1970, although it may of course still appear in other Māori language contexts, and may still have a presence in oral legal texts. Nevertheless, this entry shows the waxing and waning of two quite separate senses within this limited Corpus of texts, both informed, and arguably linked by, a customary legal idea. We consider that our design of our dictionary articles enables the profiling of the relationship between these two modes of legal thought.

## Conclusion

This chapter shows how we set about creating our legal dictionary for Māori, the indigenous language of New Zealand. Invariably this dictionary is the result of the methods we chose, but also this dictionary very much reflects something of the turbulent legal history of New Zealand. The texts of our corpus reflect the impact of Crown policy on the use and dissemination of Māori language legal texts. Sources, with a few important exceptions, are not long-lived; and from the earlier decades of the nineteenth century where land deeds and official correspondence occur in Māori, the nature of the texts change significantly, and by the end of the century Crown production of Māori language legal texts had almost entirely ceased. The variability of sources provided us with problems in being able to compare texts over time in our diachronic corpus, but the complexity and richness of the texts more than compensate for problems of comparability.

The nature of the Corpus does greatly influence the nature of the dictionary itself. The fact, for example, that terms used in the twentieth and twenty-first century may differ from pre-1910 terms denoting the same concepts reflects the decline, for many decades, of Māori as a civic language. By the time Māori began to regain civic status after 1986 many of the older terms no longer appear in the corpus texts. The changing nature of Māori legal vocabulary is also reflected in the rise and fall in the use of borrowings from English, of which this chapter has provided some illustration, in regards to the terms *moni* and *pūtea.*

If the dictionary reflects the nature of the Corpus texts, it also reflects the interface between two legal worldviews. Customary legal terms and their phrasal variants form an absolutely critical core of the dictionary, in ways we had not forseen at the commencement of the Legal Māori Project in 2007. While the work of identifying how customary Māori legal terms have taken on new Western legal senses is on-going, we offer here a taste of how that change has occurred in the example of *aituā.*

There is much yet to be done to capitalise on the resources we have now identified and created. There is so much yet to be learned about Māori as a language of law and civic engagement. We are eager to move forward.

*Kua takoto te manuka. Mā wai e kawe? The challenge has been laid down. Who will meet it?*

## References

Bauer, L. 1983. *English Word-formation.* Cambridge: Cambridge University Press.

Benton, R., A. Frame P. Meredith. 2013. *Te Mātāpunenga, a Compendium of References to the Concepts and Institutions of Māori Customary Law.* Wellington: Victoria University Press.

Bergenholtz, H. and S. Tarp. 1995. *Manual of Specialised Lexicography – The preparation of specialised dictionaries.* Amsterdam/Philadelphia: Benjamins.

Boyce, M. 2006. 'A Corpus of Modern Spoken Māori'. Unpublished PhD thesis, Victoria University of Wellington Library.

Boyce, M. and M. Stephens. 2013. *The Legal Māori Corpus: Texts Printed Before 1910* http://nzetc.victoria.ac.nz/tm/scholarly/tei-legalMaoriCorpus.html [accessed: 12 February 2013].

Chung, T.M. 2004. Identifying technical vocabulary. *System*, 32, 251–63.

Jones, A. and K. Jenkins. 2011. *He Korero: Words between Us – First Māori Pākehā Conversations on Paper*. Wellington: Huia Publishers.

Kawharu, I.H. 1992. 'Kotahitanga; Visions of Unity'. *The Journal of the Polynesian Society*, 101(3), 221–40.

Lipka, L., S. Handl and W. Falkner. 2004. 'Lexicalisation and institutionalisation – the state of the art' in 2004. *The Journal of Theoretical Linguistics*, 1(1), 1–19.

Lüpke, F. 2011. Orthography Development, *in The Cambridge Handbook of Endangered Languages*, edited by P. Austin and J. Sallabank. Cambridge: Cambridge University Press, 312–36.

Macalister, J. 2006. 'The Māori lexical presence in New Zealand English: Constructing a corpus for diachronic change'. *Corpora*, 1(1), 85–98.

Moorfield, J. and T. Ka'ai. 2011. *He Kupu Arotau – Loanwords in Māori*. Auckland: Pearson.

*New Zealand Parliamentary Debates* 1997, Vol. 562, 3192.

Ngata, H.M. 1993. *English-Māori Dictionary*. Wellington: Learning Media.

Parkinson P. 2001a. '"Strangers in the House": The Māori Language in Government and the Māori Language in Parliament 1840–1900'. *Victoria University of Wellington Law Review Monograph*: 32.

—— 2001b 'The Māori Language and its Expression in New Zealand Law'. *Victoria University of Wellington Law Review Monograph*: 45.

Parkinson, P. and P. Griffith (eds) 2004. *Books in Māori, 1815–1900: An Annotated Bibliography*. Auckland: Reed.

Ryan, P.M. 1995 (4th edition). *The Reed Dictionary of Modern Māori*. Auckland: Reed Books.

Scott, M. 2008. *WordSmith Tools version 5*, Liverpool: Lexical Analysis Software.

Stephens, M. 2008. '"Wrestling with the Taniwha": An Analysis of Two Māori Language Texts and their Engagement with Western Legal Concepts', in *14 Revue Juridique Polynesienne* pp. 135–56.

Stephens, M. and M. Boyce (eds). 2013. *He Papakupu Reo Ture: A Dictionary of Māori Legal Terms*. Wellington: LexisNexis.

Stephens, M. and P. Monk. 2013. A Language for Buying Biscuits? Māori as a Civic Language in Modern New Zealand Parliament. *Australian Indigenous Law Review*, 16(2) 70–80.

Te Taura Whiri i te Reo Māori – 2008. *He Pataka Kupu: Te Kai a te Rangatira*. Wellington: Penguin.

—— 1996. *Te Matatiki: Contemporary Māori Words*. Auckland: Oxford University Press.

Ward, A. 1995. *A Show of Justice – Racial Amalgamation in 19th Century New Zealand*. Auckland: Auckland University Press.
Williams, H.W. 1971. *Dictionary of the Māori Language*. Seventh edition. Wellington: Government Printer.

# Index for English Language Chapters


academics 55, 73, 115
accidental characteristics 129–130, 134
accuracy 54, 70, 283
  of predecessors 5, 45, 52–3, 126, 135–6
acronyms 127, 131
adjectival form 268, 273, 284
adjectives 51, 161, 268, 271, 275, 278, 283–5
  ascriptive 285
  ordinary 284
  verbal 269, 284–6
adjudication 193, 196–8, 273
  legal and non-legal language in Hart's theory 193–6
administrative law 2, 20–2, 129–30
admiralty 36, 49
adverbs 161, 284
agreement 270, 287, 292, 298, 300
airplanes 186, 188, 192–4
alphabetical order 11–12, 17, 20–1, 23, 69, 141
alphabetical *répertoires* 12, 18, 23
ambiguity 266, 269–70, 272
*American and English Encyclopaedia of Law* 181, 183
Ancien Régime 4, 12–13, 15, 18, 26
Anglo-American law 115, 127–9, 131, 173, 197
antonyms 162, 166–9, 174
Aotearoa 289, 305
appropriateness 133, 135
*arrêtistes* 4, 13, 19
ascriptive adjectives 285
*atua* category 314–15
Austin, JL 197–8, 299
authentic texts 8, 121
authenticated terms 267, 281
authenticity 119, 121–2, 203–4, 265
authoritative information 76–7
authority 36–7, 63–4, 66, 200–3, 207–8, 210, 219–20
automobile 177, 187, 189–92
  exception 190

Bacon, Nicholas 34–5
Baker, JH 32–3
Ballentine, JA 184, 186
basic legal concepts 6, 79
Becquet, Léon 21
Belgium 80, 123
Bergenholtz, H 126, 157, 159, 289
bi-directional bilingual legal dictionaries 85
bicycles 183–4, 187–8, 192, 194
bijural context 201–20
bijural translation 136
bijuralism 119, 202, 219
bilingual context, establishment of meaning 201–20
bilingual dictionaries 2, 38–9, 126, 153, 155, 158, 161
bilingual legal dictionaries (BLDs) 6, 75–87, 123, 125, 135; *see also* legal dictionaries
  bi-directional 85
  comparative 75–6, 79–80, 85–7
  entries for nationality 79–85
  implications of findings 86
  test case 79–85
bilingual legislation 207, 209
  dictionaries as aid to interpretation 202–4
bilingual statutes 201, 204, 207, 210, 212–13
bilingualism
  legal 204
  official 8, 201, 203, 206, 213

*Black's Law Dictionary* 45–57, 125–6, 179, 181–2, 184–5, 211–12, 214–17
BLDs, *see* bilingual legal dictionaries
Blount, Sir Thomas 31–2, 36–9, 53, 178–9
borrowed legal terms 306–7
borrowings 290, 304–7, 312, 317
boundaries 5, 8, 56, 191, 197, 199, 298
Bouvier, John 45–6, 55, 133, 184
branches of law 125, 127–8, 132–3, 142–3, 146, 150
Browne, Irving 182–3, 199
Burghley, Lord 31, 35, 39
business law 132, 143

*Caighdeán Oifigiúil, an* 265, 272
Camden, William 31
Campbell Black, Henry 5, 46–7, 50–1, 53, 56, 179, 181
Canada 3, 188, 202–3, 206, 209–11, 213–17
  bijuralism 119, 202, 219
  equal authority principle 8, 202–3, 210, 212
  official bilingualism 8, 201, 203, 206, 213
  Quebec, *see* Quebec
  Supreme Court of Canada (SCC) 201–20
  Termium 136
canon law 18, 181
Carey, Robert 34
case law 8, 13–15, 17, 19–26, 49, 132–5, 184–6
case reporters 13, 22
categories 18, 126–8, 188, 194, 197–200, 291–2, 303
centrality 3, 7, 141–2, 146
*Century Dictionary* 50, 53
certainty, legal 2, 144, 265–6, 271, 279
changeability 301, 304
Charles II 36
Church 34, 36
CISG, *see* Contracts for the International Sale of Goods
citations 5, 47–8, 65, 71, 183
key-number 54
citizens 2, 16–18, 20, 202, 272
citizenship 79, 81–3, 85, 210–11
Civil Code 16–19, 21, 135, 202
  Quebec 215, 217, 220
civil law 11, 17, 19, 35–6, 202, 213, 216–18
  concepts 216, 218
civilian dictionaries 216–17
clarity 2–3, 8, 56, 266, 269, 274, 282
classes of terms 177, 312
classifications 67, 128, 153, 194–5
  legal 7, 150, 194
Cockeram, Henry 39
codes 4, 14, 17–22, 24, 142
  annotated 4, 19
  language 116–17, 162, 169, 171
codification 11, 17–18, 21, 84–5
cognitive functions 158, 161, 175
cognitive situations 155, 159, 167, 173, 175
coherence 73, 166, 266, 274–5
Coles
  Elisha 38–9
  John 178, 183
collocations 133–4, 156–7, 161–3, 166–72, 174, 305, 311
colonisation 289, 305
commentaries 11, 17, 63, 149
Common Law 2–4, 31–2, 66, 115–16, 131–2, 134–5, 217–18
common parlance 213, 216
common verbs 277
communicative functions 117, 158, 291
communicative situations 175, 207
Company of Stationers 35, 38–9
comparability 78, 271, 289, 294, 296–7, 300–1, 304
  direct 290, 296
comparative approach 149–50
comparative bilingual legal dictionaries 75–6, 79–80, 85–7
comparative conceptual analysis 128
comparative law 3, 7, 24, 75, 119, 142
  research 75, 79, 83, 86
comparative lawyers 1, 86
comparison and precision 75–87
competence 117, 124, 159–60, 162
  linguistic 160
compilation 5, 8, 45, 116, 128, 268–9, 273

challenges 59–74
compilers 50–1, 61, 85–6, 133, 135, 154, 156–7
completeness 6, 180
complex entries 55, 186
complexity 63, 149, 165, 281, 312, 317
compound prepositions 270–1
compound terms 84–5, 186
comprehension 79, 284
concept entries 149–50
concepts
centrality in terminology 142–3
interrelatedness 7, 141, 143
legal, *see* legal concepts
national 76, 83
one per entry 145
thorough documentation 146–7
conceptual analysis 7, 128–9
comparative 128
conceptual differences 6, 131, 160, 162
conceptualisation 316
*Concise Oxford Dictionary* 208, 210–11
conjunctions 277
consistency 54, 73, 266, 269
constitutional law 46, 135, 265
constraints 7, 73, 270, 273, 287
jurisdictional 161, 165
content words 297–8
high frequency 299–300, 304
context 5–8, 62–5, 77–8, 119–21, 146–8, 210–11, 213–14
historical 18, 70–1
international 155, 161
legal, *see* legal contexts
legislative 66
linguistic 80, 130–1
contextuality 131, 137
contextualizing labels 128
continuity 16, 269, 297
contracts 47, 118, 121–3, 166, 169, 173, 271
Contracts for the International Sale of Goods (CISG) 161, 173
contrastive notes 162, 169, 173–4
conveyance 47–8, 57, 116, 177, 183–5, 187, 192–3
coordination 272, 276
Coote, Edmund 39
corpora 133–4, 136, 289–91, 293–7, 299–308, 312–14, 316–17
creation 291–4
diachronic 8, 289–317
sub-corpora 294, 306–8
corpus linguistics 3, 200
corpus texts 295–7, 301, 304, 316–17
correctness 135
costs 79
countability 162
*Cour de cassation* 17–19, 22
Cowell, Dr John 4, 31–2, 35–9, 47, 178, 180
*Crépeau's Dictionnaire de droit privé et Lexiques bilingues* 214, 216
criminal law 49, 54, 132, 135, 187–8
Cromwell, Thomas 33–5
cross-references 7, 165, 167–9, 174, 184, 186
culture 1–2, 7, 15, 32, 118, 136–7, 313
legal 26, 118, 136, 201, 213
linguistic 177, 199–200
source 117
target 117
customary law 312–16
customary legal concepts 8, 290, 312, 315–16
customary legal terms 290, 312–13, 317
Czech
case study 115–37
law 118, 120, 122, 128–30, 132, 134–5
terms 127, 132, 135

Dagar, Charles 18
Dalloz
Armand 24
Désiré 20, 23–4, 26
Danish 155, 158, 161–2, 170, 173, 175
data
grammatical 156, 162, 167
inflectional 163, 166
databases 7, 133–6, 142, 146, 153–75
relational 156–7
de Franchis, F 80
de Lacombe, Rousseau 13
de Montainville, Jean 19
de Royer, Prost 13

de Villargues, Roland 24
declension 270, 283
definiendum 116, 128
definitions 11–14, 47–56, 59–71, 76–87, 164–75, 177–93, 204–9
  abridged 86
  dictionary 192, 196, 199, 208–9, 213–15, 219
  formalities of defining words v legal substance 50–2
  judicial 47–50, 66
  legislative 60, 66–7, 76–9, 85–6, 204
  lexical 14, 177
  measuring equivalence by means of 76–7
  statutory 66–7, 182, 184, 188, 192–3, 208
demotic usage 63, 67
Denisart, Jean-Baptiste 13
Denton, Thomas 34
descriptive terminology 147
diachronic corpora 289–317
  collation challenge 294–5
  comparability problems 296–301
  corpus to dictionary 301–4
dictionaries 1–8, 59–63, 65–73, 153–66, 177–83, 201–6, 301–4; *see also Introductory Note*
  authoritative 61–3
  avoiding the normative 62–4
  bilingual, *see* bilingual dictionaries
  civilian 216–17
  definition 61–4
  and encyclopaedias distinguished 61–2
  English 31–2, 36, 39, 72, 125, 204, 212
  hard-word 31, 38–9
  identification of material for inclusion 53–7, 125, 132–5
  and interpretation of bilingual legislation 202–4
  judicial 5, 49–50, 59–61, 65–7, 69–71, 73–4, 182
  language 14, 208, 214–17, 219
  law 2–5, 45–7, 49–51, 133–5, 153–5, 178–9, 181–3
  for legal translation 125–36
  monolingual 2, 4, 86, 125, 133, 169
  multilingual 2–3, 131, 145
  online 153–6, 159, 164–5, 175
  paper, *see* paper dictionaries
  translational 116, 120, 136
dictionary definitions 192, 196, 199, 208–9, 213–15, 219
dictionary entries, *see* entries
dictionary functions 154–8, 160, 162, 165, 175
*Dictionnaire de Trévoux* 12
direct comparability 290, 296
discrepancies 203, 207, 212, 279, 282
dissemination 8, 266, 297, 317
divergences 132, 206, 213, 268, 284
doctrinal genre 11, 13, 16, 26
doctrine 2, 4, 15–17, 19, 21–4, 26, 63–4
documents
  legal 63, 67, 122, 165, 300
  legislative 5, 68, 73, 281
domains 117, 126, 179, 290, 308
dominant languages 8, 289–90, 305
dual semiotic system 6, 118, 136
Dufour, Gabriel 21

early modern English law lexicons 31–9
editorial policy 60, 67
editors 2, 4–5, 56, 59–65, 69, 73, 180–2
*EID (English-Irish Dictionary)* 267–8, 271–3, 275, 277, 280–1
Elyot, Sir Thomas 34, 38
embedded links 165, 167–9
embeddedness 142, 147–8, 150
embedding, structural 83, 148
Empson, Richard 34
encyclopaedias 11, 14, 23, 46, 48, 177, 180
  and dictionaries distinguished 61–2
  legal 12, 45, 50, 61, 69, 181
encyclopaedic information 5, 51–2, 55, 75–7, 79, 81, 85–7
  in comparative bilingual law dictionaries 75
  and efficiency 77–9
  extent required for law dictionary 45–9
  legislative definitions in 76
  without juxtaposition 85–6

English dictionaries 31–2, 36, 39, 72, 125, 204, 212
*English- Irish Dictionary (EID)* 267–8, 271–3, 275, 277, 280–1
English law 2, 60, 62, 71–2, 179, 181, 183
English-speaking countries 116, 129, 132–3, 135
entries 46–56, 69–71, 79–86, 145–50, 182–6, 300–4, 311–16
  complex 55, 186
  concept 149–50
  one per concept 145
  structure 130–2
  word-entries 32–3, 36–9
entry words 154–6, 160–4, 166–9, 171–2, 174–5
environment 118, 141, 154, 158, 297, 299
  extra-lexicographic 158–9
  legal 123–4, 148
  lexicographic 158–9
  linguistic 119, 125, 130
equal authority principle 8, 202–3, 210, 212
equivalence 6–7, 75–6, 78–9, 82–4, 128–9, 141, 147–8
  degrees of 7, 76–8, 82, 86, 129
  functional 192
  misconception 147–8
  partial 77, 131
  perfect 77, 79
equivalents 76, 129–31, 136, 147–9, 160, 162, 172–3
  potential 129, 135
  substitutable 148
  TL 130–1
  translational 116, 136
essential elements 129
etymology 33, 36
EU, *see* European Union
European Union (EU) 5, 8, 78, 132, 136, 161, 282
everyday speech 127, 193
everyday words 127, 218
excerpts 56, 131, 133–4, 209, 300
experience 7, 59, 72–3, 128, 133, 289, 312
expertise 5, 16, 49, 55, 64, 72, 137
experts 79, 141, 144
  legal 75, 144–5, 159–60, 164, 265
  substantive 5, 49
explanations 71, 75–6, 84–6, 125, 130–1, 149–50, 179–80
extra-lexicographic environment 158–9

factual knowledge 159–60
Favard de Langlade, Baron G-J 21–2, 25
Ferrière, Joseph 4, 13–14, 18–19
fictions, benign and harmful 198–200
financial meanings 310–11
Fitzherbert, Anthony 32
focus, referential 164–5
foreign languages 5, 141, 144, 157–60, 170, 172–3
  and jurisdictions 71–2
formalities 5, 45, 50
format 20, 134, 151, 163, 186, 297, 300
Foster, C 146–8
France 4, 25, 206, 217
  *Cour de cassation* 17–19, 22
  Empire 17–19
  great Répertoires 21–7
  law 2, 6, 12, 15, 23
  legal lexicography 3–4, 11–27
  Revolution to Civil Code 4, 16–21
French 2–4, 11–13, 15, 31–8, 78, 84, 202–17
  legal lexicography 3–4, 11–27
frequency 301, 304–8, 310
  rank 307, 309
Fulbecke, William 38
function theory of lexicography 157, 159
functional equivalence 192
functions 60–2, 117–18, 147–9, 154, 156–8, 161–2, 164
  cognitive 158, 161, 175
  communicative 117, 158, 291
  dictionary 154–8, 160, 162, 165, 175
  paedagogic 14, 19
Furetière, Antoine 13
Fuzier-Herman's *Répertoire* 25

Gallegos, C. 80, 82–3, 85
Gallus, C. Aelius 1, 11
gender 270
genitive 268–71, 274–5, 284
genre 11, 19, 25, 121, 124, 199
  doctrinal 11, 13, 16, 26

literary 13, 27
genre conventions 156, 168
Gény, François 17
German 6, 76–7, 84, 122, 125, 128, 143–5
German law 6, 77, 118, 122, 145
globalization 118
glossaries 11, 31, 38, 45, 142, 149, 179–80
glosses 11, 299, 304, 306, 308, 314, 316
indicative 306
*Glossographia* 36, 39, 178
goals 55, 144, 163, 165, 269, 294
grammar 162, 166, 266, 271, 283, 285
Irish 284
rules 269–70, 272–3, 281–3
grammatical data 156, 162, 167
grammatical properties 271–2
*Grand Robert de la langue française, Le* 206, 208–9, 215
Guyot, J-N 15, 19, 24–5

hard-word dictionaries 31, 38–9
Hart, HLA 193–7, 200
headwords 1, 5, 38–9, 51, 53–4, 56–7, 277
non-logical 54
plural 52
Henry VII 32, 34
Henry VIII 32–4
Hesseling, G. 80, 84–5
high frequency content words 299–300, 304
historical contexts 18, 70–1
historical researchers 69, 71
historical terms 67–71
history 3, 18, 21, 23–6, 39, 118, 179–80
homographs 165
homonym indices 162, 164, 166–9, 171, 174
homonyms 143, 145, 165–6
homonymy 144, 165, 167, 174
hyperlinks 150, 185
hyponymic relations 6

identification of material for inclusion in dictionaries 53–7, 125, 132
Imbert, Jean 13
inconsistencies 50, 116
in sources and use of Irish legal terminology 8, 265–87
indices
homonym 162, 164, 166–9, 171, 174
polysemy 162, 164, 166–9, 171, 174
indigenous languages 289–90, 294, 312, 317
inflected forms 161, 163
inflection 162, 166–9, 171, 173–4
inflectional data 163, 166
inflectional paradigms 156, 162
inflectional rules 270
information tools 154–5, 157, 175
Inns of Court 32–5
institutions 13–14, 18, 116, 122, 125, 130, 313
intended users 130, 154–5, 159–62, 164–5
intent, legislative 68, 213
intentions 60, 121, 123–4, 169, 203, 219
interlingual translation 117–18, 121
international contexts 155, 161
Internet 133, 154, 156
search engines 154
*Interpreter, The* 4, 32, 35–7, 178, 180, 217
interpreters 117, 207, 217
interrelatedness of concepts 7, 141, 143
intersemiotic translation 118, 136
intra-language translation 124
intuition 193, 199
Irish legal terminology 8, 265–87
irregular verbs 158, 277, 283
ISO standards 6
Italian 6, 81–2, 143
Italy 6, 12, 80–2, 143

Jackson, Bernard 118–20, 123
Jacob, Giles 45–6, 55
Jakobson, Roman 6, 117–18, 124
James I 32, 35–6
Janker, K 76
Jauffret, Louis-François 16–17
Johnson, Samuel 39, 50
Joscelyn, John 38
*Jowitt's Dictionary of English Law* 5, 59–60, 63–4, 69, 73
judicial definitions 47–50, 66
judicial dictionaries 5, 49–50, 59–61, 65–7, 69–71, 73–4, 182
judicial pronouncements 49–51, 65–6, 202, 216

judicial reasoning 201, 208
judiciary 3, 63, 67
  influence 65
jurilinguistics 3, *see also Introductory Note*
jurisconsults 11–12, 15, 18, 21–2, 26–7
jurisdictional constraints 161, 165
jurisdictions 22, 75–6, 83–5, 118, 124–5, 132–3, 135–6
  and foreign languages 71–2
juxtaposition 76–7, 79, 85, 87

key-number citations 54
Kischel, Uwe 117–18
knowledge 115–16, 153–5, 158, 160–1, 163, 167–8, 173–5
  factual 159–60
  linguistic 6, 158

labels 7, 131, 196
  contextualizing 128
language codes 116–17, 162, 169, 171
language dictionaries 14, 208, 214–17, 219
language for special purposes (LSP) 8, 141–2, 155, 289
language staff 157–8, 167; *see also* interpreters; translators
languages
  dominant 8, 289–90, 305
  minority 289, 312
  native 157–60, 164
  natural 117, 127, 131, 164, 194
  official 2, 132, 136, 202–4, 282
  source 75–6, 117, 121, 132, 135, 147
  target 75–7, 116–17, 121, 125, 128, 147, 149
Latin 1, 12, 32–3, 36, 117, 158, 283
  maxims 54, 181
Laud, Archbishop 36
law dictionaries, *see also Introductory Note*
  and translation 115–37
  works of original scholarship or compilations of judicial definitions 49–50
law lexicons, early modern English 31–9
law students 20, 153, 155, 157–60, 163–4
lawyers 14–16, 31–5, 72–4, 123–5, 157–60, 165–8, 172–3
  comparative 1, 86
layout 77, 142, 313
Leckey, R 203, 207
Ledru-Rollin, A 24
legal arguments 13, 201, 220, 268
legal bilingualism 204
legal certainty 2, 144, 265–6, 271, 279
legal classification 7, 150, 194
legal concepts 124–5, 128, 141–7, 149–50, 172–3, 290–1, 294
  basic 6, 79
  customary 8, 290, 312, 315–16
  Western 8, 290, 301, 303, 312
legal contexts 61, 63–4, 66, 127–8, 147, 300, 302
  technical 63–4
  Western 302, 316
legal culture 26, 118, 136, 201, 213
legal dictionaries, *see also Introductory Note*
  bilingual, *see* bilingual legal dictionaries
  challenges of compilation 59–74
  definition 59–61
  functional requirements 144–5
  scope 178–82
  suitable authors 72–3
  target audiences 73
  use in bijural legal system 213–19
  vehicle example 183–93
legal discourse 121, 124–5, 197–8, 213, 292, 301
legal documents 63, 67, 122, 165, 300
legal encyclopaedias 12, 45, 50, 61, 69, 181
legal environment 123–4, 148
legal experts 75, 144–5, 159–60, 164, 265
legal information 118, 121, 136, 148, 153, 296
legal language 127–8, 141–2, 144, 158–61, 198–9, 289–91, 293–4
  dominant 8, 289
  minority 289
legal lexicographers 5, 71, 154, 182, 312
legal lexicography, *see also Introductory Note* and *detailed entries*

practitioner view 45–57
legal lexicons 1, 12, 14, 37, 39, 118, 127–8
*Legal Māori Corpus* 291–2, 298–9, 301–5, 307–11
legal meaning 218, 266, 302–3, 305, 313
legal profession 4, 35, 39, 65, 73, 179, 265
legal reasoning 141, 219–20
legal science 11, 14, 17, 21–4, 27
legal sources 5, 45, 80, 83, 130, 150, 184
legal standing 276, 280
legal systems 116–19, 128, 131–2, 134–6, 141–50, 160–1, 218–19
legal terminology 1–3, 7–8, 126–7, 131, 177, 180, 312–13
attention merited as opposed to other segments of language of law 126–32
multinational 141–51
structure 126–30
legal terms 49–50, 86, 163–5, 169–71, 265–6, 268–70, 279–82
authenticated 267
borrowed 306–7
customary 290, 312–13, 317
legal texts 118–19, 123–4, 127–8, 144, 146, 158–62, 166–70
legal traditions 8, 79, 141, 213, 215, 217
legal translation, *see* translation
legal translators 75, 77, 86, 115–16, 118, 130, 137
legal uncertainty 16, 194
legal vocabulary 6, 26, 71, 119, 125, 127–8, 290
growth and spread 37–9
legislation 2–4, 66–7, 134–6, 216–17, 265, 272–3, 275
bilingual, *see* bilingual legislation
European 121, 281
local 68, 133
legislative context 66
legislative definitions 60, 66–7, 76–9, 85–6, 204
in encyclopaedic information 76
legislative intent 68, 213
legislatures 63, 66–7, 73, 202, 207
influence 66–7
Leigh, Edward 38
*LEME*, *see Lexicons of Early Modern English*
lemmas 127, 132
lexical definitions 14, 177
lexicalisation 304
lexicographers 3–6, 50–1, 126–30, 132–7, 154–60, 162–3, 165–6
lexicographic environment 158–9
lexicography 3–6, 48, 50–2, 71–2, 126–37, 153–60, 162–6; *see also Introductory Note*
French legal 3–4, 11–27
function theory of 157, 159
legal, *see* legal lexicography
lexicons 4, 6, 11–12, 14, 16, 301–2, 304
legal 1, 12, 14, 37, 39, 118, 127–8
*Lexicons of Early Modern English (LEME)* 31, 38–9
linguistic competence 160
linguistic context 80, 130–1
linguistic culture of law 177, 199–200
linguistic environment 119, 125, 130
linguistic knowledge 6, 158
linguistic properties 167
linguistics 3, 8, 68, 159, 180, 197, 281
corpus 3, 200
*see also* jurilinguistics
links 83, 85, 143, 156, 162, 167–8, 182
embedded 165, 167–9
literary genre 13, 27
litigation 18, 21–2, 266, 272, 276
Louisiana 49, 135
LSP, *see* language for special purposes

*McBoyle* case 186, 192–3, 196, 200
macrostructure 137
*mandamus* 67–8
Manley, Thomas 31–2, 36–8
Māori 8, 289–317
challenge of collating diachronic corpus 294–5
communities 291–4, 297
comparability problems 296–301
corpus creation 291–4
corpus to dictionary 301–4
customary law as dictionary organising principle 312–14
dictionaries and wordlists 303–4

expressing 'money' 307–11
Kāhiti Published Between 1867 and 1933 296
*Legal Māori Corpus* 291–2, 298–9, 301–5, 307–11
Legal Māori Project 8, 289–90, 293, 303, 313, 317
legal terms derived from English 305–11
lexical change over time as reflected in *He Papakupu Reo Ture* 311–12
lexicon 290, 296, 312
*Māori Broadcast Corpus* 298–301, 307–10
*moni* 9, 298–9, 306–8, 310–11
MPs 293, 295, 297–9
Native Affairs Committee/Māori Affairs Committee Reports published from 1876–1962 296–7
pilot project 302–3
*pūtea* 9, 308–11, 315, 317
reader lists 303
reflecting primacy of customary terms in dictionary format 314–16
speeches of Māori Members of Parliament 297–8
worldview 314–15
*Māori Broadcast Corpus* 298–301, 307–10
Mattila, Heikki 1, 142, 144, 147, 218
maxims 53–4, 132, 181, 184, 192
meanings 201, 203, 215–20, 282–5, 301, 304–5, 310
establishing in bilingual and bijural context 201–20
financial 310–11
legal 218, 266, 302–3, 305, 313
ordinary 204, 206, 208, 212–13, 216–19
plain 199–200
shared meaning rule 209–10
*Méga-Code* 20
Melby, A 146–8
Mellinkoff, David 56, 127
Meriton, George 38
Merlin de Douai 18, 22, 24–5
Merrill, John Houston 181, 183
metalanguage 131, 137
methodology 6, 22, 142, 177, 179, 208, 216
Meynial, Edmond 17, 23–4, 26
microstructure 137
minority languages 289, 312
*moni* 9, 298–9, 306–8, 310–11
monolingual dictionaries 2, 4, 86, 125, 133, 169
More, Sir Thomas 31–2
Morison, Richard 33–4
Morton, John 34
motor homes 189–90
multi-word terminological phrases 127, 133
multi-word units 161, 305
multilingual dictionaries 2–3, 131, 145
multinational legal terminology 141–51
mundane objects 177–200

Napoleonic Codes 17, 19
national concepts 76, 83
nationality 76, 79–86
native languages 157–60, 164
natural language 117, 127, 131, 164, 194
neologisms 149–50, 305, 308
New Zealand, *see* Māori
nomenclatures 126
*Nomo-Lexikon* 36–8, 179
non-equivalence 129–30; *see also* equivalence
non-lawyers 32, 63, 67, 74, 116, 124, 129
non-legal terms 50, 52, 182–3
non-logical headwords 54
norms 13, 18, 144, 153, 196
notes
contrastive 162, 169, 173–4
usage 7, 162, 166–9, 174
noun phrases 52, 285
nouns 51, 161, 165–6, 205, 268, 270–1, 283–5
phrase 270–1
verbal 269, 283–4

obsolescence 18, 67, 73, 180
*OED*, *see Oxford English Dictionary* 38–9, 49–50, 53, 62–3, 177–8, 205–6, 208
official bilingualism 8, 201, 203, 206, 213

official languages 2, 132, 136, 202–4, 282
omissions 62, 70, 192, 267
one-word terms 127
online dictionaries 153–6, 159, 164–5, 175
data repository 155–7
project introduction 154–5
search options reflecting user needs 163–75
selection of function specific data 160–3
theoretical basis focussed on user needs 157–60
onomasiology 6
order
alphabetical 11–12, 17, 20–1, 23, 69, 141
predetermined 157, 163
random 157
ordinary adjectives 284
ordinary language 3, 7–8, 72, 195–200, 205
construction 196–8
definition of ordinary words for mundane objects 177–200
vehicle example 183–93
ordinary meanings 212–13, 216–19
independent assessment of 'two' ordinary meanings 204–8
simultaneous identification of 'one' ordinary meaning 208–10
unilateral description of a single ordinary meaning 210–13
ordinary words 1, 49, 177–200
original scholarship 49–50
orthography 265–6, 272; *see also* spellings
*Oxford English Dictionary (OED)* 39, 49–50, 53, 62–3, 177–8, 205–6, 208

paedagogic function 14, 19
Palsgrave, John 34–5
*Pandectes françaises* 26
paper dictionaries, multinational legal terminology 141–51
Parliament 36, 66, 68, 203, 293–6, 298, 306
parts of speech 52, 161, 165, 283
passive forms 162, 169
*Petit Robert, Le Nouveau* 205–6, 208, 215
Phillips, Edward 36, 38–9
philosophy of law 23, 26
phonology 270, 272
phrasal verbs 161
phrase nouns 270–1
phraseological units 7
phraseology 166
phrases 47–51, 156–8, 170–2, 180–7, 196, 199, 303–5
multi-word terminological 127, 133
noun 52, 285
self-explanatory 5, 51
terminological 127, 132–3, 137
pictures 168, 177–8, 193, 270, 308
plain meaning 199–200
plural headwords 52
polysemy 144, 165–6
indices 162, 164, 166–9, 171, 174
potential users 125, 131, 157–8, 160
practitioners 12, 14, 22, 24–5, 72–3, 179, 266
precedent 51, 63–5, 280
precision 56, 143, 182, 266
and comparison 75–87
predecessors 12, 15, 25, 37, 46, 52, 135
accuracy of 5, 45, 52–3, 126, 135–6
predetermined order 157, 163
preferred spellings 167
preliminary qualification 17
prepositional verbs 277
prepositions 122, 270, 272, 277
compound 270–1
private law 122, 133, 216–18
professional translators 155, 158–60, 170, 175
properties 34, 146, 167, 179, 270–2, 281
grammatical 271–2
linguistic 167
syntactic 270, 281
prototypes 163, 175, 199, 275
public domain 191, 282, 298
public law 23, 115, 132–3
*pūtea* 9, 308–11, 315, 317

quality assurance processes 159
Quebec 135, 202, 216–18
Civil Code 215, 217, 220

*Questions de droit* 18, 21–2
quotations 4–5, 39, 49, 65, 70, 84, 186
  illustrative 49, 54

random order 157
rank frequency 307, 309
rank types 307
Rannóg, an 265, 280, 282
Rastell
  John 31–3, 35–9, 45, 55
  William 31, 35
Rawle, Francis 46, 184
reader lists 303
reasoning
  judicial 201, 208
  legal 141, 219–20
referential focus 164–5
register 4, 35, 39–40, 128
relational databases 156–7
reliability 49, 54, 206, 210
*Répertoire universel et raisonné de jurisprudence* 13
*Répertoire universel Guyot* 18
*répertoires* 11, 14–15, 18, 20–2, 24–7
  alphabetical 12, 18, 23
repertories, *see répertoires*
researchers 69, 71, 303, 313
resources 16, 35, 146, 295, 305, 313, 317
revisions 34, 36, 72, 166, 184
Roman law 11–12, 18–19, 49, 53, 142, 213
rules 14–15, 17–19, 48–9, 70, 117–18, 192–5, 206–7
  grammar 269–70, 272–3, 281–3
  inflectional 270
  legal 14, 142, 194–7, 199
  spelling 166, 283
  syntactic 270, 283

samples 7, 75–6, 79–81, 86, 276, 302
Šarčević, Susan 117, 123, 128–9, 148
Schauer, Frederick 193, 195
Scotland 72, 161–2
search engines 7, 129, 156, 163, 167–8, 175
search options reflecting user needs 163–75
searches 153–4, 156, 163, 167–9, 171–2, 175, 189–90
selection 66, 69, 129, 133, 154, 161, 303
selectional restrictions 7–8, 270–1
self-explanatory phrases 5, 51
semantic rules 270, 283
semi-experts 6, 159–60, 164
semiotic system, dual 6, 118, 136
semiotic theory of translation 6, 118
sentences 49, 120–1, 162, 172, 195, 283, 286
shared meaning rule 209–10
*Shorter Oxford English Dictionary on Historical Principles* 205, 209
similarities 76–7, 149–50, 297, 299
simultaneous identification of 'one' ordinary meaning 204, 208
Sirey, Jean-Baptiste 19–20, 25
SL, *see* source language
Solan, L 201, 203
source culture 117
source language (SL) 75–6, 116–17, 121, 123, 131–2, 135, 137
source text (ST) 117–18, 121, 123–4, 145–6, 148, 296–7, 301
sources
  Irish legal terminology 8, 265–87
  legal 5, 45, 80, 83, 130, 150, 184
  Māori language 294–5
  online/Internet 86, 129
specificity 83, 119, 143
speeches 63, 291, 293–4, 297, 303
  parliamentary 297, 299–301
spelling rules 166, 283
spelling variants 161, 304
spellings 128, 266, 268–9, 272, 277, 305, 308–9; *see also* orthography
  preferred 167
Spelman, Henry 38, 179–80
ST, *see* source text
standing, legal 276, 280
statutes 59–60, 66, 178–9, 187–8, 191–3, 201–5, 207–15
  bilingual 201, 204, 207, 210, 212–13
  federal 207, 215, 217
statutory definitions 66–7, 182, 184, 188, 192–3, 208
statutory interpretation 47, 203, 213

*Stroud's Judicial Dictionary* 5, 59–60, 66–7, 70–1, 125, 182, 184
structural embedding 83, 148
sub-corpora 294, 306–8
sub-domains 179
subcategories 119, 178, 200
subentries 47, 53–4, 115, 127, 186
subject fields 142–3, 145, 160, 162
sublanguages 1, 119
substantive experts 5, 49
substitutability 51–2
suggested translations 173
Sullivan, R 201–2, 204, 206–7, 209–10, 216–19
Supreme Court of Canada (SCC) 201–20
Switzerland 123, 143
synonyms 83, 126, 128, 143–5, 162, 166–70, 174–5
synonymy 83, 144
syntactic properties 270, 281

target cultures 117
target language (TL) 75–7, 116–18, 121, 123, 125, 128–35, 137
    equivalents 130–1
target text (TT) 117, 121, 123–4, 128, 145–6, 148, 207
Tarp, S 126, 157, 289
Tate, Francis 31, 38
*TD, see Téarmaí Dlí*
*Téarmaí Dlí (TD)* 265–77, 279–85
Teissier-Esminger, Anne 17
terminographers 147–8
terminographical products 146, 148
terminography 6, 126, 142, 145, 149–50, 157, 159
terminological phrases 127, 132–3, 137
    multi-word 127, 133
terminological products 141, 143–4
terminology 6–7, 119, 142–3, 146–7, 165–6, 216–18, 282
    background 141–4
    centrality of concept 142–3
    descriptive 147
    interrelatedness of concepts 7, 141, 143
    legal, *see* legal terminology
    univocity 143–4
Termium 136
terms
    borrowed, *see* borrowings
    compound 84–5, 186
    historical 67–71
    legal, *see* legal terms
    non-legal 50, 52, 182–3
    one-word 127
textbooks 86, 133–4, 155, 219
TL, *see* target language
tokens 291–2, 295
tools 12–13, 32, 35, 38–9, 74, 76, 200–1
    information 154–5, 157, 175
    translation 79
Tottel, Richard 35, 38
traditions 1, 11, 18, 24–5, 49–50, 116, 118
    legal 8, 79, 141, 213, 215, 217
transcripts 292, 294, 297, 303
transition 4, 16, 18–20
translation 158–9, 161–2, 168–71, 173–5, 202–3, 206–7, 268–71
    actors 123–5
    bijural 136
    interlingual 117–18, 121
    intersemiotic 118, 136
    intra-language 124
    and law dictionaries 115–37
    meaning of legal translation 116–18
    process 116, 118–23, 137, 207, 215
    semiotic theory of 6, 118
    technique 204, 207–8
    tools 79
translational equivalents 116, 136
translational solutions 116–17, 135
translators 75–9, 115–17, 119–25, 128–30, 144–6, 166–8, 170–3
legal 75, 77, 86, 115–16, 118, 130, 137
professional 155, 158–60, 170, 175
transliterations 9, 305, 308, 311–12
treaties 84, 132, 161, 281, 299, 306
TT, *see* target text

uncertainty, legal 16, 194
United Kingdom 59, 66, 71–2, 83
United Nations Multilingual Terminology Database 136
United States 80, 181, 184, 186, 189, 191–3, 196

universities 15, 33, 36, 115
univocity 7, 141, 144
usage 63–8, 70, 76, 166–9, 217–18, 290, 304–5
- demotic 63, 67
- evidence 65, 67–8, 72
- examples 62, 65, 303, 312
- notes 7, 162, 166–9, 174
- ordinary 194, 212
- situations 155, 157–8, 162–3

use, Irish legal terminology 8, 265–87
user competences 159, 164
user needs, search options reflecting 163–75
users 1–2, 144–6, 149–51, 153–65, 167–8, 175, 315–16
- intended 130, 154–5, 159–62, 164–5
- potential 125, 131, 157–8, 160

vagueness 144
vehicle
- in case law 186–91
- in the 'common mind' 192–3
- as example of ordinary language in legal dictionaries 183–93

verbal adjectives 269, 284–6
verbal nouns 269, 283–4
verbs 166, 169, 270, 275, 278, 283, 285–7
- common 277
- irregular 158, 277, 283
- phrasal 161
- prepositional 277

verifiability 130, 150
vernaculars 1, 12
vocabulary 127, 290–1, 293, 296, 301–2, 305, 312
- legal 6, 26, 37, 119, 125, 127–8, 290

*Webster's* 50, 53, 133, 177–8, 185, 192, 199
Western legal concepts 8, 290, 301, 303, 312
Williams dictionary 308, 310
word-entries 32–3, 36–9
words
- entry 154–6, 160–4, 166–9, 171–2, 174–5
- everyday 127, 218
- hard 31, 38–9, 178

WordSmith Tools 293, 305–6, 310
Wüster, E. 141, 144

XML 151

Zgusta, L 1

# Index for French Language Chapters


abréviations 240
abstraction 89, 112
adjectifs 98, 225, 238–9, 247–8
adverbes 225, 238–9, 247
affinités 226, 230
aide à la traduction 105, 109
allemand 91, 95, 104, 106, 108–9
alphabétisation juridique 90–2
anglais 91, 94–6, 112, 235, 238
antonymie 238
apprenants étrangers 230–1
approche onomasiologique 95, 101
approche statistique 228
arrêts 105, 107, 250
attestés, termes 91, 97, 240

bases de données 90, 97–8, 103, 105–7, 109, 111–13, 236
  principes terminologiques pour la constitution des 103–13
    format TBX pour la représentation des données terminologiques 112
    niveau conceptuel 111–12
    niveau de la langue 109–11
    niveau de la translation 108–9
    niveau lexical 105–8
    structure de la fiche terminologique 113
bloc-définition 237–40
bloc-entrée 237–8
bloc-lexique 237–8, 241
bloc-occurrence 237
bloc-remarque 237
bloc-renvoi 237–8
bruits 100, 228

Canada, Québec 103, 235–7
caractère idiomatique 225, 235
caractère statistiquement significatif 228–9, 234
catégories 106, 226, 230, 247
  catégorie grammaticale 238
  grandes 227, 232
  intermédiaires 228
catégorisation 106–7, 227
chaînes de caractères 90
champ d'application 107
champs 106–9, 224
  de description sémantiques 107
  réservés aux collocations 108–9
chercheurs 225, 229, 243
choix 99, 111, 242–3, 245
  des exemples linguistiques 243, 245
choses 101, 246,
citations pertinentes 99
citoyen européen 89–101
classe conceptuelle 232, 243
classement 228, 239, 246–7, 249, 258
classes de mots 105–6
co-hyponymes 107, 113
collocatif 229–30, 232
collocations 99, 105–6, 108–9, 113, 224, 227–8, 231–2
  conceptuelles 227, 231–3, 241, 245
  lexicales 227, 232–3, 241, 245
  spécialisées 232
  typiques, signalisation 98
combinaison/suite de mots typique 228, 257
combinaisons 94, 226–34, 245, 249
  libres 226–8, 233
combinatoire 106, 224, 227, 230, 238, 242–3, 246
Comité de rédaction 238, 240–1, 243–5, 256–8
Comité Technique 37 104
comparaison 100, 231, 242
complémentarité 238

complexité 106
compositionnalité 229–33
compréhension 103, 110
conception 104, 106, 225, 229, 241, 244
concepts
  dénotés 239–40
  et signifié 93
  juridiques 90, 97, 233, 257
    partagés 89–90
  opératoires 90, 94, 100
conceptualisation 90, 93
conceptuel
  classes conceptuelles 232, 243
  collocations conceptuelles 227, 232–3, 241, 245
  réseau 233, 237
concordance 236
connaissances 91, 93–4, 111, 225, 235, 258
consensus 96, 231
constituants lexicaux 229–30, 234
consultation 90, 99–100
contenus 91, 93, 100, 113, 236–7, 241, 249
contexte 105–7, 109–10, 113, 228, 230, 240, 242
contraintes 224, 226, 230
cooccurrences 229, 232, 243
corpus 99, 108, 223, 228–9, 234
  parallèles 108
couples de langues 89, 231
*Crépeau* 225, 235–40, 242, 244, 246, 256, 259
critères 91, 225–8, 230–4, 239
culture
  générale 89, 94
  juridique 95
  nationale 90, 95
cumul 92, 97

Dechamps, Christina 233
décisions arbitraires 244
décodage 92, 230
définisseurs 95–7
définitions 91–4, 97, 100, 109–11, 113, 238–40, 258
  courtes 110
  minimales 96
  partagées 96
  synonymiques 240
définitions-renvoi 240
dénominations 91, 97, 104–5, 108
détermination 228, 234–6, 241
*Dictionnaire de droit privé* 223–5, 235–59
  en tant que projet 235–6
  et phraséologie, cas des exemples linguistiques 241–59
  structure de l'article 236–41
dictionnaires 90–1, 93, 106, 223–5, 227, 235–46, 256–9
  bilingues ou multilingues sur support papier, écueils 92–4
  de langue 93, 224, 238
  de mots, *voir* dictionnaires de langue
  juridiques 93, 97, 106, 109–10, 244
    multilingues 89–101
  papier 91, 97, 109
  spécialisés 258
discours juridique 225, 240–4
domaine d'application 107, 110
domaine juridique 108, 111
données 90, 103, 105–7, 109, 111–13, 223
  bases de, *voir* bases de données
  lexicales 103, 109
  terminologiques 97–8, 108, 112
doublets fonctionnels 236
droit centrifuge 104, 112
droit civil français 103–4, 108, 112
droit européen 104, 108, 112
droit privé 104, 108, 223–5, 235–8, 240–2, 244–7, 256–9
  québécois 236, 239, 241

échange de données 112
échanges internationaux 104
écueils du dictionnaire bilingue ou multilingue sur support papier 92–4
encodage 92, 235, 241
encyclopédies 93, 99
engouement pour la phraséologie 223–4
entrées 97–8, 100, 106–10, 232
  conceptuelles 100
équivalences 91–2, 95, 108, 110, 112, 238
étiquettes 95–8, 100

exemples linguistiques (EL) 223, 225, 227, 235, 237, 239–42, 244
  analyse des résultats et vérification des hypothèses 256–9
  choix 243, 245
  contenu et méthode de la rubrique 241–4
  de la deuxième édition du *Dictionnaire de droit privé* 244–58
  hypothèses de recherche 244–5
  structures sémantico-syntaxiques 246–55
expérience 90–1, 106, 243–4
experts du domaine 225, 227, 234–5, 241, 258
explications 110–11, 113, 239

faux positifs 228, 246
fiches terminologiques 111–13
  structure 113
fonctions 92, 104–8, 110–12
  lexicales 106–7
fondement onomasiologique 98
formalisme 106
français 91, 95–7, 107, 110–11, 224, 235, 238
fréquence 97, 225, 227–9, 231, 234

genre 106, 110, 246
grammaire 97, 99, 106–8, 113
  limitation à l'essentiel 98
*Grand dictionnaire terminologique du Québec* 103

hétérogénéité 105, 226
hiérarchisation des termes 98
hypéronymes 107, 113
hypothèses de recherche 244–5, 256–8

IATE 90, 103
identifiants uniques 111–12
idiomaticité 108, 233–4, 245, 258
idiomatique, caractère 225, 235
idiosyncrasies 108
illustrations juridiques 225, 240, 242
infinitif 98, 247
innovations 94
interprètes 112, 258
intuition 243–5
ISO 94, 103–6, 109–12
  normes 104, 106, 108–9, 111

jurilexicographes et phraséologie 223–59
  jurilinguistique 258,
jurisprudence 93, 242, 254
juristes 90, 94, 103, 224–5, 237, 244–5, 258–9
  non-linguistes 244

langue cible 101, 103, 108–11
langue-culture 95
langue d'origine 238
langue générale 93, 105, 224–8, 231–3, 243, 245–6, 257–8
langue maternelle 231
langue source 101, 103, 108–11
langues de spécialité 104–5, 224–8, 230–5, 241, 243–4, 256, 258
  UP, *voir* UP (unités phraséologiques), en langue de spécialité
Legallois, Dominique 223, 226, 229, 231
lexicultures 95, 97
lexiques bilingues 223, 225
L'Homme, Marie-Claude 224, 226, 229–30, 232–4, 238, 256, 258
linguistique 95, 104, 225., 228-229, 241-242
LISA, *voir* Localization Industry Standards Association 112
Localization Industry Standards Association 112
locutions 105, 229, 238, 245, 256–7
  adverbiales 246
  prépositives 238, 246

macrostructure 92, 98, 106
métalangage 104
méthodes/méthodologie 91, 94–5, 97–100, 109, 112, 228, 241–2
Meynard, Isabelle 224, 229–30, 233
microstructure 98, 100, 106
mise en application 106
modèles 93, 103, 106, 229, 242
monolingue, niveau 105, 113
mots cachés 100
mots vedettes 106, 238

multilinguisme, bon usage du 94–5

navigation 98
 interne 100
niveau
 de la langue 109–11
 de la translation 108–9
 global 95–7
 lexical 105–9, 112
 linguistique 95
 local 95–6
 monolingue 105, 113
 sémasiologique 96, 98
nombre 106, 108, 225, 228, 230–1, 236, 242
nomenclatures 95, 236–7, 245
noms 98, 105–6, 108, 110, 225, 228, 247
non-prédictibilité 230
non verbales, structures 247–9
normes ISO 104, 106, 108–9, 111
notions 104–5, 107–11, 225, 227, 233, 238, 240
numéro d'acception 239

obligation de résultat 89
omissions 223
onomasiologie
 approche onomasiologique 95, 101
 fondement onomasiologique 98
ontologie 95
ordre alphabétique 90, 101
ordre phraséologique 224, 258

paires de langues 108
*parties du discours* 225, 238
périphrase descriptive 96–7
phraséologie
 cas des exemples linguistiques 241–59
 et jurilexicographes 223–59
 juridique 98, 225, 258
 phénomène phraséologique 229, 231–2
phraséologisation 228, 231–2
polysémie 89, 96, 105, 238–9
 ordinaire 239
 termes polysémiques 107, 110, 238–9
 très fine 239
 vocables polysémiques 239

postulats 95, 225, 244
prédictibilité 227, 230–3
présentation 237, 239–40, 242, 244
principes 90, 93, 109–10, 227, 229, 231, 233
 terminologiques 103, 105, 107, 109, 111, 113

quasi-synonymes 100
Québec 103, 235–7

réciprocité 238
rédacteurs 90, 98, 240
rédaction 100, 238, 241, 243–5, 256–8
réduction anaphorique 229
régions 109, 111, 113
regroupements de termes 96–7
relations
 fonctionnelles 99
 génériques 98
 partitives 99
remarques 237, 239–40, 242
 contrastives 106, 109, 113
renvois 97, 238, 240, 255
 analogiques 238
 bloc-renvoi 237–8
 définitions-renvoi 240
 d'opposition 238
 synonymiques 238
rubriques 100, 225, 236–42, 258

segment type du discours juridique 225, 240, 242, 244
segments 242–3, 245
sémasiologie
 niveau sémasiologique 96, 98
 travail sémasiologique 95
 tributaire de l'ordre alphabétique 101
semi-experts 89–90, 94, 101
sens 95, 110–11, 226, 229–31, 234–6, 239, 245
 usuels 229–30
sentences 94
séquences lexicales perçues comme préconstruites 223
séquences polylexicales 235, 258
signifié 93
source 92, 101, 103, 106–11, 113, 258

sous-domaines 105, 107, 224, 237
sous-entrées 98
spécialistes 94, 96, 112, 230–4, 258; *voir aussi* experts du domaine
spécialité, langues de, *voir* langues de spécialité
spécificités 91, 95–6, 242, 258
statistiquement significatif, caractère 228–9, 234
structures
  non verbales 247–9
  verbales 241, 246–7, 249, 256–8
style juridique 242, 256
subsomption 92
support papier 89, 92
synonymes 96, 100, 107, 113, 238, 240
synonymie 89, 92

TBX (Term Base eXchange) 103–4, 112
technicité 93–4, 110
Term Base eXchange, *voir* TBX
termes 89–91, 94–8, 100–1, 105–13, 224, 230–4, 236–46
  attestés 91, 97, 240
  candidats 234
  complexes 105, 256
  hiérarchisation 98
  juridiques 103, 105, 108, 232, 235–6, 256, 258
  polysémiques 107, 110, 238–9
  regroupements de 96–7
  simples 105, 243, 247
  vedettes 106–7
terminographie orientée vers la traduction 108
terminologie 90–1, 94–5, 104–5, 107, 109, 231, 258
Termium 103
texte idiomatique 224
tournures propres au style juridique 242, 256
traçabilité des sources 91, 99–100
tradition onomasiologique 90
traducteurs 90, 95, 97, 103, 107–8, 112, 224
traduction 100, 103, 105, 108–10, 112, 224, 231
traitement de texte 90, 100
translation, niveau de la 108–9
travail sémasiologique 95

unités
  de connaissance 94, 111
  extralinguistiques 93
  lexicales 227, 232, 245, 257–8
  linguistiques 93, 104
  phraséologiques, *voir* UP
  terminologiques 233, 247, 256
UP (unités phraséologiques) 225–6, 241, 256, 258
  combinaisons dont la fréquence dans un corpus est statistiquement significative 228–9
  combinaisons non prédictibles 230–1
  combinaisons qui ne sont pas compositionnelles 229–30
  conceptuelles 227, 233–4, 245, 249, 252, 257–8
  en langue de spécialité 225–35
    collocations conceptuelles et collocations lexicales 232–3
    idiomaticité 233–5
  en langue générale, critères appliqués à la langue spécialisée 227–31
  lexicales 227, 232–3, 245, 249–50, 257–8
  verbales 256, 258
usage actuel 100
usagers 224, 235–8, 241, 258

validation 227, 229
verbes 105–6, 109, 233, 238–9, 241, 244–7, 256
  structures verbales 241, 246–7, 249, 256–8
vocables polysémiques 239
vocabulaire 90–1, 94–5, 100, 236
juridique 91, 103, 245, 257–8

Wüster, Eugen 94–5, 104–5

XML 112–13